NIBLEY ON THE TIMELY AND THE TIMELESS

CLASSIC ESSAYS OF HUGH W. NIBLEY

VOLUME ONE
IN THE RELIGIOUS STUDIES MONOGRAPH SERIES

With an Autobiographical Introduction by
Hugh W. Nibley

Foreword by Truman G. Madsen

Religious Studies Center
Brigham Young University
Provo, Utah

Copyright © 1978 by
Religious Studies Center
Brigham Young University

Library of Congress Catalog Card Number: 78-4382
ISBN 0-88494-338-0

7th Printing, 1988

Produced and Distributed by
BOOKCRAFT, INC.
Salt Lake City, Utah

Lithographed in the United States of America
PUBLISHERS PRESS
Salt Lake City, Utah

CONTENTS

FOREWORD

Truman G. Madsen

To those who know him best, and least, Hugh W. Nibley is a prodigy, an enigma, and a symbol.

The origins he pursues as a historian are sometimes obscure. His own origins are clear. More dominant than recessive is his inheritance from one of the early Jewish converts to the Church, Alexander Neibaur: that brilliant gift for language and linguistics, that perfect ease with the subtleties and technicalities of word usage. The outcome is a man whose thinking vocabulary is five times that of Shakespeare, and in foreign language ten times that of most men. Superb tools! How he has used them is the story of his life.

He was tracting in the Swiss-German mission at age seventeen. Then, as since, he was blithely unconcerned with what most people define as needs: food, clothing, shelter, recreation. At his mission end it was discovered that checks from home, several hundred dollars, had accumulated in the office unclaimed. He was still wearing the same shirts, huddling in the same ramshackle apartment, and consuming more books than food as the instruments of his ministry.

The pattern of physical self-neglect continues, the price of fierce concentration. Even now, a professor the University cannot afford to make emeritus, and the father of eight children, most of them grown-up, his diet is not high on the hog nor his home high on the hill. "If you don't have a car, thank God and walk," he says, and often comments as he walks up to his office on how lonely the campus is in the late evening hours when scholarship should be flourishing. Like the late Dr. John A. Widtsoe, he has prayed (as did his grandmother before him) that he would have a bare sufficiency of the things of this world lest they distract him from his mission. Over the years he has had no secretary, no prestigious research grants, no staff (only temporary bouts), and a mere handful of graduate assistants. He still pecks away at his own battered type-writer, not trusting anyone too close to his skyscrapers of three-by-five cards massed in shoeboxes. Rarely, if ever, has he taken an authentic vacation. During a recent spring semester, the doctor diagnosed total exhaustion and sent him to Florida. During that period, his wife Phyllis reports, for the first time since their marriage he once or twice came to bed at night without a book. A man of endearing eccentricities, he is not a misfit — he is instead a delight in any social setting. But in study he is, as he insists every genuine student must be, a loner cooped up in his rather bleak, rectangular office, which he chose because of its wide floor where he lays piles of categorized notes, leaving only a narrow path to and from his desk.

Some of the awe and even resentment of Nibley arises not from the fact that he penetrates into specialized esoterica but that he spills over into other fields with startling competence. Professor Arthur Henry King invited him casually to lecture on the Oedipus and was stunned at his grasp and insisted that the lecture be published. Francis Wormuth, University of Utah political scientist, read Nibley's "Tenting, Toll and Taxing" and responded, "There are two geniuses in the western states — myself and Hugh Nibley." He is up to date on contemporary scientific developments but also equipped to explain in detail their analogues in the seventeenth (or any other) century. Of course, it is in part the calling of a historian to learn something old every day. But Nibley insists that a student is only a student when "interest reaches excitement." For him, excitement becomes all but obsession; he finds nothing in the world boring or dull except those who are themselves bored or dull. Attend his home nights and you will hear incredibly learned presentations. If you want to swap war stories, those of Athens, Persia or Rome as those of Germany, he can provide vivid detail. Hike behind Tim-panogos and you will hear him tick off the Latin names of all the flora and flauna and tell you how dikes are built. Break into an opera solo and he will hum the parts of the instruments, offer commen-taries, and even take on something of a dramatic performance himself. Talk up the latest article on black holes, or parapsychology, or brain-study, or Gödel's proof, or Nigel Calder, on the brain, or astrophysics. He will disappoint you in that he has already read it and impress you to go back to reread what you missed.

Students often lament Nibley's packed and even cramped style both in lecture and writing. Robert K. Thomas says of him, "He is always the classical satirist." It is so; if he ever really gave that flair its head, he could be a ruthless cynic. In fact, however, as the present set of essays demonstrates, he has many styles. Early on he was immersed in British poetry, and such is his gift for powerful imagery that, even in sober articles, he slips into hyperbole. He has memorized half of the Greek poets, and when at a Biblical Society meeting Jesuit George MacRae heard him discourse without notes and then spontaneously quote thirty lines in the original, he put his hands over his face and said, "It is obscene for a man to know that much."

One Nibley style is a horse laugh, as is his response to the *Myth Makers*, including that to Mrs. Brodie in *No, Ma'am, That's Not History*. There he savors her delicious prose style and regrets that she ignored nine-tenths of the relevant data. But his hints are stronger; what is really wrong with Brodie is not just her debunking tone but her uncritical presuppositions and her amateur psychologizing. That's where non-Mormon analysts have come down hard on her later efforts. A more systematic style appears in three books and over three decades — *Lehi in the Desert, An Approach to the Book of Mormon,* and *Since Cumorah* — in which Nibley has provided an Old World Middle East check on the Book of Mormon. Now John L. Sorenson has done the same for the Meso-American context of the book. These efforts undercut what Richard L. Bushman calls the "sponge theory" of the Book of Mormon — that Joseph Smith simply absorbed what was "in the air" in his boyhood, then squeezed it and out came the Book of Mormon. Nibley cannot help smiling at this irresponsible "explanation." His style changes when he turns to the questions of parallels in ancient cultures, finding in Israel's Dead Sea Scrolls revealing traces of the people of the desert, in the Nag Hammadi literature evidence that some forms of Gnosticism may very well have been a graduate course in early Christianity, and in Syria the new discovery that Abraham was, after all, likely a historical character.

Students often ask how Nibley is viewed elsewhere. He has made a dent if not a breakthrough with preeminent men. In addition he has generated much heat and, for a mild man, it is surprising how gracefully he can take it. ("We need more anti-Mormon books. They keep us on our toes.") In some quarters he is impressive enough to be carefully ignored. Some of those who wish to champion him are themselves academic outcasts. Such men as anthropologist Cyrus Gordon of Brandeis, for example, take seriously a pre-Columbian origin of Meso-American peoples at their own peril, but cannot say enough good about Nibley's work. On the other hand, America's highly honored Catholic exegete, Raymond E. Brown of Union in New York, has read Nibley's work and now says in learned company that the Book of Mormon is "authentic pseudepigrapha." Chicago's Egyptologist Klaus Baer refused to comment for or against Nibley's latest book on the Egyptians but shares Nibley's thesis that no able Egyptologist can confidently assert that Joseph Smith's reading of the Abraham facsimiles is fraudulent. ("Revelation is not a puppet affair for Mormons. If God wanted to bestow the mummies and scrolls upon Joseph Smith to prepare him for revelatory understanding of Abraham, why not? If his readings don't agree with the scholar's, a proper Mormon answer might be 'Do we have a right to tell God his business?' ") Hebraist, and colleague, Sidney B. Sperry wished Nibley had focused his talent on the Church Fathers, expanding into volumes what he only skirmishes with in articles — a documentary tracing of the decline and fall of the Christian Church. Classicist Jacob Geerlings remarked shortly before his death: "Hugh Nibley is simply encyclopedic. Though I do not agree with his views I hesitate to challenge him; he knows too much."

A persevering jibe at Nibley is that, for all his learning, he is a hop, skip and jump scholar, who is too hard on reason, other disciplines, and the consensus of mainstream academia. Such writers take Nibley's jokes seriously and his serious work as a game. Sterling W. McMurrin, a historian of ideas, sees him as a kind of latter-day Tertullian putting faith ahead of critical intelligence and, like Karl Barth, as utterly opposed to the natural intelligence. To such generalizations Nibley, it must be admitted, is an unsatisfactory answerer. He will not sit still long enough to be classified. But he is no Barth. For all his plasticity and pot-shotting, he has the highest respect for scholarly endeavor, even that which is infected with vanity. But he has the heartiest and sometimes wittiest contempt for academic pretension. He is hard on abstract theology, harder on philosophy, and hardest of all on his own institution. More than once he has walked into a seminar or workshop and announced: "None of us has any business being here. We don't know enough." In this same spirit he says to students who suppose verbalizing is proof of insight, "If we really cared about this subject we would be in the library studying the documents."

As a teacher, he is, at least at the outset, terrifying. He does not lecture; he explodes. He brings source materials in the original to class, translates them on the spot, and lapses into spasms of free association as he sees linguistic connections. He teaches whatever he is working on that day, allowing students to look over his shoulder. His long paragraphs go by at approximately the speed of light. Students who learn the most learn to interrupt and to probe; it is like trying to count machine-gun shots while able at best to take notes on the tracers. Because the fine tuning of his mind is to written materials, it is as if he is listening to them more than to his students; he is utterly oblivious to electronic trappings like microphone, blackboard or TV camera. Most of the time he talks as if everyone present has just read everything he has. This is less a Germanic or Olympian detachment than a temperamental unwillingness to put anyone down. He exhibits patience with questions which show no one was listening a minute ago. When he does not want to answer, he trails away into a closely related area and his listeners are not brave enough to request backtracking. Once a student asked him the question, "What is a symbol?" The answer slowly expanded to cosmic proportions and Nibley stopped for breath an hour and twenty minutes later. It is not surprising that few professors have generated more stories about absentmindedness. He offers no defense, but demonstrates that no mind is really absent; it is only present on other — and in his case more important — things. If you watch his lips move, during moments of partial seclusion or even in the middle of a slow-moving conversation, you can catch him reviewing any one of the dozen languages he wants to keep fresh. He is usually talking before and after the bell rings for any given class period, and the lecture only begins and ends with your being in earshot. He does have "an infinite capacity for taking pains." This means he has little truck with haste. He is slow to print, quick to revise and supplement (just ask his editors, who groan as they see "final" galleys torn to shreds) and perennial in his retreat from what cannot hold water. Much of his most significant work still lies on his shelves unpublished because it requires, by his standards, more work. More and more.

How, in book form, represent his writing? How select thirteen out of three hundred essays?[1] We began with the premise that Nibley is a phenomenon. (He receives hundreds of letters a month from around the world inquiring on more topics than can be found

1. The selections were made by a committee: Poet Arthur Henry King, Philosopher C. Terry Warner, Classicist Douglas Phillips, Political Scientist Louis W. Midgley, Ancient Studies' S. Kent Brown. Several of Prof. Nibley's former students were also consulted.

in the *Britannica*.) We envisioned the rising wave of college-age students and the wider-reaching waves of adult education. We selected essays that are not exactly popular but which, on the other hand, are not (except for the notes) unduly technical. Our criteria were loose: range of subject matter, diversity of style, controversiality. In some cases we consulted (and more than once overruled) Nibley's own appraisal as to relative significance. No strict logical connection holds the essays together. But they do fall into a sequential order: they begin with materials that relate to the premortal realm of existence and then move down through the dispensations. We also included important samplings of Nibley's hard-won as well as whimsical, sometimes startling, and always disquieting comments on education, society, and politics. Thanks to the careful compilings of Professor Louis Midgley, the reader may, if he chooses, follow any one of these essays into the wider world of Nibleyophilia in the complete bibliography.

Ill-wishing critics have suspected over the years that Nibley is wrenching his sources, hiding behind his footnotes, and reading into antique languages what no responsible scholar would ever read out. Unfortunately, few have the tools to do the checking. For purposes of this volume we have assigned ten linguists to go through every note for typographical accuracy. Some slips and discrepancies have been discovered and corrected (and others, no doubt, missed). But our greater effort has been to check fidelity in translation and relevance to the points Nibley presses in his text. Some stretchings beyond a minimal "given reading" have been noted. But in most cases Nibley clearly states where his readings are not in harmony with other scholars; and, on the other hand, where they would be defended by an increasing minority. It is the latter situation, for example, which explains his ritualistic account of the Book of the Dead materials. But he well knows that his notes will stand or fall with the scrutiny of oncoming generations. "You don't need to check them," he has said more than once. "I must stand behind them." So, indeed, he must.

If there is general agreement among most high-school students that "history is bunk" and boring bunk at that, a little maturity and some exposure to Nibley may reverse the verdict. He observes that no culture in the world is more superficial than that of America, where change, adaptation and fad are as fleeting as popcorn. He thinks both Protestant and Catholic culture (less so among the Jewish) are likewise massively undernourished in terms of the classical insights and perspectives of the ancients. He is not talking simply of wisdom nor even of moral lessons. He is talking in the larger pattern of what is today called "apocalyptic." Far from living too much in the past, he sees the past as the clearest "clue" to the future; but only if one defines past and future in a way that reaches, at both ends, to God. Latter-day Saints themselves, history-minded as few others, are slow to recognize that "the restoration of all things" included restorations of key books for every major dispensation; a Book of Adam, a Book of Enoch, a Book of Noah, a Book of Abraham, a Book of Melchizedek, a Book of Elijah, a book of the intertestamental period, three books on the dispensation of Christ, and vast apocalyptic visions of the consummation of world history.

Nibley has given flesh, in all this, to a "patternist" or "diffusionist" theory of history. The premise is at work in almost everything he has written since his Berkeley days. On the negative side he refuses to accept the conventional dogma of social Darwinism — that society has emerged from simpler, cruder, more primitive forms. He never tired of pointing this out on a recent tour of Athens and visits to its museums, to Sounian, Corinth, and then again in Egypt at the Tombs of Theban Royalty, and in Luxor and Karnak, and again at the ruins of Qumran at the Dead Sea: Full-blown cultural and spiritual splendor can be found in some of these early stages of civilization. Neither the evolutionary nor the revolutionary conception of religion will do. On the positive side he sees strands of eternal meaning in pockets as rare and neglected as the Hopi Indian Year Rites. Critics say he has broken some of his own rules on "parallels" and that the similarities that seem to appear in, say, the Book of Mormon matrix and the Dead Sea Scrolls or the Coptic materials are only superficial. He himself admits that some of these materials may turn out to be "poor stuff." But in them are echoes, echoes of something at the core of the authentic influence of Christ. And these echoes, as scholars increasingly acknowledge, require reevaluation of all that has heretofore been called Christianity. Nibley's thesis is that those reevaluations, as often as not, point in the direction of Mormon doctrine.

If one studies Nibley's writing output not chronologically but thematically, one can see a pattern, both in the foreground and in the background. It is the temple. His mastery of Arabic, Greek, Hebrew (and a little Aramaic), Latin, German, French and Spanish, and more recently of Coptic and Egyptian, have given him access to world liturgy. In historic and comparative terms he has done for the western world what Mircia Eliade has done phenomenologically for the ceremonial life. He is incurably literalistic, never capitulating to the notion that religious expression is quasi-real without a tie in terra firma, yet, simultaneously, perhaps more than any one of his colleagues, alert to the rich nuances of symbolic significance, especially as these are manifest in ordinances. He has offered specialized courses in world liturgy for three decades and enlisted the aid of some bright and newly competent graduate students. He wrote "What Is a Temple?" for the dedication of the London Temple, and says now, with a wave of the hand, "a lot has been learned since then." The Mormon fourfold canon (the standard works) and books of remembrance of our own century help one understand what the temple is all about. It is Christ. Nibley has done his homework on both counts. But what he has published to the world is really something else — and may be one of his lasting contributions: Authentic records, to which there was no access in the nineteenth century, show that jewels and nuggets as well as twists and distortions and inversions of temple ceremonies have reached into almost every society. He has shown that Joseph Smith's full-bodied presentation of ordinances, with the temple at their climactic apex, could not have been simply a nineteenth-century aberration nor warmed-over Masonry. By and large, and point for point, what takes place in Mormon temples is closer to presently describable ancient practice than to any modern ritual. Of course, the hard question remains, Where did the ancients get them? Nibley has more than enough evidence gathered that it is not implausible to postulate a common source. But the question, Nibley's leading question, and which puts the burden of proof on the nay-sayers is, Where did Joseph Smith get them?[2]

Nibley's literary legacy will survive him. So will his zest for life, even in its most grim and agonizing hours (we watched him dance with joy at King Tut's Tomb as he saw firsthand and in color what he had previously seen only in photographic reproductions). And for those who find the idea of eternal ordinances and covenants and ceremonies foreign to authentic religious life, his personal embodiment of his writings will always beckon to deeper second thoughts. Some months after he had completed his volume on the Egyptian ritual he emerged elated from the Provo Temple one afternoon, saying, "I have learned more today in one session of the temple than

---

2. "I am prepared to admit," a well-known scholar confessed to Wilford Griggs after scanning Nibley's footnotes on "What Is a Temple?" "that Joseph Smith knew things about the ancient world that no one in the nineteenth century could know." That pretty well sums it up.

ever I knew before." When pressed, he offered that kindly smile which, loosely translated, means, "These are things I would rather not talk about." ("He can mumble in more languages and say more in his asides than any man alive.") He did, however, provide in his own terms a clue "that the idea of beauty in divine creation came fresh." He saw, again but as if for the first time, what he had seen in the rain forests of Oregon — "the kind of world God intended this to be." At this level there is nothing of the pedant about him, but all the uncomplicated wonderment of a child. William James somewhere observes that one may define a Bach quartet as "the moving of horsehair over catgut," or he may be transformed by the music. Something of the temple's transformation, its power, impact, and revelatory lift, can be seen exuding from Nibley's pores.

In his study of the nature of genius, Ernest Jones says "an essential prerequisite" is "a particular skepticism." The genius must be original. He "must have refused to acquiesce in certain previously accepted conclusions. This argues a kind of an imperviousness to the opinions of others, notably of authorities." (See the *Scientific Monthly*, February 1957, page 80.) One must know the authorities well in order to know where to disagree. In history, Nibley knows them cold. But he also has the requisite imperviousness, even to some of his own opinions. "Things are never settled," he keeps saying, and "my conclusions are momentary." Constantly he sees problems and perplexities that others do not and is incessant in pursuing them. Who else, for example, would have thought of tracing the role of the notched arrow in the formation of the state? On the other hand, in religious realms where others see huge problems he sees no problems at all. The one refusal to acquiesce accounts for his colossal erudition; the other for his breathtaking assurances of faith.

To students of all kinds, that combination, that balance, is sometimes confusing but always exciting. ("There may be things about the Church that I find perfectly appalling. But I know the gospel is true.") To his critics it is maddening. And to his disciples? Well, Hugh Nibley could have had disciples lined up four abreast from here to the library. He has, instead, sent them on to the only One who deserves disciples.

AN INTELLECTUAL AUTOBIOGRAPHY

Hugh W. Nibley

Those who ask, "What is the meaning of life?" and get no reassuring answers have been known to conclude that the whole thing is a cruel joke. If we are supposed to find the answers, they say, why are they hidden? Precisely because we are supposed to find them, which means we must look for them; the treasure is buried to keep us digging, the pearl of great price lies glittering in the depths where we must seek it out. Treasure hunts can be both instructive and fun, provided the clues are not too discouraging and kind Providence has strewn the most exciting and obvious clues all over the place. It is only when we choose to ignore them, like the pig-headed constable in the English murder-mystery, blind to all but his own opinion, that we court frustration and cynicism.

As an infant I entertained an abiding conviction that there were things of transcendent import awaiting my attention. So I kept wandering away from where I was supposed to be. Adults find that attitude upsetting: the scientist or scholar who looks twice before formulating a conclusion has only scorn for the layman who looks only once; but he will give a bad time to any student of his who presumes to look farther than he has, and can never forgive the younger person who actually discovers something. Yet from every side the hints continue to pour in, as they have since the beginning of time; every decibel or photon brings to our human perceptors more information than anyone has yet deciphered. My own reactions to these generous stimuli have been inadequate and hesitant, but the hints themselves may be worth mentioning. Here are some of the more potent ones, registered decade by decade.

The 1910s: In Portland in 1910 the great rain forests began a few miles from our home on every side, proclaiming in their primal magnificence the kind of world God intended this to be. But the world that men were hewing out of the forest was something else. My grandparents, especially Grandma Sloan, still believed that we were in the Last Days, and could tell us why. Everybody else, including my parents, was cool to that idea — progress and prosperity were the watchword. And what did the signals say? As we stood on the little station platform at Gearhart Beach at the end of our last summer there, the family could hear a lumber company a mile away in the towering woods noisily beginning what was to be the total destruction of the greatest rain forest in the world. My father obligingly explained that the lumber company was only acting in the national interest, since spruce wood makes the best propellors, and a strong air force is necessary to a strong and free America. But it was another message that reached and offended childish ears from that misty battleground of man against nature. A little later I understood better what was going on.

The 1920s: I began my second decade in Southern California as a compulsive reader, memorizing Shakespeare plays and aspiring to add something to the Bard's modest contribution. But English literature I soon found to be derivative, and so took to Old English to find what was behind it; what was behind it was Latin, and what was behind that was Greek. In those days we thought that you had reached the beginning of everything with the Greeks. Ministers and missionaries retiring to Southern California in the twenties flooded the dusty bookstores on Main, Spring and Los Angeles streets with an astonishing wealth of antique and exotic texts (at two bits a volume), thus abetting and implementing my undisciplined researches. But if you really want to get back of reality, science is the thing; and, as Popper assures us, all science is cosmology: I became a passionate amateur astronomer. Only to discover that everybody wanted to be a scientist, while all the written records of the race, as legitimate an object of purely scientific interest as any fossil or spectrum, were consigned to all but total neglect in the hands of esthetes and pedants. I began to suspect that the records had something very important to convey to us, hints and clues that lay waiting in densely compacted deposits of the human past — others were busy in the lab, but who really cares what is in the stacks?

In the twenties business was booming, as you may have heard, and I got a good look at some Big Men who played golf at Brentwood, Wilshire, and the L.A. Country Club; dull, profane men they were, who cheated on every stroke, just about. When my admiring father asked one of them at dinner what he considered to be his greatest achievement in life, the man unhesitatingly replied that it was his celebrated filibuster to keep James Joyce's *Ulysses* (a book of which, as literature, I was very fond) out of the land. One summer, at fifteen, I worked in the Nibley-Stoddard sawmill in the Feather River Canyon and came to know all manner of men. The thing for schoolboys to do in those halcyon days was to work in mills or ranches in the summer, or to become seasonal tramps. Full of the Concord School, I spent six weeks alone in the Umpqua forest between Crater Lake and the Three Sisters, quite a wild place then, and learned that nature is kind but just and severe — if you get in trouble you have yourself to thank for it. It was another story down in the valley, where I learned that there were kindhearted tramps who knew far more than any teacher I had had — I mean about literature and science — but tramped because they preferred passing through this world as observers of God's works. For such a luxury they paid a heavy price: in any small town in the nation anyone not visibly engaged either in making or spending money was quickly apprehended and locked up as a dangerous person — a vagrant. Everywhere, I learned very well, the magic words were, "Have you any money?" Satan's Golden Question. Freedom to come and go was only for people who had the stuff — in fact you could have anything in this world for it.

Within a year the tramping continued, this time among the amused or resentful villagers of the Black Forest and the Rhine Plain. President Tadje, one of the few great men I have known, allowed me to do it my way. By bicycle in summer and afoot in winter I went alone (my companions thought I was overdoing it) carrying the gospel to Catholic, Lutheran, and Calvinist (they were the toughest) villages. The people were still peasants in those days, living in the Middle Ages in their wildly picturesque storybook towns. Surprising enough, the work was not entirely unsuccessful — the gospel message readily leapt the immense cultural gap, passing through the ever-so-tenuous medium of faith that is common to all cultures and all religions. It was a different story when I knocked on the doors of professors and industrialists in the university and factory towns. German Wissenschaft had long since severed all ties with any gospel but its own proud, self-contained positivism; literally they were without a culture and without religion. The hints were clear enough: the infernal machine of our age was made in Germany.

At the end of my mission President Tadje let me go to Greece to carry messages to some native members of the Church and to make contact with some who had recently migrated from Turkey in a great influx of refugees. Those marvelous Greeks, cheerful and courteous, exuding the spirit of good will, with nothing to eat and nowhere to live! I took long walks, sleeping in the hills, and had a shock from which I never recovered. While I was circulating among displaced persons (under surveillance, of course) my stuff was stolen from the flea-bag hotel where I was staying. That made me an outcast among the outcasts. I spoke English, but also German and French, and my clothes were certainly not American — how could suspicious officials know where I really came from or what I might be running away from? My passport turned up at the American Express, but that was not the problem. By what right did I lay claim to affluence and security while all the people around me had none? How could a few rubber stamps place me in an exalted station? True, the stamps were only symbols, like money, but symbols of what? Hadn't those others worked as hard as I? Worse still, what was I if my sacred identity depended on who somebody *else* said or believed I was? If a bored petty official had decided not to make some phone calls, I could have become a nonperson forever. Legal fictions had supplanted intrinsic worth and faith in God and man; it was the papers that everybody was grabbing for in those desperate times. And what were the papers really worth? I soon found out when I returned to the big house in Glendale on January 1, 1930, and was told how many thousand American millionaires had just become paupers overnight.

The 1930s: At UCLA I quickly learned the knack of getting grades, a craven surrender to custom, since grades had little to do with learning. Still, that was during the Depression, when people of little faith were clinging to institutions for survival, and so I went along, as timid and insecure as the rest of them. What sort of thinking went on there? The man I worked for as an assistant refused to read Spengler, "because he is not even a full professor!" Staggering, isn't it? I have never thought of an answer to that one. Nobody stood alone; the only way they all stayed on their feet was by leaning on each other for support, like a stand of toothpicks. Berkeley was more of the same, with one difference — they had a library. I decided to put it all together in the stacks beginning at the southwest corner of the ninth level and working down to the northeast corner of the first level, book by book, stopping whenever something significant caught my eye. It took four years, and then one day a cardboard tube came in the mail. It contained another passport, this time even more magical than the one with the rubber stamps. I may have forgotten the very names of the courses and teachers that qualified me as a Ph.D., but this pretty document assured me that from here on it was all safely stored in steel filing cabinets in the registrar's office.

I had started out at Berkeley as Professor Popper's only pupil in Arabic (next year there were three of us in Hebrew), and spent an awful lot of time at it, which could have been better spent elsewhere. But what an Aladdin's cave of hints! All an Arabic writer will ever give you is hints, and you build up your world from them. The most illustrious visiting scholar of the time was Werner Jaeger, who favored me with long chats and frank revelations over the teacups (my refusal to drink the stuff made an indelible impression on him and his wife). Professor Jaeger knew very well, he told me, that the Greeks were part of a wider Oriental complex, but he had to bypass all that in his study of the Greek mind, because it tended to disturb the neatness and balance of his great work on Greek Education. Typical was the Committee's rejection of my first subject for a thesis: I wanted to write about the perennial phenomena of the mob in the ancient world; but the Committee found the subject altogether too unreal, too irrelevant to the mood and spirit of the modern world, to appeal even to normal curiosity. How could you expect such men to be aware of the desperately lonely and unhappy young people all around them, seething with resentment and building up to some kind of an explosion (which occurred in the '60s), frustrated at every turn as they asked for the bread of life and got only processed academic factory food served at an automat?

At Claremont Colleges I taught everything under the sun, including American Civilization on alternate days with Everett Dean Martin (who was still famous then) and Junior Humanities alternating with Ed. Goodspeed, retired from the University of Chicago. I also taught the History of Education and received the most sinister vibrations of all: it took no prophetic gift to see that no good could come of the highly successful efforts of Dewey, Kilpatrick and the rest, to supplant all religion and culture by their own brand of the new, emancipated, manipulated society. At the request of President Russell M. Storey (the second great man I have known) I took notes when a few celebrities would gather at his house in connection with the work of a committee on war objectives and peace aims. There we could talk with such notables as Lewis Mumford, T. V. Smith, Thomas Mann, and Edward S. Corvin. It was heady stuff, but very soon I was getting a much more instructive view of the scene from closer up.

The 1940s: In high school I had won the Proficiency Medal as the best soldier in the ROTC. Now I was as a master sergeant doing paper work in military intelligence at every level and keeping my eyes open. Mr. Tucker used to come down from Washington to Camp Ritchie with exciting news of what went on in High Places; for example, there was the fabulous Miss Crawford in the British War Office who knew every secret of the German Army; and in time behold it was I who ended up as Miss Crawford's assistant, she being a fussy red-headed spinster who got all her information from newspapers and magazines and kept all the clippings stirred up in a shoebox. That is how it is done. The army is correctly defined (by R. Heinlein) as "a permanent organization for the destruction of life and property." The business of the 101 A/B Division, to which I was attached through the winter of '43 and all of '44, was to search out and destroy; all the rest of the vast military enterprise was simply supportive of that one objective. "Good hunting!" was the general's stock admonition before take-off. My business was to know more about the German Army than anyone else and to brief division personnel at every level on that meaningful subject both before and during operations. What I saw on every side was the Mahan Principle in full force, that "great secret" of converting life into property — your life for my property, also your life for my promotion (known as the Catch 22 Principle). Attached to army groups and various intelligence units during 1945, I took my jeep all over western Europe and beheld the whole thing as a vast business operation. I well remember the pain and distress expressed at headquarters as the war wound down and twilight descended on brilliant military careers, high living, and unlimited financial manipulations; and how great was the rejoicing when the new concept of "brush-fire wars" was announced to the staff — a simple plan to keep the whole thing going, safely contained and at a safe distance. O peace, where is thy sting? The Mahan Principle was still in full force and remains so to this day.

After the War I worked for the *Improvement Era* on the top floor of the stately Church Office Building on South Temple Street in Salt Lake City, and came to know another kind of headquarters. I also got to know some of the General Authorities quite well. There were scientists, scholars and even poets among their number. One useful thing on the premises was a good collection of anti-Mormon literature. So when Mrs. Brodie's highly fictitious biography of Joseph Smith appeared I became involved in that direction: what I said about Mrs. B. and her methods is exactly what more competent reviewers have said about her more recent Life of Jefferson. The

bona fides of the Prophet centers around the Book of Mormon —
another happy coincidence: on the eve (week) of the Normandie
invasion I had in London blown all my savings on Arabic books from
the collections of Howells and Ellis, both of whom had conveniently
died at that point in time. Lacking other sources, I turned to my own
books for an Old World approach to the Book of Mormon that kept
me going for years.

The 1950s: In 1950 the Dead Sea Scrolls began to come out,
along with the equally interesting Coptic texts from Nag Hammadi
in Egypt, fusing early Judaism and Christianity in a way that conventional churches and scholars found very disturbing but which
fitted the Book of Mormon like a glove. Then in 1951 Brigham Young
University acquired both the Greek and Latin *Patrologiae* and the
Egyptian collection of the venerable S. A. B. Mercer, he who had
spearheaded the attack on the Book of Abraham back in 1912. Here
indeed was a treasure trove of hints, including some very enlightening ones about Mercer himself. At last we had something to work
with in the *Patrologiae.* But to be taken seriously one must publish,
and I soon found that publishing in the journals is as easy and
mechanical as getting grades: I sent out articles to a wide variety of
prestigious journals and they were all printed. So I lost interest:
what those people were after is not what I was after. Above all, I
could see no point to going on through the years marshalling an
ever-lengthening array of titles to stand at attention some day at the
foot of an obituary. That is what they were all working for, and they
were welcome to it. But there were hints I could not ignore and
answers I must seek for my own peace of mind. There was one thing
every student of the past has overlooked: here at our doorsteps
among Arizona Indians lies the world's best clue to the spiritual
history of the race; nowhere else on earth will one find the old cycle
of the Year Rites still observed in full force and unbroken continuity
from the beginning. When Brother Vergil Bushman, a great missionary to the Hopis, started taking me to the villages with him I
could hardly credit the devotion and courage with which a little
band of less than five thousand people had kept alive a language
and a culture which preserved the practices and beliefs of our own
ancestors from prehistoric times until nineteenth-century in-
dustrialism severed the umbilical cord. Here the clues are both
exhilarating and depressing, hopeful and sinister as nowhere else.

The 1960s: The fifties ended in Berkeley as a visiting professor
in humanities, with Classical Rhetoric as the main subject. As in the
novels of C. P. Snow, the faculty there had but one objective in life —

to achieve eminence — and all labored under the pathetic illusion that mere association with a prestigious institution was the nearest thing to human satisfaction that this life could offer. At Berkeley I put too much religion into my teaching; one young man came to me with a delicate problem — his parents, he said, had been careful to give him the most proper and respectable education available, and now he was going to have to break the painful news to them — that he had discovered that there is a God. How could he do it gently?

Along with teaching I sweated for a year at Egyptian and Coptic with a very able and eager young professor. The Coptic would be useful, but Egyptian? At my age? As soon as I got back to Provo I found out. People in Salt Lake were preaching around that Joseph Smith's fatal mistake was to commit himself on matters Egyptian — safe enough in his own day, but now that Egyptian could be read it was a trap from which there was no escape. This pressure kept me at Egyptian, in which I was still far from competent, but gradually it began to appear that it was really the experts who by their premature commitments were getting themselves into a trap. A trip to Jordan in 1964 cooled me somewhat towards the Arabs and turned me more than ever to the Scrolls. Then in 1966 I studied more Egyptian in Chicago, thanks to the kind indulgence of Professors Baer and Wilson, but still wondered if it was worth all the fuss. When lo, in the following year came some of the original Joseph Smith papyri into the hands of the Church; our own people saw in them only a useful public relations gimmick, but for the opposition they offered the perfect means of demolishing Smith once and for all. Not yet confident in Egyptian, I frankly skirmished and sparred for time, making the most of those sources which support the Book of Abraham from another side, the recent and growing writings, ancient and modern, about the forgotten legends and traditions of Abraham: they match the Joseph Smith version very closely.

The 1970s: The reading of the Abraham apocrypha inevitably led to Enoch documents and the discovery that Joseph Smith had given us among other things a perfectly good Book of Enoch which rang up an astonishing number of stunning parallels when I started to compare it with the growing catalogue of newly discovered Enoch manuscripts. But my obsession of the 1970s has been the Temple.

The essential information for solving almost any problem or answering almost any question is all *brought* together in the scriptures; but it is not *put* together for us there. Learned divines for sixty generations have argued about that, and the vast bulk of their writings is eloquent witness to their perplexity. And this is where the *Temple* comes in. Without the Temple any civilization is an empty shell, a structure of custom and convenience only. The churchmen, posting with too much dexterity to accommodate their teachings to the scientific and moral tenets of the hour, present a woeful commentary on the claims of religion to be the sheet anchor of civilization and morality. Where is the unshakable rock, the *shetiyah?* It is the Temple.

Five days a week between three and four o'clock in the morning, hundreds of elderly people along the Wasatch Front bestir themselves to go up and begin their long hours of work in the Temple, where they are ready to greet the first comers at 5:30 A.M. At that time, long before daylight, the place is packed, you can't get in, so I virtuously wait until later, much later, in the day. Whatever they may be up to, here is a band of mortals who are actually engaged in doing something which has not their own comfort, convenience, or profit as its object. Here at last is a phenomenon that commands respect in our day and could safely be put forth among the few valid arguments we have to induce the Deity to spare the human race: thousands of men and women putting themselves out for no ulterior motive. There is a touch of true nobility here. What draws them to the Temple? There is no music, pageantry, or socializing to beguile the time; none of us begins to grasp the full significance of what is going on, yet nobody seems bored. Why is that? I can only speak for myself, harking back to the subject of hints, those countless impulses with which our perceptors are being bombarded by day and night. For thousands of years the stars have gone on sending us their hints, broadcasting unlimited information if we only knew it; now at last we are reacting to a narrow band on the informational spectrum, putting clues together in a way the Ancients never did. But also we are beginning to suspect that there were times when the Ancients reacted to another band of the spectrum which is completely lost on us. The Temple, as the very name proclaims, is a place where one takes one's bearings on the universe. What goes on there is confidential, and must remain so until both the Mormons and the outside world are in a better position to understand it. Meanwhile, I write this almost fifty years to the day since the bewildering experience of my own endowment; I have just returned from the Temple again where this day I made a most surprising and gratifying discovery. If I went to the Temple five times and nothing happened, I would stop going. But I've gone hundreds of times, and the high hopes of new knowledge with which I go up the hill every week are never disappointed.

Since a highly competent young man has become the Director of Ancient Studies, the BYU campus has been visited by a dozen or so top authorities in biblical and related studies. Though they are far ahead of me, they are nonetheless schoolmen like myself, and it is only fair to let the ingenuous reader know that we are for the most part simply conscientious grinds, who got good grades and stayed on at school, moving into departmental slots conveniently vacated by the death of older (and usually better) scholars; then travelling all over to exchange commonplaces and read papers with our peers abroad in the world. As to research, we paw over large deposits of neglected material until we find something that nobody has noticed for a long time; then we write about it, and that is a contribution. The discovery of new documents has turned scholarship to translating again, which is too bad, because translating is the last resort of the resourceless mind — anybody can do it, and nobody can be expected to do it perfectly. Today as ever, to be a diligent tabulator keeping well within party guidelines is what passes as scholarly integrity. What can I say when we cautious, mincing souls, who consider ourselves illustrious if we can come up with an idea or two in thirty years, presume to take the measure of Joseph Smith?

At the present moment the hints and clues are pouring in from all sides with the accelerating tempo of a Geiger-counter gone mad, and the interpretation thereof is as certain as it is disturbing: good news for those who wait with the Saints, disturbing news for all the rest. Grandma was right.

To Open the Last Dispensation: Moses Chapter 1

After all these years it comes as a surprise for me to learn that the Book of Moses appeared in the same year as the publication of the Book of Mormon, the first chapter being delivered in the very month of its publication. And it is a totally different kind of book, in another style, from another world. It puts to rest the silly arguments about who really wrote the Book of Mormon, for whoever produced the Book of Moses would have been even a greater genius. That first chapter is a composition of unsurpassed magnificence. And we have all overlooked it completely.

The Joseph Smith controversy is silly for the same reason the Shakespeare controversy is silly. Granted that a simple countryman could not have written the plays that go under the name of Will Shakespeare, who could? If that man is hard to imagine as their author, is it any easier to imagine a courtier, or a London wit, or a doctor of the schools or, just for laughs, a committee of any of the above as the source of that miraculous outpouring? Joseph Smith's achievement is of a different sort, but even more staggering: he challenged the whole world to fault him in his massive sacred history and an unprecedented corpus of apocalyptic books. He took all the initiative and did all the work, withholding nothing and claiming no immunity on religious or any other grounds; he spreads a thousand pages before us and asks us to find something wrong. And after a century and a half with all that material to work on, the learned world comes up with nothing better than the old discredited Solomon Spaulding story it began with. What an astounding tribute to the achievement of the Prophet; that after all this time and with all that evidence his enemies can do no better than that! Even more impressive is the positive evidence that is accumulating behind the Book of Moses – which includes fragments from books of Adam, Noah and Enoch; for in our day ancient books that bear those names are being seriously studied for the first time in modern history, and comparison with the Joseph Smith versions is impressing leading scholars in the field. But even without external witnesses, what a masterpiece we have in that first chapter of the Book of Moses! Consider the below.

W as the great last dispensation to be brought on with old shopworn forms and ceremonies? A dispensation is a period of the world's history during which the church of God with its covenants and ordinances is upon the earth; in the apocalyptic scheme of things it is a comparatively brief period of light following a long period of darkness. What would be an appropriate ensign to announce and inaugurate such a happy time? The single civilization that embraces the world today, whichever way it turns, sees only itself, a great all-confining cliché in which one can think only of what is being thought and do only what is being done. It cannot even imagine a new dispensation, let alone supply one. Like a heavy galleon it labors on into ever-deepening gloom, prodded on its way from time to time by promising puffs of a New Order, New Method, New Education, New Deal, New Life, New Cure, New Light, New Way, etc., but ever and again losing momentum as the fleeting winds quickly blow themselves out, leaving the old scow to wallow on as best it may towards the dawn of nothing. To want something totally new and different is one thing; to supply it is another. Dr. Johnson, Boswell reports, "projected . . . a work to shew how small a quantity of real fiction there is in the world; and that the same images, with very little variation, have served all the authors who have ever lived." Who, then, is going to come up with anything really new? It would help also, since we are asking for the impossible, for this new thing to be vast in scope and glorious in conception and compounded of truth rather than fiction. From what source can we look for comfort? From none on this distracted globe.

It came from the outside, the Mormons said: The long, long silence was broken by an angel from on high. At once the whole world exploded in one long hoot of derision — adequate witness to the total novelty of the thing; here was something utterly alien and retrograde to everything the world taught and believed. It wasn't only that the boy Joseph Smith had an idea about an angel — it was the clear, detailed, factual, clinical account of the visits that left his fellowmen incoherent with rage. Even more outrageous was his vision of the Father and Son: the mere idea of it was astoundingly original, but again, the simple, straightforward, noble manner in which he reported it left no room for contention; it was "yea, yea, and nay, nay," for as the only witness to the most astonishing of his experiences, Joseph could not be confounded by any contrary evidence; and by the same token neither could anyone be asked to take him seriously were it not that he came before an unbelieving world with boundless riches in his hands.

For one thing, he brought out three formidable volumes of scripture. One need look no farther than the opening chapter of each of these to realize that a new dispensation is indeed upon us, with all the visions and blessings of old. The first section of the Doctrine and Covenants, or Book of Commandments, takes up all the main themes of the gospel that had been the burden of every former dispensation, and had been lost in all the dark intervals between them, and weaves them together into one strong texture in which warning and deliverance are equally balanced. The emergence in our day of the old apocalyptic literature, heretofore unrecognized for what it was, though it has suddenly become clear that the Bible teems with it, now supports Doctrine and Covenants, section 1, as new-found text after text echoes its message in identical terms.

At the same time, the opening chapter of the Book of Mormon emerges as the perfect model and type of those more specialized apocalypses or testaments attributed to individuals that are now taking up their position in the growing procession of early Jewish and Christian Apocrypha. The standard scenario which they follow is the story of the righteous man, distressed by the evils of his time and deeply concerned for the future of his people, for whom he weeps and prays until one day he is carried away in a vision in which he makes a celestial journey culminating with the view of God upon his throne; on his journey he learns the plan of salvation as well as the secrets of the universe, and receives a call to teach and admonish God's children on earth. Returning to earth, he first bears witness of divine providence to his immediate family, and bestows patriarchal blessings and prophetic warnings on his sons (hence the designation of his story as a "testament"), and then goes forth among the people to preach repentance and warn of judgments to come (that makes the account an "apocalypse"). Usually his message is rejected and he with a faithful band retires from the scene as destruction descends upon the wicked. Today we have testaments and apocalypses bearing the name of almost every patriarch, prophet, and apostle from Adam on down, some of them very old, and all of them connected in with each other and with the Bible at crucial points. Hence, we can say without hesitation that the first chapter of the Book of Mormon, the testament of Lehi, has the authenticity of a truly ancient pseudepigraphic writing stamped all over it. It is a well-nigh perfect example of the genre.

But it is the first chapter of the Book of Moses that commands the most boundless wonder and esteem. It was brought forth in the very month that the Book of Mormon came from the press and no one less inspired than the man who produced the one could have produced the other. Find the author of the Book of Moses and you have found the author of the Book of Mormon. All other candidates may withdraw. And yet, what a difference! The one is a collection of the writings of pious sectaries in the wilderness — the Rekhabite motif resounds on almost every page: chronicles and annals, letters and sermons, commentaries, hymns and meditations; the other, the voice of Moses booming down the corridors of time as he transmits to us the words that come down to him from the beginning — he sings Enoch's song, and Noah's and Adam's, to which Abraham's is added in another book. But it is that opening chapter to which we turn with awe. What other prelude could there be to the history of the race, what other prologue could ever give it such depth of meaning and such gratifying consistency? First, we find Moses in the presence of God and the bosom of eternity, being apprised of a special calling to which he has been appointed as co-worker with the Savior. (Moses 1: 3-9.) A preliminary test is indicated — suddenly the lights go out and Moses is found lying unconscious and helpless upon the earth; as he slowly comes to himself, he recognizes the misery and the glory of fallen man: "Now . . . I know that man is nothing, which thing I never had supposed." And then, in the same breath: "But now mine own eyes have beheld God . . . his glory was upon me . . . I was transfigured before him." (Moses 1:10-11.)

Weakness is his present condition, glory his everlasting birthright. It is in this moment of man's greatest helplessness and vulnerability that Satan chooses to strike, attempting first by persuasion and then by intimidation to get Moses to worship him as the god of this world. But Moses has not wholly forgotten who he is, "a son of God, in the similitude of his Only Begotten," and denounces Satan as a sham, while professing himself awaiting further light and knowledge: "I will not cease to call upon God, I have other things to inquire of him." (Moses 1:13, 18.) The humiliating exposure of Satan becomes unendurable when Moses announces that he actually is what his adversary falsely claims to be, "a son of God, in the similitude of his Only Begotten; and where is thy glory that I should worship thee?" This is too much for Satan, who casts aside his celebrated but now useless subtlety and launches a frontal attack of satanic fury, a tremendous tantrum, as he "cried with a loud voice, and rent upon the earth, and commanded, saying: I am the Only Begotten, worship me." (Moses 1:19.) The whole scene is presented in dramatic form as a ritual combat, a stychomachia, and true to the ancient pattern, the hero is momentarily bested, overcome by the powers of darkness, as he "began to fear," and "saw the bitterness of hell." But with his last ounce of strength he calls upon God from the depths and is delivered: he has won the fight, he has prevailed against the power of him who "sought to destroy the world, for he knew not the mind of God."

And now the scene changes (verses 23 and 24 read like stage directions); the lights go up, the music soars and Moses, though remaining on earth, is again invested with glory and hears the voice of God proclaiming him victor, worthy and chosen to lead God's people "as if thou wert God" — the type and model of the ancient Year King proclaimed after his victory over death as God's ruler on earth. He is specifically told that he shall "be made stronger than many waters" — for he has just passed through the waters of death and rebirth, *de profundis;* and shown himself capable and worthy of the mission which is now entrusted to him. After this royal acclamation, reminiscent of combat and coronation episodes dramatized in the earliest year rites throughout the ancient world, after the coronation, the scene again changes, as Moses and the reader view the field of labor in which the prophet is to work; he receives a thorough briefing, an intimate knowledge of the earth in its cosmic setting, its physical makeup ("every particle" of it), and everything that lives upon it. Naturally, he wants to know what is behind the behind and beyond the beyond, but God assures him that such knowledge is not for now: "But only an account of this earth, and the inhabitants thereof, give I unto you" (Moses 1:35), with which knowledge Moses is finally "content." Nevertheless, quite fundamental to a correct understanding of this world is its relationship to the wider structure of things, to heavens without end and worlds without number, constantly coming into existence and passing away in an endless processing; " . . . and there is no end to my works, neither to my words." (Moses 1: 38.) And this cosmic discourse is summed up and concluded in the most comforting proclamation of all: "For behold — this is my work and my glory — to bring to pass the immortality and eternal life of man." (Moses 1: 39.) All this becoming and passing away, the endless processing of the same elements, would offer only the overpowering and depressing prospect of science fiction, were it not for that ultimate assurance: man is going somewhere after all; in the course of nature he is doomed (2 Nephi 9:7) but the course of nature does not have the last word — God is on top of the problem and he is working for us.

The three concluding verses of the chapter place upon it an undeniable seal of authenticity. Of careful concern in each of the records handed down through the Prophet Joseph is the establishing of the exact manner in which the work has been preserved. This is another mark of the newly discovered pseudepigrapha: these verses of Moses might have been taken out of any number of Jewish or Christian Apocrypha; especially those writings from the "Forty-day Literature" in which the Coptic records are so rich: "And now Moses, my son . . . thou shalt write the things which I shall speak. And in a day when the children of men shall esteem my words as naught and take many of them from the book which thou shalt write, behold, I will raise up another like unto thee; and they shall be had again among the children of men — among as many as shall believe." (Moses 1:40-41.) And so the present dispensation gets them: "And now they are spoken unto you. Show them not unto any except them that believe." (Moses 1:42.) Such is the standard formula for the preservation and transmission of apocalyptic writings.

As a literary tour de force, Moses chapter 1 is awe-inspiring. Equally impressive is the way it takes up a position alongside other ancient writings that tell the same story in much the same way. Of particular relevance are the apocalypses of Abraham and Adam, from both of which Joseph Smith has conveyed purported writings. Let us turn to them for some illuminating comparisons.

Those who wish to credit Joseph Smith with a comprehension of comparative literature and ritual far beyond his time and training are free to do so. They may even insist, as they have with the Book of Mormon, that this is the way any uneducated rustic would tell the story. Today, however, we have several very ancient and significant parallels to Moses 1, which lie far beyond the reach of coincidence or daydreaming. The number of details and the order in which they occur make it perfectly clear that we are dealing with specific works of great antiquity which come from a common source. To show what we mean, let us compare Moses', Abraham's, and Adam's confrontations with Satan; these stories themselves contain pointed references to Enoch, with whom each here is duly compared. Let it be remembered that these accounts are not scripture, but are simply ancient records that help us understand the Enoch story.

First the Apocalypse of Abraham, an Old Slavonic account discovered in 1895 and first published by Bonwetsch in 1897.[1] K. Koch has recently ranked it as one of the six definitely authentic early Hebrew apocalypses.[2] Let us place it in parallel columns against our book of Moses, chapter 1.

Moses Chapter 1	Apocalypse of Abraham Chapter 9 (Ch. 1 of the Apocalypse proper)
The setting:	
1:1. The words of God . . . unto Moses . . . when Moses was caught up into an exceedingly high mountain.	9:8 [Abraham, in order to receive the vision, must] "Bring me the sacrifice . . . upon a high mountain."
God will show him everything:	
4. I will show thee the workmanship of mine hands; but not all, for my works are without end, . . .	6. In this sacrifice I will show forth to thee the ages of the world,
	and show thee that which is hidden. Thou shalt behold great things, which thou hast never seen before,
5. Wherefore, no man can behold my works . . . and no man can behold all my glory. [See Abr. 2:12: "Thy servant has sought thee earnestly; now I have found thee."]	because thou delightest to seek after me,

6. And I have a work for thee, Moses, my son. . . .

8. And . . . Moses, looked, and beheld the world upon which he was created . . . and all the children of men which are, and which were created. . . .

The hero is helpless after the vision:

9. And the presence of God withdrew from Moses . . . and [he] was left unto himself. And . . . he fell unto the earth.

10. And . . . it was for the space of many hours before Moses did again receive his natural strength. . . .

Satan takes advantage of his weakness:

12. Behold, Satan came tempting him, saying: Moses, son of man, worship *me*. (Italics added.)

and I have called thee my friend.

9. And I will show unto thee, the ages of the world fixed and created by my word, and show thee what is going to happen to the children of men as they shall do good or evil.

Ch. 10.

1. [Hearing a voice] I looked here and there.
2. It was not a human breath, and so my spirit was afraid, and my soul departed from me. And I became as a stone, and fell to the earth, for I had no more strength to stand;
3. And as I lay with my face to the ground I heard the voice of the Holy One say,
4. Go, Jaoel, in the power of my name, and raise that man up! Let him recover from his trembling.

(Chaps. 11 & 12 are a detailed description of Abraham's sacrifice, during which, Chap. 13):

1. I carried out everything according to the angel's instructions . . .
3. Then an unclean creature with wings alighted upon the sacrificial victims . . .
4. The unclean bird said to me: What are you doing, Abraham, in this holy place . . . where you yourself may perish in the fire!
5. Leave the man [angel] standing beside you and flee!

8

13. And . . . Moses . . . said: Who art thou? . . .

15. I can judge between thee and God. . . .
16. Get thee hence, Satan; deceive me not. . . .

Satan put to shame by humiliating contrast with the hero:

13. I am a son of God . . . and where is thy glory, that I should worship thee?

14. For behold, I could not look upon God, except . . . I were strengthened before him. But I can look upon thee in the natural man. Is it not so, surely?
15. . . . Where is thy glory, for it is darkness unto me? And I can judge between thee and God. . . .

16. Get thee hence, Satan; deceive me not;

for God said unto me: Thou art after the similitude of mine Only Begotten.

The hero is strengthened for the contest:

6. And I asked the angel, "Who is this, my Lord?"

7. He said: This is ungodliness: this is Azazel [Satan]!

8. [Michael:] Shame upon you, Satan!
9. For Abraham's part is in heaven, and thine is upon this earth.
10. God has placed thee upon this earth as the Adversary, to lead dishonest spirits and practice deception.
12. Listen, my friend, and I will put you to shame,

13. Thou has not the power to tempt all the righteous.

14. Depart from this man! Thou canst not lead him astray, for he is thine enemy and enemy to all those who follow thee and love after thy desire.

15. For behold, the garment [of glory] which once fitted you in heaven, is now laid up for him. And the decay to which he was fated now goes over to thee!

17. And he also gave me commandments ... saying: Call upon God in the name of mine Only Begotten, and worship me.
18. ...I have other things to inquire of him: for his glory has been upon me, wherefore I can judge between him and thee. Depart hence, Satan.

14:3. Take heart, exercise the power that I give thee over this one, who hateth truth ...
4. ...who rebelled against the Almighty ...
5. Say to him: ...Depart, Azazel ...
6. Thy lot is to rule over those who are with thee ...
7. Depart from me ...
8. And I spoke as the angel instructed me.

The hero is overcome but calls out and is saved:

19. And ... Satan cried with a loud voice, and rent upon the earth, and commanded, saying: I am the Only Begotten, worship me.

9. He [Satan] spoke: Abraham! And I said: Here is thy servant.

20. And ... Moses began to fear exceedingly; and ... saw the bitterness of hell. Nevertheless, calling upon God, he received strength, and he commanded, saying: Depart from me, Satan. ...

10. But the angel said to me: O, do not reply to him! For God has given him power over those who answer him ...
11. ...no matter how much he speaks to thee, answer him not, lest his will overpower thine.
12. For the Eternal One has given him a powerful will. Answer him not! (See Testament of Abraham [Falasha p. 100ff.] where he says to Isaac approaching the altar: "Come near, my son, so that thou mayest perceive the one ... who frightened me and because of whom I was afraid ..." referring to his own jeopardy on the altar.)

21. And now Satan began to tremble, and the earth shook; and Moses received strength,

(This detail is found in *Enoch's* meeting with Satan in Giz. 13:1-3. "And Enoch said to and called upon God, saying: In the name of the Only Begotten, depart hence, Satan.

Azazel, Depart! Thou shalt have no peace, a great sentence has gone forth against thee to bind thee. 2. And there will be no further discussion or questioning with thee, because of thy dishonest and deceitful works among men.")

22. And . . . Satan cried with a loud voice, with weeping, and wailing, and gnashing of teeth; and he departed hence, even from the presence of Moses, that he beheld him not.

Gizeh 13:3. Then he departed and spoke to all of them [his followers] and they all feared, and trembling and terror seized them.

The hero is borne aloft:

24. And . . . when Satan had departed . . . Moses lifted up his eyes unto heaven, being filled with the Holy Ghost. . . .

15:2. The angel in charge of the sacrifice . . . took
3. me by the right hand, and set me on the right wing of the dove while he sat on the left side.

25. And calling upon . . . God, he beheld his glory again. . . .

4. So it bore me to the limits of the flaming fire
5. and then on into heaven, as if on many winds, which was fixed above the firmament. *Bait ha-Midrash.* 5:170. R. Ishmael [double for Enoch]: When I went up to the mountain top . . . arriving at the seventh temple. I stood to pray before God: and I lifted up my eyes and said . . . deliver me from Satan. And the Metatron [also Enoch!] came who [served?] the angel, even the Prince of the Presence, and spread his wings and came to meet me with great joy . . . and he took me with his hand and raised me up.]

(See 2 Ne. 4:25 — "Upon the wings of his Spirit hath my body been carried away upon exceeding high mountains. And mine eyes have beheld great things, yea, even too great for man.")

24. And . . . when Satan had departed from the presence of Moses . . . Moses lifted up his eyes unto heaven, being filled with the Holy Ghost. . . .

11

25. ...And he heard a voice, saying: Blessed art thou, Moses, for I, the Almighty, have chosen thee, and thou shalt be made stronger than many waters; for they shall obey thy command as if thou wert God. (Here Moses is hailed as the victorious sacral king.)

17:1. And while he was speaking, fire surrounded us and a voice... like the voice of many waters like the raging of the sea in the surf.

27. And... Moses cast his eyes and beheld the earth....
28. And he beheld also the inhabitants thereof, and there was not a soul which he beheld not... and their numbers were great, even numberless.

15:6. And I saw a mighty light... and in the light a mighty fire in which was a host, even a great host of mighty beings [forms] constantly changing shape and appearance, moving, changing, praying, and uttering words I could not understand.

He is shown the field of his mission:

In the "testamentary" literature, each patriarch takes a journey to heaven and is given a view of the entire earth, an account of which then becomes an integral part of his missionary message upon his return. (Compare 1 Ne. 1:4-15, Abr. 3:15, Moses 1:40.)

27. ...As the voice was still speaking, Moses cast his eyes and beheld the earth, yea, even all of it; and there was not a particle of it which he did not behold....

21:1. He said to me: Look beneath thy feet upon the Firmament. Recognize at that level the creation there presented, the creatures that are in it, and the world that has been prepared for them.

28. And he beheld also the inhabitants thereof, and there was not a soul which he beheld

2. And I looked down, and behold... the earth and her fruits, and all that moves upon

not ... and their numbers were great, even numberless as the sand upon the sea shore.

29. And he beheld many lands; and each land was called earth, and there were inhabitants on the face thereof.

Confrontation with God:

31. And ... the glory of the Lord was upon Moses, so that Moses stood in the presence of God, and talked with him face to face.

30. And it came to pass that Moses called upon God. . . .

33. And worlds without number have I created; and I also created them for mine own purpose. . . .

38. And as one earth shall pass away ... even so shall another come; and there is no end to

her ... and the power of the people ...

3. the lower regions ... the pit and its torments ...

4. I saw there the sea and its islands, the beasts, its fishes, leviathan and his sphere ...

5. the streams of water, their sources and their courses ...

9. I saw there a mighty host of men, women, and children half of them on the right side of the picture and half on the left.

16:1. I said to the angel: I can see nothing, I have become weak, my spirit leaves me!

2. He said to me: Stay with me; be not afraid. He whom thou now beholdest coming towards us ... is the Eternal One, who loves thee.

3. But He himself you do not see ...

4. But do not be overcome, I am with you to strengthen you.

17:5. So I continued to pray ...

6. He said: Speak without ceasing!

7ff. (Abraham calls upon God naming his attributes.)

11. Eli, meaning My God ... El! El! El! El! El Jaoel!

13. Thou who bringest order into the unorganized universe, even the chaos which in the perishable world goes forth from good and evil.

Thou who renewest the World of the righteous.

14. O light, that shone upon

my works, neither to my words.

The Epic Question and Answer:

30. And ... Moses called upon God, saying: Tell me, I pray thee, *why* these things are so, and by *what* thou madest them? (Italics added. Cf. Abr. 1:2. "I sought for the blessings of the fathers, ... desiring also ... to possess a greater knowledge.")

31. ...And the Lord God said unto Moses: For mine own purpose have I made these things. Here is wisdom and it remaineth in me.

33. And worlds without number have I created; and I also created them for mine own purpose....

35. But only an account of this earth, and the inhabitants thereof, give I unto you. For behold, there are many worlds ... that now stand, ... but all things are numbered unto me, but they are mine and I know them.

Left alone a second time:

9. And the presence of God withdrew from Moses, that his glory was not upon Moses; and Moses was left unto himself.

thy creatures before the morning light ...

16. Hear my prayers!
17. Look with favor upon me: Show me, teach me. Give thy servant all that which thou hast promised him.
26.1. Eternal, Mighty, Only One! *Why* hast thou so arranged things, that it should be so?

26.5. As thine own father's [Terah's] will is in him, and as thine own will is in thee, so the resolves of mine own will are set for all the future, before you knew there even was such a thing ...

19:3. Look upon the places beneath the firmament, upon which thou standest [Cf. this formula in Abr. 3:3, 4, 5, 7 etc.!] Behold there is not a single place nor any spot at all but what is occupied by Him whom thou seekest.
4. And as he spoke the place opened up and beneath me there was heaven.
5. And upon the seventh Firmament on which I stood ... I saw the splendor of invisible glory investing living beings.

30:1. And as he was still speaking I found myself upon the earth.
2. I spoke: Eternal, Mighty,

And as he was left unto himself, he fell unto the earth.

(Abraham 2:12: "Now, after the Lord had withdrawn from speaking to me, and withdrawn his face from me, I said in my heart: Thy servant has sought thee earnestly; now I have found thee.")

Only one!
3. Behold I am no longer in the glory in which I was above! And what my heart sought to know I did not understand.

4. And he said to me: What in thy heart thou didst so desire, that I will tell thee, because thou hast sought diligently to behold, etc.

These parallel accounts, separated by centuries, cannot be coincidence. Nor can all the others. The first man to have such a confrontation with Satan was Adam. A wealth of stories about it closely matches the accounts of Abraham, Moses, Enoch, and other heroes. Perhaps the oldest Adam traditions are those collected from all over the ancient East at a very early time, which have reached us in later Ethiopian and Arabic manuscripts under the title of "The Combat of Adam and Eve against Satan.[3] It contains at least thirteen different showdowns between Adam and the adversary, of which we present a few of the most striking. Since the motif was characteristically repeated with variations (the monkish mind could not resist the temptation to work a good thing to death) it will be necessary to repeat some passages from the book of Moses.

Moses Chapter 1	Combat of Adam (direct quotations from the document are indicated with quotation marks)
9. And the presence of God withdrew from Moses, that his glory was not upon Moses; and Moses was left unto himself. . . . He fell unto the earth.	Column 297-98. Leaving the glorious garden, they (Adam and Eve) were seized with fear and "they fell down upon the earth and remained as if dead."
10. And it came to pass that it was for the space of many hours before Moses did again receive his natural strength like unto man; and he said unto himself: Now, for this cause I know that man is nothing,	299. While Adam was still in that condition, Eve, stretching high her hands, prayed: "O Lord . . . thy servant has fallen from the Garden" and is banished to a desert place. (Gen. 3:18f.)

which thing I never had
supposed.

11. But now mine own eyes
have beheld God; but not my
natural, but my spiritual eyes,
for my natural eyes could not
have beheld: for I should have
withered and died in his
presence; but his glory was
upon me: and I beheld his face,
for I was transfigured before
him.

299. They say: "Today our eyes
having become terrestrial can
no longer behold the things
they once did."

12. And it came to pass that
when Moses had said these
words, behold, Satan came
tempting him, saying: Moses,
son of man, worship me.

306. Satan, seeing them at
prayer, appears to them in a
great light and sets up his
throne on the site, thus
claiming the earth as his
kingdom while his followers
sing hymns in his praise.

13. And it came to pass that
Moses looked upon Satan and
said: Who art thou? For
behold, I am a son of God, in
the similitude of his Only
Begotten; and where is thy
glory, that I should worship
thee?

307. Adam, puzzled, prays for
light, asking: Can this be
another God here hailed by his
angels? An angel of the Lord
arrives and says: "Fear not,
Adam, what you see is Satan
and his companions who wish
to seduce you again. First he
appeared to you as a serpent
and now he wants you to
worship him so he can draw
you after him away from
God."

15-18. ...Where is thy glory,
for it is darkness unto me?...
Get thee hence, Satan; deceive
me not.... I can judge
between [God] and thee.
Depart hence, Satan.

Then the angel exposed and
humiliated Satan in Adam's
presence and cast him out
saying to Adam:

13. I am a son of God....
14. ...I could not look upon
God, except... I were

"Fear not: God who created
you will strengthen you!"

strengthened before him. (See 20: "Calling upon God, he received strength.")

307-8. The next morning as Adam prayed with upraised hands, Satan appeared to him, saying, "Adam, I am an angel of the great God. The Lord has sent me to you." It was his plan to kill Adam and thus "remain sole master and possessor of the earth." But God sent three heavenly messengers to Adam bringing him the signs of the priesthood and kingship. 309. And Adam wept because they reminded him of his departed glory, but God said they were signs of the atonement to come, whereupon Adam rejoiced.

12. Satan came tempting him, saying: Moses, son of man, worship me.
19. ...I am the Only Begotten, worship me.

323-24. After a forty-day fast Adam and Eve were very weak, stretched out upon the floor of the cave as if dead, but still praying. Satan then came, clothed in light, speaking sweet words to deceive them saying: "I am the first created of God... now God has commanded me to lead you to my habitation... to be restored to your former glory."

325. But God knew that he planned to lead them to far-away places and destroy them. Adam said, Who was this glorious old man who came to us? Answer: He is Satan in human form come to deceive you by giving you signs to prove his bonafides but I have cast him out.

13. Moses looked upon Satan and said: Who art thou?

17

21. Now Satan began to tremble. . . .
22. And it came to pass that Satan cried with a loud voice, with weeping, and wailing, and gnashing of teeth; and he departed hence. . . .

18. I have other things to inquire of [God]: for his glory has been upon me, wherefore I can judge between him and thee. Depart hence, Satan.

5:6. And after many days an angel of the Lord appeared unto Adam, saying: Why dost thou offer sacrifices unto the Lord? And Adam said unto him: I know not, save the Lord commanded me.
7. And then the angel spake, saying: This thing is a similitude of the sacrifice of the Only Begotten of the Father, which is full of grace and truth.
9. . . .As thou hast fallen thou mayest be redeemed, and all mankind, even as many as will.

10. . . .Adam . . . was filled, . . . saying: . . .In this life I shall have joy, and again in the flesh I shall see God.

326. Adam and Eve, still weak from fasting and still praying, are again confronted by Satan who, being rebuffed, "is sore afflicted" and weeping and wailing says, " 'God has wrecked my scheme . . . he has rendered worthless the plan which I contrived against his servants.' And he retired in confusion."

327. Adam asked, Why is this? Answer: "God wanted to show you the weakness of Satan and his evil intentions for since the day you left the Garden he has not let a day pass without trying to harm you, but I have not let him have the victory over you." (Adam thus learned to distinguish between good and evil.)

329. Again Adam and Eve were sacrificing with upraised arms in prayer, asking God to accept their sacrifice and forgive their sins. "And the Lord said to Adam and Eve: As you have made this sacrifice to me, so I will make an offering of my flesh when I come to earth, and so save you. . . . And God ordered an angel to take tongs and receive the sacrifice of Adam."

At this Adam and Eve rejoiced. God said: When the terms of my covenant are fulfilled, I will again receive you into my

Garden and my Grace. So Adam continued to make this sacrifice for the rest of his days. And God caused his word to be preached to Adam.

1:20. ...Moses began to fear exceedingly; and as he began to fear, he saw the bitterness of hell. Nevertheless, calling upon God, he received strength. (See Book of Abraham, Facsimile No. 1!) 5:7. This thing is a similitude of the sacrifice of the Only Begotten of the Father, which is full of grace and truth.

330. On the fiftieth day, Adam offering sacrifice as was his custom, Satan appeared in the form of a man and smote him in the side with a sharp stone even as Adam raised his arms in prayer. Eve tried to help him as blood and water flowed on the altar. "God ... sent his word and revived Adam saying: 'Finish thy sacrifice, which is most pleasing to me. For even so will I be wounded and blood and water will come from my side; that will be the true Sacrifice, placed on the altar as a perfect offering.' ... And so God healed Adam."

Plainly, others knew the story long ago, but who could have taught it to Joseph?

NOTES

1. For the sources, Paul Riessler, *Altjüdisches Schrifttum ausserhalb der Bibel,* 3rd ed. (Heidelberg: F. H. Kerle, 1975), p. 1267. It has been traced to Ebionite and Essene circles closely related to the communities of the Dead Sea Scrolls. Unfortunately, we are here reduced to using Riessler's German translation of the Old Slavonic text.

2. K. Koch, *Ratlos vor der Apokalyptik* (Gütersloh: G. Mohn, 1970), pp. 16, 19ff.

3. The sources are discussed and some of them are collected and translated in J. P. Migne, *Encyclopedie Théologique* (Paris: 1856), Cols. 289ff. It is to this work that our page numbers refer.

The Expanding Gospel

2

Moses takes us back to the beginning — but which beginning? Nothing in the restored gospel is more stimulating to the inquiring mind than the infinitely expanded panorama of time and space it spreads before us. Our existence is viewed not as a one-act play, beginning with instantaneous creation of everything out of nothing and ending with its dissolution into the immaterial nothing from which it came (as St. Jerome puts it), but as a series of episodes of which for the present we are allowed to view only a few. The play has always been going on and always will be: The Man Adam played other roles and was known by different names before he came here, and after his departure from mortal life assumes other offices and titles. Even in this life everyone changes from one form to another, gets new names and callings and new identities as he plays his proverbial seven parts — but always preserving his identity as the same conscious living being. The common religion of the human race centers around that theme: the individual and the society pass from one stage of life to another not by a gradual and imperceptible evolution but by a series of abrupt transformations, dramatized the world over in Rites of Passage, of which birth and death are the prime examples coming not unannounced but suddenly and irresistibly when their time is ripe; other passages, as into puberty and marriage, follow the same pattern.

In such a perspective of eternity the stock questions of controversy between science and religion become meaningless. When did it all begin – can you set a date? Were there ever human-like creatures who did not belong to the human race? (There still are!) How old is the earth? the universe? How long are they going to last? What will we do in heaven forever? etc. Nothing is settled yet, not only because the last precincts are never heard from in science – and their report always comes as a shocker – but because we are far from getting the last word in religion either; for us the story remains open-ended – at both ends – in a progression of beginnings and endings without beginning or end, each episode proceeding from what goes before and leading to the next. The Absolutes of the University of Alexandria to which the Doctors of the Christians and the Jews were completely in the thrall from the fourth century on, simply do not exist for Latter-day Saints. Instead of that, they have a much bigger book to study; it is time they were getting with it.

The expression "expanding gospel" is not a contradiction of terms. Even the Roman Catholic authorities concluded after much thought that the proper business of theology and philosophy is to expand men's *knowledge* of the gospel while leaving the scriptures, the sacred deposit and source of that knowledge, untouched by the addition or subtraction of so much as a syllable.[1] Thus men, by the exercise of their intellects, may add to the gospel, but God may not. But this puts the thunder before the lightning: where has God imposed any limits on his own prerogative of imparting his word to man? The scriptural warnings against adding or subtracting, aside from being limited to specific individual books, are addressed specifically to men — no *man* may add to the scriptures. That imposes no restriction on God. But it is men who have expanded and contracted the scope of the holy writ to conform to their broad or narrow views of the gospel; it is men who have selected the books that make up the word of God, and these men have not been in agreement. The debate has raged for centuries about certain well-known writings, and still remains undecided.[2]

Now we are faced by a new and important development. A sizable number of writings have recently been discovered claiming apostolic or otherwise inspired authorship and enjoying unprecedented antiquity. What is to be done with them? Of the author of some of the prophecies in the Dead Sea Scrolls Father Danielou writes:

> A revelation was made known to him . . . that the Messiah was near. . . . Now what is amazing is that this prophecy was verified exactly. Thus between the great prophets of the Old Testament and John the Baptist he emerges as a new link in the preparation for the Advent of Christ: he is, as Michaud writes, one of the great figures of Israel's prophetic tradition. It is amazing that he remained so unknown for so long. Now that he is known the question arises as to what we are going to do about this knowledge. . . . Why does not this message, then, form part of inspired Scripture?[3]

This question, says Danielou, now confronts equally the Jewish and the Christian world. How can they expand their gospel to include the words of a newly found prophet? If the new discoveries only contained exactly what was already known and accepted, there would be no objection to admitting them to the canon; but neither would they have any message for us, save to confirm what is already known. But what makes the documents so exciting is that they follow along familiar grooves to the end and then continue onward into new territory, expanding the confines of the gospel. Are we to assume that their writers, so strict and upright in their ways and so conscientious in their teachings, are saints as far as we can follow them only to become deluded purveyors of fraud and falsehood the moment they step beyond territory familiar to us?

Before reaching a decision on this important head, our first obligation is to inform ourselves as to what it is that these writings teach over and above conventional Jewish and Christian doctrine. What they teach, that is, seriously and as a whole. Speculative flights and picturesque oddities can be expected in any sizable apocryphal writing, and when such are confined to one or two texts they can be ruled out as serious doctrine. But in working through the newly found documents one soon becomes aware of certain themes that receive overwhelming emphasis and appear not in a few texts but in many or most of them. Such deserve our serious attention. Among the most conspicuous of these is the matter of a certain council held in heaven "at the foundation of the world" where the divine plan of salvation was presented and received with acclamations of joy; joined to this we are presented almost invariably with some account of the opposition to that plan and the results of that opposition. Around these two themes of the plan and the opposition a great deal of the old apocryphal writing revolves. But it is in the very oldest records of the race that we find some of the clearest statements of the doctrine, which in the oldest fragment of all, actually goes under a recognized label as "the Memphite theology."

The antiquity of the material contained in the so-called Shabako stone of the British Museum has been fully demonstrated and is today not seriously questioned.[4] The only puzzle to scholars has been how anything so completely thought-out and sophisticated could turn up in what may well be the oldest known text in existence. There is nothing "primitive" in this dramatic presentation which was to mark the founding of the First Dynasty of Egypt. It is divided into two parts, a historical and a theological, the former explaining how the kingdom came to be established and organized after its peculiar fashion, and the latter how and why the world itself was created. The beholder of the drama, which was enacted by priests with the king taking the leading role, is never allowed to forget that what is ritually done on earth is but the faithful reflection of what was once done in heaven.[5] Since a number of scholars today see an unbroken line of succession between the "Memphite theology" and the Logos-theology of John, the Shabako stone may not be out of place as the starting point in a study of the expanding gospel.[6] But quite aside from that, it deserves mention as the earliest and one of the best descriptions of the council in heaven.

In the beginning, we are told, " . . . all the gods assembled in the presence" of Ptah, who "made a division between Horus and Seth, and forbade them to quarrel," giving each his assigned portion.[7] Then for some reason he decided that his first-born, Horus, should be his unique heir, and solemnly announced to the assembled gods, pointing to Horus, "I have chosen thee to be the first, thee alone; my inheritance shall be to this my heir, the son of my son . . . the first-born, opener of the ways, a son born on the birthday of Wep-wawet," that is, on the New Year, the Day of Creation.[8] Thus, instead of being two portions, they were both united under Horus, while the controversy with Seth was patched up for the duration of the festival.[9] The entire middle portion of the Shabako Text is obliterated, but from countless other Egyptian sources, we know that the conflict between Horus and Seth never ceased on this earth, the combat and victory of Horus being ritually repeated at every coronation.[10] After rites dealing with a baptism, resurrection and the building of the temple at Memphis, the texts break off completely to resume with a catalogue of Ptah's titles as "he who sitteth upon the great throne, heavenly father who begot Atum, heavenly mother who bore Atum, the great one, the mind and mouth [heart and tongue] of the council of the gods [the ennead]."[11] "In the heart [of Ptah] was conceived the image [form, likeness] of Atum, on the tongue [by the word] was the image of Atum. Great and mighty is Ptah through whose mind and word all the spirits were brought forth.[12] And through the mind and word [of God] all physical members were invested with power, according to the doctrine that he [God] is as that which is in every body [i.e., the heart] and in every mouth [i.e., the tongue] of every god, of every human, of every animal, of every creeping thing, of whatsoever possessed life; for whatever is thought and whatever is uttered is according to his will. The council of the gods brought forth the seeing of the eyes, the hearing of the ears, the breathing of the nose, that these might convey information to the heart, which in turn became aware of things, to which awareness the tongue gives expression, giving utterance to the mind. In such a way were all the gods brought forth — Atum and the council of the Nine. But the word of God was first that which was conceived in his mind and then what was commanded by his tongue. In such a way were the spirits brought forth and the *hmswt-spirits* elected, for the provision of all nourishment and food, according to the mind and word of God."[13] The best interpretation of *hmswt-spirits,* following Sethe's long discussion of the word, would seem to be spirits chosen for specially high callings, in particular to have progeny.[14] The spirits having been thus created and a physical basis for life supplied, a law was laid down, "that he who does what is good [lovable, desirable] shall be given life to be in a state of peace [or salvation], while he who does evil [that which is hateful] shall be given death to be in a state of punishment [or condemnation]. All the works [of men], all the arts and crafts, the labors of the arms and the goings of the legs, the motion of all the members are subject to this law, conceived in the mind and declared by the tongue [of God], which law shall be the measure [*yimakh*] of all things."[15] All this was done and nourishment and food and all other good things provided by God alone and he saw that his work was good.[16] "And thus it was that all the gods and all the spirits assembled" before the throne of God, the source of all life and joy.[17] The king, representing Osiris, who is the dead king, his own predecessor, "goes through the secret gates in the splendor of the lord of Eternity, in the footsteps of Re of the great throne, to enter the courts on high and become united with the gods and with Ptah, the ancient of days [lord of years]." In the concluding scene the earthly king publicly embraces his son and heir, declaring his calling and succession, even as the god did in the beginning.[18]

That the picture actually goes back to Menes, the founder of the First Dynasty, is confirmed right at the beginning of the Pyramid Texts in a writing for Teti, the second king of the dynasty and immediate successor of Menes: "Spoken by the great heavens in the midst of the lower hall of Geb [i.e., the temple of Memphis as the earthly counterpart of the heavenly court]. This is Teti, my beloved son, who sits upon the throne of Geb [the principle of patriarchal succession], who is well pleased with him; he hath declared him to be his heir in the presence of the great assembly of all the gods; every god hath acclaimed him joyfully with upraised hands, saying, Worthy is Teti with whom his father Geb is well pleased!"[19] In the Coffin Texts the theme is carried on as Ptah summons the Great Assembly, "they who share the secrets," gives them formal greeting, and introduces his son and heir to them, who acclaim him as Prince of Peace and Righteousness, shouting for joy.[20] The earthly rites reflect the heavenly, and the king (or noble) announces in his Coffin Text, "I am in the human assembly what he is in heaven. I am ... the seed of Atum, the issue of him who gave the names in the day when Atum discussed it with the gods."[21]

The great Babylonian creation text, the Enuma Elish, begins and ends with the great assembly in heaven. "As once above," it starts out, "when the heavens had not yet received their name and the earth below was not known, ... the Creator, he of vast intelligence, omniscient, omnipotent," presided over "a great assembly among his brethren the gods."[22] Since the purpose of this version of the hymn is to exalt Marduk of Babylon, he takes over the principal functions of creating man and settling the score with the adversary. The most concise statement is on Tablet VI: "Then Marduk resolved upon a wondrous work. He opened his mouth and addressed Ea [his father], and told him of what he had conceived in his heart: 'I wish to bring blood and bone together and to organize them into a human being, whose name shall be man; let it be his duty to serve the gods and satisfy them.' " To provide satisfaction, however, was beyond the power of man, and "Marduk, in order that there be satisfaction, proposed a plan to the gods: 'Let one of their race be put to death that humanity might be. Let one of the assembled gods be delivered up as a guilty one, that they might subsist.' "[23] But Kingu opposed the plan; it was he who made

Tiamat rebel and caused the war. But he was defeated and cast down by Marduk, and the great assembly gave all the power of heaven and earth to Anu and through him to Marduk for carrying out the execution of the plan.[24] Throughout, the earthly rites are a ritual repetition of what was done (in the opening words and title of the hymn) "once above" (*enuma elish*); and the affair ends with the admonition that the rites be repeated at the same place from year to year forever: "Let them rehearse throughout the ages to come at this spot what God has done, that they may never forget it. . . . For this is the earthly image of that which is done in the heavens. . . . Great planner, full of loving-kindness, may he forgive their sins and deliver them by his grace. . . . Let us praise his name. They who have taken their places in the assembly to declare his names, in the holy place let them all together proclaim his name."[25] Though the texts are full of repetitions, contamination, overlapping of different versions coming from different times and places, the main themes of the council and the plan recur consistently.[26]

We know today that the religion of Israel cannot be studied in isolation from that of its neighbors, and for many years the experts have recognized affinities between the documents just cited and certain biblical texts. We have referred to them here, however, primarily to forestall the claim commonly made that the doctrines we are considering are of late, even Gnostic origin. The newly discovered Jewish and Christian Apocrypha have so much to say about the council in heaven and the plan laid down at the foundation of the world that every student should be aware of the very great antiquity and wide ramifications of the idea. According to Ben Sirach, the great assemblies of Israel were the ritual repetition not merely of the gathering at the foot of Sinai but specifically of the great assembly at the creation of the world, when "God set before them [the human race-to-be] a covenant, the Law of Life . . . and showed them his judgments. Their eyes beheld His glorious majesty and their ears heard his voice."[27] According to II Baruch the whole plan of the history of the world was set forth in detail "when the Mighty One took counsel to create the world."[28] According to the Book of Enoch, in the beginning "the Head of Days, his head like white wool, sat with the Son of Man beside him upon the throne of his glory, and the books of the living were opened before him," the books of the living being the register of names of those who were to live upon the earth.[29] Then the calling or mission of the Son and the plan, both of which had been kept secret until then, were "revealed to the Elect."[30] It is not too much to say that the dominant theme of

27

the Thanksgiving Hymns of the Dead Sea Scrolls is an ecstatic contemplation of the wonder of man's participation in heavenly affairs going back to the beginning. Consider a few lines from Hymn VI (or F):

> Thou hast caused me to mount up to an eternal height and to walk in an inconceivable exaltation. And I know that there is a hope for everyone whom thou didst form of dust in the presence of the eternal assembly; and that the sinful spirit whom thou hast purified of great sin may be counted with the host of the saints and enter the society of the congregation of the Sons of Heaven. Thou didst appoint unto man an eternal share with the Spirits that Know, to praise thy name in joyful unison with them and to recount thy wondrous works in the presence thereof.[31]

The whole point of this is that man actually belongs by prior appointment to that community of the Elect who share in the knowledge of the plan and who shouted for joy at the foundation of the world. In the preceding hymn, God is hailed as "prince of the gods and King of the Venerable Ones" and we must remind ourselves that this is neither a Gnostic nor a pagan production.[32] The baffling tenth and eleventh pages of the Manual of Discipline come to life in the light of this imagery. To refer their message to prayers at various times of day makes good sense, since, as we have noted, earthly rites are but the reflection of heavenly events; but if we leave it there much is left unexplained. "He has placed them as an eternal treasure, and established for them a share with the saints, and has joined their society to the family of the Sons of Heaven, the council of the Church and the assembly of the Temple, an establishment [lit. "planting"] which reaches forever into the future and the past."[33] The word which we have translated as "share" above is usually rendered as "lot" (it occurs seventy-six times in the Old Testament), but it is not the gift of chance, but is rather one's "lot" in the sense of having been appointed by God ahead of time. If we turn back to the opening lines of the preceding section of the hymn (p. x), we may see in prayers at dawn a conscious counterpart of the celestial drama: we are told of God's blessing "at the times which he fixed at the beginning of the rule of light, along with his cycles, and in the assembly at the place appointed by him, when the Watchers of Darkness also began." The Watchers, as is well known, were fallen angels, here the equivalent of those who first opposed the Rule of Light. At that time, the text continues, God "opens his treasury and shows his plan." The treasury is referred to many times in the apocrypha, especially in the *Hodiyot* Scroll, as that knowledge which was with God in the beginning, and which he imparted to his Elect.[34] The last word of the phrase is in code — a plain indication that the text does indeed have a double meaning, as it goes on to tell us in terms of lamps in a shrine, of the shining ones being received in the mansion of glory. We are even told that the great light of the Holy of Holies here actually signifies something else.[35]

This interpretation is borne out at the beginning of the Clementine Recognitions, a work having the closest affinities to the Dead Sea Scrolls, in which Peter tells of "the plan (*definitio*) of God which he announced (*promisit*) as his own will and desire in the presence of the First Angels, and which he established as an eternal law for all."[36] This is from a very early and strongly anti-Gnostic work, but the Gnostics have preserved the teaching and given it a characteristic Gnostic twist: "My Father, the joyful glorious light," says the Psalm of Thomas, "summoned all the Aeons of Peace [the First Angels have here become mere abstractions], all his sons and all the angels, and established them that they might rejoice in his greatness [i.e., share it][37]. . . . All bowed the knee before him and sang his praises together, hailing him as the Illuminator of the Worlds."[38] The newly discovered Creation Apocryphon, another "Gnostic" interpretation, tells us that this earth is the result of a discussion in heaven: "On that day began the discussion in which gods, angels, and men participated. And the decisions of the discussion were then carried out by gods, angels, and men. But the Prince Jaltabaoth did not understand the power of faith," and so was denied "the authority over matter" which the others shared.[39] The power of faith, it will be recalled, was the power "by which the worlds were created."

The unimpeachable orthodox Pastor of Hermas is quite as specific: "Behold God, constructing the world in accordance with the great council [in some Mss. "the most honored council"] . . . creating the beautiful world and turning it over to his chosen ones, that He might carry out his promise to them, which he gave in the midst of great glory and rejoicing, that is, if they keep his laws (*legitima*) which they accepted in great faith."[40] The Mandaean version is interesting because it calls the Creator Ptah-il, combining the archaic Egyptian and Semitic names,[41] and while giving the familiar account of the great council, adds the important detail that three messengers were sent down to supervise the work and to instruct Adam, these three being glorious angels who were later to live upon the earth as ordinary mortals and prophets.[41]

So far we have only mentioned the bare fact of an assembly in the presence of God at the foundation of the world, but even so it has not been possible to do so without giving some indication of what the business of the meeting was, namely, the agreement upon the great *plan* which is to be "the measure of all things" for those who live upon the earth. Recently J. Fichtner has pointed out that the preoccupation with "Yahweh's *plan*" is the very core and center of Isaiah's thinking, and scholars are now noting that the presence of a heavenly council from the beginning has been part and parcel of Jewish thought from the earliest times.[42] In fact, it was concentration on God's preexistent plan, Seligmann avers, which freed the Jews from the danger of falling into the "naturalistic fatalism" that engulfed the religions of their neighbors.[43] Before the Creation, according to IV Ezra, "even then I God had these things in mind, even to the end thereof";[44] and at the Creation itself "when the Most High made the world and Adam . . . he first of all prepared the judgment and the things which pertain to the judgment."[44] Where there is a purpose there is a plan; where there is neither there is only chaos and chance, leading to the "naturalistic fatalism" of the pagans and the philosophers. God knew, Enoch tells us, "before the world was created what is forever and what will be from generation to generation."[45] Or, in the words of Ben Sirach, "When God created his works in the beginning, after making them he assigned them their portions. He set in order his works for all time, and their authority unto their generations; and after this God filled the earth with good things, and then finally created man, and gave him a fixed number of days, and gave him authority over all the earth."[46]

When the plan is discussed, we usually hear of a definite time schedule as part of it, with set ages, dispensations, and ends carefully worked out and determined ahead of time, along with a definite and fixed number of spirits appointed to go to the earth in each of those dispensations. The so-called Manual of Discipline has a positive obsession with times and periods as part of God's plan: "From God is the knowledge of all that is and all that will be; and before they existed he established their whole plan (*makhshevtam*), and when they exist [upon the earth] he prescribes the conditions of their existence according to his glorious plan."[47] Since God created man "according to his own plan [or purpose]," says a Thanksgiving Hymn, " . . . before thou didst create them, thou didst know all their doings from eternity to eternity."[48] This writer often reminds us that man was allowed to share in the plan: "In the wisdom of Thy knowledge thou didst establish their knowledge before they existed . . . and without thy knowing nothing was done."[48] The Battle Scroll reminds us that both blessing and cursing are but the faithful working out of God's plan, that a definite day "has been appointed for the overthrow and humbling of the rule of Wickedness," and that the saints should never despair in their time of probation "until God gives the sign that he has completed his test."[49] The Zadokite documents teach that the wicked on this earth were those who were not chosen and called up in the preexistence; thus Rabin translates a key passage on the subject:

> For God has not chosen them 'from of old, (from the days of) eternity,' and before they were established He knew their works and abhorred the generations (when they arose), and He hid His face from the land from their arising (or: and from Israel) until their being consumed. And He knows (or: knew) the years of their existence and the number (or: set times) and exact epochs of all them that come into being in eternity (or: in the worlds) and past events, even unto that which will befall in the epochs of all the years of eternity (or: the world). And in all of them He raised for Himself 'men called by name,' in order 'to leave a remnant' for the land and to fill the face of the universe of their seed, and to make (or: and he made) known to them by the hand of His anointed ones His holy spirit and shew *them* (or: demonstration of) truth. And with exactitude He set out their names; but those whom He hated He caused to stray.[50]

Rabin has taken liberties with the next-to-last sentence which, as many have pointed out, states as clearly as possible that God has made known the truth to chosen spirits, called up in the preexistence, through the Holy Ghost, bestowed "by the hand of His Messiah."[51]

Almost always when the plan is mentioned something is said about its glad reception, "when the Morning Stars sang together and all the Sons of God shouted for joy." The great year-rites, common to all ancient societies, are a rehearsal of the Creation, usually presented in dramatic form; invariably the rites end with a great and joyful acclamation.[52] Thus the concluding lines of the Shabako stone, with which we began our story: "So all the gods and all the spirits came together to hail God upon his throne . . . and they rejoiced before him in his temple, the source of all good things."[53] And the Mesopotamian Enuma Elish ends with an exhortation to all men to "come to this place and rejoice and celebrate the festival," hailing God for his wonderful deeds and his loving kindness, even as was done "once above."[54] In the Asmavedha, the oldest recorded rites of India, the king is joyfully hailed at the Creation as "the Morning Star," a title that often occurs in this connection.[55] This is a reminder that the question put to Job, "Where wast thou when I laid the foundations of the earth, when the morning stars sang together and all the sons of God shouted for joy?" was not a rhetorical question at all, for Job is expected to give the right answer — "answer, for thou knowest!" This is confirmed in the testament of Job, where that prophet says, "The Lord spake with me in power, and showed me the past and future."[56] The same writing recommends study of the hymns of Job's daughter, designating them as inspired poems. The word *poema*, meaning literally creation, owes its prominence, as Walter Otto has shown, to the circumstance that the first poets were all inspired people who sang one and the same song, namely the Song of the Creation: that was the standard ritual hymn at all the ancient cult centers where the Muses were housed and the royal year-rites rehearsed and performed.[57]

The whole purpose of the Book of Jubilees is to show that the great rites of Israel, centering about the temple and the throne, actually originated with the "the celebration in heaven on the Day of Creation."[58] All who were present on that occasion, according to I Enoch, took an oath to abide by the proposed order and then burst forth into a mighty spontaneous shout of joy.[59] Like Job, the psalmist of the Thanksgiving Hymns is frightfully downcast until he is reminded that "the humble bless Thee, while the Sons of Heaven jubilate in eternal glory. . . ."[60] "Thou hast placed the lot of man eternally with the eternal spirits to shout for joy and to tell thy wonders. . . ."[61] The thing to notice here is that man shares fully in these heavenly jubilations; the poet is simple intoxicated with the assurance that man, a mere speck of "wet dust" is allowed not only to know about the secret councils of the beginning, but actually to share in them, not only as a participant but as one of the directors! The words *marvellous, knowledge, treasures, secrets, counsel, intelligence, understanding*, etc., occur in constant and varied association in the scrolls. "Mere man is to be raised up to join the heavenly hosts . . . and be among Those Who Know in the great choir of jubilation."[61] "Who is man that God gives him intelligence to share

32

in such marvels and lets him know his true secrets?"[62] "Thou hast given to thy children a rich portion of the knowledge of thy Truth, and to the degree of a man's knowledge will he be glorified."[63]

This equating of knowledge with glory may lie at the root of the unique Jewish reverence for things of the mind: "Endowed with intelligence, O Lord, I have known thee.... I have learned sure and certain things regarding thy marvellous secrets, thanks to Thy Holy Spirit...."[64] And in the wisdom of thy knowledge didst thou establish their knowledge before they existed."[65] The same thoughts preoccupy the author of the Manual of Discipline, who also asks, "Who is man... that he should take his place before thy face.... How can the clay and the potter sit together; or who understands thy wonderful plan of God?"[66] And he supplies the answer: "For eternal glory he has chosen me, and for that he teaches me...."[67] the Way of Light itself is "the spirit of the understanding of all the Plan.... Without thee nothing came into existence — and he instructed me in all knowledge." Even the Battle Scroll recurs to the theme: "Thou hast engraven them," speaking of the elect of Israel, "on the Tablets of Life for Kingship... in all the promised ages of the eternities."[68] Hence if it should happen that the hosts of Israel are defeated in battle, one seeks the explanation where Job found it, in the economy of heaven; the ultimate victory of the earthly hosts is assured by their close cooperation with the heavenly hosts, of which they are but a local extension: "... the rule of Michael will be exalted among the angels, and the dominion of Israel among all flesh. Righteousness shall flourish in heaven while all those who embrace God's truth (on earth), shall have joy in the knowledge of eternal things. So, Sons of the Covenant of God, be of good courage in the trial which God visits upon you...."[69] This was the answer that Job received.

The oft-recurring statement that nothing exists whatever except in the will and plan of God, has led scholars to see a connection not only of the Dead Sea Scrolls but of the Shabako stone itself with the Gospel of John.[70] The suggestion of Richard L. Anderson, that the *logos* in John may sometimes be translated "council" deserves closer consideration: "In the beginning was the logos (council, discussion) and the logos was in the presence of God, and God *was* the logos. This was in the beginning in his presence. Everything was done (determined) by it, and without it not a single thing was created...." Recently C. N. Dahl has shown that the early Christian conceived of salvation "as a counterpart to the beginnings of the world.... As a divine act of creation, conforming to the creation of the world, eschatology and creation can be linked up with one another even in this way."[71] Eschatology, that is, cannot be understood without protology (Dahl uses the word), or an understanding of what took place in the beginning before the foundation of the world. The words of the early Christian Barnabas might have been taken right out of the Dead Sea Scrolls: "Praise the Lord who put wisdom and intelligence (*nous*) in us for the understanding of his secrets. Who understands the Plan (*parabolen:* project) of the Lord save the wise one who knows and loves his Lord?"[72] We have seen in the Pastor of Hermas that God's plan was "promised in the midst of great glory and rejoicing."[73] The theme is as conspicuous in the earliest Christian writings as in the Jewish, but after the fourth century the doctors of both religions rejected it completely.[74]

The early Christian Apocrypha are especially concerned with the *opposition* to the plan, which was also initiated at the foundation of the world. The combat between the powers of light and darkness enjoys a very conspicuous place in ritual, being one of the essential episodes of the worldwide creation drama of ancient times.[75] In the scroll entitled "The War between the Sons of Light and the Sons of Darkness" we have ample illustration of the ritual and doctrinal concern of the Jews for this motif, and the quotations just cited from that work show that the embattled hosts on earth were but a local version of the war in heaven.[76] Satan, who opposed the plan, led a rebellion and was cast out of heaven with his followers, to become an unwilling agent in the carrying out of the plan upon the earth. The name Mephistopheles " . . . der stets das Bose will, und stets das Gute schafft," denotes the ultimate frustration of the Evil One, who with the worst intent in the world, can only contribute to the exaltation of man by providing the opposition necessary for testing him in the time of probation upon the earth.[77] In the early Christian Apocrypha Satan's rebellion in heaven begins not with a refusal to worship God, but with his refusal to bow down to *Adam*. "I have no need to worship Adam," he says in one early writing, " . . . I will not worship an inferior and younger being. I am his senior in the Creation; before he was made I was already made. It is rather his duty to worship me! When the angels who were under me heard this, they refused to worship him also . . .", and so the revolt was on.[78] "Now the Prince," says the recently discovered Bodmer Papyrus X, "not being righteous wanted to be God," he had his own counterplan to propose, and the apostates of the Church "actually accept the plan of the serpent whenever they reject God's plan."[79] The two plans represent the two ways that confront us in life, the devil himself having a definite mission on earth. "If I am a fisherman of men," says the Lord in the Gospel of the XII Apostles (a writing which Origen says is older than the Gospel of Luke),[80] "the Devil is also a fisherman, who catches many in his nets. . . . If I have come to take for my kingdom those who are mine, why should not he do the same?"[81] "O Adam," cries the Evil One upon meeting him out in the dreary world after the fall, "I was cast forth from my glory because of thee, and behold I have caused thee to be expelled from paradise . . . because thou didst cause me to become a stranger to my home in heaven. Know thou that I shall never cease to contend against thee and all those who shall come after thee . . . until I have taken them all down into Amente with me!"[82]

The contrast and choice between the Way of Light and the Way of Darkness is made possible by Satan's presence upon the earth. "Horus has two heads," says the famous seventeenth chapter of the Book of the Dead, "the one is truth, the other is sin; he gives truth to whoever brings truth to him, and sin he gives to whoever sins."[83] The concept of this world as a double sphere of light and darkness, good and evil, war and peace, meets us in the earliest meaningful human documents, the prehistoric palette, seals, "standards," reliefs on temples, and designs on clay vessels. On these we find in dramatic opposition to the happy and orderly banquet scenes, rural charm and religious processions opposing scenes of conflict, rapine, and military aggression.[84] The contrast is shown on the shield of Achilles in the eighteenth book of the *Iliad*,[85] and Hesiod in the eighth century B.C. reminds his wayward brother that two ways are always open to man: "O Perses, the better road of the two is that of Righteousness," the hard and narrow one.[86] Evil upon the earth is not a dreadful mistake, as St. Augustine thought,[87] for, as the Zohar says, "if God had not given men a double inclination to both good and bad, he would have been incapable either of virtue or of vice; but as it is he is endowed with a capacity for both."[88] "All things have their opposites," says the old and mysterious Sefer Yeshira, "good and bad. It is the Good which is the foil and proof of the Bad, and vice versa."[89] Hence in this world "we may live either by the Law of the Lord or the Law of Belial," according to the Testament of Naphthali[90] and though the Testament of Abraham announces the alarming news that "for seven thousand who walk the road of perdition, there is hardly one soul that takes the path of righteousness . . . to find salvation!"[91] the presence of the two ways is a blessing, giving man a freedom of choice and opportunity for exaltation that makes him "envied of the angels." "Happy is the man," says Ben Sirach, "who could have fallen away and did not fall away; who could have inflicted injury but did not do so. . . . Poured out before thee are fire and water, stretch forth thy hand and take thy choice. . . . Life and death are before man, and that which he desireth shall be given him."[92] This state of things, according to Fourth Ezra, was established "when the Most High made the world and Adam," and is "the condition of the contest which every man who is born upon the earth must wage."[93] The Manual of Discipline takes up the theme with zeal: "To these two ways all the children of men are born, and to these two divisions they are heirs; every one of them each in his generation, and in his time every man shares more or less in both of them."[94] The whole human race, "all kinds of their spirits and their natures" are put to the same test, each in his own dispensation, "until the final appointed end-time." The real issue is never lost from sight, for Satan himself remains actively engaged: "All man's afflictions and tribulations are in the dominion of Mastema [the devil as a deceiver of men], and everything that makes the Children of Light to stumble is due to the operations of the angels of the Devil," while on the other hand "the God of Israel and his true angels will help every Son of Light, for He created both the spirits of the Light and of Darkness, and according to them he will determine all the deeds of their life . . . for a judgment that will last for all the eternities."[95] The main idea of "the plan which God laid down . . . in the presence of the First Angels for an eternal universal law," according to the Clementine Recognitions, is that "there shall be two kingdoms placed upon the earth to stay there until judgment day . . . and when the world was prepared for man it was so devised that . . . he would be free to exercise his own will, to turn to good things if he wanted them, or if not to turn to bad things."[96] In the Dead Sea Scrolls and the earliest Christian writings this is expressly designated as "the ancient Law of Liberty."[97]

The Didache, one of the oldest (discovered in 1873) Christian writings known, begins with the words, "There are two roads, one of life and the other of death, and there is a great difference between the two," which difference it then proceeds to describe.[98] All the other apostolic fathers so-called are concerned with this doctrine, but one of the most striking expositions is in the newly found Gospel of Philip, a strongly *anti*-Gnostic work: "Light and Darkness, life and death, right and left, are brothers to one another. It is not possible to separate them from one another," in this world, that is, though in the next world where only the good is eternal this will not be so.[99] This is the doctrine of "the Wintertime of the Just," i.e., that while we are in this world men cannot really distinguish the righteous from the unrighteous, since in the wintertime all trees are bare and look equally dead, "but when the summertime of the Just shall come, then the righteous shall bear their leaves and fruit while the dead limbs of evil trees shall be cast into the fire."[100] It is another aspect of the plan. "We believe that God organized all things in the beginning out of unformed matter," says Justin Martyr to the Jew Trypho, " . . . for the sake of the human race, that they, if they prove themselves by their works to be worthy of His plan, having been judged worthy to return to his presence (so we believe), shall reign with him, having been made immortal and incorruptible. At the creation they themselves made the choice . . . and so were deemed worthy to live with him in immortality."[101]

There are many other areas of doctrine and important rites and ordinances set forth in the newly found writings and in the longer known texts which must now be reread and reconsidered in the light of recent discoveries. In time these are bound to exert some pressure to push out the walls of conventional Christian doctrine. But before the student gets involved in them it would be well to consider one issue which forces itself on the attention of every serious student of early Christianity and Judaism. We mean the problem of literalism. Just how literal are all these things supposed to be? What we have been talking about implies a different view of reality from that of conventional Christianity; it introduces as it were a third dimension into the purely two-dimensional pictures given us by scholastic philosophy and naturalism. The great difference between the Primitive Church and conventional Christianity is that the two take different things literally.[102] The history of Christian dogma has been one long process of accommodation and de-eschatologizing by which one body of belief has been completely displaced by another, eschatological reality being supplanted by sacramental piety. The teachings with which we have been dealing in this paper definitely infer a level of reality above that of the allegory and symbolism of the schools of rhetoric which became the official teachers of Christianity. The early Christian literalism was an *horrendum* to the schoolmen, but the more we learn about the early Church the clearer it becomes that that very literalism is the distinctive stamp not only of the Christian religion but of the Jewish as well.[103] Today scholars are being forced into a compromise. A recent study of Christ's forty-day ministry concludes: "What happened after our Lord's resurrection was that He moved constantly back and forth between these two 'spaces' or worlds — the seen and the unseen. There *is* another world than this. It is not at some remote point in outer space. It exists side by side with this; . . . it is the world of the spirit, and this is the world of matter."[104] Here a rather surprising concession to literalism is made only to be promptly withdrawn as the "other world" turns out to be only the immaterial "spirit" world after all, in spite of all the pains to which the Lord went as he "moved continually back and forth" between the two worlds to make perfectly clear that he was *not* a spirit.

The earliest Christian apologist, Aristides, rejects spiritual or allegorical interpretations outright when his colleagues at Athens want to introduce them into their religious discussions. If religious stories are "mythical," he insists, "they are nothing but just so many words . . . but if they are allegorical they are simply myths and nothing else."[105] Early Christians were not interested in myths or allegories. The youthful Clement leaves the schools of the philosophers in distress because they cannot answer what he considers the important questions of life: When was the world created? What was before that? Will a man really continue to live after death?[106] Only Peter could answer such questions, and Peter opens his discourse by saying, "To begin with, we say unequivocally that there is nothing bad about material substance."[107] This was the absolute antithesis of the teachings of the schools; it was the Gnostic intellectuals who first insisted on dematerializing Christian doctrine, followed by the Neoplatonists. Between those two the attitude of Christian theology to literalism was given its fixed and permanent form. The Bodmer Papyrus X shows how early they attacked with their basic weapons: " . . .they deny the resurrection, they are ashamed of the physical birth and death of the Lord."[108] The charge is repeated by all the apostolic fathers and in all the oldest Christian Apocrypha. "Christianity," wrote Schopenhauer, "has this peculiar disadvantage, that, unlike other religions, it is not a pure system of doctrine: its chief and essential feature is that it is a history, a series of events, a collection of facts."[109]

If the eschatological drama deals with real rather than allegorical events, part of those real events took place long ago and far away, but part of them are actually being acted out here upon the earth. If the saints were taught to think of themselves as outcasts in a hostile world, it just so happened that they *were* outcasts in a hostile world; one had only to look around to see that the pitfalls and dangers were real and physical as well as "spiritual." The faithful actually have found themselves more often than not holing up in the desert places of the world — E. Kaesemann's "Wandernde Gottesvolk," and when they talked of being gathered out of the world and taking leave of it, they were thinking in the most factual and spatial terms. Even those learned doctors of the Church who utterly deplored the old-fashioned literalistic ways of thinking constantly slip back to those ways themselves, especially in times of crisis; and the spiritual miracles, spiritual parousia, spiritual pilgrimage, spiritual temple, and spiritual Jerusalem, etc., of the schoolmen never proved very satisfying to the Christian mind which displays a constant tendency to revert to the tangible article whenever possible — even the great doctors prefer the dinner to the menu, when they can get it!"[110] Today a return to literalism is part of the expanding gospel.

But there is ambiguity here. Take for example the business of light and darkness. In the thousands of passages contrasting the two they are most of the time quite plainly figurative. Yet the shining garments of heavenly beings, as of Jesus at the Transfiguration, are real; and so is the darkness: "As every man's nature in this life is dark," says Enoch, "so are also his conception, birth, and departure from life."[111] When in the *Pastor of Hermas* the Church is described as a tower built above the water, we are told that the tower is a symbol, but that the water is very real: no one can enter the typological tower without passing through real water.[112] From this we see that rites and ordinances present an ambiguous situation, with some things to be taken literally and done literally and others figuratively. But in our ancient texts the reader is rarely left in doubt as to which is which; it is only the doctors of the Church, all men of the schools, who insist on minimizing the literal at the expense of the allegorical. Once one comes to understand, Origen assures us, that the historical parts of the Bible are to be understood symbolically, the historical interpretation of the whole becomes not only expendable but actually misleading, and should be abandoned altogether![113]

The mixing of types and images with reality is of the very essence of our life upon the earth, where we see through a glass but darkly. In the scriptures and the Apocrypha we are told of things that are real and yet too wonderful for us even to imagine here, let alone describe; we simply can't conceive them: "Eye hath not seen nor ear heard, neither hath entered into the heart of man the things which God hath prepared. . . ." (1 Corinthians 2:9.) Consequently, if these things are to be mentioned at all, it must be in terms of types and images which are not real. Yet the types and images are not for that reason to be despised. A valuable commentary on this theme is supplied in the newly discovered Gospel of Philip: "Truth did not come into the world naked, but she came clothed in types and images. One cannot receive the truth in any other way." (115:10-12.) The solid reality behind the images can only be known by apocatastasis, or restoration to a former state. (115:15-18.) If people do not receive the ordinances here, we are told, they will not enjoy the real thing hereafter. (121:1-8.) Marriage, for example, has a different form in the next world to what it has here (124:6-9); but only by entering it *here* will one be allowed to enter it there: "If anyone does not receive it while he is in this world, he will not receive it in the other place" (134:6-7). So it is with all the ordinances: he who has not mastered "the places" here "will not be able to be master of that place...." (124:33-36.) "The mysteries of the truth are revealed as types and images" here, while "the veil conceals how God really governs the physical creation." (132:20-25.) The rending of the veil is not the abolition but the revelation of what is behind it, "in order that we might enter into the truth of it.... We enter in our weakness through despised symbols" (133:1-15),[114] but enter we must, for who does not "receive the light" through these ordinances "will not receive it in the other place," while he who does receive it "cannot be held back, and will be beyond the reach of all his enemies even in this world. And when the time comes for him to go out of this world he has already received the truth in the images." (134:6-13.)

If one makes a sketch of a mountain, what is it? A few lines on a piece of paper. But there is a solid reality behind this poor composition; even if the tattered scrap is picked up later in a street in Tokyo or a gutter in Madrid, it still attests to the artist's experience of the mountain as a reality. If the sketch should be copied by others who have never seen the original mountain, it still bears witness to its reality. So it is with the apocryphal writings: most of them are pretty poor stuff and all of them are copies of copies. But when we compare them we cannot escape the impression that they have a real model behind them, more faithfully represented in some than in others. All we ever get on this earth, Paul reminds us, is a distorted reflection, but it is a reflection of things that really are. Since we are dealing with derivative evidence only, we are not only justified but required to listen to all the witnesses, no matter how shoddy some of them may be. For years the evidence of the Egyptians, Greeks, Babylonians, etc., has been brought into court as powerful refutation of the Bible's claims to originality and inspiration. Their voices do indeed refute the claims of conventional Christianity to the absolute originality and exclusive inspiration of the Bible, but the

Bible itself never made such claims.[115] What the outside texts prove is the antiquity and universality of the gospel and its central position in the whole history of civilization. It is not a local or tribal tradition on the one hand, nor is it the spontaneous expression of evolving human intelligence on the other, but is the common heritage of all ancient civilizations, battered, corrupted, and distorted in most cases, to be sure, but always recognizable in its main features and much too ingenious and elaborate to be the product of independent discovery.[116]

But what are we to make of pagans possessing the gospel, and that from the most ancient times? We did not say they had it, but only that their records testify to it. If we examine those records, we soon discover that all their authors possess are mere fragments which they do not pretend to understand. For them all those elements of the gospel which fit so perfectly into the account of things given in the story of the redemption are but distant traditions, shattered remnants of a forgotten structure, completely mystifying odds and ends that once meant something but whose meaning can now only be guessed at. This attitude to the heritage of the past may fairly be called the basic mood of Egyptian religion. In the seventeenth chapter of the Book of the Dead, to which we have already referred, the question is regularly asked, "What does this mean?" and fourteen times when an answer is supplied, it is with the reservation that "others say" it means something else. From the earliest times "the impression made on the modern mind" by the Egyptians, according to I. E. S. Edwards, "is that of a people searching in the dark for a key to truth . . . retaining all lest perchance the appropriate one should be lost."[117] They know there is a key, that is, but they also know they do not have it. It would be easy to show that the keynote of the literature and religion of all ancient people who have left us their records, with the exception of Israel, is one of pessimism and despair. We would only have to quote the authors of the standard literary histories of the various nations to make that clear.[118] Israel escaped both that pessimism and fatalism by being constantly reminded by the prophets of the great preexistent plan that lies behind everything that happens. This we believe to be the most significant element in the expanding gospel.

NOTES

1. M. Grabmann, *Die Geschichte der Scholastischen Methode* (Graz: Akad. Verlag, 1957), I, 1-37; O. Chadwick, *From Bousset to Newman* (Cambridge University Press: 1959), chapters i-iii.

2. For a recent treatment of this much-treated theme, see Ol Eissfeldt, *Einleitung in das Alte Testament* (Tübingen: J. C. B. Mohr, 1964), pp. 2-9.

3. J. Danielou, *The Dead Sea Scrolls and Primitive Christianity* (N.Y.: Mentor Omega, 1957), p. 81.

4. K. Sethe, *Das 'Denkmal Memphitischer Theologie' der Schabakostein des Br. Museums* (Band X:1 of Unters. zur Gesch. u. Altertumskunde Aegyptens, Leipzig: 1928), pp. 1-5.

5. In this as in the Pyramid Texts it is often impossible to tell whether a given scene is laid in heaven, on earth or in both places. L. Speleers, *Textes des Cercueils* (Brussels: 1947) pp. xlv-xlix.

6. See for example L. V. Zabkar, in *Journal of Near Eastern Studies,* XIII (1954), p. 87; H. Jacobsohn, *Die dogmatische Stellung des Königs in der Theologie der alten Aegypter* (Hamburg, N.Y.: 1939); R. Anthes, in *JNES,* XVIII (1959), pp. 169-212.

7. Shabako stone, lines 7-8, in Sethe, pp. 23-26.

8. Lines 10c-18b, in Sethe, pp. 27-32.

9. Lines 13c-14c. The case was ritually retried at every coronation in the so-called "Justification of Osiris" before the priestly court at Heliopolis. See R. Anthes, in *Journal of Near Eastern Studies,* 13 (1954), pp. 191f.

10. Sethe, *op. cit.,* Pt. 2, *Ramesseumpapyrus,* pp. 95-96; cf. the *Victory Over Seth* papyrus (Louvre 3129; Br. Mus. 10252, 13).

11. Shabako stone, lines 48-52a, in Sethe, pp. 46-50.

12. Lines 53f, in Sethe, pp. 50-56. On the nature of Ptah as Father, Begetter, Opener, etc., M. S. Holmberg, *The God Ptah* (Lund: Gleerup, 1946), pp. 258-271.

13. Shabako stone, lines 56-57, in Sethe, pp. 59-64.

14. Sethe, pp. 62-64.

15. Lines 57f; Sethe, p. 65 renders imakh as "der die Bedeutung aller Dinge macht."

16. Lines 58ff; Sethe, pp. 66-68, notes that the passage "vividly recalls the Biblical Creation story."

17. Line 61; Sethe, pp. 70-72.

18. Lines 63fl; Sethe, pp. 73-77.

19. *Pyramid Texts,* No. 3. We here translate the entire text.

20. A. De Buck, *The Coffin Texts,* I, lllff (Spell 33); cf. II, 6f (Spell 76), 24-26 (Spell 79), etc.

21. *Ibid.*, I, 167 (Spell 39). On the possible identity of Atum with Adam, see E. Leféfure, in *Bibliothèque Egyptologique*, XXXV (1913), pp. 16-21.

22. R. Labat, *Le Poeme Babylonien de la Creation* (Paris: Maisonneuve, 1935), pp. 76f. The same situation, a great earthly assembly representing the divine council at the creation of the world, is described in early Sumerian texts supplied by E. Chiera, *Sumerian Religious Texts* (*Crozer Theol. Seminary Babylonian Publ.*, Vol. I, 1924), pp. 29-30. For an Old Babylonian parallel, W. G. Lambert, *Babylonian Wisdom Literature* (Oxford: 1960), p. 163. Hittite ritual texts contain "obvious allusion to an assembly of the gods for the purpose of 'fixing the fates'; the scene is laid in heaven... but the inference that such a gathering of gods was actually enacted in ritual form, as in the Babylonian festival, can hardly be evaded," O. Gurney, in S. Hooke (ed.), *Ritual and Kingship* (Oxford: 1958), p. 108.

23. Labat, pp. 143-5 (Tab. VI, lines 2-16). We have not given the lines here in strict sequence. The whole text is full of repetition and contamination.

24. Tab. VI, 29f. The authority is bestowed in Tab. IV.

25. Tab. VI, 105-168, from which we have selected typical expressions.

26. The mixed and derivative nature of the text is clear from the declaration in Tablet VI, 121f, VII, 140-144, that "for us, whatever name we call him by, he is indeed our god, though we have called him by fifty names."

27. Ben Sirach, 17:11-13.

28. II Baruch, 56:3.

29. I Enoch, 41: 1f; 47:3. On the nature of the Book of the Living.

30. *Ibid.*, 62:7.

31. DST VI (F), p. iii, 19fl.

32. This rendering is that of A. Dupont-Sommer, *The Dead Sea Scrolls*, (N.Y.: Macmillan, 1956), p. 77.

33. DSD XI, 7-9.

34. The treasures of wisdom are kept beneath God's throne on high, II Baruch, 54:13; this is the treasury of life on which all the heavenly hosts depend, *Psalms of Thomas*, 203:9; from this chest God took the elements in the presence of the hosts when the creation of the world was being discussed, *Ibid.*, 203: 11ff; it is "the treasure-chamber of the light," *Od. Solomon*, 16:16; Ben Sirach, 39:17; from it the worthy take the riches of knowledge, DSD X, 2; *Thanksgiving Hymn* X, 23f, 29. Cf. C. Schmidt *Das 2te Buch Jeu*, in *Texte u. Untersuchungen*, VIII, p. 193, and J. Leipoldt (ed.), *Religionsgeschichte des Orients in der zeit Weltreligionen* (Leiden: Brill, 1961), pp. 86, 109f.

35. DSD X, 1-3.

36. *Clementine Recognitions* I, 24.

37. *Ps. of Thomas*, 203:lff.

38. *Ibid.*, 8:13.

39. *Creation Apocryphon*, 148: 17, rendered by H. M. Schenke, "Vom Ursprung der Welt," in *Theologische Literaturzeitung*, 1959, Nr. 4, p. 249.

40. Pastor of Hermas, Vis. I, iii.

41. G. Widengren, in J. Leipoldt, p. 86.

42. J. Fichtner, in *zeitschrift f. Alttestamentliche Wissenschaft*, 63 (1951), 16-66.

43. C. Seligmann, in *Kernmomente*, pp. 54-56.

44. IV Ezra 7:70.

45. I Enoch 39:11.

46. Ben Sirach 16:26-29; 17:lf.

47. DSD III, 15.

48. DST I: 7-13. The whole passage is relevant.

49. DST 17:7-9, in Gaster's translation, p. 304. The "main purpose" of the Battle Scroll "is to give courage to the Sons of Light — liable to despair because of their defeats — by telling them that this sequence of defeats and victories has been determined from time immemorial," Y. Yadin, *The Scroll of the War of the Sons of Light against the Sons of Darkness* (Oxford Univ.: 1962), p. 8.

50. C. Rabin, *The Zadokite Documents* (Oxford: 1954), p. 6, citing CDC, ii: 7ff.

51. Dupont-Sommer, *op. cit.*, p. 65, points out that in this passage we are dealing with "three great divine entities." To escape such a conclusion, Rabin, *loc. cit.*, puts "messiah" in the plural and then explains in a footnote that such a plural form may refer to prophets.

52. We have described the situation in *Western Political Quarterly* 4 (1951), pp. 226ff, and *Classical Journal*, XL (1946), 521ff.

53. Line 61, in Sethe, pp. 70-72.

54. Enuma Elish, Tab. VII, 32f, 146-150; VI, 72-81, 108-113.

55. W. Neisser, in *American Oriental Soc. Jnl.*, XLV (1925), 287.

56. Text in *Jewish Quart. Rev.* XIII (1900), 112.

57. W. F. Otto, *Die Musen und der göttliche Ursprung des Singens und Sagens* (Düsseldorf-Köln: E. Diederich, 1955).

58. See the discussion by R. H. Charles, *The Book of Jubilees* (London: 1902), pp. li-lii.

59. I Enoch 61:6-10; 69:25-27.

60. DST XI, 25, 61.

61. DST III, 22-24.

62. DST X, 4f.

63. DST X, 28.

64. DST XII, 11-12.

65. DST I, 19.

66. DSD XI, 20-22.

67. DSD X, 12.

68. DSW XII, 3. See above, Note 49.

69. Y. Yadin, pp. 8, 12, 15, 237-242.

70. See above, Note 6.

71. In N. Davies and D. Daube, *Eschatological Background of the New Testament* (Cambridge Univ. Press: 1956), p. 424.

72. Ep. Barnab., c. 6.

73. Above, Note 40.

74. There is a note on this in Migne, *Patrol. Graeca*, I, 1222f (Note 20).

75. S. Hooke (ed.), *Myth, Ritual, and Kingship*, p. 8.

76. Discussed by Yadin, pp. 229-242.

77. *Ibid.*, p. 232: " . . . the Lord placed Belial to carry out his specific task," this doctrine of the DSS being "in complete agreement with the statements about Belial (or Beliar) in the Apocrypha and Pseudepigrapha," *ibid.*, p. 233.

78. *Lives of Adam and Eve*, 14:2f; 15.

79. *Papyrus Bodmer* X, 54:12.

80. See E. Revillout's discussion in *Patrologia Orientalis*, 2:126-9.

81. *Ibid.*, 2:154.

82. Timothy of Alexandria, *Discourse on the Abbaton*, fol. 21a, in E. A. W. Budge, *Coptic Martyrdoms* (Brit. Mus.: 1914), pp. 240f.

83. H. Grapow, *Das 17. Kapitel des . . . Totenbuches* (Berlin: 1912), p. 43.

84. A. Moortgat, *Tammuz* (Berlin: De Gruyter, 1949), treats the theme at length.

85. *Iliad* 18: 490ff.

86. Hesiod, *Works and Days*, ll 214ff, cf. llff.

87. " . . . misera necessitas non posse non peccandi," this being the exact opposite of the early Christian teaching that men's freedom to choose their own way "makes them envied by the angels," Irenaeus, *Contra haereses*, IV, 37, 1.

88. Zohar I, 23.

89. Sefer Yeshira VI, 2f.

90. Test. Naphthali, c. 2.

91. Testament of Abraham, cited by K. Kohler, in *Jew. Quart. Rev.*, VII (1895), 586.

92. Ben Sirach 15:14-17; 31:8-10.

93. IV Ezra 7:127.

94. DSD IV, 15.

95. DSW III, 23 to IV, 1.

96. *Clementine Recognitions* I, 24. See our discussion in *The World and the Prophets* (Salt Lake City: Deseret Book, 1954), pp. 166-173.

97. The "Law of Liberty (*khoq kherut*) of the DSS (e.g. DSD X, 6, 8, 11), can only be the Christian "*ancient* Law of Liberty" discussed in the references in the preceding note.

98. Didache I, 1. The Epistle of Barnabas after a brief introduction begins almost the same way.

99. *Gospel of Philip* 101:14ff.

100. The classic statement of the doctrine, which is very often met with in slightly altered form through the Apocrypha, is in the Pastor of Hermas. *Simil.* iii.

101. Justin, *Apology,* c. 10.

102. This is seen in the fourth-century description of a typical old-fashioned Christian, in Sozomen, *Church History* I, 10f.

103. H. Nibley, in *Jew. Quart. Rev.*, L (1959), 98-100.

104. B. Holt, in *Encounter*, XXIV (1963), 89.

105. Aristides, *Apology* 13:7. The same thing in Justin, *Cohortatio ad Graecos*, c. 3.

106. *Clem. Recog.*, I, 1, 1-2.

107. *Ibid.*, IV, 23.

108. *Papyrus Bodmer* X, 51:10.

109. A. Schopenhauer, *Essay on The Christian System.*

110. Nibley, *op. cit.*, Note 103, pp. 230ff.

111. *Secrets of Enoch* 68:4.

112. Pastor of Hermas, *Vis.* III, iii-v. In the same way the hero stands "sentry duty" not only symbolically but literally, *Simil.* V, i.

113. J. Danielou, *Origen* (N.Y.: Sheed and Ward, 1955), pp. 155-7, cf. 119, 141-4, 152.

114. The translation is that of R. M. Wilson, *The Gospel of Philip* (N.Y.: Harper & Row, 1962), pp. 43ff.

115. We have discussed this in the *Improvement Era*, LXVII (Oct. 1964ff), 816ff.

116. Lord Raglan, *The Origins of Religion* (London: Thinker's Library, 1949) Chaps. vii and viii, develops this theme.

117. I. E. S. Edwards, *The Pyramids of Egypt* (Penguin Books: 1952), pp. 27f.

118. An excellent illustration is W. G. Lambert's "Introductory Essay" in his *Babylonian Wisdom Literature* (Oxford Univ.: 1960).

Treasures in the Heavens

3

As Christianity has been deeschatologized and demythologized in our own day, so in the fourth century it was thoroughly dematerialized, and ever since then anything smacking of "cosmism," that is, tending to associate religion with the physical universe in any way, has been instantly condemned by Christian and Jewish clergy alike as paganism and blasphemy. Joseph Smith was taken to task for the crude literalism of his religion – not only talking with angels like regular people, but giving God the aspect attributed to him by the primitive prophets of Israel, and, strangest of all, unhesitatingly bringing other worlds and universes into the picture. Well, some of the early Christian and Jewish writers did the same thing; this weakness in them has been explained away as a Gnostic aberration, and yet today there is a marked tendency in all the churches to support the usual bloodless abstractions and stereotyped moral sermons with a touch of apocalyptic realism, which indeed now supplies the main appeal of some of the most sensationally successful evangelists.

Over a century ago, J. P. Migne argued that the medieval legends of the Saints were far less prone to mislead the faithful than those scientifically oriented apocrypha of the Early Church, since the former were the transparent inventions of popular fantasy which could never lead thinking people astray, while the latter by their air of factual reporting and claims to *scientific plausibility led the early Christians into all manner of extravagant speculation, drawing the faithful astray in many directions. To appreciate the strength of their own position, Latter-day Saints should not be without some knowledge of both these traditions. Since the "cosmist" doctrines have been almost completely neglected, here we offer a look at some of them.*

The canonical writings and the Apocrypha have a good deal to say about "treasures in the heavens." If we compare the "treasures" passages in a wide sampling of these writings, including those of Qumran, Nag Hammadi and the Mandaeans, it becomes apparent that "treasures in the heavens" is a part of a much larger picture, a "cosmist" view of the plan of salvation which was rejected by the official Christianity and Judaism that emerged triumphant in the fourth century but seems to have been prevalent throughout the Near East in an earlier period. There is no better approach to the study of this strange and intriguing doctrine than an examination of the Treasures in Heaven. We begin with the surprising fact that the Treasures in the Heavens were not allegorical but real.

That the life-giving treasures of earth, particularly the golden grain that was anciently kept in a sacred bin, really comes from the sky is apparent to everyone.[1] The miracle of the bounties of heaven literally pouring from "the treasure-houses of the snow... the terrible storehouses" is an awesome sight and a joyous one.[2] But without a benign intelligence to administer them, the same elements that bestow life on man can wreak frightful destruction; hence it is plain that a measure of knowledge, skill, and benevolence is necessary to convert the raw elements into useful gifts.[3] Thus when one speaks of treasures in the heavens, one means not only the vast secret chambers of the rain, snow, and hail, but also the deep hidden wisdom and the power necessary to control them; God's treasury is a source not only of the elements that sustain life but also of the light and knowledge that endow them with that power.[4]

The life-giving fusion of divine wisdom with primal element is often described in religious texts as a fountain, as "the overflowing waters which shine" coming from the "treasure-chest of radiance" along with all the other shining treasures.[5] "Thou hast established every fountain of light beside thee," says Baruch, "and the treasures of wisdom beneath thy throne hast thou prepared."[6] The concept is more than a figure of speech; "the heavenly waters . . . important for life on earth," to be effectively used must be "gathered in and assigned . . . to particular treasurehouses."[7] We are introduced to that physical part of the heavenly treasure in a grandiose scene in which we behold a great council in heaven being held at the creation of the world; there God, enthroned in the midst of his heavenly hosts, explains the plan of creation to them,[8] and then opens his treasure-chest before them to show them the wondrous store of stuff that is to be used in making a world;[9] but the new world is still in a preliminary state "like unripe fruit that does not know what it is to become."[10] It is not until we get to the doctors of the Church, wholly committed to the prevailing teachings of the schools, that we hear of creation *ex nihilo*.[11] Before then, Creation is depicted as a process of imposing form and order on chaotic matter: the world is created for the specific purpose of carrying out a specific plan, and the plan, like the Creation itself, requires strict organization — all creatures have their work assigned them in the coming world, to be carried out at predetermined times and places.[12] When the plan was announced to the assembled hosts, and the full scope and magnanimity of it dawned upon them, they burst into spontaneous shouts of joy and joined in a hymn of praise and thanksgiving, the Morning-song of Creation, which remains to this day the archetype of hymns, the great *acclamatio*, the primordial nucleus of all liturgy.[13]

The Creation drama, which is reflected in the great year-rites all over the ancient world, does not take place in a vacuum but "in the presence of God," seated in the midst of "His holy ones" with whom he takes counsel, they being his mind and mouth on the occasion as he is theirs.[14] Though the plan from first to last is entirely God's own, he discusses it with others, "consulting with the souls of the righteous before deciding to create the world," not because he needs their advice, but because the plan concerns them and requires their maximum participation in it. The discussion was a lively one — apart from those rebellious angels who rejected it entirely, there was a general protest that the plan would be too painful for some parties and too risky for all; it was the generous voluntary offering of the Son of God that settled the question.[15] Those who embrace the plan wholeheartedly on this earth are the Elect, "the people of the Plan," chosen "from the foundation of the world";[16] they form on earth a community dedicated to "the faithful working out of God's plan" in close cooperation with the heavenly hosts;[17] they alone have access to the heavenly hidden treasure, because they alone covet and seek it.[18]

What most thrills the psalmist of Qumran as he sings of the bounteous fountain of God's hidden treasures is the thought that he is not only a beneficiary of God's plan, but was actually taken into his confidence in the making of it — he was there![19] When Clement of Alexandria recalls that "God knew us before the foundation of the world, and chose us for our faithfulness," he is attesting a well-known teaching of the early Church.[20] The recurring phrase, "Blessed is he who was before he came into being," is not a paradox but refers to two states of being:[21] if (following Baruch) "we have by no means been from the beginning what we are now," it does not follow that we did not exist, for it is equally true that "what we are now we shall not afterwards remain."[22] We are dealing here not with existence and nonexistence but with a passing from one state to another, sometimes explained as a passing from one type of visibility to another.[23] It is common to speak of the Creation as a renewing,[24] even as a reorganizing of old matter, nay as the building of a world from materials taken from the dismantling of older worlds.[25] Pre-existent man had been around a long time before it was decided to create this earth: the whole thing was produced, when the time came, for his benefit; and though he was created last of all to take it over, "in his real nature he is older than any of it."[26] He is the child of an earlier, spiritual birth or creation.[27]

Nothing could be more gratifying to the ego or consoling to the afflicted spirit of mortals than the secret intimation of a glorious past and an exalted parentage.[28] The exciting foster-parent illusion was exploited by the Gnostics for all it was worth;[29] but the idea was no invention of theirs: it was the thought of his preexistent glory that was Job's real comfort — "Where wast thou when I laid the foundations of the earth . . . when the morning stars sang together and all the sons of God shouted for joy?" is not a rhetorical question. For it was the recollection of that same Creation-hymn of joy and their part in it that sustained the Sons of Light in the midst of terrible reverses.[30] "If you could see your real image which came into being before you," says a logion of Jesus, "then you would be willing to endure anything!"[31] The author of the Thanksgiving Hymn is simply drunk with the idea of his own preexistent glory.[32] Such glory, according to the Johannine writings, belongs not only to the Lord but to all who follow him.[33]

But why leave one's heavenly home for a dismal earthly one? To that question, constantly reiterated in the Mandaean writings, the Gnostic answer was that we were forced to make the move as a punishment; but the "Treasure" doctrine was the very opposite — we are here as a reward, enjoying an opportunity to achieve yet greater things by being tried and tested, "that each one might be promoted, according to his intelligence and the perfections of his way, or be retarded according to his wrong-doings."[34] This is the well-known doctrine of the Two Ways: "For this reason the world has existed through the ages," says the Clementine Recognitions," so that the spirits destined to come here might fulfill their number, and here make their choice between the upper and the lower worlds, both of which are represented here."[35] In what has been regarded as the oldest ritual document in existence, the so-called Shabako Stone from Memphis we find the concept full-blown:

> To him who doeth good will be given Life and (lit. of) Salvation (htp). To him who doeth evil will be given the Death of the Condemned (criminal) . . . according to that decree, conceived in the heart and brought forth by the tongue, which shall be the measure of all things.[36]

The element of opposition necessary for such a test is provided by the adversary, who in the beginning openly mocked God's plan and set up his own plan in opposition to it.[37] Being cast out of heaven with his followers by main force, he continues upon this earth during the set time allowed him by God's plan (for the irony of his situation is that he is Mephistopheles, unwilling if not unwittingly contributing to the operation of that plan) attempting to wreck the whole enterprise by drawing off as many spirits and as much material as possible into his own camp.[38] The devil and his hosts claim the Treasure for their own and attempt to pirate the treasure-ships that cruise between the worlds, and use the loot in the outfitting of their own dark worlds.[39] A neglected leitmotif of the New Testament is the continuation on earth of the personal feud between the Lord and the adversary begun at the foundation of the world: from the first each recognizes the other as his old opponent and rival;[40] they are matched at every point — each claims identical gifts, ordinances, signs and wonders, each had his doctrine and his glory and his plan for the future of the race.[41] Above all, each claims to possess the Treasure, the Lord promising treasures in the heavens while the adversary offers a clever, glittering earthly imitation: it is the choice between these treasures (for no man can have both) that is a man's real test here upon the earth, determining his place hereafter.[42] It is the "Poor" who recognize and seek the true treasures, since they who are "rich as to the things of this world" have deliberately chosen the fraudulent imitation.[43]

In coming to earth each man leaves his particular treasure, or his share of *the* Treasure, behind him in heaven, safely kept in trust ("under God's throne") awaiting his return.[44] One has here below the opportunity of enhancing one's treasure in heaven by meritorious actions, and also the risk of losing it entirely by neglecting it in his search for earthly treasure.[45] Hence the passionate appeals to men to remember their tremendous stake on the other side and "not to defraud themselves of the glory that awaits them" by seeking the things of the world.[46] To make the "treasure" test a fair one, the two treasures are placed before us on an equal footing (the doctrine of the Two Ways), their two natures being mingled in exactly equal portions in every human being.[47] To neutralize what would otherwise be the overpowering appeal of the heavenly treasure, the memory of its former glories has been erased from the mind of man, which is thus in a state of equilibrium, enjoying by "the ancient law of liberty" complete freedom to choose whatever it will.[48] In this state, whatever choice is made represents the true heart and mind of the one who makes it. What conditions the Elect to make the right choice is no unfair advantage of instruction — for all men are aware of the issues involved — but a besetting nostalgia, a constant vague yearning for one's distant treasure and happy heavenly home. This theme, akin to the Platonic doctrine of anamnesis, runs through all the Apocrypha and scriptures; it is beautifully expressed in the Hymn of the Pearl from the Acts of Thomas.

In this classic tale, a king's son has come down to earth to find a pearl which he is to return to its heavenly depository; here below he becomes defiled with the things of the world until a Letter from Heaven, signed by all the Great and Mighty Ones, recalls to him his true heritage and his purpose in coming to earth, whereupon he casts off his earthly garments and with the pearl returns to the waiting arms of his loved ones in the royal courts on high and to his robe of glory that has been carefully kept for him in the Treasury.[49] Our various "treasure" texts consistently refer to going to heaven as a return, a joyful homecoming, in which one follows the steps of Adam "back to the Treasury of Life from which he came forth."[50] A great deal is said about a garment that one changes in passing from one stage to another, the final garment of glory being often equated to the Treasure itself.[51] This garment introduces us to the very important ritual aspect of the treasure story, for it is generally understood that one can return to one's heavenly treasure only by the careful observance of certain rites and ordinances, which provide the means both of receiving instruction and demonstrating obedience.[52] In the Mandaean economy the ordinances *are* the Treasure, the knowledge of the proper procedures being the very knowledge by which the elements are controlled and the spirit of man exalted.[53] The other sectaries are hardly less concerned with ordinances, however, the paradox of Qumran being that a society which fled from the rites of the temple at Jerusalem should become completely engrossed in yet more rites and ordinances once it was in the desert.[54] Moreover, the most elaborate of all discourses on the initiatory rites are those of the Coptic Christians.[55]

As teacher and administrator of the ordinances, the priest holds the key to "the treasure-house of divinity," in which "the merit accruing from *ceremonial* worship is accumulated.[56] These ordinances, imported directly from that Treasury of Light to which they alone offer the means of return, are types of what is done above; through them "souls are led to the Treasury of Light. . . . Between us and the Great King of the Treasury of Light are many steps and veils," and it is only by "giving the proper replies to the Guardians" that one is able to approach and finally enter the Treasury of Light.[57] The ordinances are most secret (they are usually called "mysteries"), and it is through their scrupulous observance that every man "puts his own treasure in order."[58]

The archetype whom all must follow in the ordinances is Adam, whose true home is the "Treasury of Light," and who belongs with all his children "to the Father who existed from the beginning."[59] The preexistent Adam, "the Adam of Light," having descended to earth fell into a deep sleep from which he awoke with his mind erased like that of a little child.[60] He was thus in a state to undergo impartial testing, but in his new helplessness he needed instruction. This was provided by a special emissary from the Treasury of Light, the "Sent One." The "Sent One" is often a commission of three, the "Three Great Men" who wakened Adam from his sleep and immediately set about teaching him what he should know and do in order to return to the House of Light from which he had come.[61] The Sent One may be Michael, Gabriel, or the Lord himself, but whoever holds that office always has the same calling, namely to assist the souls of men to return to the Treasury of Light: when the Lord, as the supreme example of the Sent One, descends below to deliver the spirits that sit in darkness, they hail him as "Son of Glory, Son of Lights and of the Treasures. . . ."[62] Always a stranger on earth, recognized only by the "Poor,"[63] the Sent One comes to bring a treasure, and indeed he is sometimes called the Treasure, for he alone brings the knowledge men must have to return to the Father of Lights.[64] Letters sent from above to help men in their need — the prototype of those "Letters from Heaven" that have haunted Christian and Moslem society through the centuries — being directives or passports for getting to the Treasure-house if not written deeds to the Treasure itself (the scriptures are rated as such) are themselves included among the Treasures of Heaven.[65]

While a treasure is anything precious and hidden, the early Christian idea of what was precious differed noticeably from the abstract and allegorical "spiritual" treasures of the philosophizing churchmen of a later time. The Patristic writers, trained in the schools, are offended and annoyed by the way in which many Christians cling to the old literalism of the early Church.[66] When primitive Christians thought of a treasure it had to be something real and tangible; theirs was the tradition of the Jews before them, for whom the delights of the other world "though including spiritual and intellectual joys are most tangible delights of a completely pleasing physical and social environment."[67] Much has been written about early Christian and Jewish concepts of time, but where the other world is concerned the ideas of space are at least equally important. With what care Luke tells us exactly where the angel stood in the temple and exactly where on the map he found Mary! What tireless comings and goings and what constant concern with being in one place or another fill the pages of the gospels! If we are not to think in terms of real time and place, why this persistent use of familiar words that suggest nothing else? Scholars have pointed out that it is impossible to take such formulaic expressions as "to visit the earth" and "he went and preached" (referring to the descensus) in any but the most literal sense.[68] The insistence of our sources on depicting the hereafter in terms of "places" (*topoi*, the *ma'man* of the Dead Sea Scrolls) is a constant reminder that "heaven is not only a state but a place."[69] True, it is so far away that our sun "and all the world of men" look like nothing but a tiny speck of dust, "because of the vast distance at which it is removed"; but for all that it is still the same universe, and all made of the same basic materials.[70]

This preoccupation with locus assumes a plurality of worlds, and indeed in our "treasure" texts we often find *worlds, earths,* and *kosmoses* in the plural.[71] It is only the fallen angels, in fact, led by the blind Samael, who insist: "We are alone and there is none beside us!"[72] To the Sons of Light, on the other hand, there is opened up the grandiose vision of the "worlds" united in the common knowledge of him who made them, exchanging joyful and affectionate messages as they "keep faith with one another" in the common plan and "talk to each other . . . and establish concord, each contributing something of its own" to the common interest.[73] The members of the vast complex are kept in perfect accord by the sustaining Word of God which reaches all alike, since it possesses "through the power of the Treasure" the capacity for traveling for unlimited distances with inexpressible speed.[74] This Word is also the Son, who "has betaken himself to the numberless hidden worlds which have come to know him."[75] The messages may also be borne by special messengers and inspectors, angels with special assignments and marvelous powers of getting around, who constantly go forth on their missions and return with their reports.[76]

With all its perfect unity and harmony, the system presents a scene not of monotonous uniformity but rather of endless and delightful variety: " . . . they are all different from each other, and He has not made one of them superfluous; hence each one has good things to exchange with its neighbors."[77] At a new creation there is a reshuffling of elements, like the rearranging of notes in the musical scale to make a new composition;[78] it is even suggested, as we have noted, that old worlds may be dismantled to supply stuff for the making of newer and better ones.[79]

Beginning with the very old Egyptian idea, recently examined by E. A. E. Reymond, that the creation of the world was really a re-creation by "transforming substances" that had already been used in the creation of other worlds,[80] the Jewish and Christian apocryphal writers envisage a process by which the stuff of worlds is alternately organized into new stars and planets and when these have served their time, scrapped, decontaminated, and reused in yet more new worlds. This "Urstoff" which is being constantly recycled is the *Tohuwabohu* of some Jewish teachers, according to Weiss, who saw the ultimate forms of matter in fire and ice.[81] Likewise, according to the same authority, the world-holocaust of the Stoics was merely a necessary preparation for the making of new worlds from old materials.[82] The whole thrust of Weiss's book is that until the early Christian apologists we find no trace anywhere of a doctrine of *creatio ex nihilo,*[83] the Creation being everywhere conceived of as the act of organizing "matter unorganized" (*amorphos hyle*), bringing order from disorder, the basic prerequisites for the work being space (*chora*) and unorganized matter.[84]

And so we have in the *Pistis Sophia*, continuing the Egyptian teachings, the picture of a constant remixing (*kerasomos*) going on in the universe in which old, worn-out, contaminated substances, the refuse (*sorm*) of worn-out worlds and kingdoms (247-240), is first thrown out on the scrap-heap and returned to chaos as "dead" matter (134; 41; 68), then melted down in a dissolving fire for many years (366), by which all the impurities are removed from it (249), and by which it is "improved" (ch. 41, 68), and is ready to be "poured from one kind of body into another" (251). This whole process by which souls as well as substances are "thrown back into the mixing" (14), is under the supervision of Melchizedek, the great reprocessor, purifier, and preparer of worlds (35f.). He takes over the refuse of defunct worlds or souls (36), and under his supervision five great Archons process (lit. "knead" — *ouoshm*) it, separating out its different components, each one specializing in particular elements, which they thus recombine in unique and original combinations, so that no new world or soul is exactly like any other (338).

In this full-blown pleniarism there is no waste and no shortage: "If any were superfluous or any lacking the whole body would suffer, for the worlds counterpoise one another like the elements of a single organism."[85] The worlds go on forever: "They come and come and cease not, they ever increase and are multiplied, yet are not brought to an end nor do they decrease."[86]

It was essential to the plan that all physical things should pass away; this idea is depicted by the ancient Egyptian symbol of the *Uroboros*, the serpent with his tail in his mouth, representing the frustration of material things or matter consuming itself by entropy.[87] Indeed, the *Pistis Sophia* describes the *Uroboros* (which means "feeding on its own tail") in terms of the heat-death, when it reports that fire and ice are the end of all things, since ultimate heat and ultimate cold both mean an end to substance.[88] Though matter is replaced through an endless cycle of creations and dissolution, only spirit retains conscious identity, so that strictly speaking "only progeny is immortal," each "mounting up from world to world" acquiring ever more "treasure" while "progressing towards His perfection which awaits them all."[89] When the apostles formed a prayer-circle, "all clothed in garments of white linen," Jesus, standing at the altar, began the prayer by facing the four directions and crying in an unknown tongue, "Iao, Iao, Iao!" The *Pistis Sophia* interprets the three letters of this word as signifying, (1) *Iota*, because the universe took form at the Creation; (2) *Alpha*, because in the normal course of things it will revert to its original state, alpha representing a cycle; (3)*Omega*, because the story is not going to end there, since all things are tending towards a higher perfection, "the perfection of the perfection of everything is going to happen" — that is "syntropy." (*Pistis Sophia*, 358.)

The eternal process is thus not a static one, but requires endless expansion of the universe (*p-sōr ebol mpterf*) (193 end, 219, 225, etc.), since each dispensation is outgoing, tending to separation and emanation, i.e., fissure (220), so that "an endless process in the Uncontainable fills the Boundless" (219). This is the Egyptian paradox of expanding circles of life which go on to fill the physical universe and then go on without end.[90] Such a thing is possible because of a force which is primal and self-existent, having no dependence on other matter or its qualities. This is that "light-stream" which no power is able to hold down and no matter is able to control in any way. (*Pistis Sophia*, 227.) On the contrary, it is this light which imposes form and order on all else; it is the spark by which Melchizedek organizes new worlds (35); it is the light that purifies contaminated substances (388), and the light that enables dead matter to live (ch. 65; 134). Reduced to its simplest form, creation is the action of light upon matter (*hyle*) (64); matter of itself has no power, being burnt-out energy (65), but light reactivates it (134); matter is incapable of changing itself — it has no desire to, and so light forces it into the recycling process where it can again work upon it — for light is the organizing principle (50). If Melchizedek is in charge of organizing worlds, it is Michael and Gabriel who direct the outpouring of light to those parts of chaos where it is needed. (130.) As light emanates out into space in all directions it does not weaken but mysteriously increases more and more, not stopping as long as there is a space to fill. (129.) In each world is a gathering of light ("synergy"?) and as each is the product of a drive towards expansion, each becomes a source of new expansion, "having its part in the expansion of the universe." (193 end.)

The mere mechanics of the creation process as described in our "treasure" texts display truly remarkable scientific insight. For the making of a world the first requirements, we are told, are a segment of empty space, pure and unencumbered,[91] and a supply of primordial matter to work with.[92] Mere empty space and inert matter are, however, forbidding and profitless things in themselves, disturbing and even dangerous things for humans to be involved with —

contemplating them, the mind is seized with vertigo until some foothold is found in the void.[93] The order and stability of a foundation are achieved through the operation of a "Spark." The Spark is sometimes defined as "a small idea" that comes forth from God and makes all the difference between what lives and what does not: "Compared with it all the worlds are but as a shadow, since it is the Spark whose light moves all (material) things."[94] It is the ultimate particle, the *"ennas* which came from the Father of those who are without beginning," emanating from the Treasure-house of Light from which all life and power is ultimately derived.[95] Thanks to the vivifying and organizing power of the Spark, we find throughout the cosmos an infinity of dwelling-places (*topoi*), either occupied or awaiting tenants.[96] These are colonized by migrants from previously established *"toposes"* or worlds, all going back ultimately to a single original center.[97] The colonizing process is called "planting," and those spirits which bring their treasures to a new world are called "Plants," more rarely "seeds," of their father or "Planter" in another world.[98] Every planting goes out from a Treasure-house, either as the essential material elements or as the colonizers themselves, who come from a sort of mustering-area called the "Treasure-house of Souls."[99]

With its "planting" completed, a new world is in business, a new Treasury has been established from which new Sparks may go forth in all directions to start the process anew in ever new spaces;[100] God wants every man to "plant a planting," nay, "he has promised that those who keep his Law may also become creators of worlds."[101] But keeping that law requires following the divine pattern in every point; in taking the Treasure to a new world, the Sent One (who follows hard on the heels of the colonists) seeks nothing so much as complete identity with the One who sent him; hence, from first to last one mind alone dominates the whole boundless complex.[102] Because each planting is completely dependent on its Treasure-house or home-base, the system never breaks up into independent systems; in this patriarchal order all remains forever identified with the Father from whom all ultimately come forth.[102]

We on earth are not aware of all this because we comprehend only what *we* are like.[103] Not only is God rendered invisible by the impenetrable veil of light that surrounds him,[104] but he has purposely "placed veils between the worlds," that all treasures may be hid from those who do not seek them in the proper way.[105] On the other side of the veil of the temple lay "the secrets of heaven," the celestial spaces which know no bounds, and all that they contain.[106]

The *wilon* (veil) quarantines this polluted world mercifully from the rest. [107] "Beyond the veil are the heavens,"[108] and that goes for other worlds as well as this one, for each is shut off by its veil, for there are aeons and veils and firmaments: "He made a veil for their worlds, surrounding them like a wall."[109] Behind the ultimate veil sits Jeu, "the Father of the Treasury of Light" who is separated from all others by the veils (*katapetasmata*),[110] a veil being that which separates that which is above from that which is below.[111] When a cycle has been completed in the existence of things, "the Great Sabaoth the Good looks out," from behind the veil, and all that has gone before is dissolved and passes into oblivion.[112] Only the qualified can pass by one of these veils, of course; when *Pistis Sophia* presumed to look behind the veil before she was ready, she promptly fell from her former glory.[113] Only Jesus has passed through all the veils and all the degrees of glory and authority.[114] As one grows in faith more and more is revealed, until finally "the Watchers move the veils aside and you enter into the Presence of the Father, who gives you His name and His seal. . . ."[115]

These veils seem to serve as protecting as well as confining fences around the worlds: The light of the sun in its true nature (*morphe*) is not seen in this place, we are told, because it passes through "many veils and regions (*topoi*)" before reaching us;[116] its protective function is represented by a wonderful super-bird, called "the guardian of the inhabited earth," because "by spreading out his wings he absorbs (*dechetai*) the fire-like (*pyrimorphos*) rays" of the sun; "if he did not receive (absorb) them, the human race could not survive, nor any other form of life." On a wing of the bird is an inscription declaring, "Neither earth nor heaven begot me, but the wings of fire." Baruch was informed by an angel that this bird is the phoenix, the sun-bird which feeds on the manna of heaven and the dews of earth.[117] It blocks the sun with its wings outspread, suggesting solar prominences or zodiacal light. At any rate, it is an interesting example of how the ancients explained things which most men cannot see or comprehend in terms of things which they can.

The plan calls for universal participation in the accumulation of treasure in a course of eternal progression.[118] The "Treasures in the Heavens" is heady stuff; E. L. Cherbonnier has observed that the discovery that man really belongs to the same family as God, "to share in the same kind of existence which God himself enjoys," is "like learning that one has won the sweepstakes."[119] The Evangelium is good news — the only *good* news, in fact, since all else ends in nothing. But it is also *news*, the sort of thing, as C. S. Lewis points out, that no human being could possibly have invented. Granted that the Treasures in the Heavens are something totally alien to human experience, something which "eye hath not seen, nor ear heard, neither hath entered into the heart of man," they must be nonetheless real.[120] "For the plan of Salvation," as E. Soggin has recently put it, "only exists when we are dealing with reality, not with artificial contrivances ... as Hesse notes, 'We are only interested in what really took place, all the rest being of little or no concern whatever.' "[121] Likewise the religion of Egypt "n'est pas une mystique, mais une physique" as we are now discovering.[122] This attitude, diametrically opposite to that of Christian and Jewish scholars (e.g., C. Schmidt) in the past, is gaining ground today. The old literalism has been dismissed as Gnostic, and indeed much of the appeal of Gnosticism lay in its exploitation of certain "cosmist" aspects of early Christian teaching; but the basic teachings of Gnosticism and Neoplatonism were spiritualized concepts which followed the prevailing line of the schools and ran directly counter to the old literalism of the Treasures in Heaven.[123]

While our sources contain "extremely confused and contradictory records of creation," all seem to betray "a single organic foundation."[124] And while the relationship between them all still remains to be established, it becomes clearer every day that there was a relationship.[125] The "cosmist" idea is not the monopoly of any group, Gnostic or otherwise. Indeed, cosmism was essentially anti-Gnostic.[126] The doctors of the Christians and the Jews who adopted the Neoplatonic and Gnostic ideas of the schools opposed the old literalism with all their might, so that to this day cosmism has remained the very essence of heresy.[127] Still, the very fathers who opposed the old teaching admitted that it was the original faith of the saints, and they could not rid themselves of it without a real struggle.[128]

In view of its age, its universality, its consistency, and its scientific and aesthetic appeal, the doctrine of the Treasures in the Heavens should be studied more closely than it has been. What we have presented in intensely concentrated form is enough to show that references to treasures in religious writings may well conceal far more than a mere figure of speech.

NOTES

1. We have treated this theme in "Sparsiones," *Classical Journal*, 40 (1945), 515-43.

2. *Secrets of Enoch*, v:1, cf. vi:1; Jerem. li:16; Ps. cxxxv:7; Job xxxviii:22; *I Enoch*, xviii:1; *Slavonic Enoch* (in J. A. T. Robinson, *Apocrypha Anecdota* [Cambridge: 1897], II, lviii); *Pseudo-Philo*, xxxii:7 (in M. R. James, *Antiquities of Philo* [SPCK, 1917], 176). "Clouds of radiance drip moisture and life,"*Psalms of Thomas*, i:11 (A. Adam, in *ZNTW*, Beih. No. 24, [1959], 2); text in *A Manichaean Psalm-book* (Stuttgart: 1938), 203-228. On the heavens as a general storehouse and treasure-house, K. Ahrens, in *ZMDG*, 84 (1930), 163, discussing *Koran*, xv:21; cf. *Ben Sirach*,xliii:14ff. In the *Enuma Elish*, Tab. vii:8, God's "treasure is the abundance which is poured out over all." On the relevance of this source, see W. Bousset, *Hauptprobleme der Gnosis* (Göttingen: 1907), 246.

3. They are "for a blessing or a curse as the Lord of Spirits willeth," *I Enoch*, lix:1ff.; lx:22. They must undergo a transformation to be useful to man: Deut. xxviii:12; *I Enoch*, xviii:2; and lx:15, 21-22; *III Baruch*, x:9-10. They may serve "against the day of battle and war," Job xxxviii:22, for unless benignly restrained they are dark and destructive, J. A. T. Robinson, *Apocrypha Anecdota*, lviii, citing *Testament of Levi*, iii:2; cf. *Od. Sal.*, xvi:16; *Pseudo-Philo*, xv:5.

4. "I am the Treasure of Life who descended upon the King of Glory, so that he was radiant in his understanding," M. Lidzbarski, *Das Johannesbuch der Mandäer* (Giessen: 1905), 203, No. 57. God holds the keys to control and administer the treasure, K. Ahrens, in *ZMDG*, 84, (1930), 163; he restrains the elements as by a dam, *I Enoch*, lx:1ff., keeping them "sealed up," *Pseudo-Philo*, viii:6-10, in places of peace and order, *I Baruch*, iii:15. His treasury is a shrine of wisdom, Jerem. li:16-17; cf. Pindar, *Olymp.* vi:64ff., 109. For the Mandaeans *treasure* means "capability, ability, worthiness," E. S. Drower, *The Thousand and Twelve Questions* (Berlin: Akad. -Verlag, 1960), 117, n. 8. An impressive treatment of the theme is in the *Thanksgiving Hymns (IQH)*, especially 1 (Plate 35), 3 (Pl. 37), 10f. (Pl. 44f.), 13 (Pl. 47).

5. Quotation is from E. S. Drower, *A Pair of Nasoraean Commentaries* (Leiden: Brill, 1963), 69, n.1., Cf. *II Baruch*, liv:13; *Od. Sal.*, iv:8. The treasure is a fountain, Proverbs viii:24. "He has a multitude of waters in the heavens...," Jerem. li:16. The source of all earthly treasure is a pool in heaven, *III Baruch*, x:1-10. The "treasures of glory" are the clouds and earthly fountains, says the *Battle Scroll (IQM)*, x:12, the latter being fed by the former, *Pseudo-Philo*, xix: 10, cf. N. Sed, "Une Cosmologie juive du haut moyen-age," in *Revue des Etudes Juives*, 124 (1965), 64-5. In the treasuries of the heavens are "the living waters," *I Enoch*, xviii:2; blessings pour from "the holy dwelling and the eternal fountain that never deceives," *IQSb*, i:3 (this is also temple imagery, *I Enoch*, xxxix:5). God's creative intelligence is "a strong fountain," *IQH*, xii:11. Pindar, *Olymp.* i:lff.; iii:65ff.; ix:19, and Aeschylus, *Persians*, 234, 1022, equate the life-giving gold and silver of the divine treasure-house of oracular wisdom with golden grain and silver fountains. The light of the treasure is also a stream, *Pistis Sophia*, 65 (132f.).

The creative process is an ever-flowing Jordan of Light, *Ginza*, 67 (M. Lidzbarski, *Ginza* [Göttingen: 1925], 61f.).

6. *II Baruch*, liv:13.

7. K. Koch, "Wort and Einheit des Schöpfergottes im Memphis and Jerusalem," in *Zeitschr. f. Theol. u. Kirche*, 62 (1965), 276. This is one of many recent studies pointing out the relevance and importance of early Egyptian texts for the study of Jewish and Christian concepts. So L. V. Khybar, in *JNES*, 13 (1954), 87; R. Anthes, in *JNES*, 18 (1959), 169-212; L. Speleers, *Les Textes des Cercueils* (Brussels: 1946), xxviii. The five *stoicheia* "gush forth" from the five treasure-houses, *Manichäische Handschriften der Staatl. Museen Berlin* (Stuttgart: 1940), I, 30.

8. Such a scene is depicted in the archaic text of the so-called *Shabako stone*, K. Sethe, *Das 'Denkmal Memphitischer Theologié, der Schabakostein des Br. Museums* (Leipzig: 1928), 23-32, 60-70, in the *Pyramid Texts*, e.g., #468 (895); and *Coffin Texts*, e.g., #39 (166-67); in *Enuma Elish*, Tab. iii: 132-38; iv; vi. On the general Near Eastern background of the Council in Heaven, see F. M. Cross, in *JNES*, 12 (1959), 274-77; H. W. Robinson, in *Jnl. Theol. Stud.* 45 (1944), 151-57. On the presentation of the plan, see J. Fichtner, in *ZATW*, 63 (1951), 16-33. The scene is presented in the *Serekh Scroll (IQS)*, x:1ff.; *Ben Sirach*, xvii:11f.; *Pastor Hermae*, Vis. i:3; *The 1012 Questions* (Drower), 112.

9. Thus in the Shabako stone (see note 8) as rendered by J. Breasted, *The Development of Religion and Thought in Ancient Egypt* (London: 1912), 46; "Then he assembled all the gods and their kas (saying to them): 'Come ye and take possession of the "Meb-towe," the divine store-house . . . whence is furnished the "Life of the Two Lands." ' "Cf. Pindar, *Pyth.*, xi:5: "Come to the hidden Melian treasury of the golden tripods . . . the storehouse of true counsels, where the host of heroes assembles." Cf. Jerem. x:12; *4 Ezra* viii:20; *Ben Sirach*, xxxix:12-17; *IQH*, i:10, xiii:1, *IQS*, x:1-2; *Od. Sal.* xv and xvi; xix:1ff.; *Acts of Thomas*, c. 136 (A. F. J. Klijn, *The Acts of Thomas* [Leiden: Brill, 1962], 137); *Psalms of Thomas*, i:7-14; cciii:11ff.; the *Second Gnostic Work*, 39a (C. Schmidt, in *Texte u. Untersuchungen*, 8 [1892], 254, 301). At the great council in heaven the Son said to the Father: "If it please Thee . . . speak, open Thy treasury, and take therefrom a boon," the boon being the plan of salvation, *Prayerbook of the Mandaeans*, No. 250, in E. S. Drower, *The Canonical Prayerbook of the Mandaeans* (Leiden: Brill, 1959), 207; the scene is also described, *ibid.*, 225 (No. 318), 227 (No. 321), 228 (No. 323), 252 (No. 358, cf. 365-68), 269 (No. 375) 271ff. (No. 376). There is a dramatic description of the opening of the chest in the *Alma Rishaia Zuta*, iii:199ff. (in Drower, *Nasoraean Commentaries*, 69). So *Ginza* (Lidzbarski), 493. There are five treasuries of the senses; when the mind (*enthymēsis*) wants to create, it opens the appropriate treasure-chest to get the things it needs, *Manichäische Handschriften der staatl. Museen Berlin* (Stuttgart: 1940), I, 138-40, the things being the elements in an unformed state, *ib.* 54. Though they were later corrupted by mixture with a lower state of matter or ground-substance, the physical elements are in themselves pure and holy, *ib.*, 239; in their corrupt earthly form they are gold, silver, copper, lead, and tin, *ib.*, 33. God also

opens a treasure-chest to bring forth healing elements for man, *Manichaean Psalm-book*, II, 46.

10. *Gospel of Truth* (M. Malinine, *et. al., Evangelium Veritatis* [Zürich: 1956], fol. XIVV, 5-7. Smoke, fire, wind, and water were the chaotic contents of the divine store-house, *Manichaean Psalm-book*, II, 9. In the *Ginza*, 259, there is a leavening substance, a "Sauerteig der Welt," kept in the divine treasure-house, and from this the world and the planets are created, as higher worlds are created of a like substance, 261. God furnishes "the whole creation" from "the treasuries of all the winds," *I Enoch* xviii:1, which are in the midst of "secret things" amidst mountains of precious stones and minerals, *ib.* lii:5. On wind as the "Urstoff," *Coffin Texts*, Spell 162 (A. de Buck, ed., Univ. of Chicago: 1938, II, 401). On water, W. Lambert, in *Jnl. Theol. Stud.*, 16 (1965), 293.

11. For a thorough treatment, H. F. Weiss, *Untersuchungen zur Kosmologie des hellenistischen und Palästinischen Judentums* (Berlin: Akademic-Verlag, 1966), 59-74, and notes 81 to 84, below; also W. Richter, "Urgeschichte und Hoftheologie," *Biblische Zeitschr.*, NF 10 (1966) 97; H. A. Brongers, *De Scheppingstradities bij de Profeten* (Amsterdam: 1945), 3-18.

12. The idea is carried over into the widespread ritual dramatizations of the Creation, the essence of which is the strict regulation of persons, times, and places, S. Mowinckel, *Religion und Kultus* (Göttingen: 1953), 53-9. See esp. *Pistis Sophia* 128-135.

13. This is an unfailing part of the picture: the Hallelujah chorus with its refrain of "Forever and ever!" is the closing section of almost any ritual text. See W. F. Otto, *Die Musen und der göttlichen Ursprung des Singens und Sagens* (Düsseldorf-Köln: E. Diederich, 1956); H. Nibley, "The Expanding Gospel," *B.Y.U. Studies*, 7 (1965), 5-27.

14. K. Koch, in *Zeitschr. f. Theol, u. Kirche*, 62 (1965), 271, 281-82, shows that the "creative word of God" originally refers to a conversation, a discussion with others. The Egyptian concept is discussed by H. Junker, *Die Götterlehre von Memphis* (Berlin: Akad. d. Wiss., 1940), 36f., 42, 55; the holy ones are "as it were extensions of the Great God," H. Grapow, *Das 17. Kapitel des aeg. Totenbuches* (Berlin: 1912), 40. See above, notes 8 and 9. May not the Logos of John I also be a "council" discussion"?

15. Quotation from D. Winston, in *History of Religions*, 5 (1966), 212, citing Jewish and Persian sources. It was a real discussion, in which many divergent views were expressed, as described in Timothy Abp. of Alexandria, *Discourse on Abbaton*, fol. 10a-12a (E. A. W. Budge, *Coptic Martyrdoms* [Br. Mus.: 1914], 232-34); *Ginza* (Lidzbarski), 331-33; *Mandaean Prayerbook*, No. 361 (Drower, 255); *Alma Rishaia Zuta*, iii, 215ff (67, 70); *Alma Rishaia Rba*, iv, 150ff. (7); *Pistis Sophia*, 33ff.

16. *IQM*, xii:2-3; *IQSa*, i:1ff. The world was created on their behalf, *Ascension of Moses*, i:12; *4 Ezra* ix:13. All the elect were known and the kingdom with "the riches of his glory" (i.e. the treasure) appointed to them "from the foundation of the world," Matt. xxv:34,41; Rom. ix:23; *Od. Sal.*, xxiii:1-3; *Psalms of Solomon*, xviii:30; *Didache*, x:3; *Test. Dom. nostri J. Christi*,

xxiv (J. E. Rahmani, ed.; Mainz: 1899). They are the pearls in the treasure house of Life, *Ginza*, 590f. They alone share the secrets of the treasure, *ibid.*, 296, cf. *IQH*, xvii:9.

17. *IQM*, xiii:2; vii:6; xv:13; *IQSa*, ii:8f, 14f, 20: *IQH*, iii:20f. Every major event in the N.T. is marked by the presence on the scene of heavenly beings participating with the saints in the activities.

18. *IQM*, x:10; *Clementine Recognitions*, iii:53f, 58; v:5-7; *Oxyrhynchus Frg.*, No. 654:5ff; *Gospel of Thomas*, 80:14-18; 94:14ff, 19; 1ff; *Gospel of Truth*, fol. IXr,2-4; Lactantius, *Div. Inst.*, IV:ii. "The Chosen people alone understand what the others have rejected," K. Koch, *Zeitschr. f. Theol. u. Kirche*, 62 (1965), 292.

19. *IQH*, i:21; II:7, 13, 17; iii:19ff; iv:27; v:25; vi:10-11; vii:26-30; x:4, 14ff, 22ff, 29; xi:4-8, 10, 27f; xii:11f, xiii:18f; xv:21f. Cf. *IQS*, xi:6f; ix:16-18; Isaiah xlv:3; Matt. xi:25ff; Rom. xi:33, 12; Eph., iii:8f; Col. ii:2f, 26f; Phil. iv:19; *I Enoch*, lxiii: 3; *Ep. Barnab.*, vi; *Od. Sal.*, vi:4-5; xxx:1; *Gospel of Truth*, fol. XVIr, 17; *Test. Dom. nostri J. Christi*, xliii (Rahmanie, 103); *Ben Sirach*, xvii:11-13, *Manichaean Psalm-book*, II, 120, 126. "In a certain way, election is pre-existence," writes J. Zandee, in *Numen*, 11 (1964), 46, citing Logion No. 49 of the *Gospel of Thomas*. Not only the Son of Man but Isaac, Jacob, Jeremiah, the Twelve Apostles, Peter, etc., are specifically said to have been chosen and set apart in the preexistence.

20. Clement of Alex., *Paedagog.*, I, vii (in Migne, *P.G.*, viii:321), citing Jeremiah i:7, 5; cf. Ephes. i:4; I Pet. i:20. The awards and assignments handed out at the Creation must have been earned in a preexistent life, Origen, *De princip.*, I, viii, 4; II, ix, 6-8; cf. *Zaddokite Document*, ii:7; *IQS*, iv:22; iii:15; *IQS*, 1:7.

21. The expression occurs in *Gospel of Thomas*, 84:17; *Gospel of Philip*, 112:10; cf. *Secrets of Enoch*, xxiii:4-6; *IQH*, i:19, xiii:8; *Od. Sal.*, vii:10.

22. *II Baruch*, xxi:16. Cf. *Gospel of Philip*, 112:10: "For he who is both was and shall be." "By not yet existing, I do not mean that they do not exist at all..." *Gospel of Truth*, fol. XIVr: 35-36. The formula "out of the eternities and into the eternities" is found in *IQS*, ii: line 1, and *Ep. Barnab.*, xviii, and indicates an endless past as well as an endless future for man, "...for Thou didst establish them before eternity," *IQH*, xiii:8. "When he prepared the heavens I was there. Then I was by him, as one brought up with him; and I was his daily delight," *Proverbs* xiii:21ff; see H. Donner, in *Aegypt. Zeitschr.*, 81 (1956), 8-18, for Egyptian parallels.

23. With a new creation things become visible on new level, *Secrets of Enoch*, xxiv:5-xxv:1; xxiv:2; xxx:10-11; lxv; *II Baruch*, li:8. This is consistent with the doctrine that one sees or comprehends only what one is like, see below, note 103. In the Genesis creation hymn, "everything is as it were created twice, in two different ways," J. B. Bauer, in *Theol. Zeitschr.*, 20 (1964), 7; Albright has shown that "in the beginning" does not refer to an absolute beginning but to the start of a new phase in a going concern, *ib.*, 1. *Ex ouk onton* refers to such a phase rather than to creation *ex nihilo*, W. Richter, in *Biblische Zeitschr.*, NF 10 (1966), 97, citing 2 *Macc.* vii:28, and *Homil. Clem.*, xix:4, 9, 16, 18.

24. The concept of Gen. i and Psalms xciv and civ is the same as the old Egyptian idea that the Creation was the beginning of a new cycle of time following a different kind of age, K. Koch, *Zeitschr. f. Theol. u. Kirche,* 62 (1965), 257. At the Creation God showed his children "what they did not know before, creating new things and abolishing old agreements, to establish that which should be eternally," *IQH,* xiii:10-12; *Ben Sirach,* xxxvi: 6-8. Passing from one life to another is a renewal, *IQH,* xi:12ff; one's existence does not begin with the womb, though a new life begins there, *IQH,* xv:12-15; *Apocalypse of Adam,* 78:1. When the "treasury of the heavenly King is opened" the saints become heirs to a new kingdom by a renewal of the mind, *Acts of Thomas,* Ch. 136. To become a Christian is to accept a new creation, *Epist. to Diognetus,* xi.

25. Below, note 79. The Egyptians taught that a creation was the reuniting of existing things in new forms, R. Anthes, in *Aegypt. Zeitschr.,* 82 (1957), 3. Untamed chaotic matter is represented as a raging beast, e.g., ·*Pistis Sophia,* 54 (104); 55 (105); when the beast is subdued an orderly world is composed of its substance, *ib.,* 70 (154). Can this be the origin of the common tradition of creation from the body of some slain monster?

26. *Clementine Recognitions,* i:24. So *Ginza,* 506, 508-10, 438. The spirits are equal in age, but not in power and glory, in which they compare as fathers to sons, without any rivalry or jealousy, *Sophia Christi* (ed. W. Till), 97:2ff.

27. Every man has a *dmuta* – "likeness, counterpart, image," which is the "spiritual or ideal counterpart or double... ," E. S. Drower, *1012 Questions,* 11; it is "the pre-existent pneumatic part of man," *ib.,* 122, n. 5, 161, 173, n. 3. Thus Paul (in the *Apocalypsis Pauli,* xviii:22ff) and Tobit (in an Aramaic text of *Tobit* from Qumran) both see their spiritual doubles. In the remarkable Vision of Kenaz in the *Pseudo-Philo,* xxviii:8, that early prophet sees the spirits of men walking about in another spirit-world while waiting for this world to be created. This is the Mandaean Ether-Earth, E. Drower, *Prayerbook of the Mandaeans,* 290, n. 4. Before the creation of the world "the soul still sat in the Kanna, without pain and without defect... ," Lidzbarski, *Johannesbüch der Mandäer,* 55 (No. 13). All creature are double, *Paster Hermae,* II (Mand., viii), 1, and all souls existed before the formation of the world, *Secrets of Enoch,* xxiii:4. The related Platonic doctrine "became a prevailing dogma in later Judaism," according to R.H. Charles, *Apocrypha & Pseudepiographa of the Old Testament* (Oxford: 1913), II, 444.

28. "God has shed upon man the splendor of his glory at the creation of all things," *IQH,* xvi:9; vii:24ff; *Secrets of Enoch,* xxiv:1, 5; xxii: 8b; *Od. Sal.,* xxviii:14-15; xli; xxiv:5; xxxvi:3-5; *Gospel of Thomas,* 90:2; *Gospel of Philip,* 112:12, 14f. *The Nature of the Archons,* 144:20 (in *Theol. Literaturzeitung,* 83 [1958], p. 668); *Pastor Hermae,* Simil. I:i; Mandaean texts cited by R. Bultmann, "Die neuerschlossenen mandäischen u. manichäischen Quellen... ," *ZNTW,* 24 (1925), 108f. One is overawed by the thought that this thing of wet dust once "praised among the praising ones... was great among the mighty ones... ," *IQS,* xi:20-22; *IQSb,* iii, 28. To know one's true identity is the great treasure, *Gospel of Thomas,* 80:26; 81:3f; 87:1f. "I am a Son and come out of the Father... descended from the pre-existing Father," etc., *Apocryphon of James* (ed. W. Till), i:333, 15f.

29. Thus a fragment from Turfan, cited by Bultmann, 126: "I come from the light as one of the gods, and here I have become a stranger." With characteristic vanity the Gnostics reserved such glory for themselves alone, Irenaeus, *adv. Haeres.*, I, vi. cf. *Od. Sal.* 41:8, *The Pearl*, 11, 31-44, 56.

30. Job xxxviii:3-7, 21, this last is not stated as a question in the MT, but a flat declaration; *IQM*, xvii:20-27; " . . . peace was prepared for you before ever your war was," and God will not take back the promises made at the Creation, *Od. Sal.*, iv:12-14.

31. *Gospel of Thomas*, Log. 84. When Adam complained of his hard lot on earth, a heavenly messenger shamed him by reminding him of the throne awaiting him in heaven, Lidzbarski, *Mand. Johannesbuch*, 57 (No. 13). "Endure much; then you will soon see your treasure!" *Ginza*, 493; cf. The *Apocryphon of John*, 20:19-22; 17.

32. E.g., *IQH*, iii:22; vii:32; x:1ff, and above, note 19. Cf. Acts i:23, 26.

33. Those who will go to heaven are they who came from there in the first place, John iii:13. They recognize the Lord on earth even as they once acclaimed him above, John xvii:8; xvii:10-12.

34. Justin Martyr, *Apol.*, i:10, 59; ii:4-5, 7. So *Zadokite Frg.*, ii:3-6. "When you lay your hand on the treasure the soul enters the scales that will test her," *Alma Rishaia Rba* (Drower), 44-46. Only when you have overcome here "is your name called out from the Book of Those Who Were Valiant, and you become the heir to our Kindgom . . ." *The Pearl*, lines 46-48. For the reward aspect, Origen, *De princ.*, I, viii, 4; II, ix, 6-8. Cf. *Manichaean Psalmbook*, II, 4, 58, on this "world of testing. . . ."

35. *Clementine Recognitions*, i:24.

36. K. Sethe, *Dramatische Texte* (Leipzig: 1928), I, 64-65.

37. A specific counterplan is mentioned in *Clementine Recognitions*, iii:61; cf. *IQM*, xiii:4; *IQS*, ii:4ff.; *4Qflor.*, i:8; *Gospel of Philip*, 123:2ff.; 103:14ff.; *Apocryphon of John*, 74:1ff.; 36:16ff.; 72:10ff; *Sophia Christi*, 122:1ff. There are those in the Church who preach the doctrine of the Serpent, according to the Pseudo-Epistle of Paul to the Corinthians in *Bodmer Papyrus*, X:54:15, describing his ambitious opposition to God's plan in the beginning, *ib.*, X:53:11-15.

38. "Now the Prince, not being righteous and wanting to be God . . . enchains all the flesh of men . . . ," *Bodmer Papyrus*, X:53. So Irenaeus, *adv. Haer.*, V, xxv; *Creation Apocryphon (Ursprung der Welt)*, 151:11ff. (A. Bohlig u. P. Labib, *Die Koptisch-Gnostische Schrift ohen Titel aus Cod. II von Nag Hammadi* [Berlin:Akad. Verlag, 1962], 48f.), 155:25ff.; 150:27, 35; 151:3, 7, 15, 18, 24; 154:19ff., 14f.; 156:1; *Psalms of Thomas*, ii:1-2; 1:30-37, 22-25, 43-47; vii:1-3; *Test. Dom. nostri J. Christi*, xxiii:43; *Acts of Thomas* (A. J. Klijn), 204:22-25; *Book of John the Evangelist* (ed. M. R. James), 187-89; *Vita Adae et Evae*, xv:3; xvi:1, 4 (in R. H. Charles, *Apocrypha & Pseudepiographa of the Old Testament*, 137) *Hypostasis of the Archons* 134:9 (after Isaiah xlvi:9); 140:26; 141:1. *Abp. Timothy Ep. on Abbaton*, fol. XIIIa; *Pseudo-Phil*, xxx:5; xxxiv:2f; *Sibylline Oracles*, iii:105ff. (in Charles, 381); *Ascension of Isaiah*, ii:9; vii:3-5, 9f.,

15; *Secrets of Enoch*, x:18; xxxa:3f.; M. Lidzbarski, *Mand. Johannesbuch*, No. 2, 3 (14f., 17ff.); *Alma Rishaia Zuta*, iii:215ff. (70); *Ginza*, 18, 263.

39. When God sent forth a ship of light "laden with the riches of the Living," Satan and his pirate crew coming "I know not from where" seized "the treasure of the Mighty One" and "distributed it among their worlds" until they were forced to give it up, *Psalms of Thomas*, iii:1-15, 29-32, 35; *Manichaean Psalm-book*, II, 53, 163, 178; cf. the image of the three ships, *ib.*, 168, 171, 174; *Berlin Manich, Hs.*, I, 50; *Psalms of Thomas* xii:1-xiii. *The Second Coptic Work*, 14a (ed. C. Schmidt, in *Texte u. Unters.*, VIII:236, 286) has Christ coming out of the monas of Setheus "like a ship laden with all manner of precious things," so also the *Manichaean Psalm-book*, II, 151f; in the *Mand. Johannesbuch*, No. 58 (206), a ship moves between the worlds bearing the glory of the Treasure of Life from one to the other. In the Egyptian *Victory over Seth*, i:19-22, the god passes through dangerous straits in his ship while Seth and his robber band try to waylay him. (In the *Book of the Dead* the battle of the gods takes place on board a ship, H. Grapow, *Das 17. Kapitel des Totenbuches*, 37). When Adam returns to "the Treasure of Life" he is asked by the guardians "what wares he is bringing in his ship," J. Leipoldt, *Religionsgeschichte des Orients* (Leiden: E. J. Brill, 1961), 86. In numerous Acts of Thomas the Captain of the ship or the rich merchant is Christ in disguise, e.g., A. Klijn, *Acts of Thomas*, ii-iii. The same commercial imagery of the ship in the *Mand. Johannesbuch*, No. 18, 84-86; cf. *Ginza*, 324. The seven planets are described as floating ships, *Mandaean Prayerbook*, No. 286, 288; these seven try to rob man of his treasure, *Psalm of Thomas*, v:4 (in *ZNTW*, Beih. 24, [1925], 123); *The 1012 Questions*, 251, 258. The Ark itself was not a ship but a luminous cloud in space, according to the Apocryphon of John, 73:5f.

40. Mark v:5ff; Luke iv:34f. The recognition is mutual, Luke iv:41; viii:27f; x:17. The contest is continued in the desert, Matt. iv:1, with Satan still claiming the rule and challenging the Lord's title, Matt. iv:10, 3. The war we wage here (Eph. vi:12) is a continuation of the conflict in the beginning, *Hypostasis of the Archons*, 134:20. Those who follow either leader here, followed the same there, John viii:44, 7; *Od. Sal.*, xxiv:5, 7.

41. *Apocryphon of James*, liii:12ff (the gifts); *Apocryphon of Adam*, 85:1f (ordinances); *The 1012 Questions*, II, iiib, 86 (Drower, 226-27) (signs); 2 Thess. ii:9 (wonders); *Bodmer Papyrus*, X:54 (doctrine); *Apocalypse of Elias*, i:8ff (glory); they are even rival fishermen, Logion, No. 174, in M. Osin et Palacias, "Logia et agrapha D. Jesu," *Patro. Or.*, XIX, 574.

42. Matt. vi:19-21; xiii:10ff; xix:21, 29; Mark x:21; xii:41ff; Luke xviii:21f; xii:21, 32; Rom. ii:5, I Tim. vi:17-19; Jerem. xlviii:7; *Ben Sirach*, v:2. Many Logia deal with the theme, M. A. Palacios. *Logia et agrapha*, Nos. 34, 42, 44, 50, 53-55, 77 (in *Migne, P.O.*, XIII, 357ff.). So the *Gospel of Thomas*, 37, 137, 147; *Apocalypse of Elias*, viii:12f.; *Psalms of Thomas*, i:17-19; *Apocryphon of James*, ii:53; *Acts of Thomas*, 37, 137, 147; *Gospel of Thomas*, 85:6ff.; 86:27; 92; 94:14; 95:15; 98:31; 99:4; *Slavic Adam and Eve*, xxxiii:1. It is important not to confuse the treasures or to falsify, *Ginza*, 19, 40, 123f., 334, 392, 433; cf. *Pistis Sophia*, 100 (249-51). *Berlin Manich. Hs.* I, 223, 228f.; *Manichaean Psalm-book*, II, 75, 79, 82.

43. Hence the paradox that the "Poor" are the rich, *Epist. to Diognetus, v; Manichaean Psalm-book,* II, 157. See below, note 45.

44. Treasures now "prepared" and awaiting the righteous on the other side, Mark x:40; *Gospel of Truth,* fol. XXIv, 11-17, can only be claimed by meeting certain stipulations, *Gospel of Philip,* 108:1ff. All treasures are held in trust, "dedicated," 1 Chron. xxvi:20; *Pseudo-Philo,* xxxix:3, and will be handed over when the time comes, *I Enoch,* li:1. The righteous "without fear leave this world," because they have with God "a store of works preserved in treasuries," *II Baruch,* xiv:12; xxiv:1. Whatever part of the Treasure we enjoy on earth is not ours but has only been entrusted to our keeping, *The 1012 Questions,* I, i; 111f.; 122f. On the "treasury of good works" as "an old Oriental doctrine," K. Ahrens, in *ZMDG,* 84 (1930), 163. "One's good works are his deposits," says Ignatius, *Epist. ad Polycarp.,* vi. The Christian (Manichaean) and Chinese versions are compared by A. Adam, in J. Leipoldt, *Religionsgeschichte des Orients,* 109; for the Iranian version, D. Winston, in *History of Religions,* 5 (1966), 194f., who also mentions concealing the treasure under God's throne, 212, to which parallels are supplied by *II Baruch,* liv:13, *Ginza,* 281; the *Shabako Stone,* line 61, and the Ark of the Covenant "under the feet of the statue of god," W. H. Irwin, in *Revue Biblique,* 72 (1965), 164. This is the theme of *The Pearl.*

45. Matt. xxv:14-29. Dives is welcome to his treasures on earth, but cannot claim treasures in heaven, Luke xvi:20-5, Matt. xix:21, 24; vi:19f; Mark x:25; Luke xviii:25; xii:33f. *II Baruch,* xliv:13-15; *Secrets of Enoch,* i:5; *Gospel of Thomas,* 88:34f.; 89:1ff.; *Acts of Thomas* 146; *The 1012 Questions,* II, iv, 159 (245). It is a Jewish, Christian, and Mandaean tradition that earthly prayers are laid up in God's treasure-house, Lidzbarski, *Mand. Johannesbuch,* 10, n.2; *Mand. Prayerbook,* No. 379 (293). If a righteous one strays "his treasure will be taken from him," *Alma Rishaia Zuta,* i, in E. Drower, *Nasoraean Commentaries,* 55; *Berlin Manch. Hs.,* I, 73.

46. *Apocalypsis Pauli,* 19 (text in *Orientalia,* ii [1933], 22). Cf. *II Baruch,* lii:7; *The 1012 Questions,* vib, 379 (Drower, 279).

47. *IQS,* iv:16-18. This is an "Abbild" of the cosmic struggle, J. Schreiner, in *Biblische Zeitschr.,* NF 9 (1965), 180; J. M. Allegro, in *Jnl. of Semit. Stud.,* 9 (1964), 291-94.

48. For the erasing of the memory, see below, note 60. The "Law of Liberty" (*Khōq kherut*) of *IQS,* x:6, 11, is "the Ancient Law of Liberty" of *Clementine Recognitions,* ii:23-25; iii:26, 59; iv:24, 34; x:2; cf. Minucius Felix, *Octav.,* xxvii; Cyril of Jerusalem, *Catehesis* iv:19f, (in Migne, *P.G.,* xxiii:481). Having such freedom, the wicked have deliberately rejected God's plan, *IQS,* iv:25-26. Though the evil spirits are fiercely opposed to this liberty (*Clementine Recognitions,* i:42) the "testing of election for every single individual" goes on without coercion in "truth, righteousness, humility, judgment," etc., while the self-willed are free "to go the way of their own heart . . . according to the plan of his own devising . . ." *IQS,* v:3-5, the spirit being "immortal, rational and independent," *Const. Apostol.,* vi:11; Tatian, *Adv. Graecos,* vii. The present test was appointed from the beginning, *IQM,* xiii:14ff. "This is the condition of the contest which every man who is born

on the earth must wage; if he be overcome, he shall suffer... if he be victorious, he shall receive what I said..." 4 *Ezra*, vii:127, cf. *IQH*, xiv:23. It is "a testing-time in the common light," *Sibylline Oracles*, frg. 1:5, 18, 25-17. See further J. B. Bauer, in *Theolog. Zeitschr.*, 20 (1964), 2-3.

49. A. Adam, "Die Psalmen des Thomas u. das Perlenleid," Beiheft 24 of *ZNTW*, 1959, 49-54. The Syriac text is given by G. Hoffman, in *ZNTW*, 4 (1903), bearing the title, "Song of Judas Thomas the Apostle in the Land of India." Thomas's situation in India resembles that of the hero in the Land of Egypt. The pearl itself comes from the other world and is that part of the heavenly knowledge which is to be found here, *Mand. Prayerbook*, No. 252, 208f.; when it is taken away the world collapses, *Ginza*, 517; it is "the pure pearl which was transported from the treasuries of Life, *Mand. Prayerbook* No. 69. The robe of glory, left behind with the Treasure, is to be regained with it, Bartholomew, *"Book of the Resurrection of Christ,"* Fol. 18b (in E.A. W. Budge, *Coptic Apocrypha*, 208); *Pistis Sophia*, 6 (9f.).

50. J. Leipoldt, *Religionsgeschichte des Orients*, 86; *Abp. Timothy on Abbaton*, Fol. 20b. The joyful homecoming is a conspicuous Egyptian theme from the beginning: There is rejoicing among the Great Ones for one of their own has returned, *Pyramid Texts*, No. 606 (1696); 217 (160); 222 (201); 212, 213, etc. *Coffin Texts* (de Buck), II, Spells 31, 132. The theme is discussed by H. Brunner, in *Aegypt. Zeitschr.*, 80 (1955), 6; cf. Pindar, *Olymp.*, viii:13. The righteous are homesick, *I Enoch*, xiv:4; xlii:1ff.; *Manichaean Psalm-book*, II, 197-200, 87. Going to heaven is a return, 4 *Ezra*, vii:78, *John* xvii:5f.; iii:7-13; *Rev.* v:12. The saints desire "to be received back again" into "the first Church (that)... existed from the beginning," before the Creation, *II Clem. Epist.*, xiv: *Clementine Recognitions*, iii:26; *Test. Dom. nostri J. Christi*, xxviii (61); *Timothy on Abbaton;* Fol. 20b; 12a; *Gospel of Philip*, 115:18. The saints find the Kingdom because they came from there, *Gospel of Thomas*, 89:27; *Pastor Hermae*, III (Simil. i, the Pearl motif); *Apocalypsis Pauli*, xxiii:9; xxiv:6ff.; *Apocryphon of James*, i:27: 5ff., 12; xxxi:13-25; ii:58:2ff. "The Living Ones will return again to the Treasure which is theirs," *Psalms of Thomas*, i:49; cf. xviii:1ff.; xvii:20ff. In the end everything returns to its "root," *Creation Apocryphon*, 175:4; cf. J. Zandee, in *Numen*, 11 (1964), 66. Those above are equally impatient for the reuniting, *Pistis Sophia*, 10/16-19); *Manichaean Psalm-book*, II, 201, 72, 136.

51. In reclaiming its treasure the spirit "becomes what is was before removing its garment," *Apocryphon of James*, ii:56:11ff.; cf. *Gospel of Philip*, 105:19; *Gospel of Truth*, fol. XXIv, 24; *Psalms of Thomas*, ii:70-72, 74, 77; *Acts of Thomas*, vi-vii (lines 35-55 of The Pearl); *Second Gnostic Work*, i-a; *Ginza*, 487, 26f; *Od. Sal.*, xi:10; *Pastor Hermae*, III, Simil. viii, 2. The garment is the treasure for both men and angels, *Ginza*, 13; the garment of Adam and Eve "was like the Treasure of Life," *ib.*, 243; it is a protection for the righteous which the evil ones try to seize and possess, *ib.*, 247, 259, 132.

52. The garment represents ritual in general, C. Schmidt, in *Texte u. Unters.*, 8 (1892), 347.

53. E. Drower, *The 1012 Questions*, 212, 241; the ordinances are "the treasures that transcend the world," *ib.*, 245. "Ginza" means "a treasure,

mystery, sacrament . . . what is hidden and precious . . . ," *ib.* 12. As guardian of these secrets and mysteries the Eldest Son is called "the Treasurer," *Ginza,* 150. The eldest are they who observe the ordinances secretly in this world, *ib.* 153-54, and their highest duty is to transmit and explain these rites to their children, *Mand. Prayerbook,* No. 373, 266. See S. A. Pallis, *Mandaean Studies,* 192.

54. Discussed by B. Gärtner, *The Temple and Community in Qumran and the New Testament* (Cambridge Univ.: 1965), 16ff. The temple with its rites is the earthly counterpart of the heavenly treasury, *I Baruch,* iv:3-5. Since the Creation the ordinances have been essential to God's plan, *Jubilees,* vi:18; *Pseudo-Philo,* xxi:2. It is in the cultus that the cosmic plan is unfolded, N. A. Dahl, in W. D. Davies and D. Daube, *Background of the New Testament,* 430f., and the return of the temple is the return of the heavenly order, 4 QFlor., i; vi.

55. I.e., I and II *Jeu* and the *2nd Coptic Gnostic Work.* Without the "mysteries" one has no power and no light, *Pistis Sophia,* 55 (107); this is a Hauptthema of the *Gospel of Philip,* 124. The old temple rite of the shewbread is an initiation to the Treasury of Light, *Pistis Sophia,* iv: 370. One's station (*taxis*) hereafter depends entirely on the mysteries one has "received" on earth, *ib.,* 90 (202); 86 (195); 32 (52); *Gospel of Philip,* 125 (317); 129 (329). Without the performance of certain ordinances, no one, no matter how righteous, can enter into the Light, *Pistis Sophia,* 103 (263). Hence the rites are all-important, *ib.,* 107, 11 (279), 100 (249f). One becomes "an heir of the Treasure of Light by becoming perfect in all the mysteries . . ." *II Jeu,* lxxvi; *I Jeu,* v; *Apocryphon of John,* liii:11ff.

56. K. Ahrens, in *ZDMG,* 84 (1930), 163; quotation is from D. Winston, *History of Religions* 5 (1966), 195, giving Jewish and Avestan sources; cf. *IQS,* x:4; ii:3, *Secrets of Enoch,* xl:9f. At the fall of the temple "the heavens shut up the treasure of the rain" and the priests "took the Keys of the Sanctuary and cast them into the height of heaven," *II Baruch,* x:18. The key to the Mandaean kushta (initiation rites) is held by the Master of the Treasurehouse, *Ginza,* 429f. So also in the *Pistis Sophia,* iv (336), the ordinances are "the keys to the Kingdom of Heaven." The keys which Christ gave to Peter were those to "the Heavenly Treasure," *Epistola XII Apostolorum,* Frg. 2, in Migne, *P.O.,* II:147.

57. *II Jeu,* lxxiii (in T.U., VIII:211f.); the same image in *Pistis Sophia,* 14 (23). Cf. *IQH,* xvii:21: "God has chosen his elect . . . instructed him in the understanding of his mysteries so that he could not go astray . . . fortified by his secrets." Through definite ordinances one progresses in the community and helps others to progress, *IQH,* xiv:17-18, teaching of "the Creation and of the Treasures of Glory," *IQM,* x:12f, and testing the knowledge of the members, *IQM,* xvii:8; *IQSb,* iii:22-26. In the Coptic works all the rites "serve a single *oekonomia,* i.e., the gathering in of the spirits who have received the mysteries, so that they can be sealed . . . and proceed to the *kleronomia* (heritage) of Light . . . called in the literal sense of the word the Treasure of Light," C. Schmidt, in *Texte u. Unters.,* 8 (1892), 365. In *Pastor Hermae,* I, Simil. iii:5, the saints are raised up by degrees, being tested at each step, to the precious tower.

58. E. Drower, *The 1012 Questions*, 212, 241. See Morton Smith, *The Secret Gospel* (N.Y.: Harpers, 1972), 96, 115, 83.

59. J. Zandee, in *Numen*, 11 (1964), 45. Adam is the type of the initiate, *Ep. Barnab.*, vi:11-16, from whom the mysteries have been handed down, *Apocryphon of Adam*, lxxxv:19ff. He was privy to the whole plan of creation, *II Baruch*, iv:2; *Secrets of Enoch*, xxx:13ff, being in the "Creation Hymn" (Gen. i:26ff) "God's counterpart as a speaking, active, personal being," J. B. Bauer, in *Theol. Zeitschr.*, 20:8, a historical, *not* a mythological, character, *ib.*, 7. He "came forth out of the light of the invisible place . . ." *Pseudo-Philo*, xxviii:9, and received the first anointing, *Creation Apocryphon*, 159:5; *Clementine Recognitions*, i:47. It is "the light of Adam" that leads men back to the Light, *Psalms of Thomas*, iv:9; and the faithful are promised "all the glory of Adam," *IQS*, iv: line 23; *Zadokite Doc.*, iii:20. He is called "the son of the Treasuries of Radiance" in the *Mandaean Prayerbook*, No. 379, 290.

60. On the sleep of forgetting, *The Pearl*, line 34; *Psalms of Thomas*, xv:5; *Apocryphon of John*, 58:15ff; *Apocryphon of Adam*, 65:14-21; *Abp. Timothy on Abbaton*, fol. 15b; *Sophia Chr.*, 106:1-10; *Creation Apocryphon*, 158:25; *Apocryphon of James*, I xxviii, 14, 22f; *Hypostasis of the Archons*, 137:1-5. It is the "Sem-sleep" of the Egyptian initiation rites. It is also expressed in terms suggesting Plato's Cup of Lethe, *Manichaean Psalm-book*, II, 7, 57, 117, and as the dropping of a veil, *Sophia Chr.*, 120 (in *Texte u. Unters.*, 60:280); *Pistis Sophia*, 131 (336-38); *Ginza*, 34; the Cup-of-Lethe plays an important role in the Greek mysteries, to a lesser extent the Cup of Memory is discussed by C. Schmidt, in *Texte u. Unters.*, 8 (1892), 405f.

61. Called "Three Great Men" in *Apocryphon of Adam*, 66:12ff., they are three arch-angels, *Creation Apocryphon*, 152:23; *Sophia Christi*, 96:3ff.; *2nd Gnostic Work*, 19a. They are sent down to instruct and accompany Adam, *Ginza*, 15, 33-35; they are the Three Uthras, "sent into the world to fetch the Elect . . . back to the House of Light," R. Bultmann, in *ZNTW*, 24 (1925), 132. Thus Enoch is fetched by three men in white, *I Enoch*, xc:31; who also visit Abraham, *Genesis Apocryphon*, ii:24, xix:23ff.; xx:1-8; xxi:21f.; xxii:22f. For the Jewish version of the Three Men in White, R. Goodenough, *Jewish Symbols in the Greco-Roman Period* (N.Y.: Panteon 1958), IX, 102-4, 84-89; X, 91-96. Cf. J. Barbel, "Zur Engel-trinitätslehre im Urchristentum," in *Theological Review*, 54 (1954), 48-58, 103-112; K. Rudolph, *Die Mandäer*, I, 162, noting that these three were the arch-types of the Sent Ones in general.

62. *Od. Sal.*, xxix:1ff; xxii:1; *Psalms of Thomas*, v:28; *Gospel of Truth*, fol. XLv, 22; *I Jeu*, 3; *Epistle of the Apostles*, xii (23); *Berlin Manich. Hs.*, I, 56; not only Adam but every patriarch after him is instructed by a Sent One, *Mand. Johannesbuch*, Nos. 13, 14 (57ff) 60, n. 6. Indeed the Sent Ones are to help every mortal back "to the place from which he came," *Ginza*, 244; cf. *IQS*, xi:1; Luke i:78-79 (John the Baptist as a Sent One). The adversary also has his sent ones, *Pistis Sophia*, 66 (136).

63. Being rejected like the poor, the Sent Ones may be identified with them, R. Bultmann, in *ZNTW*, 24 (1925), 124. The evil spirits accuse the Sent Ones of being aliens and meddlers in the earth, *Ginza*, 263f., and accuse Adam and his descendants of the same thing. The poor are the true heirs, *4QpPs* 37: iii:10; *Od. Sal.*, viii:6-13; see K. Romaniuk, in *Aegyptus*, 44

(1964), 85, 88, citing Old Testament and New Testament parallels to Egyptian teachings. Their "angels" have unbroken contact with the Father, Matt. xviii:10.

64. The Sent One is the Treasure, C. Schmidt, in *Texte u. Unters.*, 8 (1892), 349. The saints receive the law "by angels" (lit. "sent ones"), Acts vii:52, each dispensation having its special angel, *Pastor Hermae*, I, iii, 4. "There has come from the plains of heaven a blessed man . . . and he has restored to all the good wealth (treasure) which the former men took away," namely, the ordinances of the temple, *Sibylline Oracles*, v:414-33. "Thou didst appoint from the beginning a Prince of Light to assist us," *IQM*, xiii:10. Enos, Enoch, Moses, and Joshua were such Sent Ones, *Const. Apostol.*, vii:38, as was John the Baptist, restoring lost ordinances and preparing the people for things to come, *John* 1:6; *Luke* i:16f; *Heb.* i:14; cf. *IQS*, ix:11. Those who accept the plan had a pure begetting through the First Sent One, *Sophia Chr.*, 82:12. Like Adam, everyone is awakened from the sleep of forgetfulness by a Sent One, *ib.*, 94:5ff. Angels and prophets are sent to bring men "what is theirs," *Gospel of Thomas*, 96:7, instructing them in the mysteries, *Mysteries of Heaven and Earth*, iv, 1, in Migne, *P.O.*, VI, 428; *Bodmer Papyrus* X:53. Adam himself became a Sent One to help his children, *Psalms of Thomas*, v:26-8; iv:1-10, 12-17. The instructions to the Sent One and his two counsellors were to teach Adam and his posterity what they must know and do to return to the Light, *Ginza*, 16, 17, 18, 41, 57ff., 113 (on the teaching of ordinances), 119; for the Sent One is in special charge of the Treasure of Life in this world and the other, *ib.* 96.

65. It was by "a letter of command from the Father" that "the Son of Truth inherited and took possession of everything," *Od. Sal.*, xxiii:15-17; *The Pearl*, lines 35-39, 63f., 50. The "King's Letter" is one's passport to heaven, *The 1012 Questions*, 198. As a knowledge of the ordinances, the Treasure is an actual scroll, written by the hand of the Lord of Greatness, *Alma Rishaia Zuta*, 72. Writing is one of the Ten Treasures of the Creation, *Pesachim*, Fol. 54a. The heavenly books are "Beweisdokumente," L. Koep, *Das himmlische Buch . . .* (Bonn: Hanstein, 1952), 54-61; e.g., The Book of Deeds is a written contract between Christ and Adam, *ib.*, 64. "Thou hast engraved them on the Tablets of Life for kingship . . . ," *IQM*, xii:3, discussed by F. Notscher, in *Revue de Qumran*, 3 (1959), 405-12. For the Mandaeans the holy books *are* heavenly treasures, E. Drower, *The 1012 Questions*, 158f, 170, 252. The holy books were often literally treasures, being inscribed on precious metals and buried in the earth like other treasures, H. Nibley, "Qumran and the Companions of the Cave," *Revue de Qumran*, 5 (1965), 191f. The idea of books as treasures is a natural one. "The treasures of the wise men of old are the books they have left us," *Xenophon, Memorab.*, I, vi, 14.

66. We have given some examples in "Christian Envy of the Temple," *Jewish Quarterly Review*, 50 (1959), 97ff.; reprinted in *When the Lights Went Out* (Salt Lake City: Deseret Book Co., 1970), 54ff.

67. J. B. Frey, in *Biblica*, 13 (1932), 164.

68. For the first formula, M. R. James, *Biblical Antiquities of Philo*, 56, 44. Luther called for second *"locus vexatissimus,"* and indeed it "makes im-

possible a spiritual interpretation" of the kerygma, M. H. Scharlemann, in *Concordia Theological Monthly*, 27 (1956), 86, 89.

69. Quotation from J. Frankowski, in *Verbum Domini*, 43 (1965), 149. See also below, notes 91, 96, 97.

70. *Pistis Sophia*, 185, 186, 189; on the basic materials, *id.*247-48.

71. In the *Genesis Apocryphon*, ii:4, Abraham and Sarah swear by "the King of all the Worlds," (cf. the common Moslem expressions); God made the "worlds," *Od. Sal.*, 10; xvi:16; xii:4, 8; all the worlds worship the Sent One as "Illuminator of their worlds," *ib.*, xii:12; so *Psalms of Thomas*, viii:13, 6ff; *The 1012 Questions*, 112; "other worlds" have been going on forever, *Gospel of Philip*, 106:18f. God "arranged all the kosmois in his glory," *Apocryphon of John*, xxi-xxii; the worlds assemble before him, *Psalms of Thomas*, viii:13. The angel who came to Isaiah was "of another firmament and another world," *Ascension of Isaiah*, vi:13. The adversary opposed the plan of God "to create another world" and put Adam in charge, *Secrets of Enoch*, xxi:3. A logion depicts the saints hereafter moving freely through space among the spheres, *Logia et agrapha*, No. 127, in Migne, *P.O.*, XIX: 547; cf. *II Baruch*, xlviii:9. The Father is in the worlds (*kosmois*) and the Son is first and highest among those worlds (*en toisde tois kosmois*) according to an early Liturgy, in Migne, *P.O.*, XVIII:445f., 448. Each heaven is completely equipped with thrones, dwellings, temples, etc., and there are many such heavens, *Creation Apocryphon*, 150:18ff., 23-25. The Archon Jaldaboth created beautiful heavens for his sons, *ib.*, 150:9f.; *Hypostasis of the Archons*, 144:5-10, furnished with stolen materials, above, note 39.

72. *Ascension of Isaiah*, x:12; *Creation Apocryphon*, 148:29f; *Ginza*, 80, they say, "There is only one world — ours!"

73. *Od. Sal.*, xii:3, 10; xvi:14-16; *Gospel of Truth*, fol. XIVr, 11-16; *Apocryphon of John*, xxvi:2f.; xxi:1ff.; *I Enoch*, ii:1, 4; xliii:1; *II Baruch*, xlviii:9; *Epist. I Clement.*, xx. When God created this world, all the other worlds rejoiced together, *2nd Gnostic Work*, 47a. The worlds borrow light from each other and exchange all they know, *Ginza*, 10-11; they form a single lively community, *Mand. Prayerbook*, No. 379, 303, 298-99, all the mysteries being "shared out amongst the worlds of light," *The 1012 Questions*, 112, 164. In a pinch the "Treasures" help each other out, *Psalms of Thomas*, xii:25.

74. Quotation is from the *Mand. Johannesbuch*, No. 59, 207. So also *Od. Sal.*, xii:4-9; *The 1012 Questions*, 213; *Mand. Prayerbook*, No. 379, 296. This seems to be an Eastern tradition, the others being more concerned with emissaries and messengers; see the following notes.

75. *2nd Gnostic Work*, 45a. Cf. *Manichaean Psalm-book*, II, 23, 66. On his visits each world implores him to stay, "and be our King and bring peace to our city!" (l.c., *Ginza*, 258) — i.e. it is a true Parousia, *Psalms of Thomas*, viii:1-13f.; cf. John x:16.

76. Two hundred angels act as interplanetary messengers, *Secrets of Enoch*, iv:1. The business of the angels is to coordinate the working of the central plan among the worlds, F. Dieterici, *Thier und Mensch vor dem König der Genien* (Leipzig: 1881), 78f. The heavenly bodies receive commands from

a single center, M. R. James, *Biblical Antiquities of Philo*, 43, the highest heaven being the "indispensable exchange-center between the spheres," K. Koch, in *Zeitschr. f. Theol. u. Kirche*, 62 (1965), 275; the affairs of "the incomprehensible expanse of the structure of heaven," are directed from a command-post in the center, *Creation Apocryphon*, 146:15-20. The rulers dispatch "letters from world to world and reveal the truth to each other, and there are some souls that travel like an arrow and cleave through all the worlds," *The 1012 Questions*, 192, cf. 164. Adakas "is a 'go-between' between the worlds," E. S. Drower, *Mand. Prayerbook*, 293, and Manda d-Haiai, called "the Capable" by his brother 'uthras, is called "to regulate and to station the 'uthras in their places" among the worlds, *ib.*, 294. In the beginning of the *Apocalypse of Paul*, i:1f., Paul is ordered "to go down and speak to the planet earth," (*le'alma de arga*). Visitors to celestial regions in the various Testaments (Abraham, Isaac, Isaiah, the XII Patriarchs, Adam, etc.) report a traffic of chariots in the spaces, e.g., *I Enoch*, lxxv:8. By whatever means, they circulate ceaselessly among the worlds with marvellous ease, *Ginza*, 13, 42. The Mandaean faithful are urged to "be informed about all worlds" as far as possible, *The 1012 Questions*, 289. The worlds of darkness also communicate, but on another level, *Berlin Manich. Hs.* I, 32.

77. *Ben Sirach*, xlii:23-5; *Od. Sal.*, xii:9; " . . . each is more wonderful than the other!" *Ginza*, 11-13; so also *Mand. Johannesbuch*, No. 59, 207, explaining that it is "the power of the Treasure" that makes such rich variety possible. Among ten thousand times ten thousand worlds "every world is different from the others," *Ginza*, 152. Even the worlds of darkness are all different, *Berlin Manich. Hs.*, I, 68. One cannot describe how another world differs entirely from every other, *Pistis Sophia*, Ch. 88 (199); no other world can be described in terms of this one, so different are they all (84, 133).

78. *Wisdom of Solomon*, xix:18. On the letters of the alphabet as elements of creation, see *Sefer Yeshira*, texts by P. Mordell, in *JQR*, N.S. III (1913), 536-44.

79. The Creation is compared to the smashing of inferior vessels to use their substance for better ones, *Gospel of Truth*, fol. XIIIf., 25ff.; or the melting down of scrap-metal for reuse, *Manichaean Psalm-book*, II, 11; or with the breaking of an egg that a more perfect form might emerge, *Clementine Recognitions*, iii, 27-29; cf. *The 1012 Questions*, 183; the *Ginza*, 83f. God spares some worlds from dismantling until they have fulfilled their purpose, *Psalms of Thomas*, ii:30-31. While treasure-ships carry matter through space (above, note 38), the Seven Planets "intercept all the goods bestowed by the constellations and divert them to the use of the demons" in furbishing out their worlds, D. Winston, *History of Religions*, 5 (1966), 2ff.; the fullest treatment in *Berlin Manich. Hs.*, I, 109, 111-14, 177; where it is even necessary to decontaminate older materials before reusing! *ib.*, 113-14, 130. *Pistis Sophia*.

80. E. A. E. Reymond, *The Mystical Origin of the Egyptian Temple* (Manchester Univ. Press: 1969), 187.

81. H. F. Weiss, *Hellenist. Judentum*, 92-99.

82. *Ib.*, 22ff.

83. *Ib.*, 146.

84. *Ib.*, 29-36, citing many sources. It is the business of the Demiurge to *organize* rather than to produce out of nothing, *ib.*, 44ff.

85. *The 1012 Questions*, 164. "There is abundant room in thy Paradise, and nothing is useless therein..." *Od. Sal.*, xi:20. There is a remarkable picture of the struggle for survival, however, when life began in the waters: " ... they attacked one another and slew one another, saying to one another: 'Move off out of my way... Move on that I may come!' " *The 1012 Questions*, 184.

86. *The 1012 Questions*, 111; *Gospel of Philip*, 104:18f.; the physis itself is "imperishable, complete, and boundless," *Creation Apocryphon*, 146:11.

87. It represents "die Begrenzung und Begrenztheit der Welt," E. Horning in *Aegypt. Zeitschr.*, 97 (1971), 78.

88. *Pistis Sophia*, 323-4; L. Kakosy, in *Aeg. Zeitschr.*, 97 (1971), 104-5.

89. Worlds come and go, only progeny (sonship) is eternal, *Gospel of Philip*, 123:6-10; "The man of heaven, many are his Sons, more than the man of earth. If the Sons of Adam are many but still die, how much more the sons of the perfect man, they who do not die but are begotten at all times," *ib.*, 106:17. "Mounting up from world to world" is from *The 1012 Questions*, 192, and "towards His perfection" from the *Gospel of Truth*, fol. XXv, 4-14. The ultimate objective is to receive the same glory which the Son received from the Father in the beginning, John xvii:22; the *Epistle to Diognetus*, x, tells us not to marvel at this — man must become the heir of divinity in the fullest sense, C. Schmidt, in *Texte u. Unters.*, 8 (1892), 319f.; *Gospel of Philip*, 100:1ff, 11; 101:1ff; *Psalms of Solomon*, i:3-4. It is important not to get stuck "in the middle" and so delay progress, Schmidt., *op. cit.*, 335, this world being merely a bridge, according to the famous logion (Migne, *P.O.*, XIII, No. 75). The fundamental nature of Godhood is to beget and create, *Sophia Christi.*, 87:1-88:1.

90. G. Thausing, in *Mitt. dt. Inst. Kairo*, VIII (1939), 63-64.

91. This is the *ametretos bathos* in which a sector is staked out for a new creation, *2nd Gnostic Work*, 9a. Ptahil-Uthra is ordered: "Go down to a place where there are no Shkinas (dwellings) and no other worlds, and make thee a world as the Sons of Salvation do..." *Ginza*, 98. God plans for the occupancy of all the "spaces" ahead of time, *Gospel of Truth*, fol. XIVr, 11-16. One seeks release by moving "from the more confined to the more spacious places," *Pistis Sophia*, 47 (83). The role of space in creation is vividly depicted in Egyptian temple-founding rites, in which the King, representing God creating the world, takes sightings on the stars in a pure and empty place, A. Moret, *Du caractere religieux de la royaute pharaonique* (Paris: 1902), 130-42; R. T. R. Clark, *Myth and Symbol in Ancient Egypt* (London: Thames, 1959), 80. Preparing for the creation of the world, "Marduk went into the heavens, inspecting the places, and there he established a new one, an exact replica... of the dwelling of Ea," *Enuma Elish*, iv:142. "Space and time are the plan of the world-system...," G. S. Fullerton, in *Philosophical Review*, 10 (1910), 595.

92. The work begins with *hyle*, C. Schmidt, *Texte u. Unters.*, 8 (1892),

365, 372, although "We do not know whether Hyle was already present in the Treasury of Light or not," there was a "kerasmos in which Light and Matter are mixed in various proportions," *ib.*, 383. "Kenaz" in the *Visio Kenaz* (M. R. James, *Apocr. Anecdota*, II, No. 3 [Cambridge: 1893], 178-79) sees "flames that do not consume and fountains stirring into life," amid a vague substance taking form at the Creation. Those who were with God "before his works of old" are later "to inherit substance, and fill their treasures," Proverbs viii:19-22, referring perhaps to a new, material phase of creation — see above, notes 80-84.

93. It is well for men not to contemplate the bathos too intently, *Gospel of Truth*, fol. XIXr, 8f.; *I Enoch*, frgs. in R. H. Charles, *The Book of Enoch* (Oxford: 1912), 297; *Evang. Barthol.*, Frg. iii, in *Revue Biblique*, 10 (1913), 326. "Matter having no fixity or stability," is repellent, *Gospel of Truth*, fol. XIIIv, 15ff; *Pistis Sophia*, 39 (63). *Apocal. of Abraham*, 16-17. Sophia's first advice to her son was, "Get a foothold, O youth, in these places!" *Creation Apocryphon*, 148:12; 149:6. The foothold idea may have inspired the ubiquitous image of the "Rock," e.g., *IQS*, xi:5; R. Eisler, *Iesous Basileus* . . . (Heidelberg: 1930), II, 286f. Preparing for the Creation, Marduk, having found his space, established the stations (fixed points of reference) beside the star *Nibiru*, firmly bolted on the left and on the right, *Enuma Elish*, v:8-10.

94. *2nd Gnostic Work*, 2a-3s; 18a. The *fundamentum* of a world begins to take form when touched by a *scintilla*, but "the spark ceases and the fountain is stopped" when the inhabitants transgress, *Visio Kenaz, l.c.* Matter without Light is inert and helpless, *Pistis Sophia*, 55 (107); *Berlin Manich. Hs.*, I, 130; it is the "first light" which reproduces "the pattern of the heavenly model" wherever it touches, *Creation Apocryphon*, 146:20. For "rays from the worlds of light stream down to the earthly world" for the awakening of mortals, *The 1012 Questions*, 199f.; sometimes a column of light joins earth to heaven, *Synax. Arab.*, in Migne, *P.O.*, XI:754, even as the divine plan is communicated to distant worlds by a spark, *2nd Gnostic Work*, 29a-30a; it is the "dynamis of Light" that animates one world from another, C. Schmidt., *Texte u. Unters.*, 8 (1892), 331. God's assistants, "the faithful servants of Melchizedek," rescue and preserve the light particles lest any be lost in space, Schmidt, *Texte u. Unters.*, 8 (1892), 404, cf. *2nd Gnostic Work*. The spark is also called a "drop," *Sophia Christi*, 104:7ff.; it is "the divine drop of light that he (man) brought with him from above," *ib.*, 119:1ff. The Spark can reactivate bodies that have become inert by the loss of former light, *Pistis Sophia*, 65 (134). It is like a tiny bit of God himself, "die kleine Idee" Schmidt, *Texte u. Unters.*, 8 (1892), 396; *I Jeu*, 7; H. Zandee, in *Numen*, 11 (1964), 67. Thus Christ calls upon the Father, addressing him as "Spinther," to send light to the Apostles, *Pistis Sophia*, 130 (35). This light comes from the Treasury, *Berlin Manich. Hs.*, I, 44.

95. C. Schmidt, *op. cit.*, 333. Knowledge of the divine plan is communicated to the worlds by a spark, *2nd Gnostic Work*, 29a-30a; the Father "let an idea come out of His Treasury . . ." *I Jeu*, 7, even as "the Son of Radiance" is sent forth to enlighten the worlds, *Psalms of Thomas*, viii:12; such an ambassador is himself a "treasure-chamber of Life . . ." *ib.*, iii:18. All the mysteries are "shared out" among 380 Worlds of Light "as they emanate

from that Supreme Celestial world," *The 1012 Questions,* 112. God is "pure radiance, a precious Treasure of Light, the Intelligence which correcteth the hearts of all our kings!" *ib.* 123. The "Emanation" (*probole*) is a sharing of treasures, so that "das Lichtschatz ist also der Gipfelpunkt des Universums," C. Schmidt, *Texte u. Unters.,* 8 (1892), 325, 266. "The sparks from the Crown scatter to every Place," *Ginza,* 7; the Power of the Light, radiating into surrounding Chaos, produces a higher type of *topos* wherever it goes, *Pistis Sophia,* 58 (112), the creation process being the adding of Light and its power to dark chaotic matter, *ib.,* 50 (94), 48 (85f.), 50 (90). Every *phōster* goes back to the same Root, *Manichaean Psalm-book,* II, 26, 138.

96. An important part of God's plan is the providing of a proper *topos* for the saints, *Pastor Hermae,* III, Simil. v:6. Each *topos* awaiting occupants is the result of the diffusion of the Treasure, *I Jeu,* 11. For "there has previously been prepared a topos for every soul of man," *Secrets of Enoch,* xlix:2; lviii:4ff., "mansions without number," lx:2. The work of Jesus was to collect the treasures of the Father into one blessed *topos* of meeting, *Acts of Thomas,* xlviii. While the elect have their mansions, *I Enoch,* xli:1-9, there are special places set apart for spirits in transition, *ib.,* xxii: 3, 9. For each specific group yet to be born a place has been prepared, *II Baruch,* xxiii:4. The earthly and heavenly hosts alike have their assigned places, *IQM,* xii: 1-2. There is an assigned place of glory for each hereafter, *Epist. I Clem,* v, vi; Polycarp, *Epist. ad Phil.,* ix; *Apocryphon of Adam,* 69:19ff.; everyone should know to what *topos* he has been called and live accordingly, *Epist. II Clem,* i; v; Ignatius, *ad Magnes.,* v; Polycarp, *op. cit.,* xi; *Oxyrhinchus Frg.,* No. 654:22. No one gets a *topos* without earning it, Ignatius, *ad Smyrn.,* vi; *Pastor Hermae,* III, Simil. viii, 3, 5, 8; *Apocalypse of Elias,* vi:6ff. The *topothesias* of the angels greatly interested the early saints, Ignatius, *ad Trall.,* v.

97. The central *topos* is the Treasury of the true God, C. Schmidt, *Texte u. Unters.,* 8 (1892), 367; it is "the topos from which all aeons and all cosmoses take their pattern and their origin . . ." *Sophia Christi,* 116 (in *Texte u. Unters.* 60:266ff.). It is "the self-produced and self-begotten topos" from which all others are derived, *2nd Gnostic Work,* 1a; it is called "the God-bearing" *topos,* or "land of the begetting of gods," *ib.,* 21a. The Egyptians regarded the "werden der Welt als ein Kolonisati onsvorgang . . ." W. Richter, in *Biblische Zeitschr.,* NS, 10 (1966), 101f. The colonization is always a family affair: God wants "all of those he raised up for Himself" to "fill the face of the universe with their seed . . ." *Zadokite Doc.,* ii:10. The inhabitants are the progeny or seed of those who sent them, *I Enoch,* xxxix:1; *The 1012 Questions,* 118, 170f.; *Sophia Christi,* 88:7ff.; 98:1-99:5ff.; *Apocryphon of James,* 1:43:5ff; called "chosen seed, or seed of promise . . .," J. Zandee, in *Numen,* 11 (1964), 45f., 72f. When "the elect . . . descend from heaven . . . their seed will become one with the children of man," *I Enoch,* xxxix:1. Simat-Hiia, the primordial Eve is "mother of all kings, from whom all worlds proceeded," *Alma Rishaia Rba,* vi:388ff. (29). A colonizing activity is described in *Pistis Sophia,* 26f. (36f.), 24 (34f.). Lactantius presents the idea of real seeds floating around in space, *Div. Inst.,* III, xvii.

98. "Planting" can here mean create, beget, establish or assist, i.e., it is the proper work of the "Sent One," according to M. Lidzbarski, *Mand.*

Johannesbuch, 60, n.6, and *Berlin Manich. Hs.* I, 53f. Eden was God's planting on earth, W. Richter, *Biblische Zeitschr.,* NF, 10 (1966), 101f. "I said that the world should be . . . (saying) I will plant a great vineyard, and out of it I will choose a plant," i.e. the Chosen People, *Pseudo-Philo,* xxviii:4; the Qumran community calls itself a planting, *IQS,* viii:5, 20-2; ix:15, as does the early Church, Irenaeus, *adv. haeres.,* V, xxxvi, 1. God's "planting in the world of men" includes providing necessary physical substances, *Psalms of Thomas,* iii:29-35, and the "planting" of light in a place of darkness, *ib.,* vii:17. God before the world existed planted the earth and then planted the Garden in it, *4 Esdras* 3:4, 6; He is the "Greatest of Gardeners," "the Planter" par excellence, H. F. Weiss, *Hell. Judent.,* 50. Those who share in God's plan are his "plants," *The 1012 Questions,* 127, 140, 150, who in turn have their disciples or plants, *ib.,* 130, 216f. The human race is Adam's "planting," *Mand. Prayerbook,* No. 378, 283, 286; No. 386, 290. The Elect are "the plants that God has planted," and must plant their own plants through marriage, *Ginza,* 61f. The "planting" of the earth is described as a colonizing enterprise in *Ginza,* 335, 337; they move from place to place in winged wagons, looking for places to settle, *ib.,* 337-40; the Planter is expected to provide the necessary helpers for new settlers, *ib.,* 404. Ritually, the planting is a *sparsio,* a sowing or begetting of the race, H. Nibley, "Sparsiones," *Classical Journal,* 40 (1945), 515ff.

99. On the "Treasure-house of Souls," see R. H. Charles, note on *4 Ezra.* iv:35 (*Apocrypha & Pseudepiographa of the Old Testament,* II, 567); *II Baruch* xxx:2; *Pseudo-Philo,* xxxii:13; C. Schmidt, in *Texte u. Unters.,* VIII: 368. The souls of the righteous like the Treasure itself are beneath the throne of God, *Bab. Sabbath,* fol. 152b; cf. Rev. vii:9. The "planting" of a world is always from the "House of Light, the shining Home," i.e., the Treasure-house, *Mand. Johannesbuch,* No. 63, 218. It is "through the power of the Treasure" that "earths of radiance" are created, "thrones of glory are established and Chiefs of worlds appointed," *ib.,* No. 59, 207; the Treasure being the source of everything within as well as between the worlds, *ib.,* No. 57, 203-5. Every world comes into existence by a sort of fission from the Treasure of the Secret Mysteries, *Oxford Mand. Scroll,* 55f. What Adam plants then grows and so increases his Treasure, *Mand. Prayerbook,* 285. The bestowing of the "Treasure of the Mighty One" on men to test them is called a "planting of plants," in *Psalms of Thomas,* xiii:5-14; iii:24-7; *Acts of Thomas,* Ch. 10.

100. On the hierarchy of emanations, Schmidt, *Texte u. Unters.,* 8 (1892), 367. In the system of *I Jeu,* 5-7, one put in charge of a new *topos* as "Chief" is a Jeu, who then becomes the Father of "other emanations to fill other toposes," each of which in turn becomes a "Father of Treasures"; in the end "myriads of myriads will go forth from them," *ib.,* 6. Every Son begets sons, and these in turn consult in the making of "other worlds," *Ginza,* 240; just so "a Jordan produces Jordans without number and without end — living waters," *ib.,* 65-67. Through the power of the Treasure earths are created, places made inhabitable, "chiefs of worlds are appointed," so that the Treasures may be handed down from the older worlds to newer ones, *Mand. Johannesbuch,* No. 59, 207. It is perhaps from his Manichaean experience that St. Augustine derives the image of sparks springing from a

central fire, each becoming a focal center for more sparks, an idea conveyed in the *Berlin Manich. Hs.*, I, 35f.

101. Quotation from the *2nd Gnostic Work*, 49a. He who is begotten is expected to beget, Gen. 1:29; ix:1. In the Egyptian rites the First-born is commanded "to create men, to give birth to the gods, to create all that should exist," R. Reymond, in *Chroniques d'Egype*, 40 (1965), 61; the work of the Creation is repeated indefinitely and daily in ritual, H. Kees, in *Aegypt. Zeitschr.*, 78 (1942), 48. One becomes a Son in order to become a Father; one receives in order to give, *Gospel of Philip*, 123:10-14. The Son is commanded, "Go, confirm kings, create new Jordans, and help Chosen Ones (to) arise with thee to the Father," *The 1012 Questions*, 123. The Sent Ones say to the Father, "O our Lord, Lord of all worlds, Thou didst command that we should create worlds and propagate species!" and God informs them that that is the secret treasure, bestowed only on "one who is our son (plant)," *ib.*, 137. All who behold the creative process have a normal desire to become creators themselves, *Ginza*, 67f., creation being the essence of godhood, see above, notes 8, 9, 14.

102. The patriarchal line is never broken: "Let us, Father, create other worlds in order to raise to *Thee* a planting . . . ," *Ginza*, 241. One does not create without the express permission of the "Creator of the Treasures," *ib.*, 67f. He who is "planted from above" does his own "pure planting" under the auspices of *his* Planter, *Mand. Johannesbuch*, No. 59, 207. Hence "all gloried in the knowledge that their Father had transplanted them from the House of life," *Alma Rishaia Rba*, 1; in the end, all come "into existence for his sake," *Mand. Johannesbuch*, iv, 30-35, 70. Even to the greatest Sent Ones he is the "lofty King by Whom our Treasure ascends!" *Alma Rishaia Zuta*, 64f. At the Council in Heaven the Son was hailed as "the Father of those who believe," *2nd Gnostic Work*, 29a-30a; this identity of Father and Son to and with believers is a basic teaching of the Fourth Gospel, R. Bultmann, in *ZNTW*, 24 (1925), 122.

103. "The dwellers upon the earth can understand only what is upon the earth . . ." and the same applies to other worlds, *4 Ezra*, iv:21. Beings comprehend only what they are like, so that the Lord must take the form of those to whom he appears, C. Schmidt, *Kopt.-Gnost. Schrift*, I, 342; *Gospel of Philip*, 101:27-36; 105:29-106:10; *Ascension of Isaiah*, vii:25; *Pistis Sophia*, 7 (12); cf. U. Bianchi, in *Numen*, 12 (1965), 165; *Manichaean Psalmbook*, II, 42.

104. *Gospel of Thomas*, 95:20-23; *II Jeu*, 54; cf. *Gospel of Truth*, fol. xv, 20-23: Exod. iii:6; Matt. xvii:5-6; Mark ix:5-6; E. L. Cherbonnier, in *Harvard Theological Review*, 55 (1962), 195-199. So also the Son, *Gospel of Thomas*, 87:27, whose "true name man is not able to hear at this time," *Psalms of Thomas*, xiii:14, xiv. "He . . . is within the Veil, within his own shkinta" (dwelling tabernacle), *Mand. Prayerbook*, No. 374, 267; His *topos* is completely out of our cosmos, being the ultimate Treasure, "the Treasure of the Outer Ones," *I Jeu*, 47; 59; *2nd Gnostic Work*, 2a, surrounded by veils and guarded gates, C. Schmidt, *Texte u. Unters.*, 8 (1892), 402; hence it is "beyond the veil, a place of shadowless light," *ib.*, 366; *Sophia Christi*, ix:116, "the great secret Dwelling of Light," *The 1012 Questions*, 163. By night all the

outer worlds strain to see the Father... because of the invisibility that surrounds him," *2nd Gnostic Work*, 5a, even as the angels yearn to see the ultimate place of the saints, L. Guerrier, in *Patrol. Or.*, IX, 153; cf. I Peter i:12.

105. *Sophia Christi*, ix:118; *2nd Gnostic Work*, 47a; *Berlin Manich, Hs.*, I, 118; "the veil at first concealed how God controlled the creation," *Gospel of Philip*, 132:23; there is a veil between us and the heavens, N. Sed, in *Revue des Etudes Juives*, 124 (1965), 39. All treasures are hidden treasures until God reveals them, *Zadokite Doc.*, v:1; *II Baruch*, li:7-8; *Evang. Barthol.*, iii:2-7; *Gospel of Thomas*, 86:4f., 24. "If you want to go to the Father you must pass through the veil," *I Jeu*, 42. God isolates hostile worlds from each other lest they unite against him, *Ginza*, 177. "As the doctrine of the body is hidden in its treasure-house, so God the Father is hidden in his Kingdom, invisible to the wastelands without," *Berlin Manich. Hs.*, I, 151.

106. A. Pelletier, in *Syria*, 35 (1958), 225f.

107. M. J. bin Gorion, *Sagen der Juden* (1913), I, 59.

108. N. Sed, in *Revue des Etudes Juives*, 124 (1965), 39.

109. *2nd Gnostic Work*, 47a; *Pistis Sophia*, 317; in *Texte u. Unters.*, 60:118.

110. C. Schmidt, in *Texte u. Unters.*, 8 (1892), 368.

111. *Hypostasis of the Archons*, 143:20.

112. *Pistis Sophia*, 366.

113. *Ib.*, 42-44.

114. *Ib.*, 23.

115. *I Jeu*, 39; *Pistis Sophia*, 317-18.

116. *Pistis Sophia*, 184.

117. *Apocalypse of Baruch* (3rd Bar.), VI, 3-6.

118. The progress of the soul in the afterworld, with three main degrees of glory is found in Egyptian funerary literature, e.g., *Book of Breathings*, lines 2-3, in Biblioth. Egyptol. 17:113. So Pindar, *Olymp.*, ii:75. For Jewish and Christian concepts, H. P. Owen, in *New Testament Studies*, 3 (1956), 243f., 247-49; K. Prumm, in *Biblica*, 10 (1929), 74; K. Kohler, in *Jewish Quarterly Review*, 7 (1894/5), 595-602; C. Schmidt, in *Texte u. Unters.*, 8 (1892), 478, n. 1, 489-91, 496f., 519-21, 524f. Eternal progression is indicated in *IQH*, vii:15, and in the formula, "out of the eternities and into the eternities," *IQS*, ii:1; *Epist. Barnab.*, xviii; " ... press on from glory to glory," says a Hymn of Serverus, in Migne, *P.O.*, v:683; *I Jeu*, 54f., 58f.; *2nd Gnostic Work*, 5a; *Gospel of Thomas*, 90:4ff. (" ... a forward motion, and then a resting-time ...."). You master the places in this world so that you can master them in the next, *Gospel of Philip*, 124:33f.; *Gospel of Truth*, fol. XIIr, 11-14, the ultimate object being to "share in the treasury of light as immortal gods," *II Jeu*, 58. He who receives all the ordinances "cannot be held back in the way," *Ginza*, 19.

119. E. L. Cherbonnier, in *Harvard Theological Review*, 60 (1962), 206.

120. This idea is forcibly expressed in the *Pistis Sophia*, 88f. (199), 84 (183); *Ginza*, 14, 493-94.

121. J. Soggin, in *Theologische Literaturzeitung*, 89 (1966), 729. Those who receive the mysteries of the gospel will also come to know the mysteries of the physical Cosmos, *Pistis Sophia*, 232.

122. A. Piankoff, in *Inst. Francais Archeol. Orient.*, Bibl. Et., 19, 1.

123. The Schoolmen have always avoided "cosmism" and still do, H. F. Weir, *Hell. Judaism.* 79ff; Klaus Koch, *Ratlos vor der Apokalyptik* (Gütersloder Verlag, 1970) esp. 55ff.

124. The contradictions are emphasized by S. A. Pallis, *Mandaean Studies*, 1, 2, 4, 8, 188, and A. Brandt, *Mandäische Religion*, 48ff., while the "einheitliche und organische Grundlage" is noted by K. Rudolph, *Mandäer*, I, 141, following H. Jonas. The Mandaeans frequently refer to other sects, Jewish and Christian, as bitter rivals, not because of the differences but because of the many resemblances and common claims between them, e.g. *Ginza*, 28-30, 48-52, 135, n.4, 223-32; *Mand. Prayerbook*, No. 357, 251; *Berlin Manich. Hs.*, I, 21. While A. Loisy, *Le Mandeisme et les Origines Chretiennes* (Paris: Nourry, 1934), 142, maintains that "le Mandeisme n'est intelligible qu'en regard du chretianisme," M. Lidzbarski, *Ginza*, ix, insists that it is older than the captivity of 587 B.C. Such disagreements are typical.

125. See K. Rudolph, *Mandäer*, I, 19-22, 36-41, 59ff., 112ff., 173-75, 251-54, seeing the common source in the early Taufsekten. Since the rites are "sinnlos und unerklärbar" without the peculiar doctrines (K. Rudolph, *Mandäer*, I, 254), the common rites indicate a common doctrinal tradition, E. Drower, *Nasoraean Commentaries*, vii.

126. In their main points the two doctrines are in striking contrast, e.g., (1) The idea that all matter is evil heads the list of "orthodox" charges against the Gnostics, *Bodmer Papyrus* X:51: 10: *Const. Apostol.*, vi:10; C. Schmidt, *Texte u. Unters*, 8 (1892), 402f.; cf. *Clementine Recognitions*, iv:23: ". . . absolute dicimus in substantia nihil esse mali." Cf. the Gnostic denial of a physical resurrection with the attitude of the *Gospel of Philip*, 105:9-19. (2) The Gnostic idea that Adam was "predisposed to evil" and that souls come to the earth to be punished is the opposite to that of man's preexistent glory, J. Zandee, *Numen*, 11 (1964), 31; *Creation Apocryphon*, 171:10ff.; Cyril of Jerus., Migne, *P.G.*, XXXIII:481. (3) Gnostic dualism — between physical and non-physical states of being — is *anti*-cosmist, U. Bianchi, in *Numen*, 12 (1965), 165-66, 174, 177; S. Giverson, in *Studia Theologica*, 17 (1963), 69f. (4) The Gnostics put God utterly beyond man's comprehension, not in the same family as the "Treasure" concept does, *Bodmer Papyrus* X:51:10; *Const. Apostol.*, vi:lo; Ignatius, *Tartens.*, incip., Israel means "man who is God," according to the *Creation Apocryphon*, 153:25. (5) Whereas the true Gnostic achieves complete spirituality on earth and goes directly to heaven (or the sun) at death, Schmidt, *Texte u. Unters.*, 8 (1892), 521ff.; *Epist. to Rheginos*, Puech in *Vigiliae Christianae*, 8 (1956), 44-46, the idea of a long and gradual progress of the soul is older than the Gnostics, K. Kohler, in *Jewish Quarterly Review*, vii:598; cf. *IQS*, ii:23ff; *IQH*, x:28. (6) Whereas pessimism is the hallmark of all Gnostic systems, in *Numen*, 11 (1964), 17; Bianchi, in *Numen*,

12 (1965), 165, the "Treasure" doctrine is completely optimistic and joyful. (7) The Gnostics show the influence of the schools, Bianchi, 162, while the other teaching is characteristic neither of the schools nor of religions in general, K. Koch, *Zeitschr. f. Theol. u. Kirche,* 62 (1965), 263. (8) Following the schools, Gnosticism shuns literalism and turns everything in abstraction and allegory: it is not a real system but poetic fantasy, C. Schmidt, *Texte u. Unters.,* 8 (1892), 397, 413, 421-22; but "of mystical rapture there is no hint" in the other tradition, H. P. Owen, in *New Testament Studies,* 3 (1965), 251; Koch, *loc. cit.*

127. C. Schmidt, *Texte u. Unters.,* 8 (1892), 345f.: there was nothing the Patristic Fathers combatted more vigorously than "the cosmist heresy." Having chosen the way of the Gnostics and Neoplatonics, they condemned all literalism, *ib.,* 421, and *Texte u. Unters.,* XLIII:524-25.

128. Tertullian and Irenaeus wavered between the two views, Schmidt, XLIII:520f. The fundamental "Treasure" doctrine of the descensus disappears after the 3rd century, F. Kattenbach, *Das Apostolische Symbol* (Leipzig: 1894), I, 104; II, 913f. The *Epist. to Diognetus,* vi, compromises, but for Athanasius, Basil, John Chrysostom, etc., heaven has become a state of mind pure and simple.

Subduing
the Earth

4

Ever since the days of the Prophet Joseph, presidents of the Church have appealed to the Saints to be magnanimous and forbearing towards all of God's creatures. But in the great West where everything was up for grabs, it was more than human nature could endure to be left out of the great grabbing game, especially when one happened to get there first, as the Mormons often did.

One morning just a week after we had moved into our house on Seventh North, as I was leaving for work, I found a group of shouting, arm-waving boys gathered around the big fir tree in the front yard. They had sticks and stones and in a state of high excitement were fiercely attacking the lowest branches of the tree, which hung to the ground. Why? I asked. There was a quail in the tree, they said in breathless zeal, a quail! Of course, said I, what is wrong with that? But don't you see, it is a live quail, a wild one! So they just had to kill it. They were on their way to the old B.Y. High School, and were Boy Scouts. Does this story surprise you? What surprised me was when I later went to Chicago and saw squirrels running around the city parks in broad daylight – they would not last a day in Provo.

Like Varro's patrician friends, we have taught our children by precept and example that every living thing exists to be converted into cash, and that whatever would not yield a return should be quickly exterminated to make way for creatures that do. (We have referred to this elsewhere as the Mahan Principle – Moses 5:31.) I have heard important Latter-day Saint leaders express this philosophy, and have seen bishops and stake presidents teaching their reluctant boys the delights of hunting for pleasure. The earth is our enemy, I was taught – does it not bring forth noxious weeds to afflict and torment man? And who cared if his allergies were the result of the Fall, man's own doing, and could be corrected only when he corrects himself? But one thing worried me: If God were to despise all things beneath him, as we do, where would that leave us? Inquiring about today, one discovers that many Latter-day Saints feel that the time has come to put an end to the killing.

The contemporary reappraisal of man's relationship to his environment now confronts society at large with a question that has always been of major concern to the leaders of Israel, namely, What is man's dominion? The key scriptural passage on the subject reads: "And God blessed them, and God said unto them, Be fruitful, and multiply, and replenish the earth, and subdue [*kivshū*] it: and have dominion over [*rdū b*] . . . every living thing that moveth upon the earth." (Genesis 1:28.) The words *kivshū* and *rdū* both have a basic root-meaning of exerting pressure, that being, however, merely a point of departure for a whole spectrum of derivatives, so that scholars have translated the words according to individual taste and temperament to convey various ideas and types of dominion. Thus the dictionaries tell us that *radad*, with the basic meaning of trampling the earth, in Genesis 1:28, specifically means "to plow," while *kavash*, with the original idea of squeezing or hugging, can mean everything from "violate" to "cherish."[1]

In all the interpretations we are confronted by two opposing concepts of dominion that have always divided the human race. From the beginning men have been asked to choose between them. Thus the Clementine Recognitions tell us that Abel's claim to dominion was challenged by Cain, that Noah was challenged by the giants (the "Watchers" of Enoch's day), Abraham by Pharaoh, Isaac by the Philistines, Jacob by Esau, Moses by the magicians of Egypt, Christ by the adversary in person, Simon Peter by Simon Magus, the apostles by the whole world, and finally, in the last days, Christ by the anti-Christ again.[2] In each case the challenger argued from a position of strength and promised "all the kingdoms of the world" with all their power and glory to those who would worship and follow him, while the other offered the kingdom of heaven hereafter to those who worship the Lord and serve him only. (Luke 4:5-8.)

Each of the great leaders before entering upon his mission was allowed to make his own choice between the two ways, the case for each being presented personally to him by the highest authority on either side. Thus Adam, Enoch, Noah, Abraham, Moses, the ancient apostles, Joseph Smith, and, of course, the Lord himself were not only privileged to speak with God face to face, "even as a man talketh one with another," but were also exposed to intimate and personal interviews, however harrowing and unsolicited, with the prince of darkness as well. Their opponents in each of the dispensations were also favored with direct ministrations from both sides, and each made his choice between enjoying power and dominion here or hereafter.

In commanding Adam to "be fruitful, and multiply," God also informed him that he had given the identical command to all his other creatures, furthermore that he was putting Adam in charge of things to see to it that his purposes were fulfilled. Specifically, he was to "replenish the earth, and subdue *it*, and to have dominion over " every *living* thing in the biosphere. (Abraham 4:28.) There are two clearly marked departments — the earth itself as a storehouse and source of life, which Adam is to keep replenished (*filled* is the word), and the creatures that move about on and over the earth, over which he is to have dominion. As Brigham Young explains it, while "subduing the earth" we must be about "multiplying those organisms of plants and animals God has designed shall dwell upon it,"[3] namely "all forms of life," each to multiply in its sphere and element and have joy therein.

As usual, it is the Prophet Joseph who sets the record straight with an inspired translation: "And it came to pass that after I, the Lord God, had driven them out, that Adam began to *till* the earth, and to have *dominion* over all the beasts of the field, and to eat his bread by the sweat of his brow." (Moses 5:1. Italics added.) Here, in the place of the "subdue" of the King James version, we have explicitly the word "till" applied to the earth alone, while "dominion" is reserved for the animal kingdom. And what is dominion? After commanding every form of life to multiply for the express purpose of having joy, God gave the identical command to Adam, at the same time putting him in charge of the whole operation, making him *lord* over the whole earth and giving him *dominion* over everything on the face of the earth. Lordship and dominion are the same. The word *lord* is the usual English slurring of *hlaf-weard, hlaford*, the loaf-ward or keeper of the bread, because according to the Oxford English Dictionary, "in its original sense the word (absent from other Teutonic languages) denotes the head of a household in his relation to the servants and dependents who 'eat his bread' . . . the development of sense has been largely influenced by the adoption of the word as the customary rendering of the Latin *dominus*."

Which brings us in the dictionary to "dominion, derivative of *domini-um*, property, ownership, from *dominus*, lord, specifically "the lord of the household," in his capacity of generous host, *"pater familias* and owner of the house" [*domus*]. The title of dominus designated the Roman Emperor himself as the common benefactor of mankind inviting all the world to feast at his board. In short, lordship and dominium are the same thing, the responsibility of the master for the comfort and well-being of his dependents and guests; he is the generous host, the kind pater familias to whom all look for support. He is the lord who provides bread for all; but how? By tilling the earth that he may "eat his bread by the sweat of his brow" — he is not a predator, a manipulator or an exploiter of other creatures, but one who cooperates with nature as a diligent husbandman.

The ancients taught that Adam's dominion was nothing less than the priesthood, the power to act for God and in his place. The idea is that God, while retaining his unshakable throne in the heavens, "extended his glory to a new world below in the work of the Creation, then as the culmination of that work he created man to be in charge [*li-mshōl*] of all the beings he had created"[4] with the understanding that "from this time forth man must work to improve the earth and preserve and take care of all that is in it, exactly as God had done before."[5]

"The Spirit of the Lord and the keys of the priesthood," said Brigham Young, "hold power over all animated beings. . . . In this dispensation the keys will be restored."[6] God is a god of the living (See Matthew 22:32) and gives Adam dominion over every *living* thing, so that his rule ceases where life ceases. A king's glory and success are measured by the happiness, prosperity, and increase of his subjects, even as the power and glory of God show forth, according to the Sefer Yeshira, in the exuberance of living things upon the earth;[7] his "work and his glory" are to bestow the prerogatives of divinity on those below him. (Moses 1:39.) "From the hour in which I created the world it was my task to bless my creatures," the Lord tells Abraham in making the covenant of the priesthood with him, "but from now on it will be you who bestows the blessing."[8] "As I put Adam and then Noah in charge of all my creatures, so now I put you in charge, in order that you might bestow my blessing on them."[9]

All creatures are duly overawed by the presence of God's representatives and image: "Even the fierce beasts of prey fear man," says the Zohar, "as long as he keeps his covenant, his kingly dignity, and his eye fixed on God in whose image he is."[10] For "God formed man in his own heavenly form and made him to be Lord over them. Whenever man stands upright and lifts his eyes toward heaven, then all the animals raise their heads too, and look to man, fearing and trembling in his presence."[11] Throughout history an indispensable fixture of royalty has everywhere been the great animal park, paradise, or royal forest in which majesty could display itself in the role of God on earth, parent of the human race, and patron and protector of all lesser beings. In a word, the concept of man's dominion as a holy calling and high responsibility has been the common heritage of the human race throughout history.[12] God's rule is before all a rule of love: "I love my creatures far more than you ever could!" the Lord tells Esdras in a vision.[13] There is a tradition that Melchizedek, instructing Abraham in the things of the priesthood, explained to him that Noah earned his blessings by his charity to the animals, recalling how in the ark, "We did not sleep because all night long we were setting food before this one and before that one." Taking this lesson to heart, Abraham himself made a sort of Garden of Eden near Hebron, and there practiced charity toward all creatures that thus he might "become a possessor of heaven and earth."[14] Adam, according to many accounts, was the great friend and companion of all the animals when they lived together in perfect peace and happiness, and they continued true to him even after the Fall.[15] Indeed, "Adam before he came to this earth was intimately acquainted with all the great spirits in heaven, and also with all the holy beasts," so that he was peculiarly fitted in his priestly office to serve as mediator between the worlds as well as between higher and lower forms of life.[16]

The teaching of Israel laid the heaviest emphasis on responsibility. Since man is quite capable of exercising the awesome powers that have been entrusted to him as the very image of God, he must needs be an example to all, and if he fails in his trust, he can only bring upon himself the condemnation of God and the contempt of all creatures.[17] "When men lose *their* vicious dispositions," said the Prophet Joseph, " ... the lion and the lamb will lie down together."[18]

A favorite theme of Brigham Young was that the dominion God gives man is designed to test him, to enable him to show to himself, his fellows, and all the heavens just how he would act if entrusted with God's own power; if he does not act in a godlike manner, he will never be entrusted with a creation of his own worlds without end.[19] So there is risk involved: "The rule over the world is in the hand of God," says Ben Sirach, "and at the right time He sets over it one that is worthy"; but if that rule is ever exercised in an arbitrary or arrogant manner, it is quickly taken away and given to someone else.[20] "If you fail in your duty," God tells Adam, "the beasts over which you ruled shall rise up against you, for you have not kept my commandment";[21] and all creatures are quick to recognize the hand of the oppressor and impostor.

Some of the profoundest human commentary is contained in the vast and ancient corpus literature of the animal fables, a protest literature in which the beasts bring accusation against the human race for their shabby performance in the days of their probation.[22] They are, moreover, responsible for more than their own survival, "For by God's rule for the animals, if humanity perishes, then all perish; but if man lives, then all may live."[23] What kills men destroys other forms of life as well, and having dragged them down with us in the Fall ("On account of thee," they say, "our natures have been transformed ... "[24]), we are answerable for them: "The Lord will not judge a single animal for its treatment of man, but He will adjudge the souls of men towards their beasts in this world, for men have a special place."[25] A familiar early Jewish and Christian teaching was that the animals will appear at the bar of God's judgment to accuse those humans who have wronged them.[26] "Happy is he who glorifies all the works of the Lord, but cursed is he who offends the creation of the Lord; for nothing will go unnoticed and unrecorded."[27] Jesus referred to God's intimate concern for all when he said of the sparrows, " ... not one of them is forgotten before God" (Luke 12:6), and has declared in these last days: " ... I, the Lord ... make every man accountable, as a steward over earthly blessings, which I have made and prepared *for my creatures*" (D&C 104:13).

The traditions that Adam dwelt with beasts in the preexistence, and that the animals will accuse man at the judgment, call attention to the ancient teaching, restored in this dispensation, that animals have spirits. "The spirits of all beasts have their proper paradise in the great plan of things, and at the judgment all the spirits of beasts will accuse man."[28]

G. R. Driver has recently called attention to an important but forgotten teaching: "Few, if any, readers of the Old Testament seem to have noticed that, as our text stands and as it can only be read without violating normal standards of interpretation, they are committed to the strange doctrine of resurrection not only of man and of birds and beasts but also of . . . 'gliding things innumerable' which swim in the sea."[29] Modern revelation confirms this: "For I, the Lord God, created all things, of which I have spoken, spiritually, before they were naturally upon the face of the earth . . . in heaven created I them. . . ." (Moses 3:5.) " . . . every tree . . . that is pleasant to the sight of man . . . became also a living soul. For it was spiritual in the day that I created it. . . ." (Moses 3:9.)

"Always keep in view," Brigham Young exhorts us, "that the animal, vegetable, and mineral kingdoms — the earth and its fulness — will all, except the children of man, abide their creation — the law by which they were made, and will receive their exaltation."[30] We are all going to move together into the eternities, and even now look forward to "heaven, the paradise of God, the happiness of man, and of beasts, and of creeping things, and of the fowls of the air; that which is spiritual being in the likeness of that which is temporal . . . the spirit of man in the likeness of his person, as also the spirit of beast, and every other creature which God has created." (D&C 77:2.) What an admonition to proceed with reverence and care! It is only because the Latter-day Saints are ignorant of these things, according to President Young, that God has not already cursed them for their brutal and callous treatment of God's other creatures.[31]

Normative Judaism and Christianity, following the lead of Aristotle and the doctors of Alexandria, have always rejected and resented the idea that animals might in any degree be classed with men, who alone, according to the perennial doctrine of the schools, enjoy the powers of speech and reason, the mark of divinity that sets them uniquely and absolutely apart. "Man is bound to treat dumb animals kindly and abstain from unneccessary [sic] cruelty," an eminent churchman has recently written, "not because these animals possess any real rights (for only intelligent beings can have real rights) but because they are creatures of God. . . ."[32] The Latter-day Saints, on the other hand, "have divine knowledge that they [animals] think . . . and reason,"[33] and do possess real rights,

"For all things have an *equal* right to live!" as President Joseph F. Smith would say.[34] We are told that early Christian groups avoided the eating of meat, "not as the flesh of irrational beasts, but as belonging to creatures having rational souls."[35] Schopenhauer observed that the two most serious defects of Christian teaching are (1) the denial of spirits to all creatures but man, and (2) of life to all worlds but this one. These closely related doctrines have formed the common ground on which fundamentalism and scientism have joined hands, the former horrified at the thought of being related to lower creatures than man, the latter scorning any suggestion that we might be related to higher ones.[36]

God and Satan both presented plans of dominion to Adam and then to his son Cain. The father chose one plan, the son the other. It must be admitted that the second proposition was a very tempting offer and very skillfully presented — "Satan tempted me" is the stock excuse for giving in. But we must go back to Adam to see how clever the thing really is.

The story is told not only of Adam but of the other great patriarchs as well. Noah was confronted by the same party with the same proposition while he was working in his garden after the flood.[37] Abraham too had an Eden and an altar, and while he was once calling upon God in prayer, Satan suddenly showed up with an insolent, "Here I am!" and proceeded with his sales pitch.[38] Moses like Christ was tempted on a mountain, by the same person and with the same proposal: "If thou . . . wilt worship me, all shall be thine."[39] Adam is thus only the first; the elements of the story that follow are found in various combinations among the many texts of the growing Adam literature that is coming to light in our generation. The texts often take dramatic form indicative of ritual origin.[40]

As Adam was praying one day, runs the story, a distinguished gentleman appeared on the scene and engaged him in conversation. There was nothing of the hippy or tramp about the stranger; he was well-dressed, and came to Adam with "cunning and smooth talk, as a true friend genuinely concerned for his welfare."[41] He began with some harmless generalities — the weather and the scenery: it was, he observed, a most glorious and beautiful world. This, however, by way of leading up to his next point, which was that he happened to be the owner and proprietor of it all. Yes sir, as far as the eye could see it was all his, and he tolerated no nonsense in it: nobody dared make trouble where he was in charge. This was all hokum, of course; "Satan never owned the earth; he never made a particle of it," said Brigham Young, "his labor is not to create, but to destroy."[42] But to demonstrate his authority, when three strangers (usually described as angels)[43] appeared on the scene at this moment, he at once challenged them as trespassers, asking them if they had any money. He explained to Adam that everything in his world could be had for money,[44] and then got down to business. For the fellow was all business, a person of integrity, ready to keep his part of an agreement (the agreement always turns out to be a trap for the other party), pious and God-fearing,[45] dedicated to hard work — he works, in fact, "like a demon." He was there to offer Adam the chance of a lifetime to buy in on a scheme that would give him anything he wanted in this world. It was an ingenious and simple self-financing operation in which one would buy power with wealth and then more wealth with the power, until one might end up owning and controlling everything. The initial capital? It was right under their feet! You begin by taking the treasures of the earth, and by exchanging them for the services of important people in key positions; you end up running everything your way. What if your rule is one of blood and terror? Better to rule in hell, as Milton's Satan puts it, then to be ruled in heaven!

Satan's tempting proposition has been the theme of much popular legend and great literature. A transitional figure between the ritual and the literary is Pluto of Hades, the god of wealth: "All the riches of gems and precious metals hidden beneath the earth are his, but he owns no property above the ground. . . ."[46] So he brutally kidnaps the fair Proserpine, who represents all the beauty and harmony of nature, to establish his claim over the earth[47]; but the marriage is barren — Pluto can intimidate and coerce, but like his Egyptian counterpart Seth he can neither beget nor create; what he buys with the treasures of the earth is nothing but a rule of blood and horror.[48] But Greek comedy and Roman satire depict with agonizing frankness the irresistible success of Pluto's program in a decadent world. In Aristophanes's last play, the *Pluto*, Hermes the messenger of Zeus comes to earth as a prophet to denounce mankind for having turned from the worship of heaven to the worship of wealth or Pluto: "You have all committed a great sin," he says, "and must be destroyed." But seeing how well the people are living he soon decides to change sides and asks for a job with the establishment; next, the high priest of Zeus, finding himself unemployed, is forced to apply to Pluto for a job; what is his surprise when he finds none other than Zeus himself now working in the front office of Pluto Inc.[49] The cynical conclusion is that no one can resist Satan's bargain, and in the history of the world very few people have. The first to accept was Cain, who "loved Satan more than God," though at the latter's advice he continued to make offerings to the Lord. Moses 5:18, 21.) The "great secret" of success that he learned from his new teacher was that he could get anything in this world by the calculated use of force, with no need to be ashamed since it could all be done in the sacred name of freedom; instead of being appalled at the blood on his hands, Cain "gloried in that which he had done, saying: "I am free; surely the flocks [wealth, *pecus, Vieh*] of my brother falleth into my hands." (Moses 5:31-33.) Cain slew Abel not, as we like to think, in a fit of passion but with cold calculation, "for the sake of getting gain." (Moses 5:50, 38.) He was all business. As for the victim, he was quite able to take care of himself, and if he failed, that, by the rules of the new game, was his hard luck: "Am I my brother's keeper?" Significantly enough, when this forthright, no-nonsense economy, unencumbered by enervating sentimentality, worked against Cain, he straightway became a bleeding heart in his own behalf, and appealed for the mercy he would not give. "My punishment is greater than I can bear!" (Genesis 4:13.) In making an example of Cain, God absolutely forbade the use of Cain's own methods against him: "Whoever slayeth thee, vengeance shall be taken on him sevenfold." (Moses 5:40.)

One of the best-known teachings of the Jews is that when man (Israel in particular) falls away from God, all nature becomes his enemy.[50] Modern revelation confirms this: when all the people became wicked in Enoch's day, "the earth trembled, and the mountains fled . . . and the rivers of water were turned out of their courses; and the roar of lions was heard out of the wilderness. . . ."[51] Just so, in the last days "all the growing things will be blighted by the . . . great lawlessness, and plagues will come over all creatures of all the earth. . . ."[52] Where people refuse the gospel, according to Brigham Young, "that land will eventually . . . become desolate, forlorn, and forsaken," as nature refuses her bounties.[53]

The explanation of this all-out hostility is simple. The animal, vegetable, and mineral kingdoms abide the law of their Creator; the whole earth and all things pertaining to it, except man, abide the law of their creation," while "man, who is the offspring of the Gods, will not become subject to the most sensible and self-exalting principles."[54] With all things going in one direction, men, stubbornly going in the opposite direction, naturally find themselves in the position of one going the wrong way on the freeway during rush hour; the struggle to live becomes a fight *against* nature. Having made himself allergic to almost everything by the Fall, man is given the choice of changing *his* nature so that the animal and vegetable creation will cease to afflict and torment him,[55] or else of waging a truceless war of extermination against all that annoys him until he renders the earth completely uninhabitable.

This second course is Cain's dominion. Satan, spitefully determined to destroy everything that God has commanded to live and multiply, began his earthly career by making war on the birds and fishes and systematically destroying the animals and trees. This, we are told, was because he was envious of the beautiful rapport that existed between Adam and the animals.[56] Next, under the administration of his pupil Cain, all the forests of the earth rapidly disappeared, while that hero "wandered through the earth with his bow for 130 years, looking for anything to kill — a human angel of death."[57] While Noah refused Satan's plan to divide up the world and rule with an iron hand,[58] his sons accepted it, each driving out from his property all the animals as trespassers, so that the beasts that had loved Noah began to fear and hate man.[59] In particular, Ham organized secret combinations "to work iniquity and to shed blood . . . and after that, they sinned against the beasts and birds, and all that moves and walks on the earth."[60] Next Ham's son Nimrod, the mighty hunter who boasted that no animal could escape his bow, turned that bow against men as well as animals and so subdued all things to his will, ruling all the earth with his inspired violence. He was the mortal enemy and rival of Abraham and whereas Abraham gave Adam's blessing to the beasts, "Nimrod assembled all the animals and slaughtered them."[61] This he was able to do through possession of the garment of the priesthood that had once belonged to Adam and that Ham had stolen from Noah. Seeing him in this garment, all creatures willingly came and submitted to him, mistaking the dominion of Cain for the dominion of Adam.[62] From Nimrod, Esau, another hunter, inherited the garment but lost it to Jacob from whom it passed down to Moses, who when it wore out replaced it with a garment of cotton or hair rather than skins to avoid the shedding of animal blood.[63]

These interesting old stories might be dismissed as literary oddities were it not that the annals and chronicles of real history, "a continual scene of wickedness and abominations" (Moroni 2:18), are completely dominated by the Nimrod type. "The greatest acts of the mighty men" proclaim the nature of their dominion. "Before them the earth was a paradise," said Joseph Smith, "and behind them a desolate wilderness." There is another plan: "The designs of God, on the other hand" are that "the earth shall yield its increase, resume its paradisean glory, and become the garden of the Lord."[64] Meanwhile, when "we see all the world trying to lord it over God's heritage," we can be sure that "it is in this spirit that the evil principle and power is trying to overcome and rule over the divine principle planted here. This constantly leads the children of men astray."[65] To render its appeal irresistible, the program is pushed by a clever rhetoric and high ethical tone; Babylon has never wanted for dedicated and highly paid apologists to justify the ways of those who "seek for power, and authority, and riches." (3 Nephi 6:15; Hebrews 13:26-28.)

Man's dominion is a call to service, not a license to exterminate. It is precisely because men now prey upon each other and shed the blood and waste the flesh of other creatures without need that "the world lieth in sin." (D&C 49:19-21.) Such, at least, is the teaching of the ancient Jews and of modern revelation.

NOTES

1. The Septuagint renders the two words "rule throughout" (*katakyrieusate*) and "be first" or "govern" (*archete*). Both the Hebrew words have the *two* main ideas of (1) bringing pressure to bear, and (2) treading the earth and walking about on it. Very ancient parallels suggest that the original idea was that of the new master of the earth going about on his royal rounds of inspection and discovery, as we read in the Egyptian *Coffin Texts*, Spells 80, 132, 136.

2. Clementine Recognitions III, 61 (Migne, *Patrol. Graec.* 1, 1308f).

3. *Journal of Discourses*, vol. 9, p. 168: hereafter cited as *JD*.

4. N. Sed, "Une cosmologie Juive." *Rev. des Etudes Juives*, vol. 124 (1965), pp. 48-51, for the text.

5. M. J. bin Gorion, *Sagen der Juden* (Frankfurt: 1913), I, 83, 354 (for sources).

6. *Brigham Young History*, s.v. April 26, 1846 (Church Historical Department).

7. *Sefer Yeshira*, p. 148f.

8. Rab. Nehemiah, in M. G. Braude, *The Midrash on Psalms* (Yale University, 1959), p. 8.

9. Bin Gorion, *S.J.*, II, 137, 424, citing a number of sources.

10. Zohar, 27a, 57b, 58a, 93b.

11. 4 Esdras 8:47.

12. Discussed by us in *Western Political Quarterly*, vol. 4 (1951), pp. 235-44.

13. 4 Esdras 8:47.

14. Braude, *Midr. Ps.* 37:1 (pp. 422-3); *Midr. Prov.* 23:17a; bin Gorion, II, 268f, 428.

15. Vita Adae et Evae 8:3 (in R. H. Charles, *Apocrypha and Pseudepigrapha of the Old Testament* (Oxford: 1964), II, p. 135.

16. Bin Gorion, *S.J.*, I, 288.

17. Ever since Cain slew Abel, the animals have followed the example of Man" according to the Pure Brethren of Basra, text in F. Dieterici, *Thier un Mensch* (Leipzig: 1881), p. 36; cf. A. Vaillant, *Livre des Secrets d' Henoch* (Paris: 1952), p. 57f, chap. 15 of the text. The teaching is attested to in very early times: L. Kakosy, in *Acta Orientalia*, vol. 17 (1964), p. 205.

18. Joseph Fielding Smith, Comp. *Teachings of the Prophet Joseph Smith*, (Salt Lake City: Deseret Book Co., 1947), p. 71. Hereafter cited as *TPJS*.

19. Discussed in *BYU Studies*, Summer 1972; cf. The Gospel of Philip, 112:14f, and E. Brunner-Traut, in *Ztschr. f. aeg. Sprache*, vol. 80 (1955), pp. 27, 29.

20. Ben Sirach, 10:4.

21. Book of Adam and Eve, 24:4, in R. H. Charles, *op, cit.*, p. 147.

22. Perhaps the most impressive treatment of the theme is the entire volume of F. Dieterici, above, no. 17.

23. Bin Gorion, *S.J.*, I, 198.

24. Apocal. of Moses, 11:2; Jubilees III, 28; R. Eisler, *Iesous Basileus*, I, 523.

25. Secrets of Enoch 58:4f (in R. H. Charles, *op., cit.* II, 464); cf. the Vaillant text, chap. XV.

26. *Ibid.* chap. XV.

27. Vaillant, *Secrets d' Henoch*, chap. XIII, pp. 46, 55, and chap. XV, p. 57.

28. *Ibid.*, chap. XV.

29. G. R. Driver, in *Journal of Semitic Studies*, vol. 7 (1962), p. 12ff.

30. *JD* 8:191.

31. *JD* 15:227.

32. F. J. Connell, in *American Ecclesiastical Review*, vol. 146 (1962), p.270f.

33. Joseph Fielding Smith, *Man's Origin and Destiny*, p. 194.

34. Joseph F. Smith, *Gospel Teachings* (1971 Melchizedek Priesthood Manual), I, 372. cf. 337-9.

35. Apostolic Constitutions, 6:10, Philastrius in Migne. *Patrol. Lat.* 12, 1209, 1214.

36. On the problem of preserving man's uniqueness and dignity. A. Lovejoy, *The Great Chain of Being* (Harper Torchbooks: 1960), p. 121ff. Synesius, in *Patrol. Graec.* 66:1289, 1292, recognizes both upward and downward relationships.

37. Midr. Rab. Noah 36:3; bin Gorion, I, 228.

38. Ginsberg, *Legends of the Jews*, I, 269f; Genesis Apocryphon, p. 23; Testament of Abrahamin, *Jewish Quarterly Rev.*, vol. 7 (1895), p. 584f.

39. Moses 1:12-19, Luke 4:7.

40. The writer is preparing an extensive study on the subject. Some of the old sources describing the confrontation of Adam and Satan are the Testament of Adam, various "Adam Books," the Lives of Adam and Eve, the Cave of Treasures, Flavius, Encomium of Demetrius, the Conflict of Adam and Eve with Satan, sources in bin Gorion I, 92ff, 254ff, Manichaean Hymns, Tha' labi, Testament of Abraham, Apocalypse of Moses, Slavic Adam and Eve, Secrets of Enoch, Bp. Theodosius on the Abbaton, the Precious Jewel, Midrash, etc.

41. *JQR* 7:584f.

42. *JD* 10:320.

43. They are the "Sent Ones" who come to instruct Adam.

44. The theme is dramatically treated in the Testament of Job, chaps. vi, vii, xxii-xxiii, where Satan says, "For money you can have anything you want!"

45. To Moses he even claims to be the Son of God, Moses 1:19; he speaks only with reverence of the Father as his father.

46. R. Graves, *The Greek Myths* (Penguin Books: 1955), 31e (I, 122).

47. Homer, *Hymn to Demeter*, lines 16-19ff.

48. Graves, 31f; on Seth, E. Hornung, *Orientalish Litteraturzeitung*, vol. 65 (19), p. 19; S. Schott, *Sieg ueber Seth*, p. 18.

49. G. Murray, *Aristophanes* (New York: Oxford University Press, 1933).

50. Discussed by O. Holtzmann in *Ztschr. f. Neutest, Wissenschaft*, vol. 11 (1910), pp. 231, 226f.

51. Moses 7:13; Zohar, Vayera, 97a, bin Gorion, I, 153.

52. Apocal. of Abraham, 29:16.

53. *Millennial Star*, vol. 38 (1876), p. 344.

54. *JD* 9:246.

55. When man changes his nature, "every animal and creeping thing shall be filled with peace; and the soil of the earth will bring forth in its strength." *JD* 1:203.

56. Psalms of Thomas, I, 35f; bin Gorion I, 151, on the destruction of the forests; *ibid.*, 151, on Satan's jealousy of the animals.

57. Bin Gorion, I, 151, 148ff.

58. Midr. Rab., Noah 36:3.

59. Bin Gorion, I, 226.

60. Jubilees, VII, 14, 23.

61. *Jewish Encyclopedia*, s.v. Nimrod.

62. Pirke Rab. Eleazer, chap. xi; Zohar, Noah 73b.

63. R. Eisler, *op. cit.*, II, 34.

64. *TPJS*, p. 248.

65. *JD* 9:107.

Genesis of the Written Word

5

The most interesting thing about this article is that, within a month after it was printed, a cover story appeared in the prestigious journal Science recounting the strange achievement of an Apache Indian by the name of Silas John, who not only claimed to have had a whole writing system revealed to him in a dream for holy purposes, but actually produced the system, which turns out to be a highly efficient one; an instant alphabet, not out of nothing, but out of a dream. If it could happen in 1904 to a semi-literate Apache, could it not have happened earlier?

Only such evidence could break the vicious circular argument which has long prevented serious investigation into the origins of writing. Many writers in scientific journals have recently deplored the way in which scientific conclusions reached long ago and held as unimpeachable truths turn students away from avenues of research which might well prove most fruitful. The evolutionary rule-of-thumb, convenient, satisfying, universal, is cited as the prime offender. Here is a test of how it works: Ask your students to write a paper on "A Day in the Life of a Primitive Man." None of them has ever seen a primitive man or ever will, but does that stop them? Before the question is on the board they are off and running, and can go on writing at top speed indefinitely. They all know exactly how it should have been; evolution emancipated them from the drudgery of research. And in all of science there never was a more open-and-shut case than the origin of writing: intuitively we know it must have begun with pictures, and traditionally we know it can have developed in only one way – very slowly and gradually from simple to more complex forms, and all that. Some may elaborate on the theme with tree-alphabets, ogams, runes and (as we have) arrow-markings, but if there ever was a hypothesis which enjoyed complete and unquestioning obedience, the origin of writing has been it. Yet the discerning Kipling, taking a hard common-sense look at the official solution, found it simply absurd. It is the same hypothesis that we now dare to question, grateful for the support of the noble Silas John.

We have all grown up in a world nurtured on the comfortable Victorian doctrine of uniformitarianism, the idea that what happens in this world is all just more of the same: what lies ahead is pretty much what lies behind, for the same forces that are at work on the earth today were at work in the same manner, with the same intensity and the same effects at all times past and will go on operating inexorably and irresistibly in just the same way forever hereafter. There is no real cause for alarm in a world where everything is under control beneath the watchful eye of science, as evolution takes its undeviating forward course, steady, sure, reliable, imperceptibly slow and gentle and gratifyingly predictable. According to an eminent British scholar of the 1920s:

> The skies as far as the utmost star, are clear of any malignant Intelligences, and even the untoward accidents of life are due to causes comfortably impersonal. . . . The possibility that the Unknown contains Powers deliberately hostile to him is one the ordinary modern man can hardly entertain even in imagination.[1]

In such a world one needed no longer to run to God for comfort. The matter-of-fact, no-nonsense approach of science had since the days of the Miletian school and the ancient atomists banished all childish fears and consigned the horrendous and spectacular aspects of the human past and future to the realm of myth and fantasy.

Quite recently, however, scientists have noted with a shock that in looking forward not to the distant but to the immediate future what they discern is not just more of the same but something totally different, something for which they confess themselves entirely unprepared, since it is all entirely unexpected.[2] The idea that what lies ahead is by no means the simple and predictable projection of our knowledge of the present has, as John Lear points out, reconditioned our minds for another look at the past as well as the future. Since the past is wholly a construction of our own imaginations, we have always found there just what we expected to find, that is, more of the same. But now "future shock" has prepared us for "past shock," and we find ourselves almost forced to accept a view of the past that is utterly alien to anything in the experience of modern man.[3]

Joseph Smith as a prophet also looked both ahead and behind, and came up with a picture of both worlds that violently shocked and offended his Victorian contemporaries. He presented his peculiar picture of the past in the most daring possible way, in the form of a number of books which he claimed to be of ancient origin, their contents given to him "by the Spirit." But his image of the future and the past was not conveyed in mystical utterances in the manner of Swedenborg, Jakob Boehme, or the "Urantia Volume," whose assertions may be tested only by waiting for history to catch up with them. His story was rather to be found in the pages of ancient books that purportedly existed and either still survived in the world or had left unmistakable marks behind them.

In the first lesson of the 1972 Melchizedek Priesthood Manual President Joseph Fielding Smith brought this formidable contribution to our attention:

> The Latter-day Saints are doubly blessed with the word of the Lord which has come to light through the restoration of the gospel. We have been given the records of the Nephites and the Jaredites. . . . The Lord restored much that had been originally revealed to Adam and Enoch and Abraham . . . and it is to their condemnation when members of the Church do not take advantage of their opportunities to read, study, and learn what the records contain.[4]

Few people realize that in Joseph Smith's day *no* really ancient manuscripts were known. Egyptian and Babylonian could not be read; the Greek and Latin classics were the oldest literature avail-

103

able, preserved almost entirely in bad medieval copies no older than the Byzantine and Carolingian periods. The oldest text of the Hebrew Bible was the Ben Asher Codex from the ninth century A.D. Today we have whole libraries of documents more than four thousand years old — not just their contents, but the actual writings themselves going back to the very beginnings of civilization. It is just as easy to dig back six thousand years as it is to remove the dust of five thousand years; and when we do so, what do we find in the way of written documents? Let us consider three main points: 1) what can be inferred from Joseph Smith's statements as to the nature of the oldest human records; 2) what the ancients themselves have to say about those records: and 3) what the actual condition of the records indicates.

First, if Joseph Smith is right, the written records should be as old as the human race itself, for, he tells us, "a book of remembrance was kept, . . . in the language of Adam." (Moses 6:5.)[5] Now what do the ancients themselves have to say on the subject? Surprisingly, a great deal, of which we can give only a few quotations here. According to them, the king had access to that divine book which was consulted at the time of the creation of the world: "I am a scribe of the god's book," says one of the earliest Pharaohs, "who says what is and brings about what is not. . . ."[6] A later but still ancient (Thirteenth Dynasty) Pharaoh recalls, "My heart yearned to behold the most ancient books of Atum. Open them before me for diligent searching, that I may know god as he really is!"[7] Over the lintel of the ancient library of the great temple at Edfu was a relief showing two kneeling figures giving praise to the heavenly book descending to earth; hieroglyphs above their heads show them to represent Sia and Hw, or the Divine Intelligence and the Divine Utterance (the Word) by which the world was created.[8] In Egypt every step of the founding of a new temple had to follow the prescriptions given in the heavenly book, since such a founding represented and dramatized the creation of the earth itself.

And what does the actual state of the documents attest? If writing evolved gradually and slowly as everything is supposed to have done, there should be a vast accumulation of transitional scribblings as countless crude and stumbling attempts at writing would leave their marks on stone, bone, clay and wood over countless millennia of groping trial and error. Only there are no such accumulations of primitive writing anywhere. Primitive writing is as illusive as that primitive language the existence of which has never been attested. And indeed the very nature of writing precludes anything in the way of a slow, gradual, step-by-step evolution: one either catches on to how it is done or one does not, and once one knows, the whole mystery lies revealed. All the evidence shows that that is the way it actually was. "Suddenly . . . graves in the pre-dynastic cemeteries" display "the art of writing . . . with a fairly long period of development behind it," writes Engelbach, " . . . In fact it was writing well past the stage of picture writing. . . ."[9] Both the long period of development and a primal picture writing must here be assumed, since there is no evidence for them. If writing did evolve in Egypt, the process took only "a few decades," after which the art remained unchanged "for thousands of years," according to Capart.[10] Sir Alan Gardiner notes the same strange and paradoxical state of affairs: hieroglyphic "was a thing of rapid growth," but "once established remained immutable for fully 3,000 years."[11] So also A. Scharff assures us that with the First Dynasty "writing was introduced and perfected (*ausgebildet*) with astounding speed and detail."[12] "There is no evidence of a *gradual* development of script in Egypt," writes Miss Baugartel,[13] and yet there is no evidence of that script anywhere else. There is something wrong with this evolution-ary process by which one and the same people develop a system of writing almost overnight, and then refuse to budge an inch on the way of progress forever after. Stuart Piggott finds that *immediately* after "ambiguous stammerings . . . on the slate palettes . . . a rapid cursive form of writing with pen and ink" is in evidence.[14] Stranger still, on the most famous of those predynastic slate palettes with their ambiguous stammerings that suggest only the dawn of writing we see clearly depicted a king (Narmer) following behind an atten-dant (*tt*) who is carrying the classic two inkpots of the Egyptian scribe. The tombs of the First Dynasty "show that they had a well-developed written language, a knowledge of the preparation of papyrus. . . ."[15] Inscriptions found on tags and labels of First-Dynasty jars, often regarded because of their crudeness and brevity as primitive attempts at writing, are crude and brief because they were meant to be identification tags and nothing more — not literary compositions; actually, as S. Schott points out, "they are written in a sophisticated cursive writing."[16] For though "hiero-glyphics appear all at once in the world as an Egyptian invention cir. 3000 B.C.," hieratic, the cursive writing of the same symbols was also in use just as early.[17]

All of which is most retrograde to tenaciously held theories of the evolution of writing in Egypt. But how about the rest of the world? Wherever we look the earliest systems of writing are somehow connected with the Egyptian and appear suddenly in the same paradoxical way. Though there is "a prehistoric connection with Babylonian cuneiform" and Egyptian, according to Sethe,[18] and though J. Friedrich has demonstrated the connection by an impressive catalogue of striking parallels,[19] the gap between the two systems is still too wide to allow any thought of deriving the one from the other.[20] "The writing which appeared without antecedents at the beginning of the First Dynasty (in Egypt) was by no means primitive," writes Frankfort, "It has, in fact a complex structure of . . . precisely the same state of complexity which had been reached in Mesopotamia. . . . To deny . . . that Egyptian and Mesopotamian systems of writing are related amounts to maintaining that Egypt invented independently a complex and very consistent system at the very moment of being influenced in its art and architecture by Mesopotamia where a precisely similar system had just been developed. . . ."[21] Not only are these two systems related, but they show remarkable affinities to the earliest Chinese writing,[22] as well as the Hittite, proto-Indian,[23] and proto-Elamitic scripts.[24] P. Mordell insists that the Hebrew alphabet is related to an Egyptian linear writing system, a real alphabet, which "evolved at a date when hieroglyphic writing was unknown, then persisted with a strange vitality, and was never absorbed or ousted."[25] This was that mysterious prehistoric "Mediterranean" alphabet which is said to be older than hieroglyphic,[26] and which suddenly spread all over the Near East at the end of the second millennium B.C.[27]

"Evolved"? Many scholars have pointed out that the alphabet is the miracle of miracles, the greatest of all inventions, by which even the television and jet-planes pale in comparison, and as such a thing absolutely unique in time and place; they also agree that it was of Egyptian or West-Semitic origin.[28] It is also argued that by the very nature of the thing it can only have been the work of a single inventor.[29] "The gulf between the idea and the written word," writes H. Schmitt, "could only have been bridged once, by a miracle of invention."[30]

Given the evolutionary hypothesis, any healthy, normal, growing boy can describe in convincing detail how long ago "the naive child of nature" everywhere drew crude pictures to convey his simple thoughts,[31] and how out of this the process moved "everywhere inexorably . . . towards the final stage, the alphabetic writing."[32] To save our eager high school student from undue embarrassment, we have just quoted two eminent scholars. But if it really happened that way, then we would find traces of evolving writing "everywhere"; veritable middens of scratched rock and bones and shells would attest the universal groping toward the inexorable final stage over tens of thousands of years, while the clumsy transitional forms should outnumber proper writing by at least a million to one. But the vast accumulations of attempts at writing simply do not exist; there is no evidence whatever of a worldwide groping towards the goal. Having made his lucid and logical statement, the author of our last quotation observes with perplexity that "it is surprising that the ultimate stage in evolution . . . was only achieved in a very few spots on the globe."[33] That is, we do not find a multiplicity of writing systems throughout the world; in fact when we come right down to it there seems to have been only one! We find "only a very few systems of writing," says David, " . . . and even these are so much alike and so closely related in time and space that their independence appears at least problematical."[34] The vast worldwide corpus of embryonic scribblings that should attest the long ages of slow transition from picture writing to true writing simply is not there, and the innumerable systems of writing which must have resulted from the basic psychological need of men everywhere to express themselves can be counted on the fingers, and most probably on the thumbs, of one hand.

People have always drawn pictures, but was that the origin of writing? Was there ever a real picture writing? E. Doblhofer defines "pictorial writing" which he says is "incredibly ancient," as "a series of images (which) can possibly be 'read' accurately by any spectator."[35] K. Sethe would agree: a "pure" picture writing is one which "could be read in any language at sight."[36] And right here the issue is settled: if there ever was a true picture writing it has not yet been discovered. Where on earth is a single inscription to which any and all beholders, scholars or laymen alike, regardless of their own language and culture, would give the identical interpretation? When Sethe sought for a true picture writing to illustrate the process by which hieroglyphic emerged, the only examples he could find in all the world were North American Indian petroglyphs, which no one can "read" or interpret to this day.[37] "True picture-writing," wrote Alan Gardiner, "makes excessive demand upon the skill and ingenuity of the writer, and its results are far from unambiguous. . . ."[38] It takes special skill, that is, to execute "true picture-writing" and special skill to read it: which is to say that it is not the simple and uninhibited drawing and viewing of pictures at all. Doblhofer himself confirms this when he assures us that "the *most primitive* pictorial writings ... translate ... abstract ideas with the aid of *symbolical signs*," for symbolical signs are not plain pictures but conventional devices which must be learned; that is, even "the most primitive" picture writing is not just picture writing as he defines it.[39] In the very earliest Egyptian writing it is impossible to interpret the pictures as such, and there is no evidence of pictograms in Egypt at any time, according to Sethe.[40] Also, we must not forget that along with the most "primitive" Egyptian writing in prehistoric times we find a genuine alphabetic writing flourishing most paradoxically.[41] Long wrestling with the problem of deriving the alphabet from a syllabic writing, that is, from a system in which the names of things depicted supplied certain sound combinations, has led to the general conclusion that syllabic writing was "a blind alley which could not lead to alphabetic writing."[42]

Like the earliest Egyptian documents, the Babylonian tablets bearing "the *oldest* written signs thus far known" are highly stylized and cannot be read.[43] Granted they are picture writing, no two scholars "read" them the same. Mesopotamia offers to date the only chance of presenting the evolutionary sequence of the development of writing by a stratigraphic pattern. Only, alas, it doesn't work. Though it is assumed, of course, that "the earliest examples of writing in Mesopotamia are pictographs ... very few of these were actually excavated scientifically, so that, from the chronological point of view, there is little help to be obtained from stratigraphic connections," according to Burton-Brown, who should also have pointed out that the inscriptions which have been scientifically excavated have a way of refuting the expected patterns, since some of the most primitive writing is found in late strata and vice versa.[44]

The paradox that anything as advanced and sophisticated as writing should come into the world full-blown and all at once is invincibly repugnant to the evolutionary way of thinking. Of recent years the anthropologists have taken a strong stand on the "tool" theory of civilization. The idea is that primitive hominids quite thoughtlessly and accidentally blundered on the use of this or that piece of wood, bone, or rock as a tool, and that "it was the success of the simplest tools that started the whole trend of human evolution and led to the civilizations of today."[45] It is the primitive tool, falling fortuitously into its hands, which draws mankind irresistibly forward to new levels of attainment, for "when men make a tool, they commit themselves, man depends upon his tools for his very humanity."[46] In a word, "social evolution is a consequence of technological evolution."[47]

Some of the scientific speculators, however, take the opposite position, that man "has always had reservoirs of response far more than his devices (tools) asked of him," and that in "his attempts to transcend his biological limitations" his mind always runs ahead of his tools, not behind them.[48] When men need a tool they invent it, not the other way around.[49] Men themselves decide what tools they will have, so that one evolutionist notes with perplexity that "one of the most puzzling aspects of the culture" of the "caveman" is "their heavy dependence on tools whose use is now a complete mystery."[50] C. H. Coon observed that "for the simple reason that human beings are not equipped by nature to live without tools," we must suppose that they always had all the tools they needed for survival, even in Pliocene.[51] Petrie in a significant and neglected study pointed out that instead of eagerly adopting a superior tool as soon as it was made known to them, human beings have shown "a resistance of almost 100 percent" to any new tool coming from the outside.[52] Though all the neighbors of the Egyptians knew about their superior axe forms for thousands of years, the only other ancient people to adopt them were of all things the South Americans.[53] Petrie knows of seventeen Egyptian tools and weapons, some of unsurpassed efficiency, which are over the centuries never found outside of Egypt, and, he observes, "the converse is equally true."[54]

Then whatever induced one people to adopt *writing* from another? The interesting thing here is that though the idea quickly caught on, each people in adopting it insisted on making it its own exclusive possession and devised from the first a native style that set it off from all the others. Both the popularity and the variety of ancient writing is to be explained by its religious nature. Avon Mulinen has noted that new scripts invariably appear as the vehicles of new religions,[55] while J. Smolian points out that all of man's greatest inventions or discoveries seem to have the primary purpose of putting him into communication with the other world.[56] If Joseph Smith was right, books and writing are a gift to man from heaven, "for it was given unto as many as called upon God to write by the spirit of inspiration." (Moses 6:5.) The art of writing was a special dispensation, an inestimable boon, enabling the righteous to retain the memory of divine visitations and communications ever fresh before them, and assisting them in coordinating their earthly activities with the heavenly order: "The *immediate* will of heaven is contained in the Scriptures," said the Prophet Joseph.[57]

The earliest records of the race have much to say "about the miracle of writing, which the Ancients regarded as a gift from heaven."[58] The Egyptians believed that writing was a sacred trust given to the king as "high-priest and scribe" to keep him and his people ever in touch with the mind and will of heaven.[59] Thus the Book of the Foundation of Temples was thought to have been sent down from heaven to the immortal genius Imhotep, the Vizier of King Zoser of Dynasty III and the greatest builder of all time, after which the book "was taken away to heaven at the time the gods left the earth," but was sent down again by Imhotep at a later time, when he "caused it to fall from heaven at the place north of Memphis."[60] In Babylonia

> the King is the Sent One. He has ascended to heaven to receive . . . the tablets of destiny and to get his commission. Then he is sent out, i.e., he descends again. . . . And so the knowledge is communicated to the king, it is of a mysterious character, bearing upon the great mysteries of heaven and earth, the hidden things, and is a revelation of the hidden knowledge by the gods (the god). Can we style it "primordial revelation"?[61]

The idea of a primordial revelation is that a complete knowledge of the world from its beginning to its end is already written down and has been vouchsafed to certain chosen spirits from time to time, a doctrine familiar to Latter-day Saints.[62] The heavenly origin of writing is constantly referred to anciently in the doctrine that writing and the symbols of writing are derived from the starry heavens. The Tablets of Destiny which contain all knowledge and impart all authority "are the divination of the world, the stars and constellations form the writing."[63] As Clement of Alexandria observed, both in Egypt and Chaldaea "writing and a knowledge of the heavens necessarily go together."[64] How this is can be seen if one considers where all of the oldest writings of the race are found.

If we turn from ancient doctrine to concrete discovery we are soon made aware that the oldest writings are always found in *temples*. "It is in these temples that we find the first signs of writing. . . . The script appears from the first as a system of conventional signs . . . such as might have been introduced all at once. We are confronted with a true invention, not with an adaption of pictorial art."[65] For Egypt, Steindorff maintained that "the birthplace of this 'hieroglyphic system' of writing was the sacerdotal school of Heliopolis."[66] In Babylonia, according to Hrozny, it was in the Uruk period, 3200 B.C. that "there originated . . . from the records of business transaction in the temple enclosure, the picture writing which in later times developed into cuneiform writing."[67] Though these symbols cannot be read (i.e., they were not picture writings, but "a collection of abstract tokens eked out with pictograms"),[68] it is apparent that they "were for the most part lists of commodities supplied to or delivered by officials and others concerned with the administration of the Temple."[69]

Here we have a combination of business and religion which has given rise to the discussion of the rivalry of *Kultschrift* (cultic or religious writing) and *Gebrauchschrift* (practical business writing). Actually no rivalry exists between them: the consensus is that the oldest written symbols are property marks, such as arrow markings and cattle brands, and in order to be respected as such they have to be sacrosanct, holy symbols duly registered in the temple.[70] If the oldest writing is used for business, it is always temple business, and the writing is also used for other — far more important — purposes. Examining the claims of the two, Helmut Arntz concluded that the holy or cultic writing has clear priority.[71] One can, like old Commodore Vanderbilt, carry on business in a state of total illiteracy, and indeed men of affairs have always viewed men of letters with suspicion: "Writing is an art despised by the Roman businessman," wrote Cornelius Nepos, "who have all their writing done for them by hirelings."[72] But one cannot carry on the holy business of the temple without the divine gift of writing.[73] "Hieroglyphic is correctly named," Sethe observed, being devised "only for the walls of temples . . . it is a survival from prehistoric times."[74] It is no accident that temple architecture and writing appear suddenly together.[75] The *Templum* is, as we have shown elsewhere, an observatory, where one takes one's bearings on the universe.[76] There the heavens are carefully observed, and to be of value those observations must be recorded. Alphabet, calendar, and temple naturally go together, all devised for handling messages from the stars and planets.[77] "We may think of the stars as letters inscribed on the heavens," said Plotinus, and we may think of the heavens as a great book which men copy and project on tangible materials at the holy places.[78] Recent studies by Gerald Hawkins, Peter Tompkins, Giorgio di Santillana, and others have given vivid reality to the heretofore vaguely surmised existence of ritual complexes of great antiquity where men observed the heavens and acquired an astonishing amount of knowledge about them, which in order to use, they faithfully committed to their books.

From first to last, ancient writing remains in the hands not of businessmen but of priests; it is a holy and a secret thing, imparted only to the elect and zealously withheld from all others. "He who divulges it," we read of a typical holy book, "dies a sudden death and an immediate cutting-off. Thou shalt keep very far away from it. It is to be read only by a scribe in the workshop, whose name has been duly registered in the House of Life."[79] "Only the prophets may read and understand the holy books" is the rule.[80] Each system of writing itself is an effective seal on the holy books, a cryptogram, "a secret formula which the profane do not know."[81] The key to power and priesthood lies "in the midst of the Sea of Coptos, in a box of iron in which is a box of kete-wood, in which is a box of ivory and ebony in which is a box of gold in which is *the* BOOK."[82] The idea of the holy book that is taken away from the earth and restored from time to time, or is handed down secretly from father to son for generations, or hidden up in the earth, preserved by ingenious methods of storage with precious imperishable materials to be brought forth in a later and more righteous generation (e.g., Moses 1:41) is becoming increasingly familiar with the discovery and publication of ever more ancient apocryphal works, Jewish, Christian, and others.[83] But nowhere does the idea find clearer or more complete expression than in the pages of the Book of Mormon and the Pearl of Great Price.

What is perhaps the oldest book known, the so-called Shabako stone, instead of the primitive mumbo jumbo one might expect, contains a story strangely familiar to Latter-day Saints. It is the text of a ritual drama enacted in the temple to celebrate the founding of the First Dynasty of Egypt, and it depicts the council in heaven, the creation of the world, the fall of man, and the means by which he may achieve resurrection and be reinstated in his primal glory. The book, on a leather scroll, was hidden up in the wall of that same temple in the time of Menes, the first Pharaoh, and was discovered by a later king, Shabako, who followed the same text in the rites establishing his own (Twenty-fifth) Dynasty.[84]

Another king reports that "when His Majesty settled the lands (*grgtawi*) . . . he mounted the throne of Horus . . . he spoke to his noble ones, the *Smrw* of his immediate presence, the faithful writers-down of the divine words, who were in charge of all the secrets."[85] Writing, here shared only with his intimates, is par excellence "the King's Secret" which gives him all advantage over his fellows and the ability to rule them. The technique of writing is the foundation of empires, for only the written document can overcome the limitations of space and carry a ruler's word and authority out of sight and beyond the hills, and even defeat the inroads of time on human memory by preserving the words of command and judgment for unlimited numbers of years.[86] The king describes himself as the mediator and scribe of the god in heaven in the administration of empire: "I sit before him, I open his boxes, I break open his edicts, I seal his dispatches, I send out messengers."[87] In Mesopotamia also "the supreme sovranty of the universe is connected with the tablets of destiny, the possession of which could give even a robber possession of the rulership of the world."[88] The Pharaoh was authorized to rule only when "the master of the house of the divine books" had inscribed his royal names "on the true records deposited in the heavenly archives."[89] The archives were known in Egypt as the House of Life, housing the writings upon which the life of all things ultimately depended.[90] It was a powerhouse humming with vital electricity, transmitting cosmic forces from heaven to earth, a place of deadly peril to any mortal not holding the necessary priestly credentials.[91] Wherever the heavenly book is mentioned, the heavenly scribe appears as king, priest and mediator, in early Jewish and Christian as well as older traditions.[92] Pharaoh is preeminently "He who knows, being in possession of the divine book."[93] Like the Egyptian Thoth, the Babylonian Nabu, the prophet and scribe writes all things down in the "unalterable tablets" of destiny which determine all that happens upon the earth.[94] In the earthly as in the heavenly court everything was written down, not only to follow the divine example but to coordinate earthly with celestial proceedings. In Persia, for example, "the entire administration, as was customary from the earliest times in the Orient, was carried on by written documents, as it was in the courts of Egypt, Babylonia, and Assyria . . . everything is carefully written down; even in battle the King's secretary is beside him taking notes; every royal remark is written down and then gathered into 'Daybooks' or 'Memorandabooks', such as have been found in the archives of Suza, Babylonia, Ecbatana, etc."[95] The Myth of Irra, one of the oldest stories in existence, shows "that Mesopotamian theologicans were not ignorant of the concept of a 'sacred book' that is a divinely inspired, even dictated text, which contains the only correct and valid account of the 'story' of deity."[96] In Egypt it is "the King who is over the spirits, who unites hearts — so says He who is in charge of wisdom, being great, and who bears the god's book, even Sia ('the personification of intelligence and understanding' — Faulkner) who is at the right hand of Re."[97] The relief, mentioned above, from the temple library of Denderah shows us the scribe's palette, at all times the Egyptian symbols of writing and all that it implies, descending from heaven; it is supported by two figures who strike the pose signifying "eternity" and who face each other, denoting "from eternity to eternity," while four other figures are in the attitude of adoration; hieroglyphic symbols above the head of each show them to represent the ear that hears, the eye that sees, the mind or intelligence (*Sia*) which conceives, and the word of power (*Hw*) which consummates the creation of all things.[98]

The books were consulted on every occasion: "Copy thy fathers who have gone before thee. . . . Behold, their words are recorded in writing. Open and read and copy."[99] When King Zoser away back in the Third Dynasty asked his all-wise minister Imhotep to explain a seven-years' famine, the latter "begged permission 'that I may enter into the Mansion of Life, and may open the books and may seek guidance from them.' "[100] Interestingly enough, the most important of all writings were genealogical records, and Gardiner concluded not only that the House of Life was, properly speaking, nothing more or less than the genealogical archives, but that the Great Pyramid itself was built to contain the royal genealogical records.[101] The astonishing mass and charge of ancient book making may be attributed to the basic doctrine that everything must be written down: "The Babylonian conception of Canonicity . . . that the sum of revealed knowledge was given once for all by the antediluvian sages," necessarily posits the existence of the Primordial Book that contains everything that was, is, and is to come, and presents "a remarkable parallel to the Rabbinic view that God's revelation in its entirety is contained in the Torah," according to W. G. K. Lambert.[102]

This is consistent with the marvelous function of writing as the great synthesizer. To write is to synthesize. The basic idea of writing is that symbols represent sounds and that smaller units make up larger units — not compounds or composites, but true units. Thus a letter by itself is without significance; there must be a reference to something which goes beyond it — other letters making a word or a name. A single letter, heraldic mark, tally, crest, or *wasm* has no meaning without reference to the official heraldic list of such and the names they represent. The word in turn is also meaningless without reference to other words; even a one-word sentence such as "Alas!" takes its meaning from other unspoken words. The meaning of every sentence also depends on its larger context; even a short aphorism must be understood in its cultural context. For the ancients, any self-contained message was a *book*. They were not disturbed by the extreme brevity of many "books," because they regarded every book also as part of a larger context — for the Egyptians the "Hermetic" books. Every proper Arabic book, regardless of its subject, still opens with a paragraph praising God for his creation and the place in it which this particular writing occupies. Ancient records come to us not in single books but in whole libraries. These are not mere collections but organic entities, as the archaic Egyptian sign of the Book-lady Seshat attests: her seven-pointed star goes with her seven books, representing every department of human knowledge, being let down from the opened heavens.[103]

The House of Life where the books were copied and studied had from the earliest times the aspect of a university, a super graduate-school;[104] "there it was that all questions relating to ... learned matters were settled."[105] The place was always part of the temple, and the books contain the earliest *poetry*, for *poema* means "creation" and the business of the Muses at the temple was to sing the Creation song with the morning stars;[106] naturally the hymn was sung to *music*, and some scholars would derive the first writing from musical notation.[107] It was performed in a sacred circle or *chorus*, so that poetry, music and the *dance* go out to the world from the temple, called by the Greeks the Museon, or shrine of the muses. The Creation hymn was part of the great dramatic presentation that took place yearly at the temple, dealing with the fall and redemption of man, represented by various forms of combat, making the place the scene of the ritual *athletic* contests sanctified throughout the world. The victor in the contest was the father of the race, the priest-king himself, whose triumphant procession, coronation, and marriage took place on the occasion, making this the seat and source of *government* (the king was always crowned in the temple rather than the palace).[108] Since the entire race was expected to be present for the event, a busy exchange of goods from various distant regions took place, the booths of pilgrims serving as the market booths for great fairs, while the necessity of converting various and bizarre forms of wealth into acceptable offerings for the temple led to an active *banking* and *exchange* in the temple courts; the earliest "money," from the shrine of Juno Moneta at Rome, is temple money. Since the place began as an observatory, and all things were tied to the calendar and the stars, *mathematics* flourished and *astronomy* was a muse. *History* was another muse, for the rites were meant for the dead as well as the living, and memorials to former great ones (believed to be in attendance) encouraged the production of a marvelous art of portraiture, of *sculpture* and *paint-*

ing, which would have flourished anyway as architectural adornments, since the design and measurements (the *middoth*) of the temple structure itself as a sort of scale model of the universe and cosmic computer were all-important; the *architecture* of the hierocentric structure was of primary concern. And since from that central point all the earth was measured and all the lands distributed, *geometry* was essential: "In the Beginning the One God promised Horus that he should inherit the land of Egypt, which was written in the Books by order of the Lord of All . . . at the Division of the Lands it was decreed in writing."[109]

The writings produced and copied in the House of Life were also discussed there, giving rise to *philosophy,* but concerned largely with cosmology and natural science. In short, there is no aspect of our civilization that does not have its rise in the temple, thanks to the power of the written word. In the all-embracing relationships of the Divine Book everything is relevant. Nothing is really dead or forgotten; every detail belongs in the picture, which would be incomplete without it. Lacking such a synthesizing principle, our present-day knowledge becomes ever more fragmented, and our universities and libraries crumble and disintegrate as they expand. Where the temple that gave it birth is missing, civilization itself becomes a hollow shell.

In the short compass of a single lecture one always raises more questions than can be answered or discussed. The true origin of writing must remain, as Siegfried Schott observes, a subject of the purest speculation for a long time to come, and possibly forever.[110] The fact that all the scholars are merely guessing should not deter us from the fascinating game, for as Karl Popper puts it, it is only by guessing and discussing that any science makes any progress.

Some years ago there was a consensus among students that Egypt was the ultimate home of the alphabet. The decisive study was that of Kurt Sethe, who tried to follow a strictly evolutionary line with writing evolving inevitably from everyday human needs throughout the world as if by natural law,[111] "gradually and imperceptibly," culminating in a full-blown alphabet in Egypt.[112] In the beginning, he avers, humans everywhere communicated by pictures, and to prove this he cites cases in which the white man astounded the Indians by communicating in writing *without pictures;* he then furnishes as a classical example of Indian picture writing the headstone of a famous chief on which three short vertical strokes represent three seriously wounded warriors while sixteen short horizontal strokes denote sixteen war-parties.[113] And this is picture writing? Well might the white man have been astounded that the Indians could thus communicate *without letters*. None, in fact, of the more than a dozen reproductions of Indian picture writing supplied by Sethe can be read as pictures, and Sethe himself concludes that all these examples are nothing but "mnemotechnical aids" to help the *writer* fix things in his own mind rather than convey them to others; most of the sketches are so reduced and stylized as to be entirely symbolic, with no attempt at realism, reduced cues that mean nothing to those who have not already experienced what they depict.[114]

This, however, is not true picture writing, according to Sethe, that being a foolproof system in which "every single element of the thought process has its own picture." (p. 17.) But if Sethe's examples of primitive picture writing (of which he could find none in Egypt) were inadequate and even irrelevant, his examples of true picture writing leave even more to be desired — there are none. All his evidence he must find embedded in later hieroglyphic writing. (pp. 18-19.) In true picture writing, he says, every concept has its picture, so that the writing can be read by anybody anywhere in the world. (pp. 24-25.) As an example he gives the sign of the cross, which accompanying a name signifies a dead person, forgetting that it only does so as a purely abstract and highly conventionalized symbol, and not as a picture. (p. 26.) But since "man thinks in words," according to Sethe, everywhere the true picture writing was "automatically" and "very early converted to phonetic writing." (p. 26.) But if men were thinking in words all the time they were drawing pictures, how long would it take them to associate the two? Why does there have to be a gap at all? The evolutionary rule requires it: true writing being purely phonetic must necessarily be the last step in the long evolutionary process. (p. 27.) Again the evidence is missing: all known picture writings in the Old World, according to Sethe, had already become phonetic scripts *before* their earliest appearance, so that we can only infer the existence of the previous primitive — and true picture writing — systems from indications discovered in the known systems. (p. 28.) The only clear evidence that Sethe can find for the evolutionary process is the existence of *independent* systems of writing, all of which, according to him, must have emerged in the same way from primitive picture writing; he lists ten such systems, of which only three had been deciphered in his time. (p. 20.) Since then the list has been extended, and in the process the independence of the various systems from each other has been brought under serious questioning. Since alphabetic writing is the ultimate perfection in the chain of evolution, it is disturbing that Sethe must conclude that the less efficient, clumsier, and more primitive syllabic writing was evolved *from* the more perfect alphabetic writing, and not the other way around. (p. 29.)

Sethe's thesis is that the Egyptians, beginning with a true picture writing containing "originally a countless multitude of symbols" (p. 34) (which strangely enough have never turned up anywhere), through a series of inevitable and "purely mechanical" steps, "quite unconsciously and without intention" produced an alphabet of twenty-four letters, all consonants (p. 38), from which all the alphabets of the world were eventually derived. (pp. 45-63.) The crucial step was the adoption of these characters to their own language by the Hebrews in Sinai — possibly by Moses himself. (p. 55.) For Sethe, the "missing link" was supplied by Petrie's discovery of the Siniatic script in 1905. (pp. 57-59.) From first to last "the entire developmental process of writing from pictures to letters can be viewed in the framework of natural science. . . ." (p. 66.)

To Sethe's famous study (based on a series of lectures, 1916-1934) S. Schott added an appendage in 1964. He notes that certain conclusions of Sethe are necessarily premature: the Sinai script has not yet been read with certainty. (p. 73.) And he cites the later study of H. Bauer, who, while agreeing that "the Egyptian origin of alphabetic writing is by no means in doubt" and that "anything as rare and marvelous . . . can hardly have originated twice,"[115] sees the all-important transition to the standard Semitic alphabet taking place not in Sinai but in Canaan to the north. (p. 74.) The split between the northern and southern schools still maintains simply because of a lack of evidence. (p. 75.) Schott wonders if it is necessary to go through all that rigamarole about the various stages of picture writing, for which no rigorous test is possible. (p. 76.) If we are dealing with a "rare and marvelous" invention, where must we draw the line as to the inventor's inspiration — can he not have invented the whole thing? The trouble with the evolutionary concept in Egyptian writing, Schott observes, is that the process unfortunately runs backwards. (p. 80.) The only way to account for the total lack of evidence for all the necessary long transitional phases, according to Schott, is the assumption that everything in those days was written on perishable material, a proposition which he finds untenable. (p. 81.)

And this is where we come in — without apologies, since everything is pretty much up in the air, and there is much to be said that has not been said. Since it is admittedly poverty of evidence that leaves us all in a box canyon, one would think that the scholars, if only in desperation, would venture to consider all of the evidence and not only that which comes under the heading of natural science. With all other ways blocked, it might be a good idea to try some of the neglected passages and ask some of the unasked questions. Here are a few:

1. How are we to account for yawning gaps in the evolutionary record, the complete absence of those transitional documents which should, according to the theory, be exceedingly numerous?

2. What about the *sudden* emergence, first of hieroglyphic writing and then of the Semitic alphabet, each in its perfectly developed form? Why in the case of admitted human inventions, the work of obvious genius, must we still assume long periods of gradual, accidental, unconscious development if no evidence for such development exists outside of the theory itself?

3. The oldest writing appears side by side with the oldest legends about writing. Wouldn't normal curiosity suggest a hearing of those legends? Greek tradition attributing the origin of the alphabet to Phoenicians has been thoroughly vindicated, no scholar denies that. Then why not examine other legends seriously, at least until something better turns up?

4. Why is it that the ancients are unanimous in attributing the origins of writing, including the alphabet, to a heavenly source?

5. Why are the earliest written documents always found in temples? Why do they always deal with religious matters?

6. Whence the unfailing identification of reading and writing with divination, that is, with interpreting the will of heaven?

7. "There is in the very nature of writing something marvelous and mysterious, which at all times has exercised a powerful attraction on thoughtful minds," writes Sethe. (p. 1.) Why, then, does he insist that the first true writing, the process of an unconscious, mindless, "automatic" process *"can* contain only very trivial matters"? (p. 73.) Could anything so "wunderbares und geheimnisvolles" (p. 1) have been invented in a humdrum way for purely humdrum purposes?

8. The supernatural power of the written symbol is as old as the marking of arrows. How can one comprehend the nature of the earliest writing without considering the miraculous or magical powers it exercised over man and beast?[116]

9. The first writing appears full-blown with the founding of the First Dynasty of Egypt, and in a form far too well knit and

consistent to have evolved, according to Schott. (p. 81.) What is the significance of writing as "the King's secret," the indispensable implement to government and authority?

10. Why is writing always a mystery, a guild secret, a kingly and priestly monopoly? "The really marvelous things that writing does, the astounding feats of thought-stimulation, thought-preservation, and thought-transmission . . . are of no interest to practical people: business records, private letters, school exercises, and the like are periodically consigned to the incinerator by clerks and merchants to whom eternal preservation and limitless transmission mean nothing."[117] Why must the latter be given the credit for inventing writing?

Let these ten questions suffice to justify our own speculations. Schott rejects Sethe's main thesis, that the Egyptians had a true alphabet, on the grounds that they mingled their alphabetic signs with syllabic and picture writing (the ideograms or determinatives that come at the end of words). But whereas the scribes make constant use of the twenty-four letters or single-consonant symbols and could not write without them, they often omit the other signs and seem to be playing with them. Schott maintains that only the Phoenician genius suddenly realized the possibility of doing without the syllabic and pictographic elements entirely; yet for ages the Egyptian scribes freely dispensed with them, now in one word and now in another — they knew it could be done. Pictures? Hieratic is as old as hieroglyphic, yet it contains no recognizable pictures, and demotic is anything but picture writing. Why retain pictures in such systems, since no one can recognize them? To an Egyptian who spoke the language, the alphabetic signs would be enough, just as the same signs, without vowels, are quite adequate for the reading of Semitic languages. Granted that some of the other signs are necessary, why is the whole massive and awkward machinery of both picture writing and syllabic writing retained to clutter up an economical and efficient alphabet? I would like to suggest that those who employed the "holy engravings" (for that is what *hieroglyphic* means) had not only their own people in mind but were thinking of others as well. One need only think of countless early funeral steles, consciously addressed to distant generations yet unborn. Without ideograms any learned Egyptian scribe could still read a text, but we today could never understand Egyptian without those pictures. Can it be that they are put in there for our benefit or the benefit of others like us? Likewise the eking out of the alphabetic signs with syllabic forms suggests a patient repetition and emphasis for the benefit of stumbling children. If Egyptian writing, because of its compound nature, is absolutely unique, perhaps its intention was also unique — to communicate more widely than the other languages. There is a good deal of evidence to support this theory, but we cannot go into it here. For many years learned men guessed at the meaning of hieroglyphics, and when some of them, like Horapollo, Kircher, or Seiffert, made some happy strikes, it was the pictographs that enabled them to do so and which could have put them on the right track, had they properly pursued them. In the 1880s Egyptologists of a number of lands, under the leadership of Professor Samuel Birch of Oxford, collected and interpreted all the then available hypocephali, and came up with a surprising unity of views, based on the symbolism alone. Today, as many experts are pointing out, it is doubtful whether anyone really understands any Egyptian religious text; there is still a long way to go, though much progress has been made. But the point is that the evidence is all there before our eyes and that the Egyptians have perhaps consciously supplied us with an overload of material, a safety factor to make sure that in the end the message would get across.

As for the Semitic alphabet and our own, derived from the Egyptian and often called the greatest of all inventions, the most wonderful thing about it is that it seems to have been devised for the express purpose of recording the scriptures — our scriptures. The objection today to Sethe's suggestion that Moses himself may well have been the inventor is that the alphabet is older than Moses and seems to have been at home at an earlier time up north — in Canaan. Sethe does not apologize for citing a Jewish writer, Eupolemos, in support of the claims put in for Moses (p. 55), and so it seems only fair to point out that by far the overwhelming authority of Jewish tradition favors not Moses but Abraham as the inventor of the alphabet, though some say he inherited it from Enoch. Of recent years a number of new alphabets have turned up in the Near East, dating to 2000-1500 B.C. and all "clearly the inventions of individuals."[118] Well, why not? Once one knows it can be done, one is free to invent one's own alphabet; the Deseret Alphabet is an impressive demonstration of that. But it would seem that "the Canaanitic alphabet, which has conquered the world," is the oldest of all, and as such "a witness to the ancient origin of the Torah."[119] Some think it may be as old as or even older than hieroglyphic itself.[120]

By the most cautious estimate of the situation, it is safe to say that the scriptures are not to be taken lightly. When scholars who

121

pride themselves on their freedom from any religious commitment are found seriously considering the genesis of the written word not only in holy writings but specifically in our own scriptures, it behooves us to pay attention. Whoever reads the standard works today has before him the words of God to men from the beginning, in witness of which the very letters on the page are but slightly conventionalized forms of the original symbols in which the message was conveyed. Merely as a cultural phenomenon the possibility is awe-inspiring, but that it should all go back to Israel and Egypt is too much to hope for. As members of the human race we are bound to approach the scriptures with new feelings of reverence and respect. They are the nearest approach and the best clue thus far discovered to the genesis of the written word.

NOTES

1. E. Bevan, *Hellenism and Christianity* (London: Allen and Unwin, 1921), p. 81.

2. J. Lear, in *Saturday Review*, 10 January 1970, p. 99, speaking in particular of population and pollution problems.

3. "What is happening now is . . . an abandonment of Renaissance-inspired approaches. . . . The new approach is quite different in spirit and method. It begins with a clear acknowledgment of the impossibility of reconstructing the original order of things human." (Lear, p. 101.)

4. Joseph Fielding Smith, *Answers to Gospel Questions* (Salt Lake City: The Church of Jesus Christ of Latter-day Saints, 1972), p. 4.

5. Early Jewish apocrypha emphasize the close association between Adam and the art of writing, a theme which cannot be handled in the scope of this paper. He is called "THE FOUR/LETTERED Adam" in the Sibylline Oracles 3:24, referring to the well-known Jewish doctrine that all things were created out of letters in the first place, the theme of the Sefer Yeshirah.

6. R. O. Faulkner, *The Ancient Egyptian Pyramid Texts* (Oxford: 1969), no. 510:1146.

7. That this Atum is to be identified with Adam has been suggested by leading Egyptologists: E. Lefebure, in *Biblical Archaeological Society Proceedings*, 9:174ff; A. Moret, *Histoire de l'Orient* (Paris: Presses Universitaires, 1945), 1:209ff.

8. J. Capart, "Exaltation du Livre," in *Chroniques d'Egypte*, 41 (1946):25.

9. W. Englebach, in *Annales du Service*, 42(1942):197

10. J. Capart, in *Egyptian Religion and the East*, 1(1930):117.

11. A. Gardiner, in *Journal of Egyptian Archaeology*, 2(1916):62.

12. A. Scharff and A. Moortgat, *Aegypten u. Vorderasien im Altertum* (Munich: F. Bruckmann, 1950), p. 22.

13. E. Baumgartel, *Prehistoric Egypt* (Oxford University: 1947), p. 48.

14. S. Piggott, *The Dawn of Civilization* (New York: McGraw-Hill Book Co., 1961), p. 127.

15. W. B. Emery, in *Scientific American* 197(1957):112.

16. K. Sethe, "Vom Bilde zum Buchstaben, Die Entstehungsgeschichte der Schrift," in *Untersuchungen zur Gesch. u. Altertumskunde,* (1946; reprint ed., Hildesheim: G. Olms, 1964), 12:27-28.

17. A. Scharff and A. Moortgat, p. 46.

18. K. Sethe, p. 20.

19. J. Friedrich, in *Archiv Orientalni*, 19(1951):251.

20. H. Frankfort, *Birth of Civilization* (London: 1957), p. 110.

21. H. Frankfort, pp. 106-107.

22. A. David, in *Archiv Orientalni*, 18(1950):51-54.

23. B. Hrozny, *Ancient History of Western Asia* (Prague: Artia, n.d.), pp. 116-117.

24. J. Jordan, in *Archiv für Orientforschung*, 6(1930-31):318.

25. P. Mordell, in *Jewish Quarterly Review*, 2(1911-12):575.

26. E. Massoulard, *Prehistoire et Protohistoire d'Egypte* (Paris: Institut d'Ethnologie, 1950), pp. 323ff.

27. H. Tur-Sinaï, in *Jewish Quarterly Review*, 41(1950-51):296.

28. K. Sethe, p. 20; H. Bauer, in *Der Alte Orient*, (1937), 36:12ff; J. Friedrich, p. 259; B. Hrozny, pp. 166ff. looks for the place of origin in northern Syria, northwestern Mesopotamia, or eastern Asia Minor.

29. K. Sethe, p. 46.

30. H. Schmitt, in *Ztschr. der Dt. Morgenländischen Gesellschaft*, 97(1947):82ff.

31. K. Sethe, p. 10.

32. E. Doblhofer, *Voices in Stone* (New York: Viking Press, 1961), p. 33.

33. E. Doblhofer, p. 22.

34. A. David, in *Archiv Orientalni*, 18(1950):49.

35. E. Doblhofer, p. 22.

36. K. Sethe, pp. 24-25.

37. K. Sethe, p. 9.

38. A. Gardiner, in *Journal of Near Eastern Studies*, 2(1943):64.

39. E. Doblhofer, p. 28, italics added.

40. K. Sethe, p. 28.

41. K. Sethe, p. 18.

42. *Journal of Near Eastern Studies*, 11(1953):288.

43. H. J. Lanzen, in *Archaeology*, 17(1964):125.

44. T. Burton-Brown, *Studies in Third Millennium History* (London: Luzac, 1946), p. 66.

45. S. Washburn, in *Scientific American*, September 1960, p. 63.

46. J. K. Feibleman, in *Social Forces*, 45(1967):331ff. *See also* K. P. Oakley, in *Advancement of Science*, 18(1948):422; L. Mumford, in *Technology and Culture*, 6(1965):375-381.

47. L. A. White, in *American Anthropologist*, 45(1943):338, 347.

48. *Man on Earth*, 1, no. 4(1965):6.

49. A. Hertz, in *l'Anthropologie,* 35(1925):6.

50. W. Sullivan, in *Science Digest* 58(1965):93.

51. C. S. Coon, *The Story of Man* (New York: Alfred A. Knopf, 1962), p. 64. The Leakeys would concur with his verdict.

52. W. F. Petrie, in *Smithsonian Report,* 1918, p. 568.

53. W. F. Petrie, pp. 568-569.

54. W. F. Petrie, p. 570.

55. A. von Mulinen, in *Ztschr. der Deutsch-Palästina-Verein,* 47:88, 90.

56. J. Smolian, in *Numen,* 10(1963):203, citing as examples fire, wheel, wagon, architecture, ships.

57. Joseph Fielding Smith, Comp., *Teachings of the Prophet Joseph Smith* (Salt Lake City: Deseret Book Co., 1947), p. 54.

58. N. H. Tur-Sinai, in *Archiv Orientalni,* 17(1949):433.

59. Hermes Trismegistus, 1, cited in T. Hopfner, *Fontes Historiae Religionis Aegyptiacae* (Bonn: 1922-24), p. 393.

60. H. Brugsch, in *Aegypt. Ztschr.,* 10(1872):1-4.

61. G. Widengren, *The Ascension of the Apostle and the Heavenly Book* (Uppsala University: Aarsskrift, 1950)7:21.

62. Joseph Fielding Smith, *Gospel Questions,* p. 5; Moses 7:67.

63. A. Jeremias, *Das Alte Testament im Lichte des Alten Orients* (Leipzig: 1916), 1:51.

64. Clement of Alexandria *Stromateis* 5. 4. 20.

65. H. Frankfort, p. 59.

66. G. Steindorff, *Egypt* (New York: J. J. Augustin, 1943), p. 24.

67. B. Hrozny, p. 36.

68. H. Frankfort, p. 59.

69. S. Piggott, p. 90.

70. H. Nibley, "The Arrow, the Hunter, and the State," *Western Political Quarterly,* 2(1949):329-339; *Improvement Era,* 58(May 1955):307-308.

71. H. Arntz, in *Ztschr. der Dt. Morgenländischen Gesellschaft* 97(1947):75.

72. Cornelius Nepos *Eumenes* 1.

73. *Improvement Era,* 58(May 1955):307ff.

74. K. Sethe, pp. 7-8.

75. S. Schott, *Mythe und Mythenbildung im alten Aegypten* (Leipzig: 1945), pp. 10-11.

76. *Western Political Quarterly,* 19(1966):603-7; 4(1951):235-238.

77. A. Scharff and A. Moortgat, p. 3; there is a striking passage in Syncellus, cited in T. Hopfner, p. 74.

78. Plotinus *Euneads* 2. 7.

79. Pap. Salt 825A in A. Gardiner, in *Journal of Egyptian Archaeology*, 24:167.

80. Heliodorus *Ethiop.* 1. 28; H. Grapow, *Hieroglyphen*, p. 13.

81. E. Drioton, *Le Livre du jour et de la nuit* (Cairo: Inst. Fr. Arch. Or., 1942), p. 86.

82. F. L. Griffith, *Stories of the High Priests of Memphis* (Oxford: 1900), p. 16.

83. Leo Koep, *Das himmlische Buch in Antike und Christentum* (Bonn: P. Hanstein, 1952); G. Widengren, *The Ascension of the Apostle and the Heavenly Book.*

84. K. Sethe, *Dramatische Texte zu altaeg. Mysterienspielen* (Leipzig: 1928), 1:5, 8.

85. M. Pieper, *Die Grosse Inschrift des Königs Nerferhotep* (Leipzig: 1929), pp. 6-11.

86. A. Moret, *Histoire de l'Orient* (Paris: Presses Universitaires, 1944), 1:96ff.

87. Pyramid Texts, no. 309, p. 490.

88. G. Widengren, pp. 10-11.

89. A. Moret, *Royaute Pharaonique* (Paris: 1902), p. 102.

90. W. Barta, in *Ztschr. f. aeg. Sprache*, 97(1971):7.

91. A. Gardiner, in *Journal of Egyptian Archaeology*, 24:168ff.

92. H. Zimmern, *Keilinschriften und das Alte Testament* (Berlin: 1903), p. 405.

93. Pyramid Texts, no. 267d.

94. B. Meissner, *Babylonien und Assyrien* (Heidelberg: 1927), 2:125.

95. E. Meyer, *Gesch. des Altertums*, 4, no. 1, 42ff.

96. A. L. Oppenheim, in *Orientalia*, 19(1950):155.

97. Pyramid Texts, no. 250:267.

98. J. Capart, in *Chroniques d'Egypte*, 22:25-27.

99. A. Gardiner, in *Journal of Egyptian Archaeology*, 1(1914):25.

100. A. Gardiner, in *Journal of Egyptian Archaeology*, 24:166.

101. A. Gardiner, in *Journal of Egyptian Archaeology*, 11:4.

102. W. K. G. Lambert, in *Journal of Cuneiform Studies*, 11:9.

103. H. Schaefer, in *Ztschr. f. aeg. Sprache*, 42(1905):72-75.

104. S. Schott, in "Nachwort" to K. Sethe, p. 71.

105. A. Gardiner, in *Journal of Egyptian Archaeology*, 24:158, cf. 174ff.

106. W. Otto, *Die Musen* (Darmstadt: Wissens. Buchgesellschaft, 1961).

107. F. M. Heichelheim, in *Epigraphica*, 12, no. 1-4 (1950):111-115.

108. We have treated the overall theme in *Western Political Quarterly* 4:226ff.

109. S. Schott, *Sieg über Seth*, p. 16.

110. S. Schott, in *Untersuchungen zur Geschichte u. Altertumskunde*, 12:83.

111. K. Sethe, pp. 2-3; the only motivating force was immediate practical need, pp. 41, 66.

112. K. Sethe, p. 32, speaking of Egyptian linear writing; p. 39, speaking of the Egyptian alphabet.

113. K. Sethe, pp. 41ff, Fig. 2.

114. K. Sethe, pp. 6, 11, 14-17. Thus the famous Mexican Catechism (p. 9, Fig. 12), could be deciphered by someone who had been told that it contains the Ten Commandments and who also knew what the Ten Commandments were; but for any outsider the whole thing might as well be written in Chinese. The numbers inserted hereafter in our text refer to pages of this study of Sethe's.

115. H. Bauer, pp. 12-13; cit. Schott, p. 75.

116. H. Nibley, "The Arrow, the Hunter and the State."

117. *Improvement Era*, 58(May 1955): 307-308.

118. A. Jirku, in *Ztschr. der Dt. Morgenländischen Gesellschaft*, 100:520.

119. H. Tur-Sinai, in *Jewish Quarterly Review*, 41:296.

120. P. Mordell, in *Jewish Quarterly Review*, 2:575.

The Sacrifice of Isaac

6

When I was in high school everybody was being very smart and emancipated and we always cheered the news that some scholar had discovered the original story of Samson or the Flood or the Garden of Eden in some ancient nonbiblical writing or tradition. It never occurred to anybody that these parallels might confirm rather than confound the scripture – for us the explanation was always perfectly obvious: the Bible was just a clumsy compilation of old borrowed superstitions. As comparative studies broke into the open field parallels began piling up until they positively became an embarrassment. Everywhere one looked there were literary and mythological parallels. Trying to laugh them off as "parallelomania" left altogether too much unexplained. In the 1930s English scholars started spreading out an overall pattern that would fit almost all ancient religions. Finally men like Graves and Santillana confront us with huge agglomerations of somehow connected matter that sticks together in one loose, gooey mass, compacted of countless resemblances that are hard to explain but equally hard to deny. Where is this taking us? Will the sheer weight and charge of the stuff finally cause it to collapse on itself in a black hole, leaving us none the wiser? We could forego the obligation of explaining it and content ourselves with contemplating and admiring the awesome phenomenon for its own sake were it not for one thing – Joseph Smith spoils everything.

A century of bound periodicals in the stacks will tell the enquiring student when scholars first became aware of the various elements that make up the super-pattern, but Joseph Smith knew about them all, and before the search ever began he showed how they are interrelated. In the documents he has left us, you will find the central position of the Coronation, the tension between Matriarchy and Patriarchy, the arcane discipline for transmitting holy books through the ages, the pattern of cycles and dispensations, the nature of the Mysteries, the great tradition of the Rekhabites or sectaries of the desert, the fertility rites and sacrifices of the New Year with the humiliation of the kind and the role of substitute, etc. Where did he get the stuff? It would have been convenient for some mysterious Rabbi to drop in on the penniless young farmer when he needs some high-class research, but George Foote Moore informs us that "so far as evidence goes," apocalyptic things of that sort were "without countenance from the exponents of what we may call normal Judaism."

Take for example the tradition that the sacrifice of Isaac merely followed the scenario of an earlier sacrifice of Abraham himself. Nobody has heard of that today – until you tell them about it, when, of course, they shrug their shoulders and tell you that they knew about it all along. Which prompts me to recommend a simple rule for the ingenuous investigator: always ask the expert to tell you the story first. I have never found anyone who could tell me the Joseph Smith Abraham story, and the apocrypha records which report it have all been published since his day. Today the story of Abraham casts a new light on the story of Isaac. Here is some of it.

W hile it is the unique and different in human experience that most engages the modern fancy, the Egyptian was intrigued by the repeated and characteristic events of life. The most important of these events were ritualized, just as we ritualize the inauguration of a President or the Rose Bowl game, repeating the same plot year after year with different actors. Hence, if Abraham and Sarah went through the same routine with King Abimelech as with Pharaoh, it is not because either or both stories are fabrications, as scholars have so readily assumed, but because both kings were observing an accepted pattern of behavior in dealing with eminent strangers. Likewise, if Abraham was put on an altarbed like dozens of others, it was because such treatment of important guests had become standard procedure for combating the drought prevailing in the world at that time.

Repeating patterns of history suggest ritual as a means of dramatizing and controlling events, but they exist in their own right — they are not invented by men. In the exodus of the Saints from Nauvoo, thousands of people suddenly found themselves moving west in the dead of winter amid scenes of some confusion. But within three days the entire host was organized into twelve main groups — one under each of the apostles — and companies of fifty and one hundred. Instantly and quite unintentionally the order of Israel in the wilderness and the Sons of Light in the Judean desert was faithfully duplicated. A student of history three thousand years from now might well reject the whole account as mythical, since it so obviously reduplicated an established pattern.

To one who is aware of the interplay of pattern and accident in history, the stories of the sacrifice of Isaac and of Sarah are perfect companion pieces to the drama of Abraham on the altar. Take first the case of Isaac, who is just another Abraham: a well-known tradition has it that he was in the exact image of his father,[1] so exact, in fact, that until Abraham's hair turned white, there was absolutely no way of distinguishing between the two men in spite of their difference of age.[2] "Abraham and Isaac are bound to each other with extraordinary intimacy," writes a recent commentator; " . . . the traditions regarding the one are not to be distinguished from those concerning the other," e.g., both men leave home to wander, both go to Egypt, both are promised endless posterity and certain lands as an inheritance.[3] What has been overlooked is the truly remarkable resemblance between Isaac on the altar and Abraham on the altar.

First, in both stories there is much made of the preparatory gathering of wood for a "holocaust" that never takes place. Abraham is commanded, "Take now thy son . . . and offer him . . . for a *burnt* offering." (Genesis 22:2. Italics added.) "Behold, I offer thee now as a holocaust," he cries in the Pseudo-Philo.[4] Accordingly, he "bound Isaac his son, and laid him upon the altar on the wood,"[5] sometimes described as a veritable tower, just like the structure that "Nimrod" had built for Abraham.[6] And while the Midrash has Isaac carrying the wood of the sacrifice "as one carries a cross on his shoulder,"[7] so Abraham before him "took the wood for the burnt offering and carried it, just as a man carries his cross on his shoulder."[8] According to one tradition, the sacrifice was actually completed and Isaac turned to ashes.[9] On the other hand, when the princes announced their intention of putting Abraham in a fiery furnace, he is said to have submitted willingly: "If there is any sin of mine so that I be burned, the will of God be done."[10] Indeed, the Hasidic version has it that "Abraham our father offered up his life for the sanctification of the Name of God and threw himself into the fiery furnace. . . ."[11] The famous play on the words "Ur of the Chaldees" and "Fire [ur] of the Chaldees" was probably suggested by these traditions — not the other way around, since Isaac escapes from the flames in the same way that Abraham does; i.e., the original motif requires a fire, not a city called Ur.

For all the emphasis on sacrificial fire, it is the knife that is the instrument of execution in the attempted offerings of Abraham and Isaac: "And Abraham stretched forth his hand, and took the knife to slay his son." (Genesis 22:10.) It was always the custom to slaughter (*zabakh*) the victim and then burn the remains to ashes; the blood must be shed and the offering never struggles in the flames. Many stories tell how the knife was miraculously turned aside as it touched the neck of the victim, whether Abraham or Isaac: suddenly the throat is protected by a collar of copper, as it turns to marble, or the knife becomes soft lead.[12] But in the usual account it is dashed from the hand of the officiant by an angel who is visible to the victim on the altar but not to the priest.[13] If the wood under Abraham and Isaac was never ignited, neither did the knife ever cut.

Being bound on the altar, Abraham, as the Book of Abraham and the legends report, prayed fervently for deliverance. Exactly such a prayer was offered as Isaac lay on the altar, but though in this case it was Isaac who was in mortal peril, it was again Abraham who uttered the prayer for deliverance: "May He who answered *Abraham* on Mt. Moriah, answer you, and may He listen to the voice of your cry this day."[14] And just as the angels appealed to God when they saw Abraham on the altar, so later when they saw Isaac in the same situation they cried out in alarm: "What will happen to the covenant with Abraham to 'Establish my covenant with Isaac,' for the slaughtering knife is set upon his throat. The tears of the angels fell upon the knife, so that it could not cut Isaac's throat. . . ."[15] It is still *Abraham* for whom the angels are concerned, even though it is the life of Isaac that is in intimate danger. Everything seems to hark back to the original sacrifice — that of Abraham. Thus, at the moment that Isaac was freed from the altar, "God renewed his promises to *Abraham*,"[16] the very promises that had been given at the moment of Abraham's own deliverance (Abraham 1:16, 19); while he in turn prayed to God "that when the children of Isaac come to a time of distress, thou mayest remember on their behalf the binding of Isaac their father, and loose and forgive their sins and deliver them from all distress."[17] Thus Abraham's prayer for deliverance is handed down to all his progeny.

In both sacrifice stories an angel comes to the rescue in immediate response to the prayer, while at the same time the voice of God is heard from heaven. This goes back to Genesis 22:11f, 15-18, where "the angel of the Lord" conveys to Abraham the words of God speaking in the first person: "And the angel of the Lord . . . said, By myself have I sworn, saith the Lord. . . ." As the Rabbis explained it, "God makes a sign to the Metatron, who in turn calls out to Abraham . . ."[18] or "the Almighty hastened to send his voice from above, saying: Do not slay thy son."[19] That this complication is ancient and not invented by the doctors, whom it puzzled, is indicated in the "lion-couch" situation in which, as we have seen, the appearance of the heavenly messenger is accompanied by the voice of the Lord of all, which is heard descending from above. It is Abraham who establishes the standard situation: how many times in his career did he find himself in mortal danger only to pray and be delivered by an angel? An angel came to rescue the infant in the cave when his mother had given him up for dead; the same angel came to rescue the child Abraham from the soldiers, saying, "Do not fear, for the Mighty One will deliver thee from the hand of thine enemies!"[20] The same angel delivered him first from starvation in prison and then from death in the flames. So it is not surprising that the angel who comes to rescue Isaac puts a stop to the proceedings by calling out "Abraham, Abraham" (Genesis 22:11f), while Isaac remains passive throughout.[21]

One of the strangest turns of the Abraham story was surely Abraham's refusal to be helped by the angel, with its striking Egyptian parallel.[22] Surprisingly enough, the same motif occurs in the sacrifice of Isaac. For according to the Midrash, God ordered Michael, "Delay not, hasten to Abraham and tell him not to do the deed!" And Michael obeyed: "Abraham! Abraham! What art thou doing?" To this the Patriarch replied, "Who tells me to stop?" "A messenger sent from the Lord!" says Michael. But Abraham answers, "The Almighty Himself commanded me to offer my son to Him — only He can countermand the order: I will not hearken to any messenger!" So God must personally intervene to save Isaac.[23] Such a very peculiar twist to the story — the refusal of angelic assistance in the moment of supreme danger — is introduced by way of explaining that it is God and not the angel who delivers; so in the Book of Abraham: "... and the angel of his presence stood by me and immediately unloosed my bands; And his voice was unto me: Abraham, Abraham, behold, my name is Jehovah, and I have heard thee, and have come down to deliver thee...." (Abraham 1:15-16.) Everything indicates that this is the old authentic version.

In both sacrifices the role of Satan is the same, as he does his best at every step to frustrate the whole business. As the man in black silk pleaded with Abraham on the altar to be sensible, yield to the king, and so save his own life, even so he addresses him at the second sacrifice: "Are you crazy — killing your own son!" To which Abraham replied, "For that purpose he was born." Satan then addressed Isaac: "Are you going to allow this?" And the young man answered, "I know what is going on, and I submit to it."[24] First Satan had done everything in his power to block their progress on the road to the mountain,[25] and then as a venerable and kindly old man he had walked along with them, piously and reasonably pointing out that a *just* God would not demand the sacrifice of a son.[26] It was even Satan, according to some, who dashed the knife from Abraham's hand in the last moment.[27] In both stories it is Satan who suggests the sacrifice in the first place,[28] and then does everything in his power to keep it from being carried out. Why is that? The explanation is given both times: Mastema suggests the supreme sacrifice in order to discredit Abraham with the angels, for he is sure that the prophet will back out in the end. As soon as it becomes perfectly clear, therefore, that Abraham is *not* backing out, Satan becomes alarmed, and to keep from losing his bet he wants to call the whole thing off.

In a recent and important study, A. R. Rosenberg has pointed out that the sacrifice of Isaac has its background in the Canaanitish rite of the substitute king, which rite was "celebrated in both Persia and Babylonia in connection with the acronical rising of Sirius ... [as Saturn] the god who demanded human sacrifices."[29] We have already noted that the worship of Sirius played a conspicuous part, according to the Book of Abraham 1:9, in the rites involving the sacrifice of Abraham. In connection with the offering of Isaac, Rosenberg lays great emphasis on a passage from the Book of Enoch: "... the Righteous One shall arise from sleep and walk in the paths of righteousness," the figure on the altar being the Righteous One.[30] At once we think of "the weary one" or "the sleeping one" who arises from the lion-couch. What confirms the association is the report that "as Isaac was about to be sacrificed, the *Arelim* began to roar in heaven."[31] For the Arelim are "the divine lions,"[31] whose role in Egyptian sacrificial rites we have already explained. Thus, even the lion motif is not missing from our two sacrifice stories.

The close resemblance between the sacrifices of Abraham and Isaac, far from impugning the authenticity of either story, may well be viewed as a confirmation of both. J. Finkel points out that there are many close parallels to the story of the sacrifice of Isaac in ancient literature, and that these are "overwhelmingly ritualistic,"[32] that is, they belong to a category of events that follow a set pattern and yet *really do happen.* "On the mountain of the Temple Abraham offered Isaac his son," according to a Targum, "and on this mountain — of the Temple — the glory of the Shekhinah of the Lord was revealed to him."[33] What happened there was the type and shadow of the temple ordinances to come, which were in turn the type and shadow of a greater sacrifice. The one sacrifice prefigures the other, being, in the words of St. Ambrose, "less perfect, but still of the same order."[34] Isaac is a type: "Any man," says the Midrash, "who acknowledges that there are two worlds, is *an* Isaac," and further explains, "Not *Isaac* but *in Isaac* — that is, a portion of the seed of Isaac, not all of it. . . ."[35] In exactly the same sense Abraham too is a type: " . . . and in thee (that is, in thy Priesthood) and *in* thy seed . . . shall all the families of the earth be blessed." (Abraham 2:11. Italics added.) Far from being disturbed by resemblances, we should find them most reassuring. Is it surprising that the sacrifice of Isaac looked both forward and back, as "Isaac thought of himself as the type of offerings to come, while Abraham thought of himself as atoning for the guilt of Adam," or that "as Isaac was being bound on the altar, the spirit of Adam, the first man, was being bound with him"?[36] It was natural for Christians to view the sacrifice of Isaac as a type of the Crucifixion, yet it is the Jewish sources that comment most impressively on the sacrifice of the Son. When at the creation of the world the angels asked, "What is man that Thou shouldest remember him?" God replied: "You shall see the father slay his son, and the son consenting to be slain, to sanctify my name."[37] When Abraham performed "the various sacrifices that should once be brought in the Temple, to atone for the sins of Israel," he was shown the whole history of the world, and the coming of the Messiah and the resurrection, and how in the end his own father would be saved by ministrations on behalf of the dead.[38] So, as Joseph Smith has told us, Abraham was perfectly aware of the entire plan of salvation and of his place in it.[39]

The importance of the sacrifice of Isaac as a type of atonement is brought out in many references to the cosmic significance of the ram which took Isaac's place. From its horn was made the *shofar* which was to be blown on New Year's Day forever after to remind the people "of the offering of Isaac as an atonement for Israel."[40] According to Rabbi Eliezer, its left horn announces the redemption of Israel at the New Year, while its right horn will be the trumpet that announces the Millennium.[41] Every part of the ram figures in the history of Israel's salvation: Its ashes form the foundation of the inner altar, its sinews make the ten strings of David's harp, its skin is Elijah's girdle, one of its horns is blown on Sinai and the other for the final gathering of all Israel.[42] Like the altar of Isaac, which is supposed to have been the same one on which Adam, Cain, Abel, and Noah sacrificed before and on which David and Solomon were to make offering thereafter,[43] the ram is one of those symbols that binds all times, places, and dispensations together in a single unified plan.

But if Isaac is a type of the Messiah as "the Suffering Servant," Abraham is no less so. Even while he labors to minimize any spiritual resemblance between Christ and Abraham, M. Soggin reluctantly confesses that the historical and literary parallels between the two are most conspicuous.[44] R. Graves has called attention to the various signs and characteristics that show that Abraham himself was a type of the sacred victim as a substitute offering for a king, just as Isaac was.[45] An important point of resemblance between the two sacrifices is the complete freedom of will with which the victim submits. "I know what is going on," says Isaac on the altar, "and I submit to it!"[46] In time the main significance of the Akedah, the binding of Isaac, was on the freewill offering of the victim for the atonement of Israel; we are even told that Isaac at the age of thirty-seven actually "asked to be bound on the Day of Atonement and Abraham functioned as the High Priest at the altar."[47] In the same way, a great deal is made of Abraham's willingness: "I was with thee," says God in the Midrash, "when thou didst willingly offer for my name's sake to enter the fiery furnace."[48] When Abraham refused to escape though Prince Jectan opened the way for him, the Prince told him, "Your blood will be upon your own head," to which the hero cheerfully agreed.[49] According to one tradition, Abraham had the choice of handing over to the king some sort of token or seal (a brick with his name on it?) or giving up his life, and he deliberately chose the latter.[50] The Hasidic teaching was that "Abraham our father offered up his life . . . and threw himself into the fiery furnace."[51] There need be no sense of competition between the merits of father and son here — others too have made the supreme sacrifice — but the significance of Abraham's test on the altar, as R. J. Loewe points out, "is that Abraham in Nimrod's furnace is the *first* of those who willingly gave up his life for the sanctification of the divine Name."[52] This assigns a very important place in the history of the Atonement to the drama depicted in the Book of Abraham and strongly attests its authenticity.

In the Egyptian versions of the "lion-couch" drama, the resurrection motif was paramount. The sacrifices of Isaac and Abraham, apart from typifying the Atonement, were also foreshadowings of the Resurrection. There are persistent traditions in each case that the victim actually was put to death, only to be resurrected on the spot. We have seen in the Abraham stories how, when no knife could cut his throat, he was catapulted into the fire, which thereupon was instantly transformed into a blooming bower of delicious flowers and fruits amid which Abraham sat enjoying himself in angelic company.[53] This at once calls to mind the image found in numerous (and very early) Oriental seals and murals of the revived or resurrected king sitting beneath an arbor amid the delights of the feast at the New Year.[54] St. Jerome cites a Jewish belief that Abraham's rescue from the altar was the equivalent of a rebirth or resurrection.[55] It is Abraham who leads out in the resurrection: "After these things," says the Testament of Judah (25:1), "shall Abraham and Isaac and Jacob arise unto life, and I (Judah) and my brethren shall be chiefs of the tribes of Israel."

The stories of the resurrection of Isaac are quite explicit. As Rabbi Eliezer puts it, "When the blade touched his neck, the soul of Isaac fled and departed . . . but at the words 'lay not thy hand . . .' his soul returned to his body and he stood upon his feet and knew that in this manner the dead in the future would be quickened. And he said: Blessed art thou, O Lord, who quickeneth the dead."[56] Another tradition is that "the tears of the angels fell upon the knife, so that it could not cut Isaac's throat, but for terror his soul escaped from him" — he died on the altar.[57] Another has it that as the knife touched his throat "his life's spirit departed — his body became like ashes," i.e., he actually became a burnt offering;[58] or, as G. Vermes puts it, "though he did not die, scripture credits Isaac with having died and his ashes having lain upon the altar."[59] But he only dies in order to prefigure the Resurrection, for immediately God sent the dew of life "and Isaac received his spirit again, while the angels joined in a chorus of praise: Praised be the Eternal, thou who hast given life to the dead!"[60] In another account God orders Michael to rush to the rescue: "Why standest thou here? Let him not be slaughtered! Without delay Michael, anguish in his voice, cried out: 'Abraham! Abraham! Lay not thy hand upon the lad. . . .' At once Abraham left off from Isaac, who returned to life, revived by the heavenly voice."[61] Isaac is a symbol of revival and renewal — "Is any thing too hard for the Lord?" (Genesis 18:14.) At his birth, we are told, both Abraham and Sarah regained their youth.[62] And "just as God gave a child to Abraham and Sarah when they had lost all hope, so he can restore Jerusalem."[63] When R. Graves surmises that "Abraham according to the custom would renew his youth by the sacrifice of his first-born son," he is referring to a custom which Abraham fervidly denounced but which was nonetheless observed in his own family, according to the Book of Abraham (1:30), which reports that his own father "had determined against me, to take away my life." The famous Strassburg Bestiary begins with a vivid scene of the sacrifice of Isaac followed by the drama of the sacrificial death and resurrection of the fabulous phoenix-bird, the Egyptian and early Christian symbol of the Resurrection.[64]

Why the insistence on the death and resurrection of Isaac? Because a perfect sacrifice must be a *complete* sacrifice, and the rabbinical tradition, especially when it was directed against the claims of the Christians, insisted that the sacrifice of Isaac was the perfect sacrifice, thus obviating the need for the atoning death of Christ. "Though the idea of the death and resurrection of Isaac was generally rejected by rabbinic Judaism," writes R. A. Rosenberg, still the proposition was accepted "that Isaac was 'the perfect sacrifice,' the atonement offering that brings forgiveness of sins through the ages."[65] Accordingly, the blood of the paschal lamb is considered to be the blood of *Isaac*,[65] and according to some Jewish sectaries the real purpose of the Passover is to celebrate the offering of Isaac rather than the deliverance from Egypt.[66] It wasn't only the sectaries, however: "In Rabbinical writings all sacrifice is a memorial of Isaac's self-oblation."[67]

But the stories of Isaac's "resurrection" are scattered, conflicting, and poorly attested, however persistent, and this leads to serious difficulty: "The main problem was, of course," writes Vermes, "the obvious fact that Isaac did not actually die on the altar."[68] The whole biblical account, in fact, focuses on the dramatic *arrest* of the action at its climax — "Lay *not* thine hand upon the lad." (Genesis 22:12. Italics added.) It has often been claimed, in fact, that the story of Isaac's sacrifice really records the abolition of human sacrifice, when Abraham decides it will not be necessary.[69] But the validity of the sacrifice, according to the Rabbis, lay in Isaac's complete *willingness* to be offered, which has been called "the most profound and anomalous religious concept ever known to the human mind," being nothing less than "the cornerstone of the whole Jewish theology of the love of God."[70] Abraham may have known that Isaac was in no real danger when he said, with perfect confidence, "My son, God will provide himself a lamb for a burnt offering" (Genesis 22:8), and when without equivocation he told the two young men who escorted them to the mountain: " . . . I and the lad will go yonder and worship, and come again to you" (Genesis 22:5); Isaac did not know it — it was he who was being tested. But Abraham had already been tested in the same way; if "Isaac . . . offered himself at the Binding," so before his day the youthful "Abraham . . . threw himself into the fiery furnace. . . . If we follow in their footsteps they will stand and intercede for us on the holy and awesome day."[71] Isaac was being tested even as other saints are tested, since, as Rabbi Eliezer puts it, "the testing of the righteous here below . . . is essential to the *plan* of the universe."[72] The Midrash, in fact, "strongly emphasized the parallelism between the sacrifice of Isaac and the willing martyrdom of *other* heroes and heroines," including many who suffered terribly painful deaths.[73] Isaac, in short, belongs to the honorable category of those who were willing to be "partakers of Christ's sufferings," as all the saints and martyrs have been. (1 Peter 4:13.)

The second problem raised by the claim that Isaac's sacrifice was the ultimate atonement is that the shedding of blood did *not* cease with it: "If Isaac's sacrifice atones," asks Vermes, "why was further daily sacrifice in the Temple necessary?"[74] Circumcision no less than the Akedah "remains a never-ceasing atonement for Israel, being performed by Abraham himself and 'on the Date of Atonement,' and upon the spot on which the altar was later to be erected in the Temple,"[75] but for all that, no one claims that all the law is fulfilled in it. "Students of Christian origins have come increasingly to realize," writes Rosenberg, a Jew, " . . . that the sacrifice of Isaac was to be reenacted by the 'new Isaac,' who, like the old, was a 'son of God.' "[76] The early Christian teaching was that, as he was about to sacrifice his son on the mountain, Abraham "saw Christ's day and yearned for it. There he saw the Redemption of Adam and rejoiced, and it was revealed to him, that the Messiah would suffer in the place of Adam."[77] But the old Isaac, called in the Targum "the Lamb of Abraham,"[78] neither suffered sacrificial death nor put an end to the shedding of blood. His act was an earnest of things to come, and that puts it on the same level as the sacrifice of Abraham.

This explains, we believe, the absence of the story of Abraham on the altar from the pages of the Old Testament. G. Vermes points out that whereas in the biblical version of the sacrifice of Abraham "the principal actors were Abraham and God," other versions, even in very early times, "somewhat surprisingly shift the emphasis and focus their interest on the person of Isaac."[79] Whatever the reason for the shift, it was a very emphatic one: " . . . the Binding of Isaac was thought to have played a unique role in the whole economy of the salvation of Israel, and to have a permanent redemptive effect on behalf of its people."[80] It completely supplanted the earlier episode of the sacrifice of Abraham on the ancient principle that "the later repetition of an event . . . causes the earlier occurrence to be forgotten."[81] The principle is nowhere better illustrated than in the story of Abraham himself: the names Abram and Sarai are unknown to most Christians, because of the explicit command, "Do *not* call Sarah Sarai" anymore; "do *not* call Abraham Abram" — those were once their names, but no more![81] When Israel finally returns to God and goes to Abraham for instruction, we are told, instead of teaching them himself, he will refer them to Isaac, who will in turn pass them on to Jacob and so on down to Moses — it is from the *latest* prophet of the latest dispensation that the people receive instruction.[82] On this principle, the only words of the Father in the New Testament are those which introduce his Son and turn all the offices of the dispensation over to him. (Matthew 3:17, 17:5.)

It was necessary to overshadow and even supplant the story of Abraham's sacrifice by that of Isaac if Isaac were to have any stature at all with posterity. Scholars long declared both Isaac and Jacob, imitating Abraham in everything, to be mere shadow figures, mythical creatures without any real personalities of their own. Jacob, to be sure, has some interesting if not altogether creditable experiences, but what is left for Isaac? The three stand before us as a trio: "Abraham instituted the morning prayer, Isaac the noon prayer, and Jacob the evening prayer," i.e., they all share in establishing a single body of rites and ordinances.[83] One does not steal the glory of the other. Great emphasis is laid by the rabbis on the necessary equality of merit and glory between Abraham and Isaac,[84] while each emphasizes some special aspect of the divine economy: Abraham was the Great One, Jacob the Little One, and Isaac who came in between was "the servant of Jehovah who was delivered from the bonds of his Master."[85] The special emphasis on Isaac is as the sacrificial victim. If his sacrifice was "an imperfect type," it was still more perfect than the earlier sacrifice of Abraham on a pagan altar, and in every way it qualified to supersede it. Though it was an equal test for both men, "purged and idealized by the *trial* motivation,"[86] the second sacrifice was the true type of the Atonement. In the long and detailed history of Abraham the story of the sacrifice in Canaan could safely be omitted in deference to the nobler repetition, which, while it added no less to the glory of Abraham, preserves a sense of proportion among the patriarchs.

Abraham gets as much credit out of the sacrifice of Isaac as he does from his own adventure on the altar — he had already risked his own life countless times; how much dearer to him in his old age was the life of his only son and heir! And since the two sacrifices typify the same thing, nothing is lost to Abraham and much is gained for Isaac by omitting the earlier episode from the Bible. But that episode left an indelible mark in the record. The learned Egyptologist who in 1912 charged Joseph Smith with reading the sacrifice of *Isaac* into Facsimile No. 1 and the story of Abraham was apparently quite unaware that ancient Jewish writers of whom Joseph Smith knew nothing told the same story that he did about Abraham on the altar. The important thing for the student of the Book of Abraham is that the sacrifice of Abraham was remembered — and vividly recalled in nonbiblical sources — as a historical event. This makes it almost certain that it *was* a real event, for nothing is less probable than that the Jews would at a very early time *invent* a story which, while adding little or nothing to the supreme glory of Abraham, would do definite damage to Isaac's one claim to fame. If the binding on the altar — the *Akedah* — was to be the "unique glory of Isaac," it was entirely in order to quietly drop the earlier episode of Abraham that anticipates and overshadows it, just as it is right and proper to forget that the hero was once called Abram.

Recent studies of the sacrifice of Isaac emphasize as its most important aspect the principle of substitution, which is also basic in the sacrifice of Abraham. As J. Finkel expressed it, "evidently the primary aim of the story (of Isaac) was to give divine sanction to the law of substitution."[87] Isaac was not only saved *by* a substitute, but he himself was substituting for another. "A ram by the name of Isaac went at the head of Abraham's herd. Gabriel took him and brought him to Abraham, and he sacrificed him instead of his son."[88] As he did so, Abraham said, "Since I brought my son to you as a sacrificial animal be in thine eye as if it were my son lying on the altar."[89]

Accordingly, "whatsoever Abraham did by the altar, he exclaimed, and said, 'This is instead of my son, and may it be considered before the Lord in place of my son.' And God accepted the sacrifice of the ram, and it was accounted as though it had been Isaac."[90] Himself noble, Isaac was saved by the substitution of "a noble victim."[91]

But, more important, he himself was a substitute. "In Jewish tradition," writes A. R. Rosenberg, "Isaac is the prototype of the 'Suffering Servant,' bound on the altar as a sacrifice."[92] Rosenberg has shown that the title of Suffering Servant was used in the Ancient East to designate "the substitute *king*" — the noble victim. Accordingly, the "new Isaac" mentioned in Maccabees 13:12 must be "a 'substitute king' who dies that the people might live."[93] The starting point in Rosenberg's investigation is Isaiah 52:13 to 53:12, which "seems to constitute a portion of a ritual drama centering about a similar humiliation, culminating in death, of a 'substitute' for the figure of the king of the Jews." If we examine these passages, we find that they fit the story of Abraham's sacrifice even better than that of Isaac.

Thus beginning with Isaiah 52:13 we see the Suffering Servant raised up on high, reminding us of the scene from the Midrash (Midr. Rab. 43:5): " . . . they cut cedar and made a great altar (*bemah*) and placed him on it on high and they bowed down in mockery before him and said to him, 'Hear us, Lord!' and the like. They said to him, 'Thou art King over us! Thou art exalted above us! Thou art a god over us!' But he said to them, 'The world does not lack its king, nor does it lack its God!' " (Midr. Rab. 43:5.) Here Abraham both rejects the office and denounces the rites. The Midrash also indicates that the rites of Isaac were matched by heathen practices, his Akedah resembling the binding of the princes of the heathen, since every nation possesses at its own level "a 'prince' as its guardian angel and patron." (Midr. Rab. 56:5.)

The next verse (52:14), the picture of the Suffering Servant with "visage . . . marred," recalls Abraham led out to sacrifice after his long suffering in prison while the princes and the wise men mock. Verse 15, telling of the kings who shut their mouths in amazement, recalls the 365 kings who were astounded to behold Abraham's delivery from the altar. In 53:1 the arm of the Lord is revealed, as it is unbeknownst to the others in the delivery of Abraham. (Cf. Abraham 1:17.) Isaiah 53:2 emphasizes the drought motif, which, as we have seen, is never missing from the rites of the substitute king. In verses 3 to 8 the Suffering Servant is beaten that *we* may be healed — a substitute for all of us. In verse 8 he is "taken from prison and from judgment" to be "cut off out of the land of the living," exactly as Abraham was according to the traditions. Verse 9 reminds us of Abraham in wicked Canaan, and verse 10 — "it pleased the Lord to bruise him..." — recalls the description of Abraham as a son being mercilessly beaten by a loving father but never complaining. Finally the reward: Because his soul was placed as an offering, he shall see his progeny, his days shall be lengthened, and he shall prosper greatly (see verses 10-12) — all "because he hath poured out his soul unto death..." (verse 12). Such was the reward of Abraham, with the assurance also that by the knowledge gained he would be able to sanctify others. (See verse 11.) In the end the Suffering Servant becomes the great intercessor: "he bare the sin of many, and made intercession for the transgressors" (53:12), just as Abraham does, as the great advocate for sinners living and dead. Thus Isaiah 52:13-53:12, while vividly recalling the suffering of Isaac, is an even better description of Abraham on the altar.

The sacrifice of the substitute king is found all over the ancient world. According to Rosenberg, the rite was "celebrated in both Persia and Babylonia in connection with the acronical rising of Sirius," sometimes identified in this connection with Saturn, "the god who demanded human sacrifice."[94] The Book of Abraham has already apprised us of the importance of Sirius (Shagre-el) in the sacrificial rites of the Plain of Olishem, and it even labors the point that human sacrifice was the normal order of things in Canaan in Abraham's day. We have taken the position from the first that Abraham was put on the altar as a substitute for the king, an idea first suggested by the intense rivalry between the two, as indicated both in the legends and in the Book of Abraham. Rosenberg's study of the sacrifice of Isaac concludes that in the earliest accounts of that event "both the Jewish and Christian traditions stem ultimately from the ancient Canaanite cult of Jerusalem, in which periodically the King, or a substitute for the King, had to be offered for a sacrifice."[95] It was to just such a cult — in Canaan — that we traced the sacrifice of Abraham, and that is why we have been at such pains to point out the close and thorough-going resemblances between the two: they are essentially the same rite and have the same background. If the one reflects "the ancient Canaanite cult" in which "a substitute for the King had to be offered," so does the other. Rosenberg says the sacrifice of Isaac most certainly goes back to that cult, and the Book of Abraham tells us flatly that the sacrifice of Abraham does. Certainly the Abraham story in its pagan setting is much nearer to the original substitute-king rite in all its details than is the Isaac story, which is a sizable step removed from it. The substitute sacrifice is a red thread that runs through the early career of the prophet: The life of the infant Abraham when his brother Haran substituted a slave child to be killed in his place;[96] then Haran himself died for Abraham in the flames;[96] and then Abraham was saved from the lion-couch when the priest was smitten in his stead (Abraham 1:17, 29); finally his life was saved by his wife Sarah, who was willing to face death to rescue him again from the lion-couch. This last much-misunderstood episode deserves closer attention.

NOTES

1. B. Beer, *Leben Abraham's*, p. 47; L. Ginzberg, *Legends of the Jews*, Vol. 1, p. 262; for Rashi's explanation, G. Abrahams, *The Jewish Mind*, p. 51, n. 1.

2. M. J. bin Gorion, *Die Sagen der Juden*, I, 325.

3. H. Seebass, *Erzvater Israels*, p. 105.

4. G. Vermes, *Scripture and Tradition in Judaism* (Leiden: Brill, 1961), pp. 199f for text.

5. *Ibid.*, p. 209.

6. Beer, *op. cit.*, pp. 66, 182.

7. I. Levi, in *Rev. des Etudes Juives*, Vol. 59 (1912), p. 169.

8. Bin Gorion, II, 300.

9. Beer, p. 67.

10. Pseudo-Philo, VI, 11. Cf. Isaac's speeches in Beer, p. 65.

11. N. N. Glatzer, *Faith and Knowledge*, p. 178.

12. Bin Gorion, II, 303.

13. Beer, p. 67: Sometimes Abraham lets the knife fall, and sometimes it is not the angel but Satan who dashes it from his hand. Cf. bin Gorion, II, p. 287.

14. Vermes, p. 195.

15. Ginzberg, *L. J.*, Vol. 1, p. 281.

16. Pseudo-Philo, 32:2-4; complete Latin text in Vermes, pp. 199-200.

17. Ginzberg, *loc. cit.*; see next note.

18. Targums cited at length in Vermes, pp. 149-50.

19. Pseudo-Philo, *loc. cit.*

20. Maase Abraham, in Jellineck, *Beth ha-Midrasch* I, 28.

21. Bin Gorion, II, 287.

22. Discussed in the *Era*, Vol. 72 (August 1969), p. 76. In all the apocryphal accounts of Abraham on the altar he refuses the assistance proffered by the angel, saying that God alone will deliver him. Maase Abraham, in Jellineck, *Beth ha-Midrasch* I, 34, and Midrash de Abraham Abinu, *ibid.*, p. 41; Ka'b el-Ahbar, text in *Rev. des Etudes*, Vol. 70 (1920), p. 37.

23. Beer, p. 68.

24. I. Levi, in *Rev. des Etudes Juives*, Vol. 59, p. 169.

25. Ginzberg, *L. J.*, Vol. 1. pp. 276-277.

26. Beer, p. 62, citing S. ha-Yashar, 77-79, and Midrash.

27. Bin Gorion, II, 287.

28. Levi, *op. cit.*, pp. 166f.

29. R. A. Rosenberg, in *Journal of Biblical Literature*, Vol. 84 (1965), p. 382.

30. *Ibid.*, p. 385, quoting the Book of Enoch 92:3, which Rosenberg calls "the most important text yet discovered of the Jewish apocalyptic literature."

31. *Ibid.*, p. 382.

32. J. Finkel, in *Proceedings of the American Academy of Jewish Research*, Vol. 3 (1930), p. 15.

33. Vermes, *op. cit.*, p. 195.

34. J. Danielou, in *Biblica*, Vol. 28 (1947), pp. 392-393.

35. M. Braude, *Midr. Ps.*, 105:1.

36. Bin Gorion, II, 307-308.

37. Vermes, p. 201; Beer, p. 68.

38. Ginzberg, *L. J.*, Vol. 1, pp. 235-237.

39. *Teachings of the Prophet Joseph Smith*, pp. 59-60, 181; cf. *Apocalypse of Abraham*, chapters 11 and 12.

40. I. Levi in *R.E.J.*, Vol. 59, pp. 169-171; Beer, p. 186.

41. Pirqe R. Eliezer, Ch. 31, pp. 229f.

42. Ginzberg, Vol. 1, p. 283. So also the donkey was likewise the same beast that would later be ridden by Balaam, Moses, and the Messiah; Beer, p. 61.

43. M. Levittes, *Maimonides*, VIII, p. 10.

44. J. Soggin, in *Theologische Literaturzeitung*, 89 (1964), pp. 732f.

45. R. Graves, *The White Goddess* (New York: Vintage, 1958), p. 355.

46. D. S. Shapiro, in *Tradition*, Vol. 4 (1962), p. 218,discusses this.

47. P. R. Eliezer, Ch. 31, p. 227.

48. Midrash Rab. Gen., 39:8; Ps. 110:3.

49. Pseudo-Philo, VI, 10; bin Gorion, II, 78.

50. Bin Gorion, *loc. cit.*

51. N. N. Glatzer, *Faith and Knowledge*, p. 178.

52. R. J. Loewe, in A. Altmann, *Biblical Motifs*, p. 166, with Tanhuma text supplied in note 35.

53. So in the *Maase Abraham*, in Beth ha-Midrasch, I, 34. According

to the Sefer ha-Yashar, 8, "Abram walked in the midst of the fire for three days and three nights," cit. Vermes, p. 73. Ka'b el-Ahbar, Qissat Ibrahim Abinu, in *Rev. Et. Juives*, Vol. 70 (1920), p. 42; cf. *Midrash de-Abraham Avinu*, in Beth ha-Midrash, I, 40-41. According to Tha'labi (Qissas, p. 55), it was the "Angel of the Shadow" who sat with Abraham in the fire, i.e., he was sacrificed.

54. A. Moortgat, *Tammuz* (Berlin: de Gruyter, 1949), pp. 63, 114, 139-142.

55. In Beer, p. 113.

56. P. R. Eliezer, Ch. 31, 38A.i.

57. Ginzberg, Vol. 1, p. 281.

58. Beer, p. 67.

59. G. Vermes, *Scripture and Tradition*, p. 205.

60. Beer, p. 69.

61. Ginzberg, Vol. 1, pp. 281-282; in another version Isaac's spirit went to paradise for three years before returning, *ibid.*, pp. 285-287.

62. *Ibid.*, Vol. 1, p. 208.

63. Cavalletti, in *Studii e Materiali*, 35: 263.

64. *Cahier des Curiosites Mystiques*, Vol. 1 (1874), pp. 152-55.

65. R. A. Rosenberg, in *J.B.L.*, Vol. 84, p. 388.

66. *Ibid.*, p. 386, citing Jubilees 18:18.

67. Vermes, *op. cit.*, p. 209.

68. *Ibid.*, p. 205.

69. So Z. Mayani, *Les Hyksos et le Monde de la Bible* (Paris: Payot, 1956), p. 21.

70. Vermes, pp. 193, 221.

71. N. N. Glatzer, *Faith and Knowledge*, p. 178.

72. Beer, p. 57.

73. Vermes, p. 204.

74. *Ibid.*, p. 208.

75. Ginzberg, Vol. 1, p. 240.

76. Rosenberg, p. 388.

77. Cave of Treasures 29:13-14.

78. Rosenberg, *loc. cit.*, citing Targ. Levi 22:27.

79. Vermes, p. 193.

80. *Ibid.*, p. 208.

81. Holtzmann, Tosephtakraktat Berakot, in *Ztschr. f. Alttest. Wiss.*, Vol. 23 (1912), pp. 12f.

82. Beer, p. 206.

83. M. Braude, *Midr. Ps.* 55:2.

84. See above, notes 37, 46-48, 70, 71, for examples.

85. Vermes, p. 203, cit. Targ. Job 3:18.

86. J. Finkel, in *Proc. Am. Acad. Jew. Research,* Vol. 3 (1930), p. 14.

87. *Ibid.,* p. 12.

88. Bin Gorion, II, 295.

89. Beer, p. 70.

90. Ginzberg, Vol. 1, p. 283.

91. Finkel, p. 12.

92. Rosenberg, in *J.B.L.,* Vol. 84, p. 385.

93. *Ibid.,* pp. 383, 385.

94. *Ibid.,* p. 382.

95. *Ibid.,* p. 388.

96. Beer, p. 15; M. Sprengling (ed.), *Barhebraeus' Scholia on the Old Testament* (Univ. of Chicago, 1931), p. 49, comments on Gen. 11:28. That Haran died as a substitute for Abraham is clearly indicated in Midr. in *Beth ha-Midrasch* I, 40; S. ha-Yashar (text in Vermes, p. 72); Ginzberg, *L.J.,* Vol. 1, p. 216; bin Gorion, II, 96f; Beer, pp. 15-17; cf. Bar Hebrews, *Scholion* to Gen. 11:2; Midr. Rab., Noah 38:13.

The Book of Mormon: A Minimal Statement

7

The following statement was written on request for a journal which is published in eight languages and therefore insists on conciseness and brevity. Teaching a Book of Mormon Sunday School class ten years later, I am impressed more than anything by something I completely overlooked until now, namely, the immense skill with which the editors of the book put the thing together. The long Book of Alma, for example, is followed through with a smooth and logical sequence in which an incredible amount of detailed and widely varying material is handled in the most lucid and apparently effortless manner. Whether Alma is addressing a king and his court, a throng of ragged paupers sitting on the ground, or his own three sons, each a distinctly different character, his eloquence is always suited to his audience and he goes unfailingly to the peculiar problems of each hearer.

Throughout this big and complex volume, we are aware of much shuffling and winnowing of documents, and informed from time to time of the method used by an editor distilling the contents of a large library into edifying lessons for the dedicated and pious minority among the people. The overall picture reflects before all a limited geographical and cultural point of view — small localized operations, with only occasional flights and ex-peditions into the wilderness; one might almost be moving in the cultural circuit of the Hopi villages. The focusing of the whole account on religious themes as well as the limited cultural scope leaves all the rest of the stage clear for any other activities that might have been going on in the vast reaches of the New World, including the hypothetical Norsemen, Celts, Phoenicians, Libyans, or prehistoric infiltrations via the Bering Straits. Indeed the more varied the ancient American scene becomes, as newly discovered artifacts and even inscriptions hint at local populations of Near Eastern, Far Eastern and European origin, the more hospitable it is to the activities of one tragically short-lived religious civilization that once flourished in Meso-America and then vanished towards the northeast in the course of a series of confused tribal wars that was one long, drawn-out retreat into oblivion. Such considerations would now have to be included in any "minimal statement" this reader would make about the Book of Mormon.

T he first step in what the Mormons consider the restoration of the gospel in the dispensation of the fulness of times was the coming forth of the Book of Mormon. More than anything else this fixed the unique status of the new religion, of which Eduard Meyer wrote: "Mormonism . . . is not just another of those innumerable new sects, but a new religion of revelation (*Offenbarungsreligion*)."[1] The Latter-day Saints "believe the Book of Mormon to be the word of God" in exactly the same sense as the Bible (Article of Faith No. 8) — a proposition which has caused great offense to many Christians and led to long and severe persecutions, the Book of Mormon being the principal object of attack.

However, the book does not take the place of the Bible in Mormonism. But just as the New Testament clarified the long misunderstood message of the Old, so the Book of Mormon is held to reiterate the messages of both Testaments in a way that restores their full meaning. Its professed mission, as announced on its title page, is "to show unto the remnant of the House of Israel what great things the Lord hath done for their fathers; and that they may know the covenants of the Lord, that they are not cast off forever — And also to the convincing of the Jew and Gentile that Jesus is the Christ, the Eternal God, manifesting himself unto all nations." Until recently, most Mormons have not been zealous in the study of the book, considering it on the whole a strange and alien document with little relationship to modern life. Its peculiar effectiveness has indeed been as a messenger (it was brought by an angel) to the world at large.

The Book of Mormon professes to present in highly abridged form the history of a peculiar civilization, transplanted from the Old World to the New around 600 B.C. Of complex cultural background and mixed racial stock, the society endured only a thousand years, of which period the Book of Mormon contains an unbroken account, taken supposedly from records kept almost entirely by the leaders of a minority religious group. The first of the line was Lehi, who with his family and some others fled from Jerusalem to the desert to live the law in its purity and prepare for the coming Messiah. Commanded by God after much wandering to cross the seas, the community reached the New World and there broke up, only a minority choosing to continue the ways of the pious sectaries of the desert. Lehi's descendants in time met and mingled with yet other migrants from the Old World, and indeed for almost five hundred years they had, unawares, as their northern neighbors warlike hunting tribes which, according to the Book of Mormon, had come from Asia thousands of years before. The racial and cultural picture of the Book of Mormon is anything but the oversimplified thing its critics have made it out to be. For the Mormons, the Book of Mormon contains "the fulness of the gospel." Six hundred years of its history transpire before the coming of Christ, and four hundred after that. In the earlier period the faithful minority formed a church of anticipation, their charismatic leaders "teaching the law of Moses, and the intent for which it was given; persuading them to look forward unto the Messiah, and believe in him to come as though he already was." There are extensive quotations from the Old Testament prophets, especially Isaiah, with remarkable variant readings, and much that is reminiscent in language and imagery of early Jewish apocryphal writings. The boldest part of the Book of Mormon is the detailed account of the visit of Jesus Christ to his "other sheep" in the New World after the Resurrection, including his instructions and commandments to the new church. This episode closely parallels certain sections of early Christian apocrypha dealing with postresurrectional teachings of the Lord to his disciples in Galilee and on the Mount of Olives, although none of these sources were available in Joseph Smith's day.

The historical parts of the Book of Mormon bear witness to its good faith, which never claims for it any sort of immunity, religious or otherwise, from the most searching scientific and scholarly criticism. Lack of comparative historical documents is offset by an abundance of cultural data: over two hundred nonbiblical Hebrew and Egyptian names offer ample material to the philologist, and a wealth of technical detail invites critical examination, thanks to precise descriptions of such things as the life of a family wandering in the Arabian desert, a great earthquake, the ancient craft of olive-culture, a major war in all its phases, the ways of the early desert sectaries, and the state of the world during a protohistoric *Volker-wanderung*.

Along with cultural-historical particulars the religious message of the book is richly interspersed with peculiar expressions, legends, traditions, and customs supposedly derived from the Old World, which may today be checked against ancient sources. Thus it describes certain practices of arrow-divination, an odd custom of treading on garments, a coronation ceremony (in great detail), the evils of the archaic matriarchy, peculiar ways of keeping and transmitting sacred records, the intricacies of an ingenious monetary system, and the like.

Of particular interest to Latter-day Saints are the prophetic parts of the Book of Mormon, which seem to depict the present state of the world most convincingly. The last 140 years have borne out exactly what the book foretold would be its own reception and influence in the world, and its predictions for the Mormons, the Jews and the other remnants of scattered Israel (among which are included the American Indians) seem to be on the way to fulfillment. The Book of Mormon allows an ample time-scale for the realization of its prophecies, according to which the deepening perplexities of the nations, when "the Lord God shall cause a great division among the people," shall lead to worldwide destructions by fire, for "blood, and fire, and vapor of smoke must come; and it must needs be upon the face of this earth." After this the survivors (for this is not to be the end of the world) shall have learned enough to coexist peaceably "for the space of many years," when "all nations, kindreds, tongues and people shall dwell safely in the Holy One of Israel if it so be that they will repent."

The Book of Mormon is the history of a polarized world in which two irreconcilable ideologies confronted each other, and is addressed explicitly to our own age, faced by the same predicament and the same impending threat of destruction. It is a call to faith and repentance couched in the language of history and prophecy, but above all it is a witness to God's concern for all his children, and to the intimate proximity of Jesus Christ to all who will receive him.

NOTES

1. E. Meyer, *Ursprung und Geschichte der Mormonen* (Halle: 1912), p. 1.

Churches
in the Wilderness

8

Long before the Dead Sea Scrolls were found, Robert Eisler called attention to the existence of societies of ancient sectaries, including the early Christians, who fled to the desert and formed pious communities there, after the manner of the order of Rekhabites (Jeremiah 35.) More recently, E. Kaesemann and U. W. Mauser have taken up the theme and now the Pope himself refers to his followers as "the Wayfaring Church," of all things. No aspect of the gospel is more fundamental than that which calls the Saints out of the world; it has recently been recognized as fundamental to the universal apocalyptic pattern, and is now recognized as a basic teaching of the prophets of Israel, including the Lord himself. It is the central theme of the Book of Mormon, and Lehi's people faithfully follow the correct routine of flights to the desert as their stories now merge with new manuscript finds from the Dead Sea and elsewhere. And while many Christian communities have consciously sought to imitate the dramatic flight into the Wilderness, from monastic orders to Pilgrim Fathers, only the followers of Joseph Smith can claim the distinction of a wholesale, involuntary and total expulsion into a most authentic wilderness.

Now, the Book of Mormon is not only a typical product of a religious people driven to the wilds — surprisingly we have learned since 1950 that such people had a veritable passion for writing books and keeping records —

but it actually contains passages that match some of the Dead Sea Scrolls almost word for word. Isn't that going a bit too far? How, one may ask, would Alma be able to quote from a book written on the other side of the world among people with whom his own had lost all contact for five hundred years? Joseph Smith must have possessed supernatural cunning to have foreseen such an impasse, yet his Book of Mormon explains it easily: Alma informs us that the passages in question are not his, but he is quoting them directly from an ancient source, the work of an early prophet of Israel named Zenos. Alma and the author of the Thanksgiving Scroll are drawing from the same ancient source. No wonder they sound alike.

I f all the Dead Sea Scrolls which are *now known* to scholars but have not yet been published were to go through the press at the same rate that the others have, we might well be talking about *new* Dead Sea Scrolls for at least two centuries to come. This is about some scrolls and some readings hitherto quite unknown to the public.

The first is the Enoch Scroll, which became accessible not long ago. I want to call attention to just one item which caught my attention. In the Joseph Smith book of Enoch is an episode that stands out conspicuously for the strangely intimate twist it gives to the story. That is when out of the blue comes "a man... whose name was Mahijah," who asks Enoch point-blank, "Tell us plainly who thou art, and from whence thou comest?" (Moses 6:40.) This triggers Enoch's great sermon in response, in which he reads to the people from the book of Adam and puts them to shame for their sins. As far as I know, the episode is not found in the Ethiopian, Old Slavonic, Hebrew, Aramaic or Greek Enoch text, so I was brought up with a start when, upon reaching the final fragments of the newly published Aramaic Enoch from the Dead Sea Scrolls, the name *MHWY* started popping up repeatedly. Before telling the story of *MHWY* from Qumran, a word about the name is in order.

It is of course the *MHWY-EL* of Genesis 4:18, where the other Enoch's grandfather is given the name, appearing in our King James Bible as Mehujael. This is not our hero, whose name lacks the -el ending; on the contrary, he belongs to the Cainite branch of the family, which would make the Sethite missionary Enoch an alien to his people. In the Joseph Smith Enoch both forms of the name appear, Mahijah and Mahujah, which should not be surprising, for in Semitic languages the consonants abide, as everyone knows, while the vowels undergo all manner of vicissitudes; and of all the vowels the *w* and the *y* are the most active. (One need mention only such obvious examples as the Hebrew *yeled* and Arabic *walad*, "boy," or the way the *w* and *y* constantly supplant each other in Egyptian participles, depending on time and place of writing.) The name *MHWY* is written exactly the same in the Qumran texts as in the Hebrew Bible. In the Greek Septuagint it is Mai-el (the Greeks, having letters for neither *h* nor *w* could end up with Ma[hu]y[ah] as Mai); the trace of the *waf* is preserved in the Latin Vulgate: Mavia-el; but in both cases the semi-vowel *waf* is weakened and the *y* sound dominates. Mahujah and Mahijah obviously have the same root. The Ma- prefix may denote the place of an action or in derived forms of the verb the person acting, reminding us that it was "upon the place Mahujah" that Enoch inquired of the Lord and received his missionary assignment in a glorious theophany (Moses 7:2), while the man who boldly put the questions to Enoch himself was Mahijah, the asker. And, since we are playing games, what the Ma- most strongly suggests is certainly the all-but-universal ancient interrogative, *Ma*, who? or what? so that the names Mahujah and Mahijah both sound to the student of Semitics like questions. In the newly discovered texts from Ebla (Tel-Mardikh) the same names are written with Ma- (Amorite) and Mi (Phoenician-Hebrew.)

But the important thing about *MHWY* in the Aramaic Enoch — by far the oldest Enoch texts so far known — is what the man does. Let me read you some parallel passages, following the translation of Professors Milik and Black so that you won't think I have been loading the dice to come out this way.

The presence of Enoch was a disturbing one, "a strange thing in the land," in the Joseph Smith version, "a wild man hath come among us." And so this is what we get (italics added):

Moses 6:39. . . .when they heard him . . . *fear came* on all them that heard him	4QEnGiants[b] 1.20 [Thereupon] all the giants [and the nephilim] *took fright*
6:40. And there came a man unto him, whose name was *Mahijah,* and said unto him: *Tell us plainly* who thou art, and from whence thou comest?	and they summoned *MHWY* [Mahujah] and he came to them. And the giants asked him and sent him to Enoch . . . saying to him: "Go then . . .

and under pain of death you
must . . . and listen to his voice;
and tell him that *he is to explain*
to you and to interpret the
dreams. . . .

So here comes Mahujah-Mahijah to Enoch, representing a disturbed constituency, to ask the holy man just what the situation is.
That *MHWY* was sent "under pain of death" shows that not only the
dreams but the presence of Enoch was a cause of dread. In reply the
messenger learns that Enoch comes from a special and holy place:

6:41. And he said unto them: I came out from . . . the land of my fathers, a *land of righteousness* unto this day	4QEnGiants^c [Ohyah, following MHWY's report]: . . . my accusers . . . they dwell in [heaven]s, for they live in *holy abodes* . . . they are more powerful than I . . .

Enoch tells the man about a revelation and call he received as he
traveled in the mountains on a missionary journey. The journey
here seems to be transferred to *MHWY* himself, who crosses the
deserts on high to behold Enoch and receive an oracle from him,
while in the Joseph Smith version Enoch himself makes such a
journey to receive instructions from God:

6:42. And . . . as I journeyed . . . by the sea east, I beheld a vision: and lo, the heavens I saw. . . . 7:2-3. . . . As I was journeying . . . I went up on the mount . . . I beheld the heavens open. . . .	4QEnGiants^b [MHWY . . . rose up into the air] like the whirlwind, and he flew . . . and crossed Solitude, the great desert . . . And he caught sight of Enoch, and he called to him and said to him: 'An oracle. . . .'

It is in reply to Mahijah-*MHWY* that Enoch refers the people to an
ancient book which he bears with him, having according to some
sources (Jubilees, XII Patriarchs) copied it with his own hand from
heavenly tablets.

6:45. Enoch: We . . . cannot deny . . . for a book of remembrance we have *written* among us,	4QEnGiants^a7 . . . to you, MH [wy . . .] the two tablets . . . and the second has not been read up till now. 8. the boo [k of . . .

According to the pattern given *by the finger* of God . . . in our own language.

The copy of the second tablet of the Epistle . . . *written] by* Enoch, the distinguished *scribe's own hand* . . . and the *Holy One,* to Shemihazah and all [his] Com[panions].

The teachings of the book (from Adam's time in the Joseph Smith version) strike home, and the hearers are overcome:

6:47. And as Enoch spake forth the words of God, the people *trembled,* and *could not stand* in his presence.

6Q8 a . . .Ohya and he said to MHWY: " . . . and [I?] do not *tremble.* Who showed you all [that] tell [us?]. . . ." And MHWY said: " . . . Baraq'el, my father, was with me."

4[En Giants ᵃ Frg.4 . . .Ohyah said to Ha]hyah, his brother. . . . they *prostrated themselves* and began to weep before [Enoch (?) . . .].

The name Baraq'el is interesting in this context, since Joseph Smith is designated in the Doctrine and Covenants both as Enoch and as Baurakale (D&C 78:9; 102:21f, etc.) Next comes a resounding declaration of general depravity, which in two verses of the Joseph Smith text powerfully sums up the same message in the longest of the Aramaic Enoch fragments:

6:48. And he said unto them . . . We are made partakers of misery and woe . . .
6:49. . . .carnal, sensual, and devilish, and are *shut out from the presence of God.*

4EnGiantsᵃFrg.8. The longest fragment: The depravity and misery of the people described. Their petition is rejected: *God has cast them out.* All is "for the worst",

But then interestingly enough, both the Qumran and the Joseph Smith sermons end on a note of hope — which is *not* found in the other versions of the Book of Enoch:

6:52. If thou wilt *turn unto me;* . . . and repent . . . *asking* all

[Closing line] And yet, *loosen your bonds* [of sin?] which tie

things in his name ... it shall
be given you.

[you] up ... and begin to *pray*.

Now comes what I consider an important theological note. Enoch
tells how the Lord told Adam of the natural inclination to sin that
came with the Fall. This is converted in the Aramaic version to a
denunciation of the wicked people of Enoch's day, who did indeed
conceive their children in sin, since they were illegitimate offspring
of a totally amoral society:

6:55. Inasmuch as thy *children*
are *conceived in sin*. even so ...
sin conceiveth in their
hearts ...
6:57. Wherefore teach it unto
your children, that all men,
everywhere, must repent.

4QEnGiants 8. Let it be known
to you that ... and your works
and those of your wives ...
themselves [and their] *children*
and the wives of [their
children ...] *by your prostitution*
on earth. And it befell you. ...

Next the wicked move against Enoch and his people in force, but are
themselves forced to acknowledge the superior power supporting
the patriarch:

7:13. And ... he [Enoch] led
the people of God, and their
enemies *came to battle against
them;* and he spake the word of
the Lord, and the earth
trembled. ...

4QEnGiant[c] [Ohyah the
enemy of Enoch]: " ... by the
strength of my power, [I had
attacked] all flesh and I have
made war with them ... they live
in holy abodes, and ... they
are more powerful than I."

And then that striking passage, so surprisingly vindicated in other
Enoch texts, of the roaring lions amidst scenes of general terror:

and the *roar of the lions* was
heard out of the wilderness;

and all nations *feared
greatly*. ...

[Thereupon ...] the *roaring of
the wild beasts* came and the
multitude of wild animals
began to cry out
And Ohyah spoke ... "My
dream has *overwhelmed* me
[... and the s]leep of my eyes
[has fled] ...

Finally the prediction of utter destruction and the confining in
prison that is to follow:

7:37 ...these shall suffer. 38. ...these... *shall perish* in the floods; and behold, I will *shut* them up; a *prison* have I prepared for them.

4QEnGiants[a] Frg. 7. Then Ohyah [said] to Hahyah, his brother.... Then he [sc. God] punished... the [sons] of the Watchers, the giants, and all [their] beloved ones *will not be spared* ... he has *imprisoned* us and you he has subdued [lit. *tqaf:* seized, *confined*].

Among new Dead Sea Scrolls we may number those found in 1966 not at Qumran but in the all but inaccessible caves that line the precipitous walls of the Nahal Khever or, as we would say, "Heber Valley." Instead of a valley it is a deep gorge, like Rock Canyon; it is the next canyon just south of En Gedi where the people bathe in the Dead Sea today. In those caves Jews fleeing from the Romans in the time of Bar Kokhba holed up with their families and their most precious portable possessions. A cave in the side of a cliff that can only be approached by one man at a time is easy to defend, and the Romans did not bother to attack them there, but simply set up camps on the flat mesas on either side of the canyon, from which they could look right down into the caves and make sure that no one escaped. Thus trapped, the poor Jews perished miserably in their hideouts, refusing to surrender, and left behind not only all manner of artifacts, kitchen-ware, clothing, baskets in excellent condition, shoes, etc., but a priceless harvest of their personal papers and books. These throw a great deal of light on practices described in the Book of Mormon.

For what these people were doing in fleeing from the farms and cities of Judea, as digging in these very caves has shown, was exactly what had been done at other times when the land was overrun by foreign armies. The evidence goes clear back to mysterious bronze vessels hidden there about 3000 B.C., supposedly by people fleeing from the armies of the first king of Egypt! I will be quoting from the review of Professor Yigael Yadin's book *Bar-Kokhba* (New York: Random House, 1971) on the subject.

First of all, there is something almost alarmingly literal about these "voices from the dust." For these documents were deliberately buried in the deep dust of the cave floors and came forth in choking clouds of dust — the finders had to wear masks: "For those who shall be destroyed shall speak unto them out of the ground, and their speech shall be low out of the dust, and their voice shall be as one that hath a familiar spirit; for the Lord God will give unto him power, that he may whisper concerning them, even as it were out of the ground; and their speech shall whisper out of the dust." (2 Nephi 26:16.) They have not survived accidentally, as most other ancient writings have, but were hidden away on purpose; nor were they simply left behind or misplaced or forgotten by people who moved on and lived out their lives elsewhere — the people who left these records died soon after they buried them and died on the spot, the victims of a savage religious war. "For those who shall be destroyed shall speak unto them out of the ground. . . ." (2 Nephi 26:16.) What do these records contain? Accounts of contemporary affairs in private letters, legal documents, military and civil correspondence, or, in the words of the Book of Mormon, "For thus saith the Lord God: They shall write the things which shall be done among them. . . . Wherefore, as those who have been destroyed have been destroyed speedily. . . ." (2 Nephi 26:17-18.) Not only all their letters and legal papers, but their household effects and their bones were left behind in the caves, for the simple reason that they did not have time to escape. As to their destroyers, "Nothing remains here today of the Romans save a heap of stones on the face of the desert," writes Yadin, "but here the descendants of the besieged were returning to salvage their ancestors' precious belongings." (p. 235.) Again the Book of Mormon: " . . . and the multitude of their terrible ones shall be as chaff that passeth away. . . ." (2 Nephi 26:18.)

With the Dead Sea Scrolls we have something new under the sun; even if they simply repeated what we already know, their principal contribution would be the same — a new dimension of reality to our religion. It has been a long time since scholars asked, "Are there really such things as this? Did this really happen?" They have learned to be content with the easy assumption that it really makes no difference in dealing with spiritual, allegorical, moral emblems whether or not there is a physical reality to our stories. The most shocking thing that Joseph Smith brought before the world was the announcement that things men had been talking about for centuries were literally true, and would have to be viewed as such. The restoration of the gospel brought a new reality, but found few believers — it was more comfortable the old way, when you could take things just as you wanted them.

But with the scrolls from the caves, the reality of things hits us in the face with a shock. How often does it happen that documents thousands of years old have been dug up by the very descendants of the people who wrote those documents, who could actually read them on the spot, not referring them to pedantic decipherment in distant studies and laboratories, but reading them right off as messages from their own grandparents? "We found that our emotions were a mixture of tension and awe," writes Professor Yadin, "yet astonishment and pride at being part of the reborn State of Israel after a Diaspora of 1,800 years." (p. 253.) Compare this with Nephi's moving lines: "And it shall be as if the fruit of thy loins had cried unto them from the dust. . . . even after many generations have gone by them. . . ." (2 Nephi 3:19-20.)

Nothing illustrates this better than Ezekiel's dry bones. The question in Ezekiel 37:3 is, "Can these bones live?" and the answer is, Yes, *when* "the stick of Ephraim, for Joseph, and for all the house of Israel" is joined "with the stick of Judah" "one to another into one stick; and they shall be one in thine hand." (See Ezekiel 37:16-19.) I once wrote a series of articles on the ancient tally-sticks. The true tally-stick was a staff (originally an arrow-shaft) on which the contract and names of the contracting parties were written; the staff was then split down the middle and one half, called "the stock" was kept by one of the parties, while the other "the bill" was held by the other. When the time came to settle the contract, the two parties would present their halves of the stick to the king. If they matched perfectly it was plain that neither party had attempted to tinker with the document, and all conditions having been met, the two halves, joined together again to make one, would be bound with string in the king's hand and laid away in the archives. The oldest known tallies are written in Latin and, surprisingly, in Hebrew. Are such the "sticks" to which Ezekiel refers? They are. The Bar Kochba cave has now produced no less than twenty-three examples of this technique in those letters of "the type commonly known as 'double deeds' or 'tied deeds,' " the use of which "is a very old and known practice in the ancient world." The idea was to write the same contract twice, once very small, roll it into a tight cylinder, sew it closed, and sign it over with the participants' signatures, not to be opened until the final settlement — plainly the technique of the tally-stick.

So here the Dead Sea Scrolls confirm our own interpretation of what the sticks of Ephraim and Judah were: matching documents to be brought together and placed side by side to make one book at that particular moment when God would set his hand to resurrecting the dry bones of dead Israel. The word of the Lord assures us now that it is indeed "Moroni, whom I have sent unto you to reveal the Book of

Mormon, containing the fulness of my everlasting gospel, to whom I have committed the keys of the records of the stick of Ephraim." (D&C 27:5.) It is specifically with the bringing forth of these documents that the work of the last days is to start moving. Moroni, who brought the book again, sealed it up anciently with the prophecy that when its word shall be "like as one crying from the dead, yea, even as one speaking out of the dust" (Moroni 10:27), *then* shall the invitation go forth to the Jews: "Awake, and arise from the dust, O Jerusalem . . . enlarge thy borders forever, that thou mayest no more be confounded. . . ." (10:31). Which is exactly what they are doing today: the only way they can keep from being "confounded" is to have defensible borders.

In 1948 the world turned a corner. Overnight modern Israel became a reality, *and so did ancient Israel.* The Battle Scroll appeared just at the moment that Israel was called to arms, and according to Yadin had not only a moral but even a practical value in that great crisis. Suddenly scriptures became "relevant." In the same year the oldest Jewish library and the oldest Christian library were discovered: both were threatened with destruction; both were challenged as hoaxes; both became the object of political and religious rivalries and deadlocks; both were viewed as the work of irresponsible and fanatic sectaries. Yet through the years there has been a growing respect for both the Nag Hammadi and the Qumran writings, both because of their impressive spiritual content and the number of other pseudepigrapha that are being discovered or rediscovered to confirm their proximity to the authentic Judaism and Christianity that flourished in the days before the Jewish and Christian doctors of Alexandria changed everything.

To me this seems to be an obvious sequel to what happened in 1830, when another book appeared from the dust, and another Israel was established. There are three main parts to the Restoration, as was made clear in a revelation given a year later: "But before the great day of the Lord shall come, Jacob shall flourish in the wilderness, and the Lamanites shall blossom as the rose. Zion shall flourish upon the hills and rejoice upon the mountains, and shall be assembled together unto the place which I have appointed." (D&C 49:24-25.) And the three shall combine their records, for "it shall come to pass that the Jews shall have the words of the Nephites, and the Nephites shall have the words of the Jews; and the Nephites and the Jews shall have the words of the lost tribes of Israel; and the lost tribes of Israel shall have the words of the Nephites and the Jews. And it shall come to pass that my people, which are of the house of

Israel, shall be gathered home unto the lands of their possessions; and my word also shall be gathered in one. And I will show unto them that fight against my word and against my people, who are of the house of Israel, that I am God, and that I covenanted with Abraham that I would remember his seed forever." (2 Nephi 29:13-14.) The Dead Sea Scrolls bind the Old Testament and the New Testament together as nothing else, and almost all the Scrolls so far published show remarkable affinity to the Book of Mormon, as well as the restored Church. Why should this be? Or am I just imagining things? The proper cure for "parallelomania" is not to avoid parallels but to explain them: every parallel has a proper explanation, even if it is only mere coincidence or illusion. There are marks on rocks that sometimes look like writing or like fossilized plants; these are not to be ignored even though they often turn out to be misleading, because once in a while they really are true writing and true fossils. Resemblances between the Bible and the Book of Mormon are not hard to explain; far from being evidence of fraud, they are rather confirmation of authenticity. If the Book of Mormon is what it pretends to be, we should expect to find a strong biblical influence in it. Its prophets sound like those of the Old Testament because they studied and consciously quoted the words of those prophets, and all prophets moreover are programmed to sound alike, being called for the same purpose under much the same conditions.

But the Book of Mormon goes far beyond such generalities when it takes us into worlds hitherto undreamed of, namely those societies of desert sectaries, Jewish and Christian, which since the discovery of the Dead Sea Scrolls and Nag Hammadi documents have come to life in our histories and commentaries. The Book of Mormon deals with both types of religious community for 3 Nephi gives us the Christian version, as other books do the Jewish. The presence of Jewish colonies that look strangely Christian and early Christian colonies that look strangely Jewish has been disturbing to both conventional "normative" Judaism and conventional Christianity, and has already called for drastic revisions of doctrine and liturgy.

In the Dead Sea Scrolls we learn of the peculiar way of life of the sectaries of the desert, whose Rekhabite tradition goes back to Lehi's day and long before, and survives long after, as is very apparent from the 2nd Sura of the Koran. The people of Lehi were rooted in this tradition. When John Welch was studying at Duke a few years ago, he was struck by the close resemblance between the story of Lehi and the writing of Zosimus, a Greek of the third century A.D. What would a Greek know about Lehi almost a thousand years after? Zosimus was looking for the model society of the saints, and affected to find it in the desert among the Rekhabites — that is the common tradition; I pointed out long ago that Lehi was in the proper sense a Rekhabite and certainly acquainted with the pious sectaries of Jeremiah 30. The writing of Zosimus shows that we are dealing with a pervasive and persistent pattern. Since the rise of "patternism" in the 1930s scholars have come to recognize all manner of common religious forms and stereotypes throughout the world. But it is important to remember that Joseph Smith in his day was running in an open field, a boundless plain where there was nothing to check or restrain him. Mrs. Brodie saw in the Book of Mormon only the product of a completely untrained, unbridled, undisciplined imagination that ran over like a spring freshet, as she put it. A hundred and forty years ago he might have gotten away with it, but now surely comes the day of reckoning! And it is not he but his critics who are confounded.

The Book of Mormon is, as it often reminds us, a selective history. It deals with small groups of pious believers, intensely conservative by nature and tradition; consciously identifying themselves with their ancestors, Israel in the wilderness of long ago. (See 1 Nephi 19:23.) It was this characteristic tendency of the sectaries to identify themselves with earlier trials and tribulations of Israel that at first made the Dead Sea Scrolls so hard to date: the same situations seem to obtain again and again through history, so that the Kittim of the Scrolls might be the Egyptians, Assyrians, Babylonians, Greeks, or Romans. Though carrying on in the New World, the Book of Mormon people preserve their ancient culture for centuries: which should not surprise us — do not the present inhabitants of America speak the English, Spanish and Portuguese and preserve the customs of the Old World after four hundred years? With this strong cultural carry-over, the Nephites are aware of being special and apart — as the sectaries always are — "a lonesome and a solemn people," is the moving expression of Nephi's brother. And strangely enough, they are peculiarly bound to the written word, as are the people of Qumran. One of the most important discoveries of the Book of Mormon was the process and techniques of recording, transmitting, concealing, editing, translating, and duplicating ancient writings. Here is something the world refused to see in the Bible, the most sealed of books, but it has been thoroughly vindicated in the Dead Sea Scrolls.

Of many striking parallels, I would like to speak of one here that goes to the root of things. It is an episode that opens in the Book of Mormon in the middle of the second century B.C. with "a man whose name was Abinadi," in deep trouble with the establishment: In the Old World we find about the same time a certain "Teacher of Righteousness" in much the same fix: his story is told in the Manual of Discipline, the Damascus or Zadokite Fragment, the commentary on Habaku and the Thanksgiving Hymns from Qumran. He is being given a bad time by certain corrupt priests who are in the saddle. In the Book of Mormon we find them cross-examining the righteous man as they sit at a special tribunal with comfortable seats,

The common formula is "lying speakers and vain seers" (*mlitse kazav w-khoze rmiyah*, 4:10)

Mosiah 11:11. . . .that they might rest their bodies . . . while they should speak lying and vain words to his people.

IQH 4:6 . . .But they lead thy people astray by speaking smooth things to them, practitioners of vain rhetoric . . . (*melitse remiuah*, preachers of deceit.)

IQH 4:20. they are men of deceit [mirmah] and seers who lead astray [*khozeh ta'ut*].

IQH 4:16. in their insolence they would sit in judgement on thee [investigate, persecute: *yidreshu-ka*] from the mouths of lying prophets led astray by error.

11:19. they did delight in . . . shedding . . . the blood of their brethren, and this because of the wickedness of their king and priests.

CD 1:20. and they took the offensive [*ya'udu*] against the life of the Righteous one and all who walked uprightly [perfectly] they hated in their hearts, and pursued them with the sword and rejoiced in controversy.

CD 19:15. The princes of Judah

have transgressed in a bond of conspiracy [*tshuvah*] ... 18. in vengeance and wrath, every man against his brother, and everyone hating his neighbor, greedy for gain

11:26. ...they were wroth with him, and sought to take away his life; but the Lord delivered him out of their hands.

IQH 2:21. The ruthless ones sought my life ... a gang of no-goods [*sodh shaweh*], a conspiracy of Belial. But they knew not that my security [*ma amadhi*] rested on Thee, 23. and that through thy mercy is my soul delivered ... 32: They sought to take away my life and shed my blood, but Thou God hast helped the weak and suffering out of the hand of the one who was stronger that he.

11:28. Abinadi ... has said these things that he might stir up my people to anger one with another, and to raise contentions among my people; therefore I will slay him.

IQH 2:14. I became a man of controversy [*ish riv*, a troublemaker] to the preachers of error ...

(Cf. Joseph Smith 2:20. I was destined to prove a disturber and annoyer of his [Satan's] kingdom ...)

12.1 ...after the space of two years ... Abinadi came among them in disguise, that they knew him not, and began to prophesy.

IQH 4:8. For they drove me out of my land, 9. like a bird from its nest, and all my friends and relatives they turned against me.
(Cf. Od. Sal. 42)

Next Abinadi uses an interesting figure, combining two elements of fire and weaving, as the Damascus text also does, but in a quite different combination:

12.3. the life of king Noah shall be valued even as a garment in a hot furnace.

CD 2:5. for those who stubbornly oppose [God] there shall be violence and overpowering of great terror by the flame of fire.

CD 5:13. they are playing with fire and throwing sparks around [or setting fires]. 14. Their weaving is a flimsy thing, the weaving of spiders.

Here both prophets are borrowing from Isaiah 50:9, 11: "... who is he that shall condemn me? lo, they all shall wax old as a garment; the moth shall eat them up. Behold, all ye that kindle a fire, that compass yourselves about with sparks: walk in the light of your fire, and in the sparks that ye have kindled...." The idea is that those who have foolishly started such fires will themselves perish by them. In the Zadokite Fragment the precarious position of the persecutors is compared with the playing with fire and a flimsy weaving of spiders. Abinadi combines the images with characteristic wit: Noah himself is the flimsy garment in the hot fire, to suffer the very death he is inflicting on Abinadi. In the next verse he employs a figure from the Scrolls:

12:10. he [Abinadi] saith that thy life shall be as a garment in a furnace of fire.

12:12. And again, he saith thou shalt be as the blossoms of a thistle, which ... the wind bloweth....

IQH 7:2 ...Thou ... scatterest the remnant of the men who fight against me like chaff before the wind [naturally suggesting Psalm 1].

12:19. [The priests] began to question him, that they might cross him, ... to accuse him; but ... to their astonishment ... he did withstand them in all their questions, and did confound them in all their words.

IQH 2:29. They spread a net to catch me, but it caught their own foot ... 3. Thou deliverest me from the spite of the manipulators [rhetoricians] of lies, 32. from the council of those who seek smooth things; thou has rescued the soul of the Poor one whom they desired to destroy because of his service to thee.

IQH 14:14. I was zealous against the deceitful men. For all who are near to Thee resist not thy mouth nor change thy words.

12:25. [You] pretend to teach this people, 12:26. If ye understand these things ye have not taught them; therefore, ye have perverted the ways of the Lord

12:27. Ye have not applied your hearts to understanding
12:28. And they said: We teach the law of Moses.
12:29. If ye teach the law of Moses why do ye not keep it? Why do ye set your hearts upon riches? Why do ye commit whoredoms and spend your strength with harlots?

12:33. I know if ye keep the commandments of God ye shall be saved; yea, if ye keep the commandments which the Lord delivered unto Moses in the mount of Sinai...
12:37. Have ye done all this?... And have ye taught this people that they should do all these things? I say unto you, Nay, ye have not.

IQH 2:15. I became an accusing spirit [of *qinah*] against all who taught smooth things; and all the men of false teaching [*remiyah*, deception, illusion] stormed against me.

16. They professed to be in the covenant of repentance.
CD 19:17. ...but they have not departed from the way of the apostates, but have wallowed in the ways of whoredoms, and godlessness... Everyone has deserted his family for immoral practices, zealous in the acquisition of wealth and property, every man doing what is right in his own eyes, confirming the people in their sins
(Cf. Alma 30:17.)

IQH 4:10. The preachers of lies and seers of illusions contrive devil's tricks against me to make me exchange the Law which thou has engraved in my heart for the smooth things they teach to the people.
11. They who shut up the drink of knowledge from the thirsting ones to give them vinegar, to turn them to false teachings that they fall into your nets!

Then comes a long sermon to the wicked priests in which he chides them with their indifference to the scriptures and lays it on with a caustic tongue, showing himself well versed in the ancient writings: "And now I read unto you the remainder of the commandments of God, for I perceive that they are not written in your hearts; I perceive that ye have studied and taught iniquity the most part of your lives." (Mosiah 13:11.) Like the Teacher of Righteousness, Abinadi sees in the law a preparation for the Messiah to come. Professor Frank Cross called the Qumran community "the church of anticipation."

13:27. I say unto you that it is expedient that ye should keep the law of Moses *as yet;* but I say unto you, that the time shall come when it shall no more be expedient to keep the law of Moses. (Italics added.)

IQS 9:9. And from no precept of the Law [Torah] shall they depart...
11. UNTIL there shall come the Prophet and the Messiah of Aaron and Israel.

13:30. Therefore there was a law given ... a law of performances and of ordinances ... which they were to observe strictly from day to day....
31. But behold ... all these things were types of things to come.
32. And now ... they did not all understand the law; and this because of the hardness of their hearts.

CD 12:21. And according to this rule shall they walk even the seed of Israel ... and this is the way [*serekh*] of living for the camp, by which they walk in the time of the wicked, UNTIL the Anointed One [Messiah] of Aaron arises.

13:33. Did not Moses prophesy ... concerning the coming of the Messiah, and that God should redeem his people? Yea, and even all the prophets who have prophesied ever since the world began — have they not spoken more or less concerning these things?

IQS 1:2. ...as was commanded by the hand of Moses and by the hand of his servants the prophets.

IQS 9:4. to atone for the sins ... to please God in the land MORE than the flesh of burnt offerings and the fat of sacrifices: the heave-offering of the lips for a mishpat, like the sacrificial odor [*k-nikhoakh*] the offering acceptable to him.

Being perfect in the way means keeping the covenants one has made: the expression is found at the opening of the Book of Luke, where we find the parents of John the Baptist following precepts like these.

Mosiah 15:10. And who shall be his seed?
11. ...whosoever has heard the words of the prophets... and believed that the Lord would redeem his people, and have looked forward to that day... these are his seed, or they are the heirs of the kindgom of God.

IQS 3:2-3. ...may he lift up his face upon all thy assembly and place upon thy head the crown.
4. in eternal glory and sanctify thy seed with eternal glory... and give thee peace and the kingdom [*malkuth*, kingship]...
5:21. A covenant of the Church to establish forever the kingship of his people.

15:26. Behold, and fear, and tremble... ye... that have known the commandments of God, and would not keep them

IQS 2:26-3:1. For his soul has turned away and departed from the knowledge [counsel] of the ordinances [*mishpate*] of truth; he did not remain firm in his dedication [changing of his life].

16:1. ...when all shall see the salvation of the Lord. 16:2. And then shall the wicked be cast out....3....and the devil has power over them....

CD 20:26. When the glory of God is openly revealed to Israel, then shall all the evil-doers of Judah be cast out from the midst of the camp and the people.

During the trial of Abinadi, Alma, one of the priests of Noah who had been converted by the teaching of the holy man, pleaded on his behalf, and being in danger of his own life (Mosiah 17:3), withdrew from circulation while he could put everything down in writing. The name of Alma, incidentally, has turned up in one of the newly discovered scrolls. In 1966, Professor Yadin found deeply buried in the floor of the Cave of Manuscripts the deed to a farm. Today the visitor entering the Shrine of the Book in Jerusalem will find the very first display on his left hand to be this deed, a strip of papyrus mounted on glass with a light shining through; and there written in a neat and legible hand is the name "Alma, son of Judah" — one of the owners of the farm. This deserves mention because the critics have always made great fun of the name of Alma (both Latin and feminine), comically out of place among the ancient Jews.

17:3. ...the king... caused

IQH 5:5. I praise THEE Lord for

that Alma should be cast out . . . and sent his servants after him that they might slay him. 4. But he fled from before them and hid himself that they found him not. And he being concealed for many days did write all the words which Abinadi had spoken.

thou didst not desert me when I was among the people . . . and didst not leave me in my secret affairs, but saved my life out of the pit and gave . . . in the midst of lions . . . 8. Thou didst take me to a place removed among the fisherfolk and hunters.

11. Thou didst hide me, O God, from the children of men, and hid thy law in me, until the time,

12. that thy help should be revealed to me.

13. Thou did preserve the life of the Poor One in the place of lions.

This is something of a standard situation — preparation for a holy mission by a retreat into the wilderness: we see the same thing in the cases of Ether, Moroni, Lehi and his sons, of Moses, John the Baptist and the Lord himself. The wilderness motif (Cf. Mauser's book, *Christ in the Wilderness*) is preparation for the more ambitious Rekhabite motif, about which Robert Eisler wrote so learnedly many years ago. Alma came out of hiding to do his work among the people; and in the Hodiyot we see the leader building up just such a following in the towns:

18:1 . . . Alma . . . went about privately among the people . . . to teach the words of Abinadi — 3. And he taught them privately. . . .

IQH 4:23. Thou hast not kept hiding for shame 24. all of those who permitted me to visit [or instruct] them, who came together in a church [*yahad*] of thy covenant to listen to me, and to follow the ways of thy heart. They rallied to my defense as a group of Saints.

And now come the New World Qumran:

18:4. And . . . as many as did believe him did go forth to a place which was called

CD 6:4. The volunteers from the people are those who bear the staff [cf. of wandering

Mormon... being in the
borders of the land...
infested, by times or at
seasons, by wild beasts.

(N.b. This is not the howling
wilderness, but the *midhbar*,
the places where desert and
cultivation or grazing
infringe upon each other;
the next verse shows that it
was a desert terrain.)

18:5. Now, there was in
Mormon a fountain of pure
water... there being near the
water a thicket of small trees
[like Ain Feshka?], where he
did hide himself in the daytime
from the searches of the king.

18:6. ...as many as believed
him went thither to hear his
words.
7. And... after many days
there were a goodly number
gathered together at the place
of Mormon, to hear the words
of Alma.... And he did teach
them, and did preach unto
them....
8. And... he said unto
them: ...as ye are... willing
to bear one another's
burdens....

Moses] and the Fountain [of
spring] is the Law... and they
are the inhabitants of Israel
who depart from the land of
Judah and dwell in the land of
Damascus as strangers. 7. The
staff is the one who teaches
them the Law, as Isaiah says.

(1 Nephi 19:23. I [Nephi in
the desert] did read unto
them that which was
written by the prophet
Isaiah; for I did liken all
scriptures unto us, that it
might be for our profit and
learning.)

IQS 8:13. At the fulfillment of
these signs they shall separate
themselves from dwelling in
the midst of a perverse people,
and go forth into the desert to
prepare a way for Him... 15.
...even by the study of the
Law as it was given to Moses
according to what has been
revealed from time to time as it
was shown to the prophet
through the Holy Ghost.

IQS 9:18. To lead and instruct
(*lehinkhotam*) in knowledge
and so give them
understanding in the hidden
wonders and truth [s] in the
midst of
19. the men of the Church; to
walk each one blamelessly
[perfect] with his neighbor in
all that has been revealed to
them in this time of preparing
the way in the wilderness, and
to instruct them in all that must
be done at this time.

Such communities were not without precedent in Israel. There were fraudulent prophets and quacks who time and again led such groups into the wilderness (see Eisler's work). The Dead Sea Scrolls have a good deal to say about such ambitious would-be Moseses. There is one instance in the early Christian literature which is interesting because it tells of one impostor who led his people to a place of filthy water — reminding us of Ignatius's charge that the apostate leaders of his day are giving the thirsting people poison to drink. What makes this case arresting is that the false prophet's name was Mormon. (Text in J. P. Migne, *Dict. des Apocryphes I.*) So too we read in CD 1:14. "The man of deception [*latson* — the phony] arose who preached lying waters to Israel and led them astray in the pathless desert, away from the paths of righteousness." In IQH 2:16 the righteous teacher tells how "all the men of falsehood [*remiyah*] stormed against me like a mass of mighty waters," 2:12. "The assembly of the wicked rushed upon me like a stormy sea, whose waves cast up all manner of mud," and 13. "filth." This is the "filthy water" of Nephi's vision, an image found also in the desert Arab poets. What could be worse to one dying of thirst in the desert than to be led to waters that could not be drunk!

18:8. [Alma says] Here are the waters of Mormon. . . . 10. . . .what have you against being baptized in the name of the Lord, as a witness . . . that ye have entered into a covenant that ye will serve him and keep his commandments. . . .	IQS 3:8. [In baptism] he submits his soul in all humility to every commandment of God, 3:9f. after which he applies himself to walking carefully [perfectly] in all the ways of God as he commanded for the specified time and conditions in turning aside to the right or to the left . . .
13. . . .as a testimony that ye have entered into a covenant to serve him. . . .	11. then he will truly be a covenant member of God's eternal church.
18:8. . . .willing to bear one another's burdens, that they may be light, . . . 9. and . . . willing to mourn with those that mourn; yea, and comfort those that stand in need of comfort. . . .	IQS 2:2-4. For all shall be united in one true church [oneness of truth], and in becoming humility, and love of mercy and fair dealing [dealings of righteousness] each man with his neighbor.

5:24. to be perfect each in supporting his fellow in truth and humility and love of mercy towards all.

18:8. ...as ye are desirous to come into the fold of God, and to be called his people....

CD 4:2. The sons of Zadok are following the patterns: The priests are penitent Israel 3. who have left the Land of Judah [and they are the LEVITES]... they are the elect of Israel who will be called up by name in the Last Days.

18:9. ...and to stand as witnesses of God at all times and in all things and in all places... even until death,

IQS 18:9. And not to turn away from him out of any fear or terror or any burning that may threaten in the government of Belial.

18:9. that ye may be redeemed, and be numbered with those of the first resurrection — that ye may have eternal life.

IQH 6:7-8. I was comforted amidst all the raging of the people gathering together. For I know that 8. after a time thou wilt raise up the Living One in the midst of thy people, and a remnant in thine inheritance, and purify them with the purification of forgiveness, for all their deed. 9. They trust on thee.

2 Nephi 9:41. ...the keeper of the gate is the Holy One of Israel: and he employeth no servant there;...
42. And whoso knocketh, to him will he open.... 43. [to them]... that happiness which is prepared for the saints.

13. And there is no go-between (*melits benayim* — servant representative) for thy Saints.... 14. for they answer in the presence of thy glory and become thy princes in an eternal inheritance.

The IQH 6:26 here uses the language of the Pastor of Hermas: "O God thou layest a foundation upon a Rock... according to the true rule and plummet [made] of thy chosen stones... and none stumbles who walketh hence. For no stranger will enter into its

wine at first before the Priest,
for he must bless the first-fruits
of the bread and wine; and he
takes the bread before them,
and after that the Messiah of
Israel puts forth his hand on
the bread, and after that all the
assembly of the church shall
bless [or be blessed, served],
each in the order of his office
[dignity],
21. and this is how they shall
do it on every formal
occasion, [*ma'rakhah*] when as
many as ten come together.

If this sounds disturbingly
Christian, it is no more so than
IQS 8:1 "In the council of the
church there shall be twelve
men, and three priests,
perfectly instructed in all that
has been revealed.

23:14. . . .trust no one to be
your teacher nor your minister,
except he be a man of God,
walking in his ways and
keeping his commandments.

2. in the entire Torah, to act in
truth and justice and judgment
and love of mercy, walking in
humility with their brethren.

23:16. Alma was their high
priest . . . [and] founder of their
church.

23:17. . . .none received
authority to preach or to teach
except it were by him from
God. . . . he consecrated all
their priests and all their
teachers. . . .

IQS 6:3f. Ten men shall not
meet without a priest to
preside.
6:7ff. There must never be a
priest failing to teach the word
of God.
6:6 And there shall not be
missing in any place where
there are as many as 10 men a
doresh [reader, expounder in
the Torah, whether by day or
night].

IQS 2:20. The priests shall enter or move on first of all, the Levites come next, and all the people in third place, for thousands and hundreds and fifties, and then tens, so that every man may know his place in the church of God for the doctrine of the eternities
6:8 the priests sit in the first place, the elders in the second and then all the other people 9. each according to his dignity. And they shall be consulted concerning the law and all decisions whatsoever that come before the congregation, so that every member
10. may place his knowledge at the disposal of all

IQSa 1:24. all things are directed by the Sons of Zadok the priests.
CD 13:2. In a place of 10 people there must a priest learned in the Book of Hagi, and all must follow his instructions. If he does not know enough, a Levite

18:19. [The priest] should teach nothing save it were . . . [what Alma] had taught, and which had been spoken by the mouth of the holy prophets.

IQS 9:7. Only the Sons of Aaron shall decide matters of law and property and administer the affairs of the society.
2:1. The priests shall bless all the active members [men who share the lot] who are in good standing [lit. who are walking perfectly].

18:23. . . . they should observe the sabbath day, . . . and *also* every day they should give thanks. . . . (Italics added.)

CD 10:14-12:4. Anyone who desecrates the Sabbath or the special day [*mo'a doth*] is put on probation for 7 years, before 6.

he is permitted again to attend all the meetings.

18:25. And there was one day in every week that was set apart that they should gather themselves together to teach the people, and to worship the Lord their God, and also, as often as it was in their power, to assemble themselves together.

IQS 6:7. the entire congregation shall watch together for a third of every night, to read in the Book, discuss the Law, 8. and sing hymns together.

18:24. ...the priests...should labor with their own hands for their support.
26. And the priests were not to depend upon the people for their support... for their labor they were to receive the grace of God, that they might... teach with power....

IQS 6:2. And the small shall heed the superior regarding work and property [Mammon, business] and they shall eat together.

CD 13:11. And everyone who joins the community shall be examined for his past activities, his knowledge and skills, his physical capacity, his energy, and his possession. (All contribute these.)

18:27. ...the people of the church should impart of their substance, every one according to that which he had....
28. ...they should impart of their substance of their own free will... to those priests that stood in need, ... and to every needy, naked soul.

IQS 6:19. Anyone accepted into the community shall turn over his property agreeable to the priests and the congregation, and receive a receipt from the official in charge.
7:6-7. Anyone careless with the common property must replace it.

18:29. ...and they did walk uprightly before God, imparting to one another both temporally and spiritually

CD 13:7. The overseer of the Camp shall direct the generality in the works of God, and teach them about the according to their needs and their wants.

wonderful things he has done, and have compassion like a father with his children, saving them from their erring ways as a Shepherd his sheep . . . that there be no oppressor or smiter in his group [*adatho*] 14:12. The gain [*shkar*] from at least 2 days a month shall be placed in the hands of the Overseer and the judges, for the support of the widows, the ailing and the poor and aged.

(In the Pastor of Hermas the rule is one day's income a month.)

As he sums up the achievements of this holy band, struggling to be real saints, and to a degree succeeding, the author of our account breaks out into an ecstatic little hymn of joy. The author of which account? Of both! The author of Mosiah 18:30 precedes the hymn with a satisfying summary to his story: " . . . and they did walk uprightly before God, imparting to one another both temporally and spiritually . . ." The writer of the Thanksgiving Hymns prefaces this particular one with an account of the wicked world in which he lived, but then he sees the community in the desert as a light shining all the more brightly by contrast:

IQH 6:11. the people of thy counsel in the midst of those of the world [the *bne* adam], telling for endless generations thy marvellous things and meditating upon thy greatness without ceasing . . . for thou sendest thy glory to all the men of thy counsel, sharing a common lot with the angels of thy presence."
IQH 6:5. from the world of *shaw* [vanity] and *khamas* [violence] . . . 8. God will establish a new life for his people, the remnant who will be his heirs.

13. Everyone who accepts his counsel receiving a common share with the angels of the presence [the Zion of Enoch motif].

There is no "go between" between the Holy One and the Saints (cf. 2 Nephi 9:41). 14. they are like a congregation of princes sharing in the eternal glory of the presence....

15. ...blossoming fruit forever, putting forth shoots to bear foliage in endless planting [renewal], to cast their shade over all the earth....

16. until ... their roots reach to the foundations of the earth [*tehom*] they strike the cosmic waters, and all the streams of Eden water them...

17. ...and has become the place of springs of light for an unfailing fountain that knows no ceasing

18. Then the account goes back to the wicked

After this brief happy vision of the community as a well-watered garden, an oasis in the desert, the poet plunges back into the dreary and wicked world. But the most remarkable parallel to Alma's hymn is No. VIII of the Thanksgiving Hymns from Qumran: The Book of Mormon hymn is divided into two stanzas, the first about the waters of Mormon, the second about the trees of Mormon. IQH VIII emphasizes the same dependence of the water and the trees on each other:

Mosiah 18:30. And ... all this was done in *Mormon*, yea, by the waters of *Mormon*, in the forest that was near the waters of *Mormon*; yea, the place of *Mormon*, the waters of *Mormon*,	IQH 8:4. I praise the Lord, for Thou didst bring me to a place of water in a dry land, to a fountain of water in a parched land, and to a water of a garden ...
the forest of *Mormon*, how	a growth [planting] of

beautiful are *they* to the eyes of
them who there came to the
knowledge of their Redeemer;
Yea, and how blessed are they,

for they shall sing his praise
forever. (Italics added.)

junipers, poplars and cedars,
along with thy glory,
trees of life are hidden
amidst secret springs in the
midst of all the trees,
by the water,
and they shall bring forth
shoots
for an eternal planting
to salvation.

Even without the last line and the formal word of conclusion —
"forever" — it would be plain that the Book of Mormon verses are a
hymn with a melody hovering about the word *Mormon*. In both
songs the imagery is that of the wanderer in the desert saved by the
water of life and the tree of life, saved from spiritual death to find
redemption and salvation. As might be expected, the trees and the
water give knowledge — life-giving knowledge as sustenance. So

1 Nephi 2:9. [Lehi's song,
qasida, in the desert] O that
thou mightest be like unto this
river, continually running into
the fountain of all
righteousness! (Cf. Ether 8:26.)

IQS 10:9. I will sing and
play . . . to
10:12. . . .the Most High, the
fountain of my good, the
source of my well-being, a
fountain of knowledge, a
flowing spring of holiness . . .I
will praise him at my going out
and coming in . . .

Even the end of the colony is much the same in the two stories.
Neither Qumran nor the waters of Mormon were unknown to the
king's men (Noah's in one case, Herod's in the other); after all the
places were not too far out in the wilderness, numbers of people
streamed out to them, and only one spy could find out or suspect all
that was necessary. What happened in the Book of Mormon
suggests quite sensibly what could have happened at Qumran, with
a jealous monarch keeping the place under surveillance until he
decided it would have to go.

Mosiah 18:32. . . .the king . . .
sent his servants to watch
them. . . . 33. And . . . said that
Alma was stirring up the
people to rebellion against
him; therefore he sent his army
to destroy them.

So they had to move on — but they were used to that, for that is the Rekhabite tradition: Israel is ever "das wandernde Gottesvolk" God's Wandering People — indeed the present Pope of Rome is partial to the title "Wayfaring Church" to describe his own flock.

Mosiah 18:34. And ... Alma and the people of the Lord ... took their tents and their families and departed into the wilderness.
35. And they were in number about four hundred and fifty souls.

Then they repeat Operation Flight into the Wilderness.

23.1 Now Alma ... made it known to his people, therefore they gathered together their flocks, and took of their grain, and departed into the wilderness....

23:3. And they fled eight days' journey into the wilderness.
4. And they came to ... a very beautiful and pleasant land, a land of pure water.
5. And they pitched their tents, and began to till the ground, and began to build buildings; yea, they were industrious, and did labor exceedingly.

CD 6:5. They went into the desert [Nu. 21:8] to dig a well, that is, to study the Law, namely the noble ones with the staff, that of Israel who had repented [been converted, *shuv*]; and they departed from the land of Judah and sojourned in the Land of Damascus, a land that was strange. 6. God has called them princes because they sought after him,
7. and the Staff [their leader] is he who studies the Law [as Isaiah 54:16 says], an implement in the hands of God to bring about his purposes.

It would be easy to supply many times more such parallels between the Book of Mormon and the other ancient records. If the latter are authentic (and both the Qumran and the Enoch writings were once challenged as late forgeries), it is hard to see how we can brush aside the Joseph Smith productions as nonsense. Even if every parallel were the purest coincidence, we would still have to explain how the Prophet contrived to pack such a dense succession of happy accidents into the scriptures he gave us. Where the world has a perfect right to expect a great potpourri of the most outrageous nonsense, and in anticipation has indeed rushed to judgment with all manner of premature accusations, we discover whenever ancient texts turn up to offer the necessary checks and controls, that the man was astonishingly on target in his depiction of general situations, in the almost casual mention of peculiar oddities, in the strange proper names, and countless other unaccountable details. What have Joseph Smith's critics really known about the true nature of those ancient societies into which his apocalyptic writings propose to take us? As the evidence accumulates, it is not the Prophet but his critics who find themselves with a lot of explaining to do.

The Haunted Wilderness

9

Exactly at noon on the winter solstice of 1964, the writer stood at the entrance of an artificially extended cave at the place then called Raqim (now Sahab), a few miles south of Amman, with Rafiq Dajani, brother of the Minister of Antiquity for Jordan, who had just begun important excavations on the spot and duly noted that the sun at that moment shone directly on the back wall of the cave, a feat impossible at any other time of the year. The ancient picture of a dog painted on the cave wall had dimly suggested to the local inhabitants and a few scholars in an earlier generation the story of the dog who guarded the cave of the Seven Sleepers – hundreds of caves claiming that title – but nobody took it very seriously. Beneath Byzantine stones, older ruins were coming to light, suggesting that the place may have been another Qumran, the settlement of early Christian or even Jewish sectaries of the desert; the region around was still all open country, mostly bare rocky ground. There it was, the beginning of an excavation that might turn up something exciting. Professor Dajani had read the article below in manuscript form and obligingly taken me for a visit to the place, where I took some pictures which were published in the Improvement Era.

Compare those pictures with what you find there today! Twelve years later I returned to the spot with a tour group in excited anticipation of the wonders I would now see laid bare. What we found was that the excavations, far from being completed, had actually been covered up, all but the cave; on the spot was rising the concrete shell of a huge new mosque, and a large marble slab, before the cave, proclaimed in Arabic and English that this was the Cave of the Seven Sleepers. The spot was being converted into a major Moslem shrine; our Christian Armenian guide was worried sick that there would be an incident, and at first hotly refused to stop the bus anywhere near the place. Naturally, I went straight for the cave and was met at the entrance by a venerable Mollah and his assistant who were selling candles; I said I wanted to see the holy dog and they led me to the back of the cave where the wall was completely covered by a large old commode through the dirty glass windows of which they pointed out some ancient brown bones and their prize – the actual jawbone of the holy dog; a relic had usurped the place of the picture. So there it was: what had been a few scattered ruins, lying deserted and completely ignored on the heath, was now being promoted as a booming cult-center, rapidly foundering in the encroaching clutter of sub-urban real estate enterprises. To a student of John Chrysostom nothing could be more instructive; it had taken just twelve years to set up an ancient and hopefully profitable center of pilgrimage. So you see, all sorts of things go on in the haunted desert, as the following article will show.

While Jewish and Christian writings have been diligently searched for possible references direct or indirect to the Qumran tradition, the Moslem commentators on the Koran have been neglected as a source of information, and that for the very quality that renders their work most valuable, namely their "uncritical" reluctance to omit from their profuse and repetitive notes any tradition, anecdote, or rumor that might conceivably cast light on a subject. Packed in among their jumbled baggage are many items that bring Qumran to mind. Whether these are significant or not remains to be decided after some of them have been examined.

The most promising place to begin a search for possible glimpses of Qumran is among the commentaries on the "Sura of the Cave" (*Sura* XVIII), and the most promising guidebook is that inexhaustible storehouse of oddities and surprises, Ahmad ath - Tha'labi's "*Accounts of the Prophets.*"[1] Following Tha'labi's lead, and eking out his reports with those of other commentators, we shall attempt to show that Moslem scholars were convinced that there had once been a singular community of saints living in caves in the Judaean desert, particularly in the region of Jericho, and that those cave people had a portentous message for the human race.

As the most fitting commentary to the thesis that all things of this earth are but "dust and dry dirt," the Prophet refers us to the *Ashab al-Kahf wa-l'Raquim*, "The Companions (often rendered simply "People" or "Inhabitants") of the Cave and the Inscription." (*Sura* XVIII, 9-10.) This was a group of holy men who had sought retreat in the wilderness in flight from a wicked and godless community and in the expectation that God would guide them in a proper way of life, fill them with grace, and provide for their wants; in due time they were hidden from the knowledge of men and their bodies were miraculously preserved in a cave, where they were at length discovered when a youth, by the providence of God, circulated old coins in a nearby town and thereby brought a rush of treasure-seekers to the scene. (*Sura* XVIII, 10-22.) Such a tradition might well look back to the sectaries of the desert — but there is a catch, for most commentators are agreed that the People of the Cave were the Seven Sleepers of Ephesus. That would settle the matter were it not that the Ephesus tradition itself rests on the flimsiest of foundations, archaeologically and philologically.[2] It is "une de ces légendes vagabondes qui n'ont pas d'attache fixe et prennent pied sur les terrains les plus divers, sans qu'aucun fait connu semble justifier le choix."[3] Scholars ancient and modern who have tried to get to the historical kernel of the story have found themselves confronted by countless conflicting traditions, and the Koran and its commentators note that every essential element of the history of the Companions is a subject of hopeless controversy among the People of the Book, who cannot agree as to where the cave was, how many people were in it,[4] what their religion was,[5] how long they stayed there, or in what condition.[6] In short, nobody really knows their history.

The main source of the confusion is not far to seek: there was more than one cave story because there was more than one cave — as the extremely popular legend spread abroad in the world the tale had to be adjusted to the interest of local patriotism, which from Andalusia to Persia enthusiastically and profitably exploited local grottoes as the authentic and original sites of the Seven Sleepers or the Companions of the Cave.[7] But amid a welter of conflicting legends and claims two main traditions have always been recognized — an Occidental, containing clearly marked pre-Christian

Classical elements as its distinctive ingredient, and an Eastern or Arabic tradition, based principally on Jewish apocryphal lore.[8] The clearest distinction between the two versions is preserved by Tha'labi. He knows the Ephesus tradition as well as anybody: the pre-Christian legends of youthful sleeping heroes are well represented in his pages;[9] he knows the resurrection miracle-stories of the early Christian apocrypha;[10] he and the other Arabs give an accurate description of the state of the Church both when the Sleepers fell asleep and when they awoke;[11] and they know the name of the mountain near Ephesus where they slept — a name which Christian scholars apparently do not know.[12]

But knowing the Ephesus version as he does, Tha'labi still gives priority to an entirely different story about a party of three refugees who were looking for a place for their families to settle when "the sky smote them" and they took refuge in a cave, only to be trapped by a rock-slide that sealed the entrance. Being thus caught, each one of them recounted some pious deed he had done in this lifetime, and with each successive story a fissure in the wall opened wider until they could all escape.[13] This tale has nothing to do with Ephesus — the men in the cave tell Jewish stories and do not even fall asleep.[14] The violence of the elements, the sliding down of the mountain, and the opening of fissures in the earth suggest an earthquake, and the sequel is that the people settled on the spot, since they left their records there.

The story of the Three is an Arabic contribution, designated by Huber as the "Raqim" version, that being the uniquely Arabic name for the locale of the Cave.[15] Since it is a perfectly plausible tale, one wonders why the Arabs, who insist on placing al-Raqim in Syria or Palestine, bother with Ephesus at all. It is because Ephesus had loudly advertised its claim to the Seven Sleepers ever since the middle of the fifth century, and our commentators are not the men to leave anything out.[16] Ephesus, however, gets into the picture only by usurping the much older credentials of Antioch — a circumstance that has been overlooked by researchers. The hero of the Arabic accounts of the Sleepers is one Tamlikh, whose name does not appear in the standard Western lists of the Seven: When he turns up in the Syriac versions his name makes an eighth in the established list, so that the older Syriac and Arabic accounts uniformly insist that there were really eight Sleepers.[17] The origin of the intruder is indicated by the epithet that Tha'labi gives him of *Ibn Falastin* — the Palestinian.[18] His Greek name of Iamblichus usually appears in Latin sources as Malchus while the Arabic writers point it variously as Tamlikh, Yamlikh, and Namlikh: all that remains is Bamlikh to remind us that, as Huber long ago suggested, the name Iamblichus-Malchus is simply Abimelech.[19] What brought Huber to that observation was the long-established identity, or at least very close parallel, between the Seven Sleepers and Abimelekh, the friend of Jeremiah who slept for seventy or one hundred years.[20] Abimelech in turn has long been identified with Onias-Honi the Circle-drawer.[21] Onias, Abimelech and Jeremiah all fell into century-long slumbers as they sat in the shade of a tree, and the tree is a peculiar detail which the Arabic writers introduce into their version of the Seven Sleepers,[22] and just as Onias was driven with his workmen to seek shelter from a storm in a cave, so the Arabs say the Cave of the Companions was discovered by a shepherd escaping from a storm, who ordered two laborers to open the mouth of the cave for him.[23] This Onias has in our day often been put forth as the leader of the Zadokite forerunners of the Qumran community in the days when they were being persecuted by Antiochus Epiphanes, and even as the founder of Qumran.[24] So we have Tamlikh, the leader of the Companions of the Cave, identified through Abimelech, with Onias, the leader of the Qumran society.

The earliest mention of the Seven Sleepers of Ephesus is in the *Itinera Theodosi*, 530 Anno Domini, which states that the Seven were brothers, and that their mother was Felicitas.[25] When one recalls that one of the first female martyrs was St. Felicitas, who heroically endured the extinction of her seven sons, and that these seven have been identified in ancient and modern times with the seven young Jewish heroes of IV Maccabees, martyred at Antioch by the brother of Antiochus Epiphanes,[26] and that Byzantine Christians also identify the Seven Sleepers with the martyrs of Antioch,[27] and when one further considers that Decius, the villain of the Ephesus story, goes by the name of Antiochus in an eastern version of it,[28] one begins to wonder if the fifth-century Ephesus story might not reflect a much earlier Syrian version. The confusion of Antioch and Ephesus is apparent in the strange insistence of our Arabic informants that the city of Ephesus changed its name to Tarsus after its conversion from paganism. Scholars have found no explanation for this strange aberration, and indeed it is hard to see how well-travelled men could have confused two of the best-known cities in the world.[29] But there is evidence that the name of Tarsus was indeed changed to Antiochia in 171 before Christ in honor of the pagan Antiochus Epiphanes, in which case it was back to Tarsus after his demise.[30] Zonaras in a rhetorical play on words calls the city Epiphanes,[31] and one wonders if the confusion of Tarsus-Epiphanes with Ephesus might not be a typical slip: the Arabs knew that the city had once had another name — and what could it have been but Ephesus, since they favored Tarsus as the site of the cave?[32] The year that the name was changed, 171 B.C., also saw a migration of Jews to Tarsus,[33] and one Arabic commentator suggests that Tarsus got its name at the time of the Cave People from a group of colonists from Tripolis in Syria.[34] At about the same time, it is surmised, the Bene Zadok were first being driven by Antiochus Epiphanes under their leader Onias III.[35] Thus there is some evidence to associate the founding of the Cave community with persons, times, places and circumstances that have become familiar in the discussions of the founding of the Qumran community.

While quite aware that the Seven Sleepers story is Christian property, our Arabic informants are inclined to favor a *pre*-Christian date for the Companions of the Cave, explaining that they later became disciples of Jesus and flourished "in the days of the kings of Tawaif, between Jesus and Mohammed."[36] This implies that the society had a fairly long life, a thing entirely out of keeping with the brief and violent episode of the Ephesians. Another thing to note is the dependence of our Arabic informants, especially Tha'labi, on Jewish sources.[37] While it was Jacobite and Nestorian leaders arguing about the People of the Cave who first asked Mohammed's opinion on the matter,[38] those who really claimed a monopoly of knowledge on the subject were the Jews. According to one account the Quraish sent a delegation to Medina to gather intellectual ammunition against the Prophet from the local Jews, who loudly insisted that they alone were qualified to speak on prophetic matters. They suggested some test questions to embarrass the new prophet, the prize one being about the People of the Cave.[39] In another version it is the skeptical Jews themselves who send the delegation to investigate Mohammed.[40] But the account favored by Tha'labi is that of a delegation of three holy men who came not to Mohammed but to Omar, looking for a true prophet. These were not the smart, proud, skeptical Jews of Medina but sincere and humble seekers, who gladly accepted the Prophet as soon as they were made sure of his calling.[41] The impression one gets is that of Hasidic Jews interviewing the sympathetic Omar during his campaign in Palestine — he calls them "brothers," and he must send back home for Ali in order to answer their questions.[42] The peculiar questions they put to him moreover bear the characteristic stamp of the nonconformist sectaries: they ask about the keys of heaven, the moving tomb of Jonah, the warning minister who is neither spirit nor man, the things that walk the earth but were not created in the womb, the speech of animals and its spiritual message, and above all "about the people of a former age who died 309 years, and then God revived them — what is their story?".[43]

That the story of the devout delegates goes back to the early sectaries is indicated in a report attributed to Ibn Abbas, the nephew of the Prophet and the star witness in all matters concerning the People of the Cave: "The followers of Jesus remained on the sacred path for 80 years after his ascension," and then "Yunus the Jew came among the Christians wearing a hermit's or monk's gown (this well before the days of Christian monasticism). . . . His devout life produced great confidence among the Christians, and . . .he said, 'Send me three of your learned men . . . that I may a divine secret before each of them separately.' " As a result "the Christians were divided into three sects" forever after — the very sects that argued about the Cave People in the presence of Mohammed.[44] Here we have a counterpart both to the three malicious questions that the Jews put to Mohammed (in nearly all the commentators the questions are three) and the delegation of three pious Jews that came to him. The oldest Syrian version of the Seven Sleepers, which some hold to be the original, places their history around sixty A.D., thus taking it entirely out of the later Ephesian setting and putting it in the orbit of the early sectaries.[45]

Tha'labi is quite at home with certain pre-Christian communities in the desert. He tells us among other things how the infant Mary was taken to be reared by "the priests of the sons of Aaron," and how the priestly society cast lots for her, standing on the banks of the Jordan to see whose rod would sink and whose would float, they being "the reeds with which they used to write the Torah." Zacharias, the father of John the Baptist, and, according to Tha'labi, "the chief of the scholars and their prophet," won the lottery; but when a famine came he could no longer support the child and it was necessary to have another casting of lots, won this time by Joseph the righteous carpenter.[46] Since "Brownlee argues that the mother of the Messiah is the 'Essene Community',"[47] Mary's prominence in such a community as this may not be without significance. The story of Joseph's winning of Mary is told in the *Epistle of I Clement*, c. 43, and indeed Tha'labi's general familiarity with Clementine motifs should be studied in view of the importance of the latter in understanding the background of Qumran.[48] His tracing of Zacharias's genealogy through both a Saduq and a Sadiq indicates access to early source material;[49] and is quite relevant to the Seven Sleeper investigation, since the oldest Western version, that of Gregory of Tours, reports, on the authority of "a certain Syrian" that the mission of the Seven Sleepers was to correct certain errors not of the Christians but of the Sadducees — a term often confused with Zadokite in the early Middle Ages in designating nonconformist sectarians among the Jews.[50] Why should the Seven Sleepers of Ephesus be emissaries to the Sadducees, of all things? The Zadokite background of Qumran needs no demonstration.

A significant aspect of the Seven Sleepers' history as told by the Arabs is that nobody ever sees them alive.[51] Even in the Western legends the ruler merely embraces the youths as they sit on the ground and after a short and formal benediction by one of them they promptly fall asleep again.[52] The miracle that proves the resurrection is never the animation of their bodies, but only their preservation;[53] no capital is made of the rich store of Jewish and Christian apocryphal lore, the "testaments" of various prophets, patriarchs, and apostles who come to life to tell of wonderful things in the worlds beyond. This remarkable reserve suggests what many students have pointed out, that the Sleeper stories may well have originated with the actual discovery of human remains in caves. The Mediterranean world had never been without local hero-cults and their grottoes: Arabic writers report visits to a center in Andalusia which had all the fixtures and purported to be the original home of the Companions of the Cave,[54] and such a shrine and cult survived at Paphos on Cyprus down to modern times.[55] But the cave best known to the Arabs was one near Tarsus, where thirteen cadavers in a remarkable state of preservation were annually propped up and groomed — their clothes brushed, the nails manicured, their hair dressed — and then laid down to sleep for another year before a devout host of Christian pilgrims who believed they were in the presence of the Seven Sleepers.[56] This reproduces exactly the drama of the original Sleepers in the presence of Theodosius and his people, and strongly suggests a cult of the dead. In the "Hunting" version of the Sleepers story, which has all the marks of the Classical Endymion cycle, our Arabic informants comment on how the spring dried up and the trees all withered while the youths slept, only to be miraculously revived at their awakening.[57] Such obvious cult-motifs serve to set the Ephesian tradition apart from the more down-to-earth "Raqim" accounts of the Arabs, which indeed contain rather surprisingly nothing of a miraculous nature.

In a much-cited passage, Ibn Abbas tells how on a campaign with Mu'awiyah or Habib ibn Maslamah he passed by a cave containing bones which were said to be those of the Companions. His friend wanted to take a look, but Ibn Abbas protested that that would be sacrilege; some men who were sent to the cave to investigate were driven in terror by a fierce wind.[58] Ibn Abbas is quoted as saying that the cave was "near Aelia," and al-Qurtubi explains that they passed by it on the way to Rum.[59] The latter authority also reports that when Ibn Abbas made a few fitting remarks at the cave site a Syrian monk who was standing by observed with surprise, "I didn't think that an Arab would know anything about that!" to which the company proudly replied by introducing Ibn Abbas as their Prophet's nephew.[60]

The key to the location of the Eastern Cave is the mysterious name of al-Raqim. The great Ibn Abbas confesses that the word is one of the four things in the Koran which he cannot understand, but is quoted by Tabari as saying that Raqim is "a wadi between 'Asfan and Aelia beyond Palestine; and it is near Aelia";[61] while Damiri has him say: "it is a wadi between Amman and Aelia, beyond Palestine between the Ghatfan (tribe) and the country beyond Palestine; and this is the wadi in which the People of the Cave live, but Ka'ab says it is their village."[62] Most Arabic authorities locate al-Raqim in the plain of Balq in southeastern Palestine, and the geographer Istakhri mentions a small town by that name in the area, apparently near the Dead Sea.[63] Some writers, however, favor the region of Damascus and others that of Amman.[64] Clermont-Ganneau noted that the village of al-Raqim 7 km. south of Amman is identified by Usama with a place called el-Kahf, where there are some remarkable tombs cut into the living rock — hence Ashab al-Kahf wa l'Raqim. In December of 1964 the writer visited this site with Mr. Rafiq Dajani of the Jordan Department of Antiquities, whose forthcoming book on the subject treats at length the features of the newly excavated site which render it in our opinion by far the most likely candidate for the original Raqim. Even Huber concedes that this was probably the al-Raqim of the Arabic commentators, but hastens to point out that it cannot possibly have been the cave of the Seven Sleepers of Ephesus.[65] But then no one says it was — our Arabic authors readily admit that they are dealing with other caves, and what interests us here is not the mythical cavern of Ephesus but real caves in the Judaean desert.

Distant candidates in Nineveh and Yemen need not detain us, though we should not overlook the suggestion that the Companions were originally wandering artisans (sayāqala).[66] Tha'labi reports that when writings inscribed on metal plates (and we shall presently see that the "inscriptions" of the Cave were such documents) were found in a cave in Yemen no one could decipher them until one of these traveling smiths or artisans was consulted.[67] This is noteworthy because some scholars have seen in these nomadic craftsmen the descendants of the Rekhabites and hence the possible ancestors of the Qumran community.[68] The earliest Oriental versions of the Seven Sleepers stories actually do come from Nejran, the borders of Yemen. Massignon explains this by showing that the feast of the Martyrs of Nejran falls on the same day as that of the Seven Sleepers of Ephesus, making it easy if not inevitable for Jacob of Sarug to confuse the two; and since Ephesus was inconveniently far away, Massignon reasons, Eastern Christians simply moved the shrine to Nejran, whence it was transplanted to "military garrisons and the hermitages of anchorites on the fringes of the deserts."[69] The objection to this theory is that the men of Nejran will have nothing whatever to do with *Seven* Sleepers, but only three or five, which is strange indeed if they imported the magic Seven directly from Ephesus.[70] Plainly the Nejran version rests on another tradition.

Al-Raqim, so Lane informs us, means writings engraved or scratched on something, "a brass plate, or stone tablet, placed at the mouth of the cave," Sale suggests, though he is not sure,[71] or else it is two lead tablets in a sealed copper box — with silver seals,[72] or it is simply a book, or even a golden tablet,[73] or perhaps it is an inscription over the cave door,[74] or else the name of the cave itself, or of the wadi where it is,[75] or possibly the mountain,[76] or it may have been the stone that blocked the entrance,[77] or else it is the ruins near the cave or even the village where the Cave People lived;[78] or it may refer to water-holes or running water in the wadi.[79] On the other hand, it may refer to coins, or to an inkstand or writing desk found on the spot;[80] or it may be the dog that guarded the cave,[81] or any number of regions claiming to possess the Cave.[82] Strangely enough, no one seeking to locate the cave ever mentions the church or mosque that is supposed to have marked the spot with perpetual ritual observances — this most obvious clue of all has no place in the Raqim tradition. Instead we are confronted with a combination of caves, writings, bones, ruins, coins, inkstands, wadis (there is no mention of a valley in any of the orthodox Ephesus stories), etc., suggesting that the would-be interpreters of al-Raqim all have in mind a type of archaeological site which the modern reader most readily associates with Qumran.

The general consensus is that al-Raqim refers to secret buried writings containing the history and even the teachings of the Companions, but "whose meaning God has kept from us, and whose history we do not know."[83] These were deliberately hidden away to come forth in later age when "perhaps God will raise up a believing people."[84] There was a tradition that Jeremiah with the same purpose had hidden such treasures in a cave near Jericho,[85] as Peter had done near Jerusalem (according to Baidawi it was Peter who discovered the documents of al-Raqim),[86] and the theme of buried holy books has a special appeal to Tha'labi, who carries the custom back to the remotest times.[87] The recently recognized possibility that the library of Qumran was deliberately buried in "a solemn communal interment," to come forth in a more righteous age thus supplies another link between Qumran and the Companions of the Cave and the Raqim, while putting a new stamp of authenticity on their existence.[88]

Let us recall how the question was put to Omar: "Tell me about the people of old who died 309 years and then God revived them — what is their story?" One wonders in passing why Jews should be so interested in a purely Christian story, and why they alone should claim to know its details, which according to Tha'labi were all to be found in Jewish books: plainly they were not asking about Ephesus at all.[89] The length of the famous sleep is reported at anything from seventy to nine hundred years. The Christians favor 372, while the Moslems accept the 309 years of the Koran.[90] The true meaning of the 309 is a great mystery, which only a true prophet can explain;[91] it comes from the beni Israel, and "the Christians of Nejran say, 'As for the 300 years we already knew about that, but as for the 9 years we know nothing about it.' "[92] But all are agreed that it represents the period of darkness during which the blessed Companions slept, like Onias, to awaken only at the dawn of a new age of faith.[93] Such was also, whatever the actual years may have been, the significance of the 390 years of the *Damascus Document* I, 5-6, "the Era of Anger" and darkness. Massignon shows the lengths to which Christians and Moslems will go to see significance in 309; it is the "anagram of the total of the 14 isolated initial letters of the Koran," namely 903, as also, of the name of Jesus: *'Isa* = 390.[94] The free juggling of figures does not draw the line at arranging them in any order, just as modern scholars are not embarrassed by the difference between 390 and 393 years or the necessity of adding or subtracting 20 or 40 to suit one's calculations. It has been recognized that the 390 of the *Damascus Document* is a symbolic number having "no more than a schematic value," and the same is held for the Koranic 309.[95] Since both have the same significance and are equally vague, distant, and mysterious, a possible confusion of the two may furnish yet another link between the two societies.

The consensus of opinion that al-Raqim were *metal* plates containing the writings of the Companions, as well as Tha'labi's preoccupation with metal documents in general, is moved from the realm of pure fantasy by the recent discovery of a number of metal documents in Palestine and Syria, the most notable being the *Copper Scrolls* from Qumran Cave 4. Tabari tells of a shepherd who discovered inscribed tablets which no one could read but an old holy man of the desert — like the Copper Scrolls, these tablets contained lists of buried treasure.[96] Another peculiarity of the Companions (which does not fit with the Ephesus scene) is the emphasis put on the formal organization of the society. After individually receiving enlightenment in the shade of a tree — like Onias, Abimelech, and the Buddha — the Seven discover to each other their like-mindedness and resolve to form a community with a nearby cave as their headquarters. They have a president and spokesman, Maximilianus, and a secretary and a treasurer, Tamlikh, the star of the play.[97] Each member fetches his property from his father's house and after giving lavishly to the poor turns the rest over to a common fund, to be shrewdly administered.[98] Such a community of property is one of the best-known features of the Qumran society.

In taking to the wilderness, the Brethren set up (according to the Arabs, but not to the Greeks) at a place where there was a good spring and some fruit trees, subsisting as did many a pious anchorite in years to come on the water and dates of an oasis.[99] "They left their homes and lands, families and children . . . and entered the caves (plural) in the year of the prophets."[100] Here we have a definitive religious movement, as against the adolescent escapade of Ephesus: in the latter case the youths (who are very young) flee to the wilderness expressly to escape the emperor, while in the former their society flourishes before the emperor ever hears of it.[101] Part of the heroic allure of the Companions is that they are high-ranking officers in the imperial army, which seeming inconsistency suits well with the image of the men of Qumran as "dedicated holy warriors."[102]

Considerable emphasis is placed by our Arabic authors on the north-south orientation of the Sleepers, who must face the north to preserve their bodies against the day of their arising. Here is a reminder of the north-south orientation of the burials at Qumran, whatever may be its significance.[103] The bodies of the Sleepers were turned from side to side by angelic ministers (to avoid corruption) every seven days, or seven years, or twice a year, or (in most writers) every year on New Year's Day.[104] Also, the sun shines into the cavern on just two days of the year — suggesting the equinoxes — and it is the sun which finally awakens them.[105] The emphasis here on a solar (resurrection) cult and calendar is a reminder that the Qumran people were peculiar for their zealous adherence to an archaic solar calendar.[106]

It was in the ancient practice of incubation at healing shrines that E. Rohde sought the origin of the Seven Sleepers tradition, and indeed our Arabic and Syriac sources tell how God speaks to the Companions as they sleep, and how one calls upon their names for healing dreams.[107] It is just possible that Qumran itself may have been such a healing shrine: " . . .the idea of a place of healing by the Dead Sea was well established in Jewish tradition and gives added reason for the Essenes' ('Physicians') choice of Qumran (Mesillah) for their desert home."[108] In this connection, Allegro dwells on the ancient designations of Qumran as meaning "shady," "sheltered" — which puts one in mind of the elaborate arrangements described by the Arab scholars for keeping the sleeping Companions in the shade,[109] though admittedly far-fetched.

The one truly moving episode in the history of the Seven Sleepers as the Arabic commentators tell it is the manner of their falling asleep. The indefatigable Tamlikh returns from the town in tears of anxiety to report to his friends that the monster (*jabbar*, a Jewish word) has returned to Ephesus and is coming out against them. This calls for a general lamentation until Tamlikh tells the brethren to dry their eyes, lift up their heads, and "eat what God has given," an expression suggestive of an exhortation to martyrdom. Accordingly, we behold the Brethren of the Cave partaking of their last sorrowful supper as the sun sets (the setting of the sun receives special emphasis), and then, as they sit upon the ground, preparing and exhorting one another in holy conversation, quietly yielding up their souls to God.[110]

The celebration of a last supper and love-feast as the sun sets brings to mind Philo's account of an Egyptian branch of the Essenes holding their solemn feast at sundown,[111] as well as al-Biruni's report that the Jewish sect of the Maghariba celebrated their rites at sunset — a circumstance which could easily lead him to omit the single *nuqfah* that makes the difference between Maghariba ("Sundown-people") and the familiar Maghariyah or "People of the Caves."[112]

The reference in *Sura* LXXXV, 4 to "the people of the pit"

(*ashabu 'l-ukhdud*) deserves mention because in the past it has commonly been interpreted as referring to the persecutors of the Christians of Nejran. This explanation was seriously questioned, and the now familiar designation of the "people of the pit" in the Dead Sea Scrolls indicates an earlier origin of the concept.[113] At the same time it vindicates the Christian Nejran tradition as an authentic echo of the old desert sectaries: it was the Christians of Nejran, it will be recalled, who first mentioned the Companions of the Cave to Mohammed.

The name given by the Companions to their settlement, according to the Arabic sources, was Hiram or Khiram, meaning "sectarians" or "separation," but also an appropriate designation for forbidden ground.[114] The wonderful dog that spoke with a human voice and faithfully guarded the threshold of the Cave usually goes by the name of Qatmir, though we also find him sharing the well-nigh universal name of Raqim, explained by Damiri's note that the Arabs often called a dog Raqmah, meaning a wadi with water in it, which he believes to be the source of the name Raqim.[115] Since the name of the dog is thus confused with that of the society, the cave, the valley and what-not, one wonders if the second commonest name of the dog might not represent a like confusion — for the name is Khumran, the closest parallel yet to "the meaningless Arabic name Qumran."[116]

Let us now briefly summarize some of the main points of resemblance between Qumran and the Companions of the Cave. First of all, the experts favor a pre-Christian origin for both; each begins its history with a persecution and migration under (possibly) Antiochus Epiphanes, at a time when both societies seem to have the same leader; both have ties with wandering artisans — the ancestors and/or descendants of desert sectarian groups; they have the same apocalyptic-mystic teachings, familiar alike from the early Jewish and the early Christian apocryphal writings; both have connections with a priestly society on the Jordan before the birth of Christ; the activities of both are reflected in the Clementine writings; both are identified with the Zadokites by name; both are near Aelia and even nearer to Jericho; both left behind the same peculiar combination of archaeological litter; both engaged in the odd practice of burying sacred records to come forth at a later time as a witness; both make use of metal plates for such records; each thinks of itself as the righteous remnant; the numbers 309 and 390 have for the Companions and Qumran respectively the same significance; both societies are well organized and practice a community of property; each community has its buildings, spring, and fruit trees as well as its caves; both were ritually oriented, dedicated to good works and religious exercises, controlled by a special solar calendar; in both the dead were laid away facing the north; both practice healing and incubation and seem to have had a solemn ritual feast at sundown; the members of both are dramatized in a military capacity; both sites are linked in later times with the mysterious word Khumran-Qumran. In both cases everything is very vague, far away, and strangely portentous.

The great mystic and symbolic appeal of the Sura of the Cave, which is recited every Friday in every mosque, rests on the concept of the Seven as intercessors for man in a wicked and dangerous world.[117] But there may be more than abstract symbolism or allegory involved here. Scattered references in Jewish and Christian writings such as the Karaite texts and the letter of Bishop Timotheus, indicate at least a dim awareness down through the centuries of the existence and the peculiar significance of writings found in caves near Jericho. When the red herring of Ephesus is removed we are faced with the very real likelihood that the people who left those records were those very "Companions of the Cave and the Writing" who made such an indelible imprint on the Islam.

The purpose of this brief exploratory study has been to raise rather than settle issues. The Arabic commentators cited are of course only a sampling, since the Arabic sources available at present in the Far West are limited, though increasing very rapidly, thanks to the titanic efforts of Professor Aziz S. Atiya. But they have given us enough to indicate that many questions still await and deserve investigation. We have not even touched upon the knotty and intriguing question of the identification and status of the all-knowing Tha'labi, nor have we examined the possible paths by which the Qumran tradition reached him and other Arabic writers; nor have we considered the wealth of literary tradition and folklore that surrounds the wonderful dog Qatmir, nor sought to trace the mysterious and significant line of Zadok in the Arabic sources; nay, we have not even mentioned the many other possible references to the Qumran tradition in the Koran itself. What we have done is simply to indicate the possibility that echoes of Qumran still reverberate in the pages of many Moslem writers, who may yet prove valuable informants to students of the Dead Sea Scrolls.

NOTES

1. "Abu Ishaq Ibn Mohammed Ibn Ibrahim ath-Tha'labi of Nishapur, the celebrated commentator, was the outstanding (Koran) interpreter of his time; he composed a great commentary which was without equal for fullness . . .": Ibn Khallikan, *Kitab wafayat al-aiyan* (Paris: 1842), I, p. 30. "Ein besonders heiss umstrittenes Feld waren altarabischen, jüdischen und christlichen Legenden des Korans und der Tradition . . . So kommt es, dass der bedeutendste Korangelehrte deiner Zeit, der im Jahre 427/1036 gestorbene Ahmed eth-Tha'labi, als bedeutendstes Werk seine "Prophetengeschichten" erfasst hat": A. Mez. *Die Renaissance des Islams* (Heidelberg: 1922), p. 190. His "History of the Prophets gives all the stories in very great detail . . . *Encyclopedia of Islam* (1934), IV, p. 736. Cf. C. Brockelmann, *Geschichte der Arabischen Literatur* (Weimar: 1898), I, pp. 350-351.

2. Baronius and Tillemont both declared it spurious. The Austrian archaeologists working at the supposed site discovered "pas un nom ni un symbole, indice d'une tombe vénérée," *Analecta Bollandiana* 55 (1937), p. 351. Philology is no less nonplussed: " . . .il ne faut pas oublier que les noms de la grotte, et de la montagne de la légende ne se retrouvent pas aux environs d'Éphèse," *Ibidem*, 24 (1905), p. 503.

3. *Analecta Bollandiana* 55 (1937), p. 351. Cf. *Ibid*, 39 (1921), p. 176, commenting on the "systèmes déja échafaudés autour de cette littérature foisonnante." There is no apparent reason why the legend should have become the special property of Ephęsus, according to Bern. Heller, *La Légende des Sept Dormants*, in *Revue des Études Juives*, 49 (1904), p. 216, note 6, though it is understandable that the city once in possession should exploit the legend to the fullest.

4. For location, see below, notes 61-65. The number of sleepers is a subject of endless debate: *Sura* XVIII, 22; al-Nasafi, *Tafsir al-Qur'an al-jalil* (Cairo: 1936-1942), II, p. 286; al-Hijazi, *al-Tafsir al-wadih* (Cairo: 1952), XV, pp. 53-54. It is one of the great mysteries, known to but a few, al-Tabari, *Kitab jami' al-bayan fi tafsir al-Qur'an* (Cairo: 1910), XV, p. 150; al-Nasafi, *loco citato*. The Jacobites said there were three sleepers, the Nestorians five, the Moslems seven: al-Qurtubi, *al-Jami' li-ahkam al-Qur'an* (Cairo: 1935?- 1950), X, p. 382; al-Damiri, *Hayat al-hayawan* (Cairo: 1867), II, pp. 353-354 (pages are incorrectly numbered, but we follow the numbers given); al-Nasafi, *opus citatum*, II, p. 285; al-Baydawi, *Anwar al-tanzil* (Cairo: 1899-1902), IV, pp. 98-99. Yusuf Ali, a modern authority, says that Mohammed "*suggested* that the youths were seven in number," *The Holy Qur-an* (New York: Hafner, 1946), II, p. 730, note 2337.

5. Some say they lived before Christ and were idolaters, others that they were Christians, others that they were Moslems: Tabari, *Tarikh al-Tabari* (Cairo: 1961), II, pp. 6-7, and *Jami' al-bayan*, XV, p. 137; some even that their people were *majus:* Damiri, II, p. 353. Yet the Jews have a special claim on them: Ibn Kathir, *Tafsir al-Qur'an al-asim* (Cairo: 1954), III, p. 74. See below, note 37.

6. Below, note 90, for the length of the stay. As to their condition, the main discussion is as to whether they were sleeping or dead, Baydawi, IV,

202

pp. 97-98; Qurtubi, X, p. 388; Damiri, II, p. 358, etc. See Michel Huber, *Die Wanderlegende von den Siebenschläfern* (Leipzig: 1910), pp. 79-99.

7. Huber, *op. cit.* pp. 17, 122. Thus after favoring Ephesus (though Ephesus is not mentioned in the Koran), Ibn Kathir, III, p. 75, concludes: "...we are not told what land the cave was in.... But Ibn Abbas says it was near Aelia, and Ibn Ishaq says it was near Nineveh, while others say it was in the land of Rum and others that it was in the plain of Balqā (southeastern Palestine), but God knows." See below, note 59.

8. Discussed by Huber, *op. cit.* in note 6 above, pp. 552-556. The distinction is clear in Huber's classification of sources into the Classical Endymion and Epimenides legends (pp. 378-390), as against the Onias-Abimelech-Ezra tradition (pp. 403-447) of the Orient. The Arabic commentators themselves admonish against confusing the two traditions. Thus al-Shirbini, *al-Siraj al-munir* (Cairo: 1868), II, p. 350, assures us that the three pious refugees (below, note 13) are "another group entirely from the (traditional) People of the Cave." Cf. al-Qurtubi, X, p. 357, and Ibn Kathir, III, p. 75.

9. The Endymion motif, in which E. Rohde, *Die sardinische Sage von den Neunschläfern,* in *Rheinisches Museum für Philologie,* Neue Folge, 35 (1880), pp. 158-159, 162-163, sees the origin of the Seven Sleepers of Ephesus, is one of the four distinct versions of the Sleepers reported by Tha'labi and others. It is the "Hunting" story in which youthful nobles go forth to hunt and celebrate a great pagan festival only to end up falling asleep in a cave, guarded by their faithful dog. The fullest account of this is in Tha'labi, *Qissas al-anbiyah* (Cairo: 1921), pp. 289-290, 292-293. Cf. Ibn Kathir, III, pp. 74-75; al-Qasimi, *Tafsir al-qasimi* (Cairo: 1957-1960), X, p. 4032. Typical of the cycle is Tha'labi's account of Saint George, pp. 299-300.

10. One of the four versions (see preceding note) is the tale of the Bath Attendant (Tha'labi, p. 293; Tabari, *Tarikh,* II, p. 8, and *Jami' al-bayan.* XV, p. 136; Damiri, II, pp. 344-345; Qurtubi, X, pp. 359-360), which consists of familiar motifs from the early apocryphal *Acts of John, Thomas, Andrew, Peter,* etc., see Huber (*op. cit.* in note 6), pp. 306-310. Also the well-known talking-dog motif, found in all the above-named Arabic sources, is familiar from the pseudo-*Acts of Andrew, Thomas,* etc. Damiri, II, p. 344, says that the official story of the People of the Cave was written down by Andrew (Mandrūs) and Thomas (Dūmās), and others say that it was "a righteous ruler of the people called Peter (Bīdrūs)" who ruled for sixty-eight years who discovered the document: Baydawi, IV, pp. 87, 90.

11. The moral decline of the Christians just before the Decian persecution, to which Eusebius and Cyprian attribute that persecution, is passed over in silence by Christian commentators on the Ephesus story, but is very well described by the Arabs: Tha'labi, p. 293; Tabari, *Jami'al-bayan.* XV, p. 133; Nasafi, II, p. 284; Shirbini, II, p. 351; Damiri, II, pp. 339-340. The state of things under Theodosius is equally well described. M. Huber (*op. cit.* in note 6), p. 567; *Analecta Bollandiana* 72 (1954), p. 265. The risen youths seem to the Emperor like the ancient disciples come to life, and he rejoices in the restoration of the old religion: Tabari, *Jami'al-bayan,* XV, p. 147; Shirbini, II,

p. 362; Damiri, II, p. 349. The righteous leader who greets the saints on their awakening sometimes bears the name of Arius: Tabari, XV, pp. 145-147; Shirbini, II, p. 361. Tha'labi, pp. 297-298, reads it *Armús*.

12. In Greek sources it is Chaos, Chileton, Chileon; in the Latin, Chilleus, Celius, Mons Celeus. *Analecta Bollandiana* 41 (1923), p. 374; 55(1937), p. 350. In the Syrian tradition it is always Mount Anchilos, of which Huber, pp. 222-223, notes that "um Ephesus herum kein einziger Berg einen auch nur halbwegs ähnlichen Namen trägt," surmising that the Christians could readily borrow the name of Mons Caelius near Rome for their Sleepers, "da der Berg selber nicht existierte... ," p. 58. The Arabs ring the changes on Anchilos with *Yanjilūs* (Baydawi, IV, pp. 85-86, 89), mispointed to read *Banāhiyūs* and even *Manhilūs* (Damiri, II, pp. 343, 350), but most commonly written as *Banjilūs* (Tabari, XV, p. 135; Shirbini, II, p. 353; Ibn Kathir, III, p. 73), this being nearest to the modern Turkish name for the real mountain east of Ephesus, Panajir-Dagh: *Analecta Bollandiana* 55 (1937), p. 350.

13. Tha'labi, p. 287, attributing the story to Mohammed. It was *thalātha nafrin*, which can mean either a party of refugees or a military detail. That it was the former may be inferred from the nature of their mission: *yarla-dūna li-ahlihim*, "looking about for some place for their families" — seeking asylum. See Damiri, II, p. 341.

14. The stories have been analyzed by B. Heller (*op. cit.* in note 3), pp. 199-202, and classified as Haggidic.

15. "So ist eine genaue *Scheidung* zwischen den Höhlenleuten (of Ephesus) un den Genossen des Er-Raqim festzuhalten... ." Huber (*op. cit.* in note 6), p. 239. See below, notes 61 and 62.

16. It is now definitely established that the story was first fastened on Ephesus by a *"pia fraus"* of Bishop Stephanus of that city in the year 449 or 450, according to *Analecta Bollandiana* 72 (1954), p. 265, citing E. Honigmann, *Patristic Studies* (Rome: Vatican, 1954).

17. M. Huber (*op. cit.* in note 6), pp. 593, 503; *Analecta Bollandiana* 39 (1921), p. 177; 66 (1948), p. 195. The Arabs explain the discrepancy by having the Seven joined by a shepherd on their way to the Cave (Tha'labi, p. 293). Tabari, *Tarikh*, II, p. 6. Baydawi, IV, p. 48 and Damiri, II, p. 339, all tell straightforward stories of eight Sleepers, in spite of *Sura* XVIII, 22.

18. Tha'labi, p. 292.

19. "Schon der Name Abimelech weist den Jamlich-und-Malchus hin": Huber (*op. cit.* in note 6), p. 22.

20. Heller (*op. cit.* in note 3), pp. 207, 214.

21. Huber (*op. cit.* in note 6), pp. 418-426. See the article *Onias (Honi)* in *Jewish Encyclopedia* (1901), IX, pp. 404-405.

22. For the three Hebrews, see B. Heller (*op. cit.* in note 3) pp. 202-206. For the tree episode, Tha'labi, p. 292; Tabari, XV, p. 136; Baydawi, IV, p. 86; Ibn Kathir, III, p. 74; Qurtubi, X, p. 359: Shirbini, II, p. 355.

23. Heller, p. 206; Cf. Tha'labi, p. 295; Tabari, *Tarikh*, II, p. 8; Baydawi, IV, p. 87; Damiri, II, 357. Down to modern times the Seven Sleepers have been protectors against storms: *Analecta Bollandiana* 68 (1950), p. 248.

24. Whether a later Onias is preferred (R. Goossens, *Onias le jusle . . . lapidé en 64 avant J.-C.*, in *La Nouvelle Clio*. 1-2 (1949f), pp. 336-353), or the earlier Onias III, *circa* 170 before Christ (M. Black, *The Scrolls and Christian Origins* (New York: Scribner's, 1961), p. 20, there is general agreement on a connection between Onias and Qumran: See H. H. Rowley, *The Zadokite Fragments, and the Dead Sea Scrolls*, in *Expository Times*, 63 (1951/2), p. 382; M. H. Segal, *The Habakkuk "Commentary" and the Damascus Fragments*, in *Journal of Biblical Literature*, 70 (1951), p. 145.

25. " . . . civitas Epheso ubi sunt septem fratres dormientes . . . quorum mater Caritina dicitur, graece, latine Felicitas," text in *Analecta Bollandiana* 41 (1923), p. 372. Cf. Gregory of Tours, in Migne *Patrologia Latina* 71, col. 787: "Septem vero germanorum. . . ."

26. The identification is recognized in *Analecta Bollandiana* 57 (1939), p. 39. Heller (*op. cit.* in note 3) p. 217, believes that the Seven heroes of Antioch are the most instructive of all parallels to the Seven of Ephesus.

27. Namely at Paphos on Cyprus, *Analecta Bollandiana* 26 (1907), p. 272. The Christians of Antioch built a basilica over the tomb of the Seven Jewish brothers, just as those of Ephesus did at the shrine of the Seven Sleepers: Heller, p. 217.

28. In an "Antiochus-Gedicht" of 1527, that ruler is designated throughout as Decius: W. Bacher, in *Jewish Quarterly Review*, 16 (1904), p. 529. "Voilà la fusion des deux légendes," cries Heller, p. 218, commenting on this.

29. Tha'labi, p. 287. Some writers simply speak of Tarsus without even mentioning Ephesus: Nasafi, II, p. 282; Shirbini, II, p. 358; al-Zamakh-shari, *al-Kashshaf* (Cairo:1890), I, p. 469. Heller, p. 200, note 5, can make no sense of this.

30. Bohlig and Steinmann, in Pauly-Wissowa, *Realencyclopädie*, IV A, col. 2419.

31. *Ibid.*, col. 2431.

32. Below, note 56.

33. *Realencyclopädie*, IV A, col. 2420-2421.

34. al-Qasimi, X, p. 4028.

35. H. H. Rowley, *The Covenanters of Damascus and the Dead Sea Scrolls*, in *Bulletin of the John Rylands Library*, Vol. 35, No. 1, September 1952, pp. 137-145; P. Kahle, *The Cairo Geniza* (London: 1947), p. 19.

36. See Tha'labi, p. 288; Damiri, II, p. 349; Tabari, *Tarikh*, II, pp. 6-7: "Some say they worshipped Jesus . . . and some say their history . . . was before Christ, and that the Messiah taught his people about them, and that

God woke them from sleep after he had raised up Jesus, in the time between him and Mohammed, but Got knows." Cf. Qurtubi, X, pp. 359, 388, and Huber (*op. cit.* in note 6) p. 21, citing Ibn Qutaiba. Damiri, II, p. 357, says they fell asleep, following one tradition, until the land became Moslem; and Ibn Kathir, III, p. 74, notes that if they had been Christians, the Jews, who do not mention such a thing, would certainly have reported it.

37. See B. Heller, *La légende biblique dans l'Islam*, in *Revue des Études Juives*, 98 (1934), p. 7, and *Ibid.*, 49 (1904), pp. 202-212. Tha'labi knows of specific Jewish informants of Mohammed, pp. 77, 137, and refers to his own Jewish teachers, pp. 137, 152, 241, 254, 257, etc. He often betrays a distinctly pro-Jewish and anti-Christian prejudice, as in the long story of Jesus' vain attempt to convert a Jew, pp. 276-279. He even knows the Pumbeditha scandal-story that Mary was once a ladies' hair-dresser, p. 131.

38. "The seyyid and the Jacobite and their Christian companions from Nejran were visiting (*kānū 'inda*) Mohammed" when the matter came up: Baydawi, IV, p. 98; Cf. Nasafi, II, p. 285; Damiri, II, p. 354.

39. Shirbini, II, p. 351; al-Hijazi, XV, p. 54; as-Suyuti, *Lubab al-nuqul* (Cairo: 1935), p. 144, emphasizes the boastfulness of the Jews.

40. Ibn Kathir, III, p. 74; as-Suyuti, *loc. cit.*; Sayyid Qutb, *Fi zilal al-Qur'an* (Cairo: 1953?), XV, p. 81.

41. Tha'labi, pp. 288-289. B. Heller (*op. cit.* in note 3) p. 200, believes this story to be a unique contribution of Tha'labi.

42. Ali and Omar in the story both address the delegates as "brothers of the arabs," who in turn are "the brothers of the Jews": Tha'labi, p. 289. The way in which Ali is greeted by Omar as he arrives wearing the robe of the Prophet suggests that he has been summoned from a distance, p. 288. As both the conqueror of Palestine and the would-be rebuilder of the temple (H. Nibley, in *Jewish Quarterly Review*, 50 (1959), pp. 118-220), Omar would be sympathetically received by the "Hasidic" sectaries of the desert.

43. The questions are given in full in Tha'labi, pp. 288-289. Most Arab writers mention only three questions: " . . .about the Spirit, the Companions of the Cave, and Dhu 'l-Quarnain," Hijazi, XV, p. 54. On the apocryphal-sectarian nature of the questions, see M. Huber (*op. cit.* in note 6) pp. 454-456; K. Ahrens, *Christliches im Qoran*, in *Zeitschrift der Deutschen Moren-ländischen Gesellschaft*, 84 (1930), p. 163.

44. H. Wernecke, in *The Monist*, 15 (1905), pp. 467-468. They became "the three chief sects of Syria," pp. 466-467.

45. This is Jacob of Sarug, discussed by Heller (*op. cit.* in note 3) pp. 260-261, who is at a loss to explain the surprisingly early date.

46. Tha'labi, pp. 260-261.

47. M. Black (*op. cit.* in note 24) p. 149.

48. Tha'labi, pp. 122-123, also tells the Clementine story of the blossoming staff. On the influence of the Clementine writing on the Koran, see K. Ahrens (*op. cit.* in note 43) pp. 56-60, 64, 174; on their importance for

Qumran, see H. J. Schoeps, in *Zeitschrift für Religions- und Geistesgeschichte*, 3 (1951), pp. 333-334; 6 (1954), pp. 277-278; 10 (1958), p. 15, and especially *Das Juden-christentum in den Pseudo-klementinen*, 11 (1959), pp. 72-77.

49. Tha'labi, p. 259. Onias, as the grandfather of John the Baptist, belongs to the same line, that of the Sadiqqim: R. Eisler, *Iesous Basileus ou Basileusas* (Heidelberg: 1930), II, p. 49.

50. Gregorius Turonensis, in *Patrologia Latina*, 71, col. 788. On the confusion of Sadducees and Zadokites, see H. H. Rowley (*op. cit.* in note 35) pp. 129-132. The Moslems designated nonconformist sectarians as *Zandakiyah*, and though the origin of the word is obscure, a *zindiq* is, according to Lane's *Arabic-English Lexicon*, I, p. 1285, "One of the thanawiyah [or asserters of the doctrine of Dualism]: or one who asserts his belief in [the two principles of] Light and Darkness: or one who . . . conceals unbelief and makes an outward show of belief." How well this applies to the dualistic theology and secretive policies of Qumran needs no illustration. Our Arabic commentators often refer to the Companions of the Cave as *thanawiyah*. When a Moslem victor asked some sectarians, "Who are you?" they replied, "Harranites." "Christians or Jews?" Neither, was the reply. "Have you holy books or a prophet?" To this they gave a guarded and confusing answer *(jamjamū)*, whereupon the official observed, "You must be Zandokiyah . . ." So in order to survive they changed their name to Ssabians. D. Chwolson, *Die Ssabier und der Ssabaismus* (St. Petersburg: 1865), II, p. 15. Sabaean denotes "irgend eine täuferische Sekte," according to K. Ahrens (*op. cit.* in note 43) p. 154. Could Zandokite and Zadokite not have been as easily confused as Zadokite and Sadducee?

51. The entire company falls asleep as soon as Tamlikh announces the approach of visitors; the entrance of the cave then becomes invisible or else all who attempt entry are driven out in terror: Tha'labi, p. 292; Tabari, *Jami'al-bayan*, XV, p. 143. Some say the purpose of the shrine is to keep anyone from entering the cave: Nasafi, II, p. 284; Zamakhshari, I, p. 724; others that the youths walled themselves in, or were killed in the city and taken to the cave for burial: Qasimi, X, p. 4051. Only one informant reports that they "arose and went out to the king and exchanged greetings," and then returned to the cave and promptly expired; but even he adds that "most of the scholars say" they died as soon as Tamlikh gave them his message: Qurtubi, X, p. 379.

52. So in the Syrian and Western texts supplied by Huber (*op. cit.* in note 6) pp. 118-127, 155-156. The same in Tha'labi, p. 298; Ibn Kathir, III, p. 77; Baydawi, IV, p. 90; Nasafi, II, p. 284. Tha'labi also tells this story, but quickly qualifies it by adding that "no man could enter into them," explaining on the authority of Ali, that as soon as Tamlikh went in to his friends God took their spirits and concealed their hiding-place, p. 298. The most convincing of all Tha'labi's accounts is his vivid description of the greedy citizens and the wild-eyed and bedraggled youth who told them the fantastic story of his grizzly companions in a nearby cave — companions that nobody ever saw alive, pp. 296-297. Here we have a story that bears the marks of plausibility.

53. "And behold their bodies were completely unchanged, except that there was not breath (*arwah*) in them." So the king said, "This is the sign which God has sent you": Tabari, *Tarikh*, II, pp. 9-10, and *Jami'al-bayan*, XV, p. 147; Damiri, II, pp. 349, 357. Much is made of their eyes being open, giving them a frighteningly lifelike appearance: Shirbini, II, p. 356; Baydawi, IV, p. 95; Nasafi, II, pp. 280-281; as-Sa'di, *Taysir al-karim al-rahman fi tafsir kalam al-mannan* (Cairo: 1954-1957), V, p. 10.

54. Qurtubi, X, p. 358. Huber, pp. 231-233, supplies translations of descriptions of this shrine by Idrisi, Qurtubi, and Yaqut.

55. *Analecta Bollandiana* 26 (1907), p. 272.

56. Al-Biruni, *Kitab al-athar al-baqiya 'an al-qurun il-khaliya* (Leipzig: 1923), p. 290. Many other sources are cited by Huber, pp. 225-226, 228-231. The extra cadavers were readily accounted for as those of devout monks who had chosen to live and die in the presence of the Seven, *Ibidem*, p. 231. M. J. DeGoeje maintained that the story of the Seven Sleepers originated with the finding of human remains in a cave near Arabissas in southeastern Asia Minor, the place being known to the Arabs as Afsus — hence Ephesus: *De Legende der Zevenslapers van Efeze*, in *Verslagen en Mededeelingen der Koninklijke Akademie van Wetenschappen*, III (1909), pp. 9-33, of which there is a lengthy summary in Huber, pp. 233-238.

57. Tha'labi, pp. 291, 293; Huber, pp. 276-277.

58. Tabari, *Jami'al-bayan*, XV, p. 143; Damiri, II, pp. 338, 353; Shirbini, II, p. 365; Ibn Kathir, III, p. 77.

59. Qurtubi, X, p. 388; Damiri, II, p. 352. Though Ibn Kathir, III, p. 77, says the cave was in the *bilad* of Rum, he explains, "We are not told in what land the cave was. . . . But Ibn Abbas says it was near Aelia, and Ibn Isaac says it was near Nineveh," *Ibid.*, p. 75. Ibn Isaac is a notoriously imaginative informant.

60. Qurtubi, X, p. 388. This may be an embellishment of an older version in which Ibn Abbas expresses some skepticism as to the possibility of recognizing bones three hundred years old: Ibn Kathir, III, p. 77; Huber, p. 233, citing Tabari and Tha'labi.

61. Qurtubi, X, p. 356; Tabari, *Jami'al-bayan*, XV, p. 131.

62. Damiri, II, p. 342.

63. Al-Qazwini, *Al-atharwa 'l-bilad* (Göttingen: 1848), I, p. 161: other sources in Huber, pp. 235-238, Al-Istakhri, *Al-masalik wa 'l-mamalik* (Cairo: 1961), p. 47.

64. Huber, p. 224, citing Yaqut and Qazwini. About the year 751 there was great excitement throughout the East in anticipation of an immediate appearance of the Seven Sleepers in a cemetery of Damascus, according to Al-Biruni (*op. cit.* in note 56) p. 285; cf. *Analecta Bollandiana* 68 (1950), p. 253. On Amman, Huber, p. 237.

65. Clermont-Ganneau, *El-Kahf et la Caverne des sept Dormants*, in *Comptes Rendus de l'Académie des Inscriptions et Belles-Lettres*, 4e série, XXVII

(Paris: 1899), pp. 564-574. Huber, pp. 238-239, accuses Clermont-Ganneau of following a false scent, yet the latter specifies that he is *not* seeking the original cave of the Seven Sleepers but only the favorite Moslem site of it: *Analecta Bollandiana* 19 (1900), pp. 356-357. L. Massignon accepts his location of al Raqim: *Analecta Bollandiana* 68 (1950), p. 254.

66. Damiri, II, p. 340; Qurtubi, X, p. 367.

67. Tha'labi, pp. 102-103. Tabari (cited by Huber, pp. 254-255) tells of a shepherd who found an inscribed tablet in a cave, which no one could read but an old holy man of the desert.

68. R. Eisler (*op. cit.* in note 49) II, pp. 35, 182-184, 190-193, 197-199. On a possible Rekhabite background for Qumran, see H. J. Schoeps, *Theologie und Geschichte des Judentums* (Tübingen: 1949), pp. 247-254.

69. *Analecta Bollandiana* 68 (1950), p. 254. It was the leaders of the Nejran Christians who first questioned Mohammed about the Cave: Nasafi, II, p. 285, etc.

70. Above, note 4.

71. The quotation is from Sale's note to *Sura* XVIII, 8, though Sale is not sure of the explanation and leaves the word *raqim* untranslated, Tabari, *Jami'al-bayan*, XV, p. 131, says it was stone tablet.

72. Tha'labi, p. 298; Baydawi, IV, p. 83 (lead or stone). The box was sealed with a silver seal. Al-Bokhari, *Jami'al-Sahih* (Leyden: 1868), III, p. 276, says there was just one lead plate.

73. Tabari, *loc. cit.*, suggests a book, Qurtubi, X, p. 357, a golden tablet.

74. L. Massignon, in *Analecta Bollandiana* 68 (1950), p. 252, discusses the significance of this.

75. Hijazi, XV, p. 50; Qurtubi, X, p. 357; Ibn Kathir, III, p. 73 (it is the wadi); Tabari, *Jami'al-bayan*, XV, p. 131; Baydawi, IV, p. 83. Al-Raqim designates "the people of the Cave who were confined (or trapped) in it" (*ashāp al-ghāri alladhī intabaqa 'alayhim*): Qurtubi, *loc. cit.*

76. Ibn Kathir, Tabari, Baydawi, *loc. cit.*

77. Qurtubi, IV, p. 357, citing al-Saddi.

78. Baydawi, IV, p. 83, and Qurtubi, X, pp. 356-358, suggest both.

79. "It is said that al-Raqim is a wadi beyond Palestine in which is the Cave; (the name) is taken from Raqmah, a wadi with water-holes in it. . . ." And Ibn Atiya says, "It is in Syria, according to what I heard from many people; it is a cave with dead people in it": Qurtubi, X, p. 357. It means running water in a wadi; Damiri, II, p. 341.

80. Qurtubi, *loc. cit.*, suggests both.

81. Qurtubi, *loc. cit.*, Hijazi, XV, p. 50; Nasafi, II, p. 277.

82. It was the name given to the Andalusian site (above note 54), and

to "a region of Rum" where there was a cave containing "twenty-one souls as if they were sleeping," Qurtubi, *loc, cit.,* who does not believe that this is *the* Cave.

83. Qurtubi, *loc. cit.* Most commentators (including those mentioned in note 84) note that the tablets contained the names and history of the Sleepers, and Qurtubi, *loc. cit.,* would even include in the writings "the rule which they embraced from the religion of Jesus" (*al-shar'tamassakūhu bi-hi min dini 'Isa*).

84. Tha'labi, p. 295; Tabari, *Jami'al-bayan,* XV, p. 135; Baydawi, IV, pp. 86-87; Damiri, II, p. 344, according to whom the book itself is to come forth as a new revelation.

85. *II Maccabees* 2, 4-8. At the time of the First Crusade local reports located this cave near Jericho: Fulcher, *Historia Hierosolymitana,* edited by H. Hagenmeyer (Heidelberg: 1913), p. 289. When the Patriarch Timotheus was informed, about the year 800, of the discoveries of documents in caves near Jericho, he assumed that it was those buried by Jeremiah: J. Hering, in *Revue d'Histoire et de Philosophie Religieuse,* 41 (1961) p. 160.

86. E. A. W. Budge, *The Contendings of the Apostles* (Oxford: 1935), pp. 394-396; Baydawi, IV, pp. 87, 90. See above, note 10.

87. He takes the custom back to the burial of Aaron, p. 171. He tells of a book sent to David from heaven sealed with gold and containing thirteen questions to be put to Solomon, p. 202; of an apocalyptic writing sealed in an iron box, p. 246; of another buried in a mountain, p. 242; of gold tablets containing the history of a vanished empire found in a cave in Yemen, p. 102; of magic books dug up from beneath Solomon's throne, p. 35.

88. M. Black (*op. cit.* in note 24), p. 12.

89. Tha'labi, p. 288. When Ali finishes his story, the most skeptical Jew confesses that he has not added nor removed a single letter from the account in the Torah; p. 292.

90. Various estimates are given by Huber (*op. cit.* in note 6) p. 102. Cf. *Analecta Bollandiana* 72 (1954), p. 266; B. Heller, in *Revue des Études Juives* 49 (1904), pp. 205, 211.

91. It "belongs to the secrets of heaven and earth": Tabari, *Jami'al-bayan,* XV, p. 152; Shirbini, II, p. 366. The Prophet spent forty nights trying to comprehend it: as-Suyuti, *Lubab al-nuqul . . .* (1935), p. 145.

92. Qurtubi, X, p. 386, who quotes Tabari as saying that the Jews also could not agree about it. It could hardly have been a Christian invention, since no amount of manipulating can fit the conventional three centuries of sleep into the century-and-a-half interval between Decius and either Theodosius. Cf. *Analecta Bollandiana* 66 (1948), p. 195.

93. Heller (*op. cit.* in note 90) pp. 206-207. Onias slept from the destruction of the First Temple to the completion of the Second: " . . . the parallel with the Seven Sleepers . . . is of course obvious," comments *The*

Jewish Encyclopedia (1902), IX, p. 405. Some say the Seven fell asleep until the land became Moslem: Damiri, II, p. 357.

94. *Analecta Bollandiana* 68 (1950), p. 351.

95. H. H. Rowley, in *Expository Times,* 63 (1951/2), p. 381; M. H. Segal, in *Journal of Biblical Literature,* 70 (1951), p. 146, note 59, and p. 130; Ysuf Ali, *The Holy Qur'an,* II, p. 720, note 2337. The 390 and the 20 years "belong to the remote past. . . . Their writers lack any real knowledge of the origin and early history of the sect; hence the: nebulous atmosphere pervading all the documents . . . the characters . . . appearing as types rather than individuals": E. Wiesenberg, in *Vetus Testamentum,* 5 (1955), pp. 304-305.

96. Above, note 87, Tabari's story is discussed by Huber, pp. 254-255.

97. Tha'labi, p. 292. They say *nakūnu 'alu amrin wahadin,* Tabari, *Jami'al-bayan,* XV, p. 132, where the last word suggests the much-discussed "*yahad*" of the Scrolls.

98. Nearly all Arabic sources mention this. Tha'labi, pp. 292-293, even notes that they gained the repute of being money-changers.

99. Tha'labi, p. 291. See above, note 79. Huber, p. 455, sees a Jewish tradition in the spring and the trees, and Heller (*op. cit.* in note 47) p. 201, notes that the society eschewed pork.

100. Qurtubi, X, p. 360; Nasafi, II, p. 278. Both mention caves in the plural. Cf. Tabari, *Jami'al-bayan,* XV, p. 132, 151.

101. On al-Raqim as a going concern, Tabari, XV, p. 135: Ibn Kathir, III, pp. 74-75. In some Western versions Tamlikh is only twelve or fifteen years old, and in all of them the youths must fetch all their food and drink from the city — they were *not* self-sustaining. There was a tradition that the activities of the Cave included even dancing, according to Qurtubi, X, p. 466, who describes the pious exercises of the community.

102. Tha'labi, pp. 289, 294; Ibn Kathir, III, p. 74, who mention the dramatic episode of the stripping of their military insignia by the enraged emperor. This is a characteristic episode in the cycle of youthful military heroes who are martyred by the emperor but then come alive to prove the resurrection. Such were St. Mercurius, St. Victor, and St. Sebastian. Tha'labi's St. George, pp. 299-305, clearly belongs to the cycle.

103. Tha'labi, p. 291; Qurtubi, X, p. 369; Ibn Kathir, III, p. 75; as-Sa'adi, V, p. 10, etc. On Qumran, M. Black (*op. cit.* in note 40) p. 141.

104. Once a week (Tabari, cited by Huber, p. 279): every seven years (Qurtubi, X, p. 370): twice a year (Baydawi, IV, p. 94); once a year at New Year's (Tha'labi, p. 291: Nasafi, II, p. 281; Qurtubi, *loc. cit*).

105. Tha'labi, p. 291; Nasafi, II, p. 281; Qurtubi, X, 369; Baydawi, IV, p. 93. Ibn Kathir, III, p. 75, sees astronomical significance in these arrangements. Huber, p. 295, discusses the awakening by the sun.

106. S. Talmon, in *Revue de Qumran*, 8 (1960), p. 475; E. Ettisch, in *Theologische Literaturzeitung*, 88 (1963), pp. 186, 188, 191-192.

107. E. Rohde, in *Rheinisches Museum für Philologie*, Neue Folge, 35 (1880), pp. 157-159, 162-163. Their names have great *"valeur prophylactique"* throughout the Moslem world: Massignon, in *Anal. Boll.* 68 (1950), pp. 249-250; for their healing offices, *ibid.*, pp. 247-248, and dreams, Huber, p. 135.

108. J. M. Allegro, *The Treasure of the Copper Scroll* (New York: Doubleday, 1960), p. 73. The Essenes specialized in "Traumdeute- und Weissagekunst"; R. Eisler, (*op. cit.* in note 49) II, p. 17.

109. Allegro, *op. cit.*, pp. 70-71. Cf. Tha'labi, p. 291; Nasafi, II, p. 280; Qurtubi, X, p. 369; as-Sa'adi, V, p. 10.

110. Tha'labi, pp. 294-295; Tabari, *Jami'al-bayan*, XV, p. 131; Damiri, II, pp. 339-340; Shirbini, II, pp. 352-353; Baydawi, IV, pp. 85-86: " . . .lift up your heads, eat, and trust in God." On the Hebrew origin of *jabbar*, see K. Ahrens (*op. cit.* in note 43) p. 19.

111. Epiphanius, *Adv. haer.*, Haer. 29, no. 5, in *P. G.*, Vol. 41, col. 397.

112. Al-Biruni, *op. cit.*, in note 56, p. 284. The added evidence of the Companions of the Cave tips the scales against the reading *maqariba*, favored by N. Golb, in *Journal of Religion*, 41 (1961), pp. 42-44.

113. This expression puzzled Huber, p. 283, as the only purely Christian tradition in the Koran, where it is accordingly strangely out of place. But J. Horovitz, in *H.U.C.A.*, 2 (1925), p. 178, showed that "it is by no means assured that . . . Mohammed really meant the martyrs of Najran," and that the only reason for such an assumption is lack of evidence as to what else the "People of the Pit" could refer to. The Dead Sea Scrolls now supply that evidence.

114. Baydawi, IV, p. 91 (Khiram); Damiri, II, p. 350 (Haram, Khadam); Qurtubi, X, p. 367 (Khiwam). The usual difficulty with pointing is apparent.

115. Damiri, II, p. 341. Nasafi, II, p. 285, also says the dog was Raqim. Tha'labi, p. 290, gives a list of suggested names, not including this one.

116. Ibn Kathir, III, pp. 73, 78; Qurtubi, X, p. 360. The quotation is from Allegro (*op. cit.* in note 108) p. 70.

117. This has been discussed by Massignon, in *Anal. Boll.* 68, pp. 245-255.

Their Portrait   **10**
of a Prophet

In the past year (1977) two full-length biographies of Joseph Smith *have appeared, both more of the same with a little more added. They all continue to miss the point: Why is Joseph Smith worth writing about? Only, apparently, because the Mormons are still going strong. He was once thought interesting as a picturesque, even fantastic, frontier character; but now that it has become the fashion to explain him away as a perfectly ordinary guy, even that has been given up. But do ordinary guys do what Joseph Smith did? It is as if the biographers of Shakespeare were to go on year after year digging up all the details of his rather ordinary life, omitting only that, incidentally, he was credited with writing some remarkable plays. The documents which Joseph Smith has placed in our hands are utterly unique; if you doubt it, please furnish an example to match the books of Moses, Abraham, any book of the Book of Mormon, or for that matter, Joseph Smith's own story. No one since Ed. Meyer has pointed out how closely Joseph's productions match those of the prophets of Israel; no one but he and E. A. W. Budge have had the knowledge to detect familiar overtones from ancient apocryphal writings in Joseph Smith's revelations and his autobiography. From the first deriding of the Book of Mormon before 1830, to the latest attacks on the Book of Abraham, the approach has always been the same: "Considering who Smith was and the methods he used, it is hardly worth the trouble to examine the writings which he put forth as holy scriptures and ancient histories." And so his work remains unread, by his critics, and the greatest of all literary anomalies remains not only unexplained but unexamined. But why should his critics not see in Joseph Smith only what they choose to see, since the Mormons themselves do the same?*

(*Scene:* — The assembly hall of a public school in Palmyra, N.Y., at the turn of the century. The hall is empty save for the presence of the chairman and his clerk, who is gathering papers together preparatory to departure. It is obviously late at night.)

Chairman: Before you go, Mr. Beckmesser, there are some things I would like to talk over with you. Since this is not a trial but only an investigation, I would like to get your reaction to Mr. Tucker's portrait of the youthful Smith. A sulky, taciturn, evil-minded brat gains a loyal and devoted following simply by telling wild and wonderful stories — how does it strike you?

Clerk: A bit odd, sir. But then, didn't a mischievous boy in East Side New York have a million people in a high state of religious excitement a few years back by announcing that the Virgin had appeared to him in a back lot?

Chairman: Yes, I recall the case. But how long did that kid's glory last — five days? A week, maybe? That only shows what a different sort of thing we are up against here. By the way, have you got that material for a portrait of Smith?

Clerk: You mean all those intimate descriptions of what he looked like? Yes, sir, I collected them as you asked. Here they are.

Chairman: Do they present a uniform picture of the man? I mean, did Smith make a consistent impression on people?

Clerk: If you mean, do they all think he is a scoundrel the answer is yes; otherwise their books would not be classified as anti-Mormon. His friends praise him, his enemies hate him, but aside from hating him they don't seem to be able to agree on a thing. Here is one, for example, who writes: "I can see him now in my mind's eye, with his torn, patched trousers held to his form by a pair of suspenders made out of sheeting, and with his calico shirt as dirty and black as the earth, and his uncombed hair sticking through the holes in his old battered hat...."[1]

Chairman: Very picturesque. The "mind's eye," indeed. Is this the child Joseph Smith?

Clerk: By no means, sir. This is supposed to describe the man "when he was about twenty-five years old," — that would be after the publication of the Book of Mormon and the founding of the Church.[1]

Chairman: But does anybody take this seriously?

Clerk: Mr. Linn accepts it as an accurate portrait. Here is a homey touch that gives it an air of simple honesty: "...Joe had a jovial, easy, don't-care way about him that made him a lot of warm friends. He was a good talker and would have made a fine stump-speaker."[2]

Chairman: A sloppy tramp with the gift to gab.

Clerk: So it seems, sir. But here is another eye-witness description from the same period: "He was always well dressed, generally in black with a white necktie. He looked like a Reverend.... Joseph was no orator. He said what he wanted to say in a very blundering sort of way...."[3] So now he's a well-dressed gent who can't talk at all. And that is typical. Mr. Tucker said taciturnity was one of Smith's most conspicuous characteristics, and here another witness says, "Joseph did not talk much in society, his talk was not very fluent, he was by no means interesting in company...."[4] S. S. Harding says, "Young Joe was hard to approach. He was very taciturn, and sat most of the time silent as the Sphinx."[5]

Chairman: Silent Smith, eh?

Clerk: That is what some say, but others say the opposite: "...very voluble in speech, having great self-confidence...."[6] "endowed with great cunning and volubility...."[7]

Chairman: But isn't that the later Smith?

Clerk: No, sir, this is the boy of Palmyra, who used to attend "revival meetings, praying and exhorting with great exuberance of words...."[6] "...used to help us solve some portentous questions... in our juvenile debating club, and subsequently... was a very passable exhorter in evening meetings...."[8] Here is another: "At times he would be very active in a religious revival, and exhorting with unusual fervor, in that exuberance of words which he had wonderfully at his command."[9] It is rather puzzling — a blundering, stammering, taciturn Sphinx with a wonderful exuberance of words. "His address is easy," wrote Mr. Howe himself of this stammerer, "rather fascinating and winning, of a mild and sober deportment, though at times inclined to jest and be exceedingly merry."[10] This is the boy whom Mr. Tucker says "was never known to laugh." And while Mr. Tucker also assures us from the most intimate experience that everything Joe and his family did proclaimed their sordid atheism, the other neighbors report him as zealously active in religious circles.

Chairman: So somebody is lying.

Clerk: At least they can't all be right. You remember Mr. Tucker said Joseph Smith was of a "plodding, evil-brewing mental composition," that "he seldom spoke to anyone," and above all that "he was never known to laugh."[11] And Mrs. Eaton, taking the cue, says "he rarely smiled or laughed. His looks were always downward bent."[12] Yet one high authority says that "a deep vein of humor ran through all he said and did,"[13] and Charles Dickens declares that "the exact adjective for Joe's religion is — jolly!"[14] The poet Whittier speaks of Smith's "rude, bold, good-humored face,"[15] and even some of the most damning "witnesses" tell us " . . .Joe had a jovial, easy, don't-care way about him," and that "he used to laugh from the crown of his head to the soles of his feet, it shook every bit of flesh in him."[16] Also, while Mr. Hendrix assures us that "he made a lot of warm friends," other neighbors say "he was shunned by the boys of his own age," and that he was " . . .an awkward and unpopular lad."[17] Here is a nice empasse: Chase and Ingersoll and Stafford, who knew him so well, describe him as a brawler, who "frequently got drunk, and when intoxicated was very quarrelsome,"[18] while Tucker and Harding, who knew him just as well, assure us that "Smith was noted as never having had a fight or quarrel with any other person. . . ."[19] Whom are we to believe?

Chairman: It might be easier to check up on his physical appearance. What do they say to that?

Clerk: He is described by eye-witnesses in 1830 as being "tall and slender — *thin favored*. . . ."[20] Dogberry calls him "spindle shanked";[21] here is a remarkable description by Stephen S. Harding, one-time governor of Utah Territory, who claims to have known Smith personally in Palmyra and "describes him as having been a tall, long-legged and tow-headed youth, who seldom smiled, hardly ever worked and never fought, but was hard on truth and bird's nests."[22]

Chairman: At least we know that Smith was tall and skinny.

Clerk: But do we? Thurlow Weed's description of Smith from that time is of "a stout, round, smooth-faced young man. . . ."²³ Tall he may have been, but how he could have been "thin-favored" and stout and round at the same time is not so obvious. And just two years later another eyewitness who claims to have known Smith very well says he is "a man of mean and insignificant appearance, between forty and fifty years of age."²⁴ Later on we are told that "the gait of this person was heavy and slouching, his hands were large and thick, his eyes grey and unsteady in their gaze. . . ."²⁵ A year after this was published another opus describes the prophet as "a tall, elegant-looking man, with dark piercing eyes, and features, which if not handsome, were imposing."²⁶ Another calls him "a man of commanding appearance, tall and well-proportioned. . . ." " . . .a noble-looking fellow," says another, "a Mahomet every inch of him."²⁷ Josiah Quincy says "he was a hearty, athletic fellow with blue eyes standing prominently out upon his light complexion. . . . '*A fine-looking* man' is what a passer-by would instinctively have murmured. . . ."²⁸ Another visitor says Smith had dark hair and eyes and "a strong rugged outline of face" with features exactly like those of Oliver Cromwell.²⁹ Charles Francis Adams described him as "a middle-aged man with a shrewd but rather ordinary expression of countenance."³⁰

Chairman: So far we have shifty grey eyes, prominent blue eyes, and dark piercing eyes.

Clerk: Yes, and while one illustrious visitor says he could not see Smith's eyes since the man refused to look people in the face,³¹ others speak of his "penetrating eagle eyes."³² Some think Smith's huge, fat, enormous, awkward hands worthy of special mention,³³ while others comment on the remarkably *small* size of his hands.³⁴ One says that he had "a Herculean frame and a commanding appearance,"³⁵ another that he was sloppy and slouching, "very lank and loose in his appearance and movements."³⁶

Chairman: A portrait artist would have a wonderful time depicting him from these honest firsthand descriptions. How do you account for the discrepancies?

Clerk: I think the report of the celebrated Mr. Conybeare, the foremost literary critic of the mid-nineteenth century, can help us out there. His classical description of Joseph Smith's appearance is warranted solely by the contemplation of a small wood-engraving of the prophet, the work of neither a sympathetic nor a skillful hand. This has been reproduced in numerous anti-Mormon books as the official non-Mormon portrait of Smith. As he views the small and clumsy drawing, Mr. Conybeare gives forth: "It is inexplicable how anyone who had ever looked at Joe's portrait, (it was not really a portrait, of course, since Smith did not pose for it), could imagine him to have been by possibility an honest man. Never did we see a face on which the hand of heaven had more legibly written rascal. That self-complacent simper, that sensual mouth, that leer of vulgar cunning, tell us at one glance the character of their owner. . . ."[37]

Chairman: Dear me, all this from a crude wood-cut the size of a postage-stamp! Our artist must have been a supreme caricaturist.

Clerk: Not at all. If you will look at the picture you will see that it is a perfectly ordinary performance — typical of the nineteenth-century school of engraving at which Robert Louis Stevenson poked fun in his *Moral Emblems*. All that consummate viciousness is simply what Mr. Conybeare reads into it. Yet a Dutch scholar has taken Conybeare's interpretation of this grotesque little vignette as solid psychological evidence for the character of Smith.[38] You get the same sort of thing when you deal with Joseph Smith's intelligence and knowledge. Here we read of "a natural genius, strong inventive powers of mind, a deep study, and an unusually correct estimate of human passion and feelings. . . ."[39] "a retentive memory; a correct knowledge of human nature. . . ."[40] "a great shrewdness and worldy wisdom . . . boundless energy and intrepidity of character, of most fearless audacity. . . ."[41] "great powers of reasoning were his natural gift . . . and a deep vein of humor ran through all he said and did. . . ."[42] "a strong mind [says Quincy] utterly unenlightened by the teachings of history. . . ."[40] "Joseph was the calf that sucked three cows. He acquired knowledge very rapidly . . . He soon out-grew his teachers. . . ."[43] "His own autobiography shows him well studied at an early period in the nice shades and differences of modern sectarian creeds, and . . . well-read in the history of Mohammed and other religious imposters."[44] " . . . a fertile and highly imaginative brain. . . ."[42] " . . . an ever-inventive and fertile genius. . . ."[43] " . . . an omnivorous reader . . . of 'buckets of blood' literature. . . ."[44] "the skill with which he carried out his im-posture . . . his eloquence, rude but powerful . . . his letters, clever and sarcastic — the manifold character and boldness of his designs — his courage in enterprise — his perseverance despite great obstacles — his conception and partial execution of the temple of Nauvoo — these and other things mark him as a man of more than ordinary calibre. . . ."[45] " . . . highly original and imaginative . . . an audacious and original mind. . . ."[46]

Chairman: A sort of superman. And on the other hand . . . ?

Clerk: On the other hand, the same Smith in 1830 is "that

spindle-shanked ignoramus, *Joe Smith*. This fellow appears to possess the *quintessence* of ignorance . . . having but little expression of countenance other than that of dullness; his mental powers appear extremely limited."[47] One of the earliest says, " . . .I thought the fellow either crazed or a very shallow imposter. . . ."[48] " . . .his knowledge was slight and his judgment weak. . . ."[49] " . . .he was lounging, idle; (not to say vicious), and possessed of less than ordinary intellect. The author's own recollections of him are distinct ones."[50] "He was as self-indulgent as he was ignorant. . . ."[51] " . . .a dissolute unprincipled young rake, and notorious only for his general wickedness. . . ."[52] "Jo from a boy appeared dull and utterly destitute of genius. . . ."[53] "his untutored and feeble intellect had not yet (in 1830) grasped at anything beyond mere toying with mysterious things. . . ."[54] "I mention these things . . . to show the weak-mindedness and low character of the man."[54] " . . .we can discover in his career no proof of conspicuous ability . . . his chief if not only talent, was his gigantic impudence. . . ."[55] He was never "noted for much else than ignorance and stupidity, to which might be added . . . a fondness for everything marvelous. . . ."[56] "Joseph was unkempt and immoderately lazy. He could read, though not without difficulty, and wrote a very imperfect hand, and had a limited understanding of elementary arithmetic. . . ."[57] "Ignorant and ill-prepared, as he confessedly was for such a work, he made no special effort to qualify himself. . . ."[58] "He had neither the diligence nor the constancy to master reality . . . a completely undisciplined imagination . . . not to be canalized by any discipline. . . ."[59] " . . .he was not liked, the young people of the town considered him not quite full-witted, and with the cruelty of youth made him the butt of their practical jokes. . . ."[60]

Chairman: So it was the village idiot who wrote the Book of Mormon. This brings up a little question of motive. Surely there are easier ways of fooling people than by composing a large and complex book which, as the book itself foretells, simply invites persecution. How do these people explain the colossally exhausting and dangerous task of writing, publishing and spreading it abroad as the enterprise of the laziest man on earth?

Clerk: There are two schools of thought. One holds that Smith was sincerely religious, the other that he was not; the latter is the larger faction by about one hundred to one. We are to believe that he undertook the writing of the Book of Mormon out of sheer impudence, "his only talent." According to Mrs. Brodie, this silly, sneaky, shallow, prevaricating boy dictated the whole Book of

Mormon as a sort of practical joke on his parents "to carry out the fun." This is her idea of fun. Here are some other verdicts: "That he was a religious enthusiast we cannot grant... one principle... actuated him through life, and that was — selfishness, which makes his religion one of the most unfounded and abominable systems that ever sprung from the depths of human or Satanic depravity."[61] His Book of Mormon is "but a wicked, silly, filthy romance, founded in ignorance, nay, the quintessence of ignorance; even the ignorance of Joseph Smith, got up for speculation, in order to gull the American Indians, and dupe the English!"[62] "You have not even the poor merit of either talent or originality," wrote Professor Turner to Joseph Smith, "...you have at once outraged and disgraced human nature itself...."[63] "If there is one fact in American history that can be regarded as definitely established it is that the engaging Joe Smith was a deliberate charlatan...."[64] "...the camel-driver of Medina was probably a sincere fanatic, whereas the seer of Palmyra was almost certainly a cunning imposter."[65] "His only object at that time was to play upon the credulous, earn applause from the debased, and extort money from the simple, under the plea of divine mission...."[66] "He was very vain of his notoriety, although it was that of a notorious liar. Indeed he had no conscience...." "The effrontery of the fellow was really superb.... Probably his well-grounded contempt for his early followers caused him to justify his methods...."[67] "He was one of those indolent and illiterate young men... who hope to shun honest labor, and who have imbibed the pernicious doctrine embraced in the phrase: 'The world owes me a living.'"[67] "...a shrewd schemer whose ethical sense was poorly developed...."[68] "Colossal egotist, ribald wit, handsome giant, ruthless enemy, loudmouthed braggart, religious charlatan, great administrator, master politician, cheap exhibitionist...."[69] "Smith was a bank-note forger... shifty, illiterate and credulous."[70] "Their leaders are evidently atrocious imposters, who have deceived a great many weak-minded but well-meaning persons, by holding out to them the promise of great temporal advantage...."[71] Joseph Smith's "own character gives no shred of prestige for his pretentious claims. Yet, most individual Mormons are sturdy, sincere, honorable, and fine citizens."[72] Mormonism grew from "the pure rascality of the Mormon prophet...." "...an uneducated youth, without wealth or social standing; indeed, without a prestige of common morality (for the founder of Mormonism is said to have been a dissolute, unprincipled young rake, and notorious only for his general wickedness)...."[73] "...a greedy speculator without conscience, and without shame. . . ."[68] " . . .I have yet to find anybody, or any book, not Mormon, that has a single good word to say of Joseph Smith."[74] For Mrs. Brodie, Joseph Smith was "utterly opportunistic." Conybeare calls him " . . .a profligate and sordid knave, making the voice of heaven pander to his own avarice and lusts."[75] And so on and so on, you get the idea: Smith was the last word in depravity, but he wanted power and money, and that explains everything. His success can be attributed either to audacity or cunning or both.

Chairman: So I ask myself, Why would a cunning and ambitious rogue too lazy to do any work invariably choose the hardest, the most dangerous, and the least rewarding ways of getting what he wanted — especially since he is supposed to have had an uncanny insight into the foibles of human nature? Or is he?

Clerk: He is, all right. E. D. Howe himself says Smith has "a natural genius, strong inventive powers of mind, a deep study, and an unusually correct estimate of the human passions and feelings."[76] He knew his public — no doubt about it. And so he proceeds to make and keep himself the most unpopular man of the century.

Chairman: Does that strike you as being believable?

Clerk: Historians admit the inconsistency, but they won't discuss it. Here is one who admits that it is "marvelously strange that . . . a dissolute, unprincipled young rake . . . should excite a revolutionary movement in the religious world . . . and that, too, in an age of refinement and scientific intelligence."[77] By admitting that this is "marvelously strange," this author seems to think he has relieved himself of any further responsibility of explaining the paradox. Mrs. Brodie has her own characteristic solution of the problem. She explains away all her whopping contradictions by what she calls "the unusual plasticity of Joseph's mind."[78] By having him sufficiently "plastic" you can have one man take any form you want to.

Chairman: But again the word simply *describes* the phenomenon — it does not *explain* a thing. Does a biographer or a portrait painter when his picture fails to resemble anything human have a right to introduce new and unexampled dimensions into his art, and attribute the weird results not to his own creativity but to the "plasticity" of his subject? Here we have a young man producing large and difficult books by his own efforts, converting thousands of deeply religious people to a willingness to give their lives for what he teaches, leading great migrations, founding many cities and societies — structures of solid and enduring quality — and all the time enduring persecution and opposition of great persistence and ferocity. And this young man is not only a complete cynic but incredibly tactless and silly; he is in fact the most unprincipled, irresponsible, shallow, undisciplined, lazy young man alive. Does it make sense to you?

Clerk: I would feel much better about it if there were some historical parallels to match this, but I know of none. In real life lazy loafers do not write big books, opportunistic charlatans do not risk their lives in hard and exhausting projects when by changing their tune they could become rich and respectable, and ambitious men with keen insight into human nature don't insist on doing and saying just the things that are bound to offend the most people the most. Here is one authority who confesses that "a mere imposter would have broken down under such a tempest of opposition and hate as Smith's preaching excited. Smith must have been at least in part honest in his delusion."[79]

Chairman: Now *there* is a generous concession — he "must have been at least *in part* honest." That explains everything; he's going to have his cake and eat it. But is anyone going to tell us in which "part" he is honest? Where was Smith's real genius?

Clerk: I think Mrs. Brodie answers that in a passage that takes all the prizes. She assures us that "the facility with which profound theological arguments were handled is evidence of the unusual plasticity of Joseph's mind. But this facility was entirely verbal. The essence of the great spiritual and moral truths with which he dealt so agilely did not penetrate into his consciousness. . . . He knew these truths intimately as a bright child knows his catechism, but his use of them was utterly opportunistic. . . ."[80]

Chairman: A remarkably revealing statement. It was Theodore Schroeder the rabid anti-Mormon who once observed that psychological studies of Joseph Smith only reveal the minds of those who make them and leave Smith untouched. Mrs. Brodie might as well have discoursed on the qualities of silent music, invisible etchings, or odorless perfume as to talk of dealing in "great spiritual and moral truths" without grasping anything of their "essence" — without such a grasp there is simply nothing to talk about; how on earth can one know things "intimately" or at all unless they do somehow "penetrate into one's consciousness"? They exist nowhere else. Since "Mrs. Brodie's intense atheism . . . actually determines . . . the content of her book,"[81] it would be interesting to know what are the "profound spiritual truths" which *she* grasps so well and which so completely escaped Joseph Smith.

Clerk: Here are some more: "...a shrewd schemer whose ethical sense was poorly developed...." "...an ever-inventive and fertile genius," who succeeded because he had no scruples whatever. It beats me how such a clever man bent on deception could be so clumsy at the same time. Josiah Canning laughs at Smith's "school-boy tact,"[82] and Peter Cartwright calls him "clumsy Joe."[83] Kidder is amazed that a "miserable plagiarist... had the unaccountable stupidity" to include extensive Bible passages in the Book of Mormon, which was designed to fool a public that knew the Bible better than any other book.[84] A classic example of his shrewdness is the oft-repeated story of how the youthful Smith went around town singing the song of his hero Captain Kidd, whose autobiography "he eagerly and often perused.... He chanted it at play, quoted it over and over at the village store until it became indelibly associated with him in the minds of the people of Manchester and Palmyra,"[85] who incidentally never mention the fact in the early period. Not a very sly way to begin a life of religious deception.

Chairman: To say the least. Yet that Captain Kidd story is a great favorite with twentieth-century writers on Mormonism. I wonder where they got it.

Clerk: I think I have a pretty good idea. In 1830 a Rochester newspaper recalled that back in 1815 there had been considerable interest "among a certain class" of people in western New York in searching for Captain Kidd's treasure. The article makes it clear that there is no necessary connection between this mania and any of Joseph Smith's activities.[86] Taking up from here, E. D. Howe reports that the Smiths went around "pretending to believe that the earth was filled with hidden treasures, buried there by Kidd or the Spaniards."[87] From there on it is easy: Joseph Smith soon emerges as the unique disciple of the terrible pirate. It is fascinating to see how Smith's critics can turn anything and nothing into direct evidence against him. But we are going to look into the treasure-digging stories in the morning. They should be good.

NOTES

1. Rev. D. H. C. Bartlett, *The Mormons or, Latter-day Saints, Whence Came They?* (Liverpool: J. A. Thompson & Co., 1911), p. 5.

2. William Alexander Linn, *The Story of the Mormons, from the Date of their Origin to the Year 1901* (N.Y.: Macmillan, 1923), p. 13.

3. W. Wyl, *Joseph Smith the Prophet, His Family and Friends* (Salt Lake City: Tribune Printing and Publishing Co., 1886), p. 26.

4. *Id.;* Maria Ward, *The Mormon Wife, or Life Among the Mormons* (Hartford, Conn.: 1873), p. 38.

5. Thomas Gregg, *The Prophet of Palmyra* (N.Y.: John B. Alden, 1890), p. 38.

6. W. Lang, *History of Seneca County* (1880), p. 649.

7. George W. Cowles, *Landmarks of Wayne County* (1895), p. 297.

8. Cowles, *Landmarks*, p. 78.

9. J. S. C. Abbott, *The History of the State of Ohio* (Detroit: New World Publ. Co., 1875), p. 697.

10. E. D. Howe, *History of Mormonism: or a Faithful Account of that Singular Imposition and Delusion* (Painesville: Printed and Published by the Author, 1840), p. 13.

11. Pomeroy Tucker, *Origin, Rise, and Progress of Mormonism* (N.Y.: D. Appleton & Co., 1867), p. 15.

12. Mrs. Dr. Horace Eaton, *Speech Delivered May 27, 1881.* (089.1 6163 in Church Historian's Office, The Church of Jesus Christ of Latter-day Saints, Salt Lake City), p. 1; also Eaton, *Address*, in *Handbook of Mormonism* (Chicago, Cincinnati, Salt Lake City: Handbook Publishing Co., 1882), p. 1f.

13. "The Yankee Mahomet," *American Whig Review*, N.S., Vol. VII, 1851, pp. 554-564 (June, 1851), p. 556.

14. Charles Dickens, *Household Words*, July 19, 1851.

15. *Howitt's Journal*, Sept. 11, 1847, p. 158.

16. Wyl, *Joseph Smith*, p. 26.

17. Ruth Kauffman and Reginald W. Kauffman, *The Latter-Day Saints. A Study of the Mormons in the Light of Economic Conditions* (London: Williams & Norgate, 1912), p. 23.

18. John C. Bennett, *The History of the Saints: or, An Expose of Joe Smith and Mormonism* (Boston: Leland & Whiting, 1842), p. 72.

19. Gregg, *The Prophet*, p. 39.

20. Francis Kirkham, *A New Witness of Christ in America, the Book of Mormon* (Independence, Mo.: Zion's Printing and Publishing Co., Vol. II, 1951), p. 68.

21. Kirkham, *New Witness*, p. 56.

22. Chas. H. Shook, *The True Origin of Mormon Polygamy* (Cincinnati: Standard Pub. Co., 1914), p. 17.

23. Thurlow Weed, *Autobiography*, I (Boston: 1884), p. 358.

24. E. S. Abdy, *Journal of a Residence and Tour in the United States of America from April, 1833 to October, 1834* (London: J. Murray, 1835), Vol. I, p. 324f.

25. *Edinburgh Review*, Vol. CII, 1854, p. 170.

26. *Female Life Among the Mormons* (N.Y.: 1885), p. 19.

27. T. W. P. Taylder, *The Mormon's Own Book*, etc., new ed. (London: Partridge & Co., 1857), p. li; also Wyl, *Joseph Smith*, p. 28.

28. Josiah Quincy, *Figures of the Past* (Boston: Little, Brown, 1926), p. 380.

29. Edwin de Leon, *Thirty Years of My Life on Three Continents* (London: Ward & Downey, 1890), p. I, 56.

30. Henry Adams, Jr., "Charles Francis Adams Visits the Mormons in 1844," *Proc. Mass. Hist. Soc.*, LXVIII, Oct. 1944-May 1947 (Boston: By the Society, 1952), p. 285.

31. Rev. H. Caswall, *The Prophet of the 19th Century: or, the Rise, Progress, and Present State of Mormons or Latter-Day Saints* (London: J.G.F. and J. Rivington, 1843), p. 223.

32. M. H. A. Van Der Valk, *De Profeet der Mormonen, Jos. Smith Jr.* Kampen: J. H. Kok, 1921), p. 28.

33. Caswall, *The Prophet*, p. 223; *Hist. of Illinois* (H. Brown: Chicago, 1844), p. 401; C. C. Weil, *The California Crusoe* (London: 1854), p. 61.

34. John Quincy Adams, D.D., *The Birth of Mormonism* (Boston: Gorham Press, 1916), p. 101.

35. *Edinburgh Review*, p. 36.

36. Wyl, *Joseph Smith*, p. 26.

37. *Edinburgh Review*, p. 36.

38. Van Der Valk, *De Profeet*, p. 28.

39. James H. Hunt, *Mormonism* (St. Louis: Ustick & Davies, 1844), p. 7; E. D. Howe, *Mormonism Unveiled* (London: 1851), p. 12f.

40. Quincy, *Figures*, p. 337.

41. *The Lamps of the Temple* (London: 1856), p. 477.

42. *American Whig Review*, p. 556.

43. Wyl, *Joseph Smith*, p. 25.

44. Benj. G. Ferris, Late Sec'y of Utah Territory, *Utah and the Mor-*

mons, *the History, Government, Doctrines, Customs and Prospects of the Latter-Day Saints* (N.Y.: Harper and Bros., 1856), p. 66.

45. Taylder, *The Mormon's*, p. li.

46. Fawn M. Brodie, *No Man Knows My History* (N.Y.: A. Knopf, 1947), p. 48f.

47. Kirkham, *A New Witness*, p. 68.

48. Weed, *Autobiography*, p. 359.

49. Schaff-Herzog, *Encyclopedia of Religious Knowledge*, Vol. VIII, p. 13.

50. O. Turner, *History of the Pioneer Settlement of Phelps and Gorham's Purchase and Morris' Reserve* (Rochester, N.Y.: W. Alling, 1851), p. 213.

51. George Townshend, *The Conversion of Mormonism* (Hartford, Conn.: Church Mission Pub. Co., 1911), p. 15.

52. *Hist. of Caldwell and Livingston Cos., Mo.* (St. Louis: National Historical Co., 1886), p. 106.

53. Rev. John A. Clark, *Gleanings by the Way* (Phila.: W. J. and J. K. Simon; N.Y.: R. Carter, 1842), p. 225.

54. Gregg, *The Prophet*, p. 4.

55. *Edinburgh Review*, p. 36f.

56. Kirkham, *A New Witness*, p. 68.

57. Schaff-Herzog, *Encyclopedia*, p. 12.

58. Gregg, *The Prophet*, p. 20.

59. Brodie, *No Man*, p. 69f.

60. Kauffman, *The Latter-Day Saints*, p. 23; Turner, *History*.

61. Taylder, *The Mormon's*, p. li-lii.

62. J. Theobald, *Mormonism Harpooned* (London: W. Horsell, 1855), p. 24.

63. J. B. Turner, *Mormonism in All Ages* (New York: 1842), pp. 300-304.

64. Earnest S. Bates, *American Faith* (New York: W. W. Norton, 1940), p. 346.

65. W. S. Simpson, *Mormonism* (London: 1853), p. 6.

66. Orvilla S. Belisle, *The Prophet; or Mormonism Unveiled* (Phila.: Wm. W. Smith, 1855), p. 55.

67. Gregg, *The Prophet*, p. 4.

68. Jules Remy, *A Journey to Great-Salt-Lake-City* 2 vols. (London: W. Jeffs, 1861), p. xxxi.

69. Sidney Bell, *Wives of the Prophet* (N.Y.: The Macaulay Co., 1935), Intro.

70. Horton Davies, *Christian Deviations* (London: SCM Press Ltd., 1954), p. 80.

71. *Hist. of Caldwell and Livingston Cos.*, p. 106.

72. Rev. P. E. Osgood, *Religion without Magic* (Boston: Beacon Press, 1954).

73. Davies, *Deviations*, p. 80.

74. Rev. T. W. Young, *Mormonism: Its Origin, Doctrines, and Dangers* (Ann Arbor, Mich.: Geo. Wahr, 1900), p. 16.

75. *Edinburgh Review*, p. 169.

76. Howe, *History of Mormonism*, p. 12.

77. *Hist. of Caldwell and Livingston Cos.*, p. 106.

78. Brodie, *No Man*, p. 70.

79. *Knowledge, A Weekly Magazine* (N.Y.: John B. Alden), Vol. I, No. 9, Aug. 2, 1890, p. 176.

80. Brodie, *No Man*, p. 70.

81. *Deseret News*, Church Section, May 11, 1946.

82. Josiah D. Canning, *Poems* (Greenfield, Mass.: Phelps and Ingersoll, 1838), p. 107.

83. Peter Cartwright, *The Autobiography of Peter Cartwright the Frontier Preacher*, 1856, p. 342.

84. Daniel P. Kidder, *Mormonism and the Mormons* (N.Y.: Carlton & Porter, 1842), p. 255.

85. Harry M. Beardsley, *Joseph Smith and His Mormon Empire* (Boston, N.Y.: Houghton Mifflin Co., 1931), p. 17; George Siebel, *The Mormon Problem* (Pittsburgh: Pittsburgh Printing Co., 1899), p. 10; Rev. R. W. Beers, *The Mormon Puzzle and How to Solve It* (N.Y.: Funk & Wagnalls, 1887), p. 27; Mrs. Ellen E. Dickinson, *New Light on Mormonism*, with an Introduction by Thurlow Weed (N.Y.: Funk & Wagnalls, 1885), p. 29.

86. Kirkham, *A New Witness*, p. 48f.

87. Howe, *History of Mormonism*, p. 11; 31f.

Educating the Saints   11

The compelling mystique of those franchise businesses which in our day have built up enormous institutional clout by selling nothing but the right to a name was anticipated in our great schools of Education, which monopolized the magic name of Education and sold the right to use it at a time when the idea of a "School of Education" made about as much sense as a class in Erudition or a year's course in Total Perfection. The whole business of education can become an operation in managerial manipulation. In "Higher Education" the traffic in titles and forms is already long established: The Office with its hoarded files of score-sheets, punched cards and tapes can declare exactly how educated any individual is even to the third decimal. That is the highly structured busywork which we call education today; but it was not Brigham Young's idea of education. He had thoughts which we have repeated from time to time with very mixed reception on the BYU Campus. Still we do not feel in the least inclined to apologize for propagating them on the premises of a university whose main distinction is that it bears his name.

A big black leather chair stood in Brigham Young's office by the Lion House; it faced the window on the opposite wall and the President's desk in the middle of the room. First-time visitors to the office were invited to sit on that chair, facing the strong light of day and the calm blue eyes of Brother Brigham, who sat there at his desk, his back to the window, quietly waiting for his guest to say something. After all, the man had come to see him, and it was only right to let him state his business. President Young, according to Grandfather,[1] would never say a word for the first three minutes. And at the end of those first three minutes he always knew exactly the sort of man he was dealing with, and the nature — greedy, benign, or sinister — of his business. "And he *never* [here Grandpa smote the arm of his chair] had to change his mind!" — his psychoanalytical techniques, black leather couch and all, were deadly accurate, and always put him on top of the situation. Brigham Young used to say that no man, if allowed to speak, could possible avoid revealing his true character, "For out of the abundance of the heart the tongue speaketh."

It is important to know this if we would understand Brigham Young himself. No man ever spoke his mind more frankly on all subjects; all his days he strove to communicate his inmost feelings, unburdening himself without the aid of notes or preparation in a vigorous and forthright prose that was the purest anti-rhetoric. It has been common practice to dismiss any saying of his of which one disapproves (and he makes no effort to please) by observing that he said so much on so many things that he was bound to contradict himself, and therefore need not be taken too seriously all the time. No view could be more ill-advised, for there never was a man more undeviatingly consistent and rational in thought and utterance. But we must let him speak for himself to see that, and that is what his critics stubbornly refuse to do, allowing him only an occasional phrase or two quoted out of context to clinch their case. The few quotations that follow are, it is true, only a tantalizingly small fraction of the prophet's inspired and resounding utterances on the subject of education, but at least there will be enough of them to establish a definite thesis. Granted that Brigham would admonish the Saints to wear overcoats one day, so to speak, and the next day turn around and advise shirt-sleeves, the element of scandal and confusion vanishes if we only get the main idea, which is that it is not the rule-book or the administration but the weather that prescribes the proper dress for the day. All the other apparent contradictions in Brother Brigham's teachings likewise vanish when we grasp the main idea behind them.

What, for example, could sound more worldy and self-centered than a remark such as, "I labor for my own dear self, I have self continually before me; the object of my pursuit is to benefit my individual person. . . ."? That is, until we read the whole statement, which continues, " . . .Men may think, and some of them do, that we have a right to work for ourselves; but I say we have no time to do that in the narrow, selfish sense generally entertained when speaking about working for self."[2] What can he possibly mean? He explains: the only way properly to serve one's self is to labor "in the . . . kingdom of God," any other course "is folly in the extreme."[3] "Do you want riches pertaining to this world? Yes, we acknowledge we do!" That again seems brutally frank until we read on: "I merely use the term 'riches' to lead the mind along, until we obtain eternal riches in the celestial kingdom of God," which is a very different thing.[4] We seem to hear the credo of the ambitious executive when we read, "We are organized for the express purpose of controlling the elements, of organizing and disorganizing, of ruling over kingdoms, principalities, and powers." But the next sentence completely reverses our verdict: "And yet our affections are often too highly placed upon paltry, perishable objects. We love houses, gold, silver, and various kinds of property, and all who unduly prize any object there is beneath the celestial world are idolators."[5] So it is all along: we may grant that Brigham Young talks like a solid, hard-headed Yankee materialist, but only as long as we understand that the only matter that interests him is the enduring substance of eternity. There is no real paradox when he says: "Then let us seek to extend the present life to the uttermost . . . and thus prepare for a better life."[6] He is thinking of this life *only* in terms of the next.

But very few people have been able to see that: "There are those in this congregation who are so short-sighted, and so destitute of eternal wisdom and knowledge, that they believe that brother Brigham is after property — after the things of this world."[7] Well, what else *could* they think of any man who rolled over all opposition, amassed substance and power, and commanded the absolute obedience that Brigham Young did? To do that in terms of our world, a man must needs be a combination of Tamerlane, Caesar Borgia, and Boss Tweed, and as such even the Latter-day Saints have pictured Brigham Young. How can you explain to the average American that there was once a shrewd Yankee farmer and builder with a passion for thrift ("I never suffered a peach-pit to be thrown away, nor ate an apple without saving the seeds to plant"[8]), who practiced and preached as the watchword of his economy the slogan, "Never count the cost"? How could you make him believe that the same dynamic character whose astounding accomplishments have made his name a synonym for work used to admonish his people: "Work less, wear less, eat less, and we shall be a great deal wiser, healthier and wealthier people"?[9] How could you ask him to take seriously the multi-millionaire who declares, "I have never walked across the streets to make a trade. I do not care anything about such things"?[10] Or the devoted family man who advised missionaries to follow his example and put all thought of family from their minds: "I am not bound to wife or child, to house or farm, or anything else on the face of the earth, but the Gospel of the Son of God"?[11] Here is the great leader who is utterly contemptuous of his "image": "I care not one groat whether they believe all that I say or not, or whether they love me or not; I have no concern about that. . . ."[12] Here is the man who worked himself almost to death to get the Nauvoo Temple built on time, and then rejoiced to see it in flames: "I was thankful to see the Temple in Nauvoo on fire . . . when I saw the flames, I said, 'Good, Father, if you want it to be burned up. . . .' "[13]

There is no paradox in all this. Brigham Young was able to master the things of the world because he would not let them master him: he took the measure of a world that could never understand him. It is not a case of physical *versus* "spiritual" values, but of eternal things, physical or not, versus things we know to be passing and therefore unworthy of our ultimate dedication. "What is this earth in its present condition? Nothing but a place in which we may learn the first lesson towards exaltation, and that is obedience to the Gospel of the Son of God."[14] That makes education the purpose of our life — a special kind of education. " . . .the world are seeking after the paltry, perishable things of time and sense. They are their glory — their pretended comfort — their god, and their daily study and pursuit."[15] But not for us! "Seek *first* the kingdom of God . . . and let the gold and silver, the houses, the lands, the horses, the chariots, the crowns, the thrones, and the dominions of this world be dead to you. . . ."[16] "The Latter-day Saints have been driven from their homes, and their goods have been spoiled; but they esteem this as nothing. What do we care for houses and lands and possessions? The whole earth is before us and all the fulness thereof."[17]

That sounds like another paradox: we do not mind the loss of earthly things as long as we get possession of the whole earth! Yes, but in the proper way: "While the inhabitants of the earth are bestowing all their ability, both mental and physical, upon perishable objects, those who profess to be Latter-day Saints, who have the privilege of receiving and understanding the principles of the holy Gospel, are in duty bound to study and find out, and put in practice in their lives, those principles that are calculated to endure, and that tend to a continual increase . . . in the world to come."[18] "As I said yesterday to a Bishop who was mending a breach in the canal, and expressed a wish to continue his labor on the following Sabbath, as his wheat was burning up, let it burn, when the time comes that is set apart for worship, go up and worship the Lord."[19] " . . . let the kitchens take care of themselves, and let the barns, the flocks and herds take care of themselves, and if they are destroyed while you are praying, be able to freely say, 'Go, they are the Lord's.' . . ."[20] The treasures of the earth are merely to provide us with room and board while we are here at school, being "made for the comfort of the creature, not for his adoration. They are made to sustain and preserve the body while procuring the knowledge and wisdom that pertain to God and his kingdom, in order that we may preserve ourselves, and live for ever in his presence."[21]

The astonishing thing is that Brigham Young, as his behavior demonstrated on innumerable occasions, really believed what he preached; which goes far to explaining his brilliant success in surmounting the most terrifying obstacles. "The Gospel of life and salvation reveals to each individual who receives it that this world is only a place of temporary duration, existence, trials, etc. Its present fashion and uses are but for a few days, while we were created to exist eternally."[22] That is the basic idea which resolves the paradoxes of Brigham Young's philosophy. No one grants more readily than this supremely practical man of affairs that "the things of this world add to our national comfort, and are necessary to sustain mortal life," and that "we need these comforts to sustain our earthly existence"; but none is more emphatic in insisting that "those things have nothing to do with the spirit, feeling, consolation, light, glory, peace, and joy that pertains to heaven and heavenly things, which are the food of the ever-living spirit within us. . . . This I know by experience. I know that the things of this world, from beginning to end, from the possession of mountains of gold down to a crust of johnnycake, make little or no difference in the happiness of an individual."[23] So we live two lives at once, taking care to keep our values straight: "I have a being and a life here; and this life is very valuable; it is a most excellent life! I have a future! I am living for another existence that is far above this sinful world."[24]

Brigham Young was the Prophet Joseph's most faithful disciple; their teachings are one as the minds of the saints and prophets have always been one. Before he met Joseph Smith, Brigham recalls, "the secret feeling of my heart was that I would be willing to crawl around the earth on my hands and knees, to see such a man as was Peter, Jeremiah, Moses, or any man that could tell me anything about God and heaven."[25] And then "when I saw Joseph Smith, he took heaven figuratively speaking, and brought it down to earth; and he took the earth, brought it up, and opened up, in plainness and simplicity, the things of God; and that is the beauty of his mission."[26] It was a mind-stretching religion: "Thy mind, O man!" said the Prophet, "if thou wilt lead a soul to salvation, must stretch as high as the utmost heavens, and search into and contemplate the darkest abyss, and the broad expanse of eternity."[27] The promise he gave to those who took the gospel and the cause of Judah to heart was that "your minds will expand wider and wider, until you can circumscribe the earth and the heavens... and contemplate the mighty acts of Jehovah in all their variety and glory."[28] What attests to him the divinity of the Bible is that it is "so much beyond the narrow-mindedness of men, that every man is constrained to exclaim: 'It came from God!' "[29] The Holy Ghost, the ultimate teacher, "has no other effect than pure intelligence. It is more powerful in expanding the mind, enlightening the understanding, and storing the intellect with present knowledge... it is... the pure light of intelligence."[30] Mind and heart must expand together, according to the Prophet: "...you must enlarge your souls towards each other.... Let your hearts expand, let them be enlarged towards others."[31] For not only is "the mind or the intelligence which man possesses... coequal with God himself" in time,[32] but "all the minds and spirits that God ever sent into the world are susceptible of enlargement... so that they... have one glory upon another...."[33]

This was what Brigham Young learned from his beloved Joseph as he "continued to receive revelation upon revelation, ordinance upon ordinance, truth upon truth...."[34] It was all good news: "What are we here for? To learn to enjoy more, and to increase in knowledge and in experience."[35] Learning is our proper calling: "We shall never cease to learn, unless we apostatize. . . . Can you understand that?"[36] "God has given us mental and physical powers to be improved . . . ,"[37] and along with them "our senses, if properly educated, are channels of endless felicity to us. . . ."[38] All systems are "go" for the expanding mind: "Let us not narrow ourselves up; for the world, with all its variety of useful information and its rich hoard of hidden treasure, is before us; and eternity, with all its sparkling intelligence, lofty aspirations, and unspeakable glories, is before us."[39] The news is all good — forever: "And when we have passed into the sphere where Joseph is, there is still another department, and then another, and another, and so on to an eternal progression in exaltation and eternal lives. That is the exaltation I am looking for."[40] " . . .when we have lived millions of years in the presence of God and angels . . . shall we then cease learning? No, or eternity ceases."[41] First and last, the gospel is learning unlimited.

The Mormons were latecomers in the learning game, and it is not hard to see why: "Most of the people called Latter-day Saints have been taken from the rural and manufacturing districts of this and the old countries, and they belonged to the poorest of the poor."[42] "We have gathered the poorest class of men to be found on the continent of America, and I was one of them; and we have gathered the same class from Europe. . . ."[43] "I never went to school but eleven days in my life."[44] "I am a man of few words and unlearned in the learning of this generation."[45] "Brother Heber and I never went to school until we got into 'Mormonism': that was the first of our schooling."[46] Such men, coming of age in the flowering of their native New England, hungered for the things of the mind, the more so since they had been denied them: " . . .we are all of the laboring and middle classes. There are but few in this Church who are not of the laboring class, and they have not had an opportunity to cultivate their minds. . . ."[47] yet they felt strongly "the necessity of the mind being kept active and having the opportunity of indulging in every exercise it can enjoy in order to attain to a full development of its powers."[48] Mormonism gave them their great chance, as it sought, in the words of Joseph Smith "to inspire every one who is called to be a minister of these glad tidings, to so improve his talent that he may gain other talents."[49]

If they were late starters, the gospel gave the Saints certain advantages which might even enable them to overhaul the more privileged. For one thing, they had motivating zeal: "Take those who are in the enjoyment of all the luxuries of this life, and their ears are stopped up; they cannot hear; but go to the poor . . . and they are looking every way for deliverance . . . their ears are open to hear and their hearts are touched. . . . These are they that we gather."[50] True, "very few of the learned or of those who are high and lifted up in the estimation of the people receive the Gospel";[51] but that is all to the good, since such haughtiness can be paralyzing. God is now working with rough but reliable materials: "The beginning of this dispensation of the fulness of times may well be compared to the commencement of a temple, the material of which it is to be built being still scattered, unshaped and unpolished, in a state of nature."[52] "A spirit and power of research is planted within, yet they remain undeveloped."[53] "When we look at the Latter-day Saints and remember that they have been taken from the coal pits, from the ironworks, from the streets, from the kitchens and from the barns and factories and from hard service in the countries where they formerly lived, we cannot wonder at their ignorance."[54]

But if their ignorance is not to be wondered at, neither is it to be condoned. Without a moment's delay the newly converted Saints were put to work on a grandiose intellectual project, which was nothing less than the salvaging of world civilization! As Brigham puts it, "the business of the Elders of this Church (Jesus, their elder brother, being at their head) [is] to gather up all the truths in the world pertaining to life and salvation, to the Gospel we preach, to mechanism[s] of every kind, to the sciences, and to philosophy, wherever [they] may be found in every nation, kindred, tongue and people, and bring it to Zion."[55] The "gathering" was to be not only a bringing together of people, but of all the treasures surviving in the earth from every age and culture; "Every accomplishment, every polished grace, every useful attainment in mathematics, music, in all science and art belong to the Saints, and they . . . rapidly collect the intelligence that is bestowed upon the nations, for all this intelligence belongs to Zion. All the knowledge, wisdom, power, and glory that have been bestowed upon the nations of the earth, from the days of Adam till now, must be gathered home to Zion."[56] "What is this work? The improvement of the condition of the human family."[57] But why do the poor struggling Saints have to do it? Because "the Lord has taken the weak things of the world to confound the . . . wise,"[58] and especially because the rest of the world is no longer up to it.

It was a daring concept, but one fully justified by history, that once "the Lord has bestowed great knowledge and wisdom upon the inhabitants of the earth — much truth . . . in the arts and sciences," it is quite possible for such treasures to be lost: "This wisdom will be taken from the wicked" — and once it is gone, "I question," says the far-seeing Brigham Young, "whether it would return again." To this impressive bit of historical insight he adds an exciting suggestion: "My faith and my desire are that there should be a people upon the earth prepared to receive this wisdom. It should not be so forfeited as to be taken from the earth."[59] The concept (recalling James Hilton's *Lost Horizon*) is an ancient one, being the idea, for example, behind the Cabbala. Repeatedly Brother Brigham admonishes the Saints that if they are to carry out such a task they must in time come to equal and even excel the learning of the world. They can do it if they work like demons: "Put forth your ability to learn as fast as you can, and gather all the strength of mind and principle of faith you possibly can, and then distribute your knowledge to the people."[60] If the world seems far ahead of us, remember, "we are not as ignorant as they are" because, like Socrates, we acknowledge our ignorance and know where we stand.[61] If the Saints "have not had an opportunity to cultivate their minds," neither had they "been educated in the devilry and craft of the learned classes of mankind," to hold them back.[62] Joseph Smith had assured them that "there is a superior intelligence bestowed upon such as obey the Gospel,"[63] and Brigham promised them, "There is nothing that the Saints can ask, or pray for, that will aid them in their progress . . . that will not be granted unto them, if they will only patiently struggle on."[64]

That last point, the patient struggling, was the rub. President Young kept after his people all the time: "After suitable rest and relaxation there is not a day, hour or minute that we should spend in idleness, but every minute of every day of our lives we should strive to improve our minds and to increase our faith in the holy Gospel."[65] A year after the arrival in the Valley, Brigham Young copied down in his journal a letter which Parley P. Pratt had written to his brother back east describing the new society: "All is quiet — stillness. No elections, no police reports, no murders, no war nor little war. . . . No policeman has been on duty to guard us from external or internal dangers. . . . Here we can cultivate the mind, renew the spirit, invigorate the body, cheer the heart and ennoble the soul of man. Here we can cultivate every science and art calculated to enlarge the mind, accommodate the body, or polish and adorn our race; and here we can receive and extend that pure intelligence which is unmingled with the jargon of mystic Babylon."[66] Wonderful to relate, for the ever practical Brigham and the struggling pioneers the improvement of the *mind* always came first. Brigham laid it on the line: "All who do not want to sustain co-operation and fall into the ranks of improvement, and endeavor to improve themselves by every good book" were invited to leave the community.[67] The challenge of nature was not the real issue — "the greatest and most important labour we have to perform is to cultivate ourselves."[68]

What the Church most urgently needed at the start was what might be called "missionary learning." It makes perfectly good sense to insist that "We should be familiar with the various languages, for we wish to send to the different nations and to the islands of the sea,"[69] or that all spend "a certain portion of the time . . . in storing their minds with useful knowledge," by "reading the Bible, Book of Mormon, and other Church works, and histories, scientific works and other useful books."[70] At an early time Brigham Young suggested the formation of independent study groups among the people: " . . . call in your brethren, and read the Bible, the Book of Mormon, the Book of Covenants, and the other revelations of God in them; and talk over the things contained in those books, and deal them out to your brethren and neighbors."[71] More formal schooling had ever an eye to the mission field: " . . .in our schools, all our educational pursuits are in the service of God, for all these labors are to establish truth on earth . . . ,"[72] specifically, "That our young men, when they go out to preach, may not be so ignorant as they have been hitherto."[73] Good missionaries should know things: "I do not wish to be understood as throwing a straw in the way of the Elders' storing their minds with all the arguments they can gather . . . [or] learning all they can with regard to religions and governments. The more knowledge the Elders have the better."[74] After all, Joseph Smith had said that the mind of one who "would lead a soul unto salvation, must stretch as high as the utmost heavens. . . ."[75]

But articulate and informed missionaries do not issue forth from a community of ignoramuses — Zion itself must be the central hearth and home of a broad and flourishing culture: "There is a great work for the Saints to do. Progress, and improve upon, and make beautiful everything around you. Cultivate the earth and cultivate your minds."[76] "Now if we can take the low and degraded and elevate them in their feelings, language and manners; if we can impart to them the sciences that are in the world, teach them all that books contain, and in addition to all this, teach them principles that are eternal, and calculated to make them a beautiful community, lovely in their appearance, intelligent in every sense of the word, would you not say that our system is praiseworthy and possesses great merit?"[77]

For Brigham, the proper study of mankind is everything: "This is the belief and doctrine of the Latter-day Saints. Learn everything that the children of men know. . . ."[78] It all comes under the heading of our religion: "Every true principle, every true science, every art, and the knowledge that men possess, or that they ever did or ever will possess, is from God. We should take pains and pride to . . . rear our children so that the learning and education of the world may be theirs."[79] "Every accomplishment, every grace, every useful attainment in mathematics, . . . in all science and art belongs to the Saints, and they should avail themselves as expeditiously as possible of the wealth of knowledge the sciences offer to the diligent and persevering scholar."[80]

A favorite with LDS schoolmen has been Brigham Young's declaration that "Every art and science known and studied by the children of men is comprised within the Gospel."[81] But this does not mean, as is commonly assumed, that anything one chooses to teach is the gospel — that would be as silly as arguing that since all things are made of electrons, protons, neutrons, etc., whenever anyone opens his mouth to speak he gives a lecture on physics. It means rather that all things may be studied and taught in the light of the gospel: ". . .if an Elder shall give us a lecture upon astronomy, chemistry, or geology, our religion embraces it all. It matters not what the subject be, if it tends to improve the mind, exalt the feelings, and enlarge the capacity."[82] It would be quite impossible to improve the mind, exalt the feelings and enlarge the capacity of any man without making him a better candidate for heaven — "it matters not what the subject be." By the same token, the reading of the scriptures if not undertaken in that spirit does *not* belong to our religion: " 'Shall I sit down and read the Bible, the Book of Mormon, and the Book of Covenants all the time?' says one. Yes, if you please, and when you have done, you may be nothing but a sectarian after all. It is your duty to study . . . everything upon the face of the earth, in addition to reading those books."[83]

"Everything on the face of the earth" is a large order, and Brigham was no fool; he knew perfectly well that "the most learned men that ever lived on the earth have only been able to obtain a small amount of knowledge,"[84] and that time, patience and method are necessary to bring the Saints around: "As Saints in the last days we have much to learn; there is an eternity of knowledge before us; at most we receive but very little in this stage of our progression."[85]

There must be a priority of things to be learned, which is what curriculum is all about: "We wish to have our young boys and girls taught in the different branches of an English education, and in other languages, and in the various sciences, all of which . . . [will] eventually . . . [be] taught in this school."[86] "We also wish them to understand the geography, habits, customs, and laws of nations and kingdoms, whether they be barbarian or civilized. This is recommended in the revelations . . . let them become more informed in every department of true and useful learning than their fathers are. . . ."[87]

Immediately after arriving in the valley President Young recommended "securing at least a copy of every valuable treatise on education — every book, map, chart, or diagram that may contain interesting, useful, and attractive matter, to gain the attention of children, and cause them to love to learn to read"; this includes "every historical, mathematical, philosophical, geographical, geological, astronomical, scientific, practical, and all other variety of useful and interesting writings."[88] To train "the whole man" was his object from the first: "Let us make mechanics of our boys, and educate them in every useful branch of science and in the history and laws of kingdoms and nations. . . ."[89] He was always fascinated with problems of communication, on which he had some interesting theories, including the improvement of English phonology: "I would also like our school teachers to introduce phonography into every school. . . . This is a delightful study! In these and all other branches of science and education we should know as much as any people in the world."[90]

But curriculum is a game for little minds; the important thing for Brigham is that the Saints use their new-found liberty and revel as he did in the things of the mind. The starving man eats thankfully what he can get and does not quibble for hours over the menu and etiquette. The decisive factor is a passion for the things of the *mind:* "We believe . . . that every man and woman should have the opportunity of developing themselves mentally as well as physically. In the present condition of the world this privilege is only accorded to a few."[91] Learning is a privilege to be eagerly exploited: "If we can have the privilege we will enrich our minds with knowledge, filling these mortal tenements with the rich treasures of heavenly wisdom."[92] The proper priority of study is not as important as study itself: "If it would do any good, I would advise you to read books that are worth reading," but "I would rather that persons read novels than read nothing"[93] — reading nothing being the normal outcome of waiting on the curriculum committee.

As the strong man loveth to run a race, so Brigham loved to exercise his brains, and constantly appealed to the people to do the same: "We are trying to teach this people to use their brains...."[94] "I pray to the Lord for you; I pray for you to get wisdom — worldly wisdom."[95] Every problem was to be approached as a mental problem, an exciting game of wits: "Whatever duty you are called to perform, take your minds with you, and apply them to what is to be done."[96] Proper pioneering takes as much brain as brawn. Intelligence is not only useful, it is a high moral quality, a holy thing, an attribute to God himself: "If men would be great in goodness," Brigham Young wrote in his history, "they must be intelligent...."[97] and he records in the same work that Joseph Smith prayed for the leaders of the Church "that God may grant unto them wisdom and intelligence, that his kingdom may roll forth."[98] And so he appeals to the people: "When you come to meeting... take your minds with you... I want [your] minds here as well as your bodies."[99]

To use one's brains is to think for one's self: "Ladies and gentlemen, I exhort you to think for yourselves, and read your Bibles for yourselves, get the Holy Spirit for yourselves, and pray for yourselves."[100] The appeal has been repeated by every president of the Church. "The catalogue of [a] man's discipline," says Brigham the sound psychologist, "he must compile for himself: he cannot be guided by any rule that others may lay down, but is... under the necessity of tracing it himself through every avenue of his life. He is obliged to catechise and train himself."[101] Even virtue is not too high a price to pay for individual responsibility: "Every mortal being must stand up as an intelligent, organized capacity, and choose or refuse the good, and thus act for himself.... All must have that opportunity, no matter if all go into the depths of wickedness."[102] We can never grow as long as we are "other-directed": "Pay no attention to what others do, it is no matter what they do, or how they dress."[103] A favorite saying of Brigham Young's was that "Men... are organized to be just as independent as any being in eternity...."[104] No one was a more passionate advocate of temperance than he, but when in his youth he was asked to sign a temperance pledge he absolutely refused: "I said, 'I do not need to sign the temperance pledge.' I recollect my father urged me. 'No, sir,' said I, 'if I sign the temperance pledge I feel that I am bound, and I wish to do just right, without being bound to do it; I want my liberty...!

What do you say? Is this correct?"[105] " . . . it would be useless for anybody to undertake to drive me to heaven or to hell. My independence is sacred to me — it is a portion of the same Diety that rules in the heavens."[106] Again, it was Joseph Smith who led the way: " . . . all have the privilege of thinking for themselves upon all matters relating to conscience. . . . We are not disposed, had we the power, to deprive anyone of exercising that free independence of mind which heaven has so graciously bestowed upon the human family as one of its choicest gifts."[107]

President Young tried to make the meetings of the Saints stimulating and adult affairs instead of humdrum routines. For one thing, "it may sometimes be just as good and profitable to stay at home as to come to meeting. . . . I do not believe that those who stay at home are, in many instances, any worse than those who come to meeting, nor that those who come to meeting are particularly better than those who stay home."[108] "If any of you feel that there is no life in your meetings . . . then it becomes your duty to go and instill life into that meeting, and do your part to produce an increase of the Spirit and the power of God in the meetings in your locality."[109] And even at conference: " . . .if any of you are not instructed to your satisfaction, be so kind as to send up a card to the stand, intimating your desire to speak, and we will give you an opportunity of doing so, to display your wisdom; for we wish to learn wisdom and get understanding."[110]

On the other hand, he rebukes senseless applause and even dampens the patriotic ardor of a Twenty-fourth of July gathering: "I have noticed that people there applaud and boys whistle when there was nothing to elicit their approbation; and I would say that it would be very gratifying to my feelings if such useless, noisy and uncalled-for demonstrations were discontinued."[111] Even high spirits and firecrackers are no excuse for turning off one's brains: "I ask . . . all the boys under a hundred years of age — never to applaud unless they know what they are applauding. It is confusing, bewildering, and making a noise without understanding."[112] Empty-headed laughter pleases him not: "Never give way to vain laughter. . . . I always blush for those who laugh aloud without meaning."[113] Children at meeting, even to attest to the growth of Zion, do not delight him: "I cannot understand the utility of bringing children into such a congregation . . . just for the sake of pleasing the mothers. . . ."[114] "If you cannot, for the space of two or three hours, forego the pleasure of gazing upon the faces of your little darlings, just stay at home with them."[115]

No matter where we begin, if we pursue knowledge diligently and honestly our quest will inevitably lead us from the things of earth to the things of heaven. All science is cosmology, says Karl Popper, and, we add, all cosmology is eschatology. For Brigham Young, since all knowledge can be encompassed in one whole, the spectrum of secular study blends imperceptibly with the knowledge of the eternities: "...in our schools, all our educational pursuits are in the service of God, for all these labors are to establish truth on the earth, and that we may increase in knowledge, wisdom, understanding in the power of faith and in the wisdom of God, that we may become fit subjects to dwell in a higher state of existence and intelligence than we now enjoy."[116] Note well that secular learning is sanctified only if it is approached in a certain spirit. Only that knowledge belongs to the gospel which is viewed and taught as such — as *all* knowledge should be...." God has created man with a mind capable of instruction," according to Joseph Smith, "and a faculty which may be enlarged in proportion to the heed and diligence given to the light communicated from *heaven* to the *intellect*...."[117]

There are three factors involved, intelligence, revelation, *and* hard work, and if the spirit may help in earthly learning, the mind is required to operate in celestial matters. The learning process begun in this life carries on into the next: "... and when we pass through the veil, we expect still to continue to learn and increase our fund of information."[118] The Saints must first learn "everything that the children of men know," and then go on and "improve upon this until we are prepared and permitted to enter the society of the blessed — the holy angels."[119] This is done by pursuing a steady course that leads from the earthly to the heavenly without a break: "We should not only learn the principles of education known to mankind, but we should reach out further than this, learning to live so that our minds will gather in information from the heavens and the earth until we can incorporate in our faith and understanding all knowledge."[120] "...teach the children, give them the learning of the world *and* the things of God; elevate their minds, that they may not only understand the earth we walk upon, but the air we breathe, the water we drink, and all the elements pertaining to the earth; and then search other worlds, and become acquainted with the planetary system." Not stopping there, they are to go on to discover "the dwellings of the angels and the heavenly beings, that they may ultimately be prepared for a higher state of being, and finally be associated with them."[121] "It is the privilege of man to search out the

wisdom of God pertaining to the earth and the heavens."[122]
" . . .learn the wisdom of the world and the wisdom of God, and put
them together and you will be able to benefit yourselves."[123] "We
try to so live as to gain more information, more light, more command over ourselves . . . until we can comprehend the great principles of existence and eternal progression."[124]

Such a concept has, of course, no conflict with science. The
motto of the Royal Society, *Nullus in verba* — "we take no man's
word for anything" — is even more strongly expressed in the first
editorial to appear in the *Times and Seasons*, written by Brigham
Young: "Remember, Brethren, that *no man's opinion is worth a straw."*
Brigham is man who wants to know: "The object of this existence is
to learn. . . . How gladly would we understand every principle pertaining to science and art, and become thoroughly acquainted with
every intricate operation of nature, and with all the chemical
changes that are constantly going on around us! How delightful this
would be, and what a boundless field of truth and power is open for
us to explore! We are only just approaching the shores of the vast
ocean of information that pertains to this physical world, to say
nothing of that which pertains to the heavens."[125] "Send the old
children to school and the young ones also; there is nothing I would
like better than to learn chemistry, botany, geology, and mineral-
ogy. . . ."[126] "In these respects we differ from the Christian world,
for our religion will not clash with or contradict the facts of science in
any particular. You may take geology, for instance, and it is a true
science; not that I would say for a moment that all the conclusions
and deductions of its professors are true [opinions are not facts!],
but its leading principles are. . . ."[127]

The basic common-sense of science appeals to Brigham Young
as being sound and true. He took the shocking position that God
works on scientific principles: "If I had the skill . . . to construct a
machine" to pass through "the atmosphere as they do now on the
terra firma on the railway, would there be any harm in acknowledg-
ing God in this?"[128] When " 'the elements shall melt with fervent
heat,' the Lord Almighty will send forth his angels, who are well
instructed in chemistry, and they will separate the elements and
make new combinations thereof."[129] That was an outrageous
statement both from a religious and a scientific viewpoint a hundred
years ago. He also propounded a doctrine which has only recently
been brought to the fore by such scientists as Giorgio Santillana:
"The people of this day think they know more than all who have
preceded them — that this is the wisest generation that ever did live

on the earth . . . but there is no question that many things of great worth known anciently have been lost. . . ."[130]

Brigham Young's sanguine discourses on education were meant to stir his people up and shame them out of their intellectual lethargy. No one knew better than he the weaknesses of human nature ("Mankind are weak and feeble, poor and needy; how destitute they are of true knowledge, how little they have when they have any at all!"[131]); the hebetude of minds used to having others think for them (" . . . the great masses of the people neither think nor act for themselves. . . . I see too much of this gross ignorance among this chosen people of God";[132] the hesitancy of the uprooted, tending either "to hide ourselves up from the world" or "to pattern after the people they had left" — both wrong;[133] the smugness of the Chosen People, who "imagine that they must begin and unlearn the whole of their former education,"[134] and who expect God to give them everything on a platter: "Have I any good reason to say to my Father in heaven, 'Fight my battles,' when He has given me the sword to wield, the arm and the brain that I can fight for myself?"[135] The Saints were much too easily satisfied with themselves: "How vain and trifling have been our spirits, our conferences, our councils, our meetings, our private as well as public conversations," wrote the Prophet Joseph from Liberty Jail, " — too low, too mean, too vulgar, too condescending for the dignified characters of the called and chosen of God."[136] "Condescending" means settling for inferior goods to avoid effort and tension. Brigham hated that: "The diffidence or timidity we must dispense with. When it becomes our duty to talk, we ought to be willing to talk. . . . Interchanging our ideas and exhibiting that which we believe and understand affords an opportunity for detecting and correcting errors" — the expanding mind must be openly and frankly critical, come hell or High Council;[137] without that we get "too much of a sameness in this community"[138] — "I am not a stereotyped Latter-day Saint, and do not believe in the doctrine. . . . Are we going to stand still? Away with stereotyped 'Mormons'!"[139]

But the foibles of human nature were but some of the timbers and cobblestones of the real barricade which the adversary has contrived to place in the way of learning. The Saints, gathered "from the poorest of the poor," had good reason to know that the imperious question put to all who presume to set foot on this world where Belial rules is not "Have you any knowledge?" (as in the ancient mysteries), but "Have you any money?" That is Satan's Golden Question. If the answer is "yes," well and good (" . . .for money answereth all things"), but if it is "no" you might as well be dead. That is the way things are set up here upon the earth; "...man has become so perverted as to debar his fellows as much as possible from these blessings, and constrain them by physical force or circumstances to contribute the proceeds of their labor to sustain the favored few."[140] It is no wonder that the Saints who had momentarily broken free from the system were obsessed with an overpowering drive to seek the only security this earth has to offer — wealth. And this passion, as Brigham Young tells them in a mounting crescendo of warning and appeal through the years, is the one absolute obstacle to their ever acquiring the knowledge they must seek.

Brigham discovered the basic conflict at an early age; he tells how at the age of nineteen he "sought for riches, but in vain; there was always something that kept telling me that happiness originated in higher pursuits."[141] At the very beginning of the Church Joseph Smith noted that "God had often sealed up the heavens because of covetousness in the Church."[142] In 1855 Brigham Young pointed out the way in which love of knowledge and love of wealth, like antipathetical sets of glands, render each other ineffective: "It is possible for a man who loves the world to overcome that love, to get knowledge and understanding until he sees things as they really are, then he will not love the world but will see it as it is...."[143] In 1859: "I desire to see everybody on the track of improvement.... But when you so love your property... as though all your affections were placed upon the changing, fading things of earth, it is impossible to increase in knowledge of the truth."[144] In 1860: "There are hundreds in this community who are more eager to become rich in the perishable things of this world than to adorn their minds... with a knowledge of things as they were, as they are, and as they are to come."[145] In 1862: "No man who possesses the wealth of wisdom would worship the wealth of mammon."[146] In 1863: If we go on "lusting after the grovelling things of this life which perish with the handling," we shall surely "remain fixed with a very limited amount of knowledge, and like a door upon its hinges, move to and fro from one year to another without any visible advancement or improvement.... Man is made in the image of God, but what do we know of him or of ourselves, when we suffer ourselves to love and worship the god of this world — riches?"[147] In 1866: "When you see the Latter-day Saints greedy, and covetous of the things of this world, do you think their minds are in a fit condition to be written upon by the pen of revelation?"[148] In 1870: "We frequently hear our merchants say that they cannot do business and then go into the pulpit to preach."[149] In 1872: "A man or a woman who places the wealth of this world,and the things of time in the scales against the things of God and wisdom of eternity, has no eyes to see, no ears to hear, no heart to understand."[150] In 1874: " . . .the covetous, those who are striving continually to build themselves up in the things of this life, will be poor indeed; they will be poor in spirit and poor in heavenly things."[151]

Over against the expanding mind, the prophets placed the contracted mind: " . . .you must not be contracted, but you must be liberal in your feelings," Joseph Smith told the people.[152] "How contracted in mind and short-sighted we must be," Brigham reflects, "to permit the perishable things of this world to swerve us in the least degree from our fidelity to the truth."[153] "Let us not narrow ourselves up; for the world with all its variety of useful information and its rich hoard of hidden treasure, is before us."[154] He illustrates this by the practice of constantly quoting a very limited number of scriptures to the exclusion of others equally important, and comments: "This same lack of comprehensiveness of mind is also very noticeable at times with some men who happen to accumulate property, and it leads them to forsake the Spirit of the Gospel. Does it not prove that there is a contractedness of mind in those who do so, which should not be?"[155] Business by its very nature is narrowing: "Take, for instance, the financial circles, the commerce of the world, those business men, where they have their opponents they . . . with all the secrecy of the grave, I might say, will seek to carry out their schemes unknown to their opponents, in order that they may win. Like the man at the table with the cards in his hands, unseen by any but himself, he will take the advantage as far as he can. So says the politician. So says the world of Christendom, so say the world of the heathens, and it is party upon party, sect after sect, division upon division, and we are all for ourselves."[156] "In our trading and trafficking we wish to confine the knowledge of our business in as small a limit as possible, that others may not know what we are doing. . . . We all wish to know something that our neighbors do not know. With scientific men you will often find the same trait of character; . . . I know more than they know; I treasure this up to myself, and I am looked upon as a superior being, and that delights me."[157]

Against this, "You see the nobleman seeking the benefit of all around him, trying to bring, we will say, his servants, if you please, his tenants, to his knowledge, to like blessings that he enjoys, to dispense his wisdom and talents among them and to make them equal with himself."[158] Brigham told the well-heeled Saints to "keep their riches, and with them I promise you leanness of soul, darkness of mind, narrow and contracted hearts, and the bowels of your compassion will be shut up. . . ."[159] Even so, Joseph Smith had warned against "those contracted feelings that influence the children of men" who judge each other "according to the narrow, contracted notions of men" while "the Great Parent of the universe looks upon the whole of the human family with a fatherly care and paternal regard."[160]

For Brigham Young the contracted mind reached its bathos in the world of fashion: "But to see a people who say, 'We are the teachers of life and salvation,' and yet are anxious to follow the nasty, pernicious fashions of the day, I say it is too insipid to talk or think about. It is beneath the character of the Latter-day Saints that they should have no more independence of mind or feeling than to follow after the grovelling customs and fashions of the poor, miserable, wicked world."[161] "To me the desire to follow the ever-varying fashions of the world manifests a great weakness of mind in either gentleman or lady."[162] Again, it is the things of the world versus the things of the mind: "Mothers. . . . We will appoint you to a mission to teach your children their duty; and instead of ruffles and fine dresses to adorn the body, teach them that which will adorn their minds."[163] So the Prophet Joseph had told the sisters at the founding of the Relief Society, "This Society shall rejoice, and knowledge and intelligence shall flow down from this time henceforth," but only if they "don't envy the finery and fleeting show of sinners, for they are in a miserable situation."[164] Status-symbols belong to the same category: "A good name! Bless me! what is a name? It may shine like the noonday sun . . . today, and tomorrow be eclipsed in midnight darkness, to rise no more! The glory of the world passes away, but the glory that the Saints are after is that which is to come in the eternal world."[165] "In all nations, or at least in all civilized nations, there are distinctions among the people created by rank, titles, and property. How does God look upon these distinctions?"[166]

Misreading the case of the ancient patriarchs, whose wealth came and went and always hung by a thread, many of the Saints dreamed fondly of a happy wedding between the good things of this earth and the blessings of the next, and sought after the death of Brigham Young to bridge the unbridgeable gulf between Babylon and Zion. We cannot go into this here, but it should be clear by now that the search for knowledge, in Brigham's book, by its very nature must be pure and disinterested: "Will education feed and clothe you, keep you warm on a cold day, or enable you to build a house? Not at all. Should we cry down education on this account? No. What is it for? The improvement of the *mind:* to instruct us in all arts and sciences, in the history of the world, in . . . laws of how to be useful while we live."[167] It is the things of the mind that are really useful. "Truth, wisdom, power, glory, light, and intelligence exist upon their own qualities; they do not, neither can they, exist on any other principle. Truth is congenial with itself, and light cleaves unto light. . . . It is the same with knowledge, and virtue, and all the eternal attributes; they follow after . . . each other. . . . Truth cleaves unto truth *because* it is truth; and it is to be adored, because it is an attribute of God, for its excellence, for itself."[168] There can be no ulterior motive in the study of heavenly things; "Knowledge is Power" is the slogan of a rascally world: " . . .what do you love truth for? Is it because you can discover a beauty in it, because it is congenial to you; or because you think it will make you a ruler, or a Lord? If you conceive that you will attain to power upon such a motive, you are much mistaken. It is a trick of the unseen power, that is abroad amongst the inhabitants of the earth, that leads them astray, binds their minds, and subverts their understanding."[169]

Here Brigham Young goes all the way: "Suppose that our Father in heaven, our elder brother, the risen Redeemer, the Savior of the world, or any of the Gods of eternity should act upon this principle, to love truth, knowledge, and wisdom, because they are all powerful . . . they would cease to be Gods; . . . the extension of their kingdom would cease, and their God-head come to an end."[170] The Saints do what they do "purely because the principles which God has revealed . . . are pure, holy and exalting in their nature."[171] How can there be compromise with the world? "Shame on men and women, professing to be Saints , who worship and love the perishing things of earth."[172] "It is disgusting to me to see a person love this world in its present organization . . ."[173] "Go to the child, and what does its joy consist in? Toys . . . and so it is with our youth, our young boys and girls; they are thinking too much of this world; and the middle-aged are striving and struggling to obtain the good things of this life, and their hearts are too much upon them. So it is with the aged. Is not this the condition of the Latter-day Saints? It is."[174]

The Latter-day Saints have always had a way of missing the bus: "Take the history of this Church from the commencement, and we have proven that we cannot receive all the Lord has for us."[175] The trouble is that "these tabernacles are dull, subject to sin and temptation, and to stray from the kingdom of God and the ordinances of his house, to lust after riches, the pride of life, and the vanities of the world."[176] "We may look upon ourselves with shamefacedness because of the smallness of our attainments in the midst of so many great advantages."[177] "...in things pertaining to this life, the lack of knowledge manifested by us as a people is disgraceful."[178] "I have seen months and months, in this city, when I could have wept like a whipped child to see the awful stupidity of the people...."[179] "I feel like taking men and women by the hair of their heads, figuratively speaking, and slinging them miles and miles, and like crying, stop, before you ruin yourselves!"[180]

In a now-classic study, R. Kaesemann showed that God's peculiar way of dealing with the chosen people, ever stiff-necked and slow to learn, was to send them wandering in the wilderness. The last dispensation has proven no exception in this regard: "Some may ask why did we not tarry at the centre stake of Zion when the Lord planted our feet there? We had eyes, but we did not see; we had ears, but we did not hear; we had hearts that were devoid of what the Lord required of his people; consequently, we could not abide what the Lord revealed unto us. We had to go from there to gain an experience. Can you understand this?"[181] "Could our brethren stay in Jackson County, Missouri? No, no. Why? They had not learned 'a' concerning Zion; and we have been traveling now forty-two years, and have we learned our a,b,c? ...I will say, scarcely."[182] "I never attributed the driving of the Saints from Jackson county to anything but that it was necessary to chasten them and prepare them to build up Zion."[183] "Are we fit for Zion? ... Could we stay in Independence? No, we could not. .... What is the matter with all you Latter-day Saints? Can the world see? No. Can the Saints see? No, or few of them can; and we can say that the light of the Spirit upon the hearts and understanding of some Latter-day Saints is like the peeping of the stars through the broken shingles of the roof over our heads."[184]

The prophecies have not been revoked, but their fulfillment can be delayed, indefinitely, if need be, until all necessary conditions are fulfilled. The Saints "will take the kingdom, and possess it for ever and ever; but in the capacity they are now, in the condition that they now present themselves before God, before the world and before each other? Never, never!"[185] "We are not yet prepared to go and establish the Centre Stake of Zion. The Lord tried this in the first place. . . . He gave revelation after revelation; but the people could not abide them. . . . They do not know what to do with the revelations, commandments and blessings of God."[186] So though this people will surely go back to Jackson County, they will none the less be *held back* until they are ready — which may be a very long time.[187]

"And so we have got to continue to labor, fight, toil, counsel, exercise faith, ask God over and over, and have been praying to the Lord for thirty-odd years for that which we might have received . . . in one year."[188] But there was nothing for it but to keep on plugging: "We are so organized that we need preaching to all the time. This is because of our weakness, and we shall have to bear with one another until we become stronger and wiser."[189] We may give up and lose the blessings, but the prophecies and promises will all be fulfilled, and "if we do not wake up and cease to long after the things of this earth, we will find that we as individuals will go down to hell, although the Lord will preserve a people unto himself."[190] "We may fail, if we are not faithful; but God will not fail in accomplishing his work, whether we abide in it or not."[191] "If we are not faithful, others will take our places; for this is the Church and people that will possess the kingdom for ever and ever. Shall we do this in our present condition as a people? No; for we must be pure and holy."[192] " . . . if my brethren and sisters do not walk up to the principles of the holy Gospel . . . they will be removed out of their places, and others will be called to occupy them."[193] It had already happened many times: "Of the great many who have been baptized into this Church, but few have been able to abide the word of the Lord; they have fallen out on the right and on the left . . . and a few have gathered together."[194] Joseph Smith stated the problem: "I have tried for a number of years to get the minds of the Saints prepared to receive the things of God," but they "will fly to pieces like glass as soon as anything comes that is contrary to their traditions: they still cannot stand the fire at all."[195]

We have felt no necessity in this brief and sketchy survey for pointing out to the reader how Brigham Young's educational concepts stand out in brilliant contrast against the background of everything that is practiced and preached in our higher schools today. But the moral of our story must not be overlooked: *Brigham was right after all.* As administrative problems have accumulated in a growing Church, the authorities have tended to delegate the business of learning to others, and those others have been only too glad to settle for the outward show, the easy and flattering forms, trappings and ceremonies of education. Worse still, they have chosen business-oriented, career-minded, degree-seeking programs in preference to the strenuous, critical, liberal, mind-stretching exercises that Brigham Young recommended. We have chosen the services of the hired image-maker in preference to unsparing self-criticism, and the first question the student is taught to ask today is John Dewey's golden question: "What is there in it for me?"

As a result, whenever we move out of our tiny, busy orbits of administration and display, we find ourselves in a terrifying intellectual vacuum. Terrifying, of course, only because we might be found out. But that is just the trouble: having defaulted drastically in terms of President Young's instructions, we now stand as a brainless giant, a pushover for any smart kid or cultist or faddist or crank who even pretends to have read a few books. That puts them beyond our depth and so we (I include myself) stand helplessly and foolishly by dangling our bonnet and plume while hundreds of students and missionaries, of members and enemies of the Church alike, presume to challenge and reject the teachings of Joseph Smith on evidence so flimsy that no half-educated person would give it a second thought. How can you hope to make these people see that the documents and discoveries they hail with such reverence and delight for the most part went out of date in the 1930s; that Huxley, Breasted, Wellhausen, and Frazer do not represent present-day scientific thought; that one book does not settle anything? No one has ever told them of the new discoveries which *every month* call for revision of established scientific and scholarly beliefs. No one has ever told them what it means to lay a proper foundation essential to any serious discussion of the things they treat so glibly and triumphantly. No one has ever told them of the millions of unread documents that already repose in our libraries, holding the answers to countless questions that must be asked before they can justify their instant conclusions. An awesome outpouring of newly discovered documents of direct bearing on the history and teachings of the Church is even now in full spate, amazing and confounding Jewish and Christian scholars, but bursting with good news for the Latter-day Saints — who ignore them completely.

It is perfectly natural for the young who discover the world of scholarship for the first time to strike in their sophomoric zeal an intellectual pose, rail in high terms against the Church that has kept them in darkness all these years, and catalogue the defects and miscalculations of the prophets in the light of their own scholarly elevation. That is perfectly natural, and if we had heeded Brigham Young, the urge to study and criticize would be running in fruitful

252

channels. Whether we like it or not, we are going to have to return to Brigham Young's ideals of education; we may fight it all the way, but in the end God will keep us after school until we learn our lesson: "Behold, you have not understood; you have supposed that I would give it unto you, when you took no thought save it was to ask me. But, behold, I say unto you, that you must study it out in your mind; then you must ask me if it be right. . . ." (D&C 9:7-8.)

NOTES

1. Charles W. Nibley. During the winter of 1921, when President Nibley was writing his reminiscences at Ocean Park, California, he used to read the manuscript to the family of the author in the evenings, telling as he went the much better stories left out of the official biography. This was one of them, and has since then been repeatedly confirmed by Preston Nibley, who had it from the same source.

2. Brigham Young in *Journal of Discourses*, 26 vols. (London: Latter-day Saints' Book Depot, 1855-86), 14:101: hereafter cited as *JD*.

3. *Ibid.*

4. *JD* 15: 35, 37.

5. *JD* 3:357.

6. *JD* 11:132.

7. *JD* 8:125.

8. *JD* 10:335.

9. *JD* 12:122.

10. *JD* 12:218f.

11. *JD* 14:19.

12. *JD* 10:302.

13. *JD* 8:203.

14. *JD* 14:232.

15. *JD* 6:40.

16. *JD* 1:266.

17. *JD* 11:16.

18. *JD* 2:91.

19. *JD* 3:331.

20. *JD* 3:53.

21. *JD* 8:135.

22. *JD* 5:53.

23. *JD* 7:135.

24. *JD* 13:220.

25. *JD* 8:228.

26. *JD* 5:332.

27. Joseph Fielding Smith, comp. *Teachings of the Prophet Joseph Smith* (Salt Lake City: Deseret Book Co., 1942), p. 137: hereafter cited as *TPJS*.

28. *TPJS*, p. 163.
29. *TPJS*, p. 11.
30. *TPJS*, p. 149.
31. *TPJS*, p. 228.
32. *TPJS*, p. 353.
33. *TPJS*, p. 354.
34. *JD* 16:42.
35. *JD* 14:228.
36. *JD* 3:203.
37. *JD* 10:231.
38. *JD* 9:244.
39. *JD* 8:9.
40. *JD* 3:375.
41. *JD* 6:344.
42. *JD* 14:103.
43. *JD* 14:121.
44. *JD* 13:149.
45. *JD* 9:287.
46. *JD* 5:97.
47. *JD* 6:70f.
48. *JD* 13:61.
49. *TPJS*, p. 48.
50. *JD* 12:256.
51. *JD* 14:75.
52. *JD* 12:161.
53. *JD* 7:1.
54. *JD* 14:38.
55. *JD* 7:283f.
56. *JD* 10:224; 8:279.
57. *JD* 19:46.
58. *JD* 14:38.
59. *JD* 8:319.
60. *JD* 8:146.

61. *JD* 14:38f.

62. *JD* 6:70f.

63. *TPJS*, p. 67.

64. *JD* 11:14.

65. *JD* 13:310.

66. Brigham Young History, manuscript in the Office of the Church Historian, The Church of Jesus Christ of Latter-day Saints, Salt Lake City, August 23, 1848, p. 57.

67. *JD* 13:4.

68. *JD* 10:2.

69. *JD* 8:40.

70. *JD* 18:75.

71. *JD* 1:47.

72. *JD* 13:260.

73. *JD* 12:31 (or 406).

74. *JD* 8:53-54.

75. *TPJS*, p. 137.

76. *JD* 8:83.

77. *JD* 13:176.

78. *JD*16:77.

79. *JD* 12:326.

80. *JD* 10:224.

81. *JD* 12:257.

82. *JD* 1:335.

83. *JD* 2:93f.

84. *JD* 3:354.

85. *Ibid.*

86. *JD* 12:116.

87. *JD* 8:40; 8:9.

88. *Millennial Star* 10:85: hereafter cited as *MS*.

89. *JD* 10:270.

90. *JD* 12:32 (or 407).

91. *Deseret News*, May 23, 1877.

92. *MS* 24:630.

93. *JD* 9:173.

94. *JD* 11:328.

95. *JD* 10:296.

96. *JD* 8:137.

97. Brigham Young History, September 22, 1853, p. 78.

98. *Ibid.*, June 1839, p. 45.

99. *JD* 8:137.

100. *JD* 11:127.

101. *JD* 6:315.

102. *JD* 8:352.

103. *JD* 15:162.

104. *JD* 3:316.

105. *JD* 14:225.

106. *JD* 10:191.

107. *TPJS*, p. 49.

108. *JD* 10:349.

109. *JD* 10:309.

110. *JD* 12:124.

111. *MS* 31:571.

112. *MS* 30:550.

113. *JD* 9:290.

114. *JD* 13:343.

115. *JD* 13:344.

116. *JD* 13:260.

117. *TPJS*, p. 51.

118. *JD* 6:286.

119. *JD* 16:77.

120. *JD* 12:172.

121. *JD* 14:210. Italics added.

122. *JD* 9:242.

123. *JD* 12:313.

124. *JD* 9:254.

125. *JD* 9:167.

126. *JD* 16:170.

127. *JD* 14:116.

128. *JD* 12:260.

129. *JD* 15:127.

130. *JD* 13:305f.

131. *JD* 3:343.

132. *JD* 9:295.

133. *MS* 29:756f.

134. *JD* 3:204.

135. *JD* 12:240f.

136. Joseph Smith, *History of The Church of Jesus Christ of Latter-day Saints*, ed. B. H. Roberts, 7 vols. (Salt Lake City: The Church of Jesus Christ of Latter-day Saints, 1932-51), 3:295-296.

137. *JD* 6:93.

138. *JD* 13:153.

139. *JD* 8:185.

140. *MS* 17:673.

141. Brigham Young History, p. xiv.

142. *TPJS*, p. 9.

143. *JD* 3:119.

144. *JD* 7:337.

145. *JD* 8:9.

146. *JD* 10:3.

147. *JD* 10:266f.

148. *JD* 11:241.

149. *JD* 13:308.

150. *JD* 15:18.

151. *JD* 17:159.

152. *TPJS*, p. 228.

153. *JD* 11:283.

154. *JD* 8:9.

155. *JD* 11:283.

156. *JD* 15:124.

157. *JD* 17:52.

158. *JD* 15:19.

159. *JD* 12:127.

160. *TPJS*, p. 218.

161. *JD* 13:4.

162. *JD* 14:16.

163. *JD* 14:220f.

164. *TPJS*, p. 229.

165. *JD* 14:77.

166. *JD* 14:83.

167. *Ibid*. Italics added.

168. *JD* 1:117. Italics added.

169. *Ibid*.

170. *Ibid*.

171. *JD* 16:70.

172. *JD* 7:271.

173. *MS* 12:275.

174. *JD* 18:237.

175. *JD* 11:103.

176. *JD* 18:238.

177. *JD* 12:192.

178. *JD* 11:105.

179. *JD* 2:280.

180. *JD* 3:225.

181. *JD* 11:102.

182. *JD* 15:4.

183. *JD* 13:148.

184. *JD* 15:3.

185. *JD* 15:2.

186. *JD* 11:324f.

187. *JD* 3:278-279; 11:324; 13:148.

188. *JD* 11:300.

189. *JD* 8:181.

190. *JD* 18:301.

191. *JD* 8:183.
192. *JD* 8:143-144.
193. *JD* 16:26.
194. *JD* 11:324.
195. *TPJS*, p. 331.

Zeal Without Knowledge

12

This talk was given on request as part of the celebration of Academic Emphasis Week. Once a year, for a whole week, our students are free to turn their minds to things of an intellectual nature without shame or embarrassment. After this cerebral Saturnalia, the young people mostly return to their normal patterns: concealing the neglect of hard scholarship by the claim to spirituality and strict standards of dress and grooming. Yet from time to time a student will confess to wayward twinges of thought and find himself wondering, "If 'The Glory of God Is Intelligence' (our school motto) might there not be some possible connection between intelligence and spirituality?" Under temporary license from the Academics Committee, we have presumed to touch upon this sensitive theme.

In one of his fascinating scientific survey books, this time dealing with the latest discoveries about the brain, Nigel Calder notes, "Two of the most self-evident characteristics of the conscious mind are that 1) the mind attends to one thing at a time, and 2) that at least once a day the conscious mind is switched off."[1] Both of these operations are completely miraculous and completely mysterious. I would like to talk about the first of them. You can think of only *one* thing at a time!

If you put on a pair of glasses, one lens being green, the other being red, you will not see a grey fusion of the two when you look about you, but a flashing of red and green. One moment everything will be green, another moment everything will be red. Or you may think you are enjoying a combination of themes as you listen to a Bach fugue, with equal awareness of every voice at a time, but you are actually jumping between recognition first of one and then another. The ear, like the eye, is, in the words of N. S. Sutherland, "always flickering about . . . the brain adds together a great variety of impressions at high speed, and from these we select features from what we see and make a rapid succession of 'models' of the world in our minds."[2] Out of what begins as what William James calls the "great blooming, buzzing confusion" of the infant's world, we structure our own meaningful combination of impressions, and all our lives select out of the vast number of impressions certain ones which fit best into that structure. As Neisser says, "The *model* is what we see and nothing else."[3] We hold thousands of instantaneous impressions in suspension just long enough to make our choices and drop those we don't want. As one expert puts it: "There seems to be a kind of filter inside the head which weakens unwanted signals without blocking them out. Out of the background of the mind constantly signals deliberate choices."[4] *Why* the mind chooses to focus on one object to the exclusion of all others remains a mystery.[5] But one thing is clear: the blocked-out signals are the unwanted ones, and the ones we favor are our "deliberate choices."

This puts us in the position of the fairy-tale hero who is introduced into a cave of incredible treasures and permitted to choose from the heap whatever gem he wants — but only one. What a delightful situation! I can think of anything I want to — absolutely anything! With this provision, that when I choose to focus my attention on one object, all other objects drop into the background. I am only permitted to think of one thing at a time, that is one rule of the game.

An equally important rule is that I must keep thinking! Except for the daily shut-off period I cannot evade the test. "L'ame pense toujours," says Malebranche: We are always thinking of *something*, selecting what will fit into the world we are making for ourselves. Schopenhauer was right: "Die Welt ist meine Vorstellung." And here is an aside I can't resist: What would it be like if I could view and focus on two or more things at once, if I could see at one and the same moment not only what is right before me, but equally well what is on my left side, my right side, what is above me and below me? I have the moral certainty that something is there and as my eyes flicker about, I think I can substantiate that impression. But as to taking a calm and deliberate look at more than one thing at a time, that is a gift denied us at present. I cannot imagine what such a view of the world would be like, but it would be *more* real and correct than the one we have now. I bring up this obvious point because it is by virtue of this one-dimensional view of things that we magisterially pass judgment on God. The smart atheist and pious schoolman alike can tell us all about God — what he can do and what he cannot, what he must be like and what he cannot be like — on the basis of their one-dimensional experience of reality. Today the astronomers are harping on the old favorite theme of the eighteenth-century encyclopedists who, upon discovering the universe to be considerably larger than they thought or had been taught, immediately announced that man was a very minor creature indeed, would have to renounce any special claim to divine favor, since there are much bigger worlds than ours for God to be concerned about, and in the end give up his intimate and private God altogether. This jaunty iconoclasm rested on the assumption that God is subject to the same mental limitations that we are; that if he is thinking of Peter, he can hardly be thinking of Paul at the same time, let alone marking the fall of the sparrow. But once we can see the possibilities that lie in being able to see more than one thing at a time, (and in theory the experts tell us there is no reason why we should not) the universe takes on new dimensions and God takes over again. Let us remember that quite peculiar to the genius of Mormonism is the doctrine of a God who could preoccupy himself with countless numbers of things: "The heavens they are many, and they cannot be numbered unto man; but they are numbered unto me, for they are mine." (Moses 1:37.)

Plainly, we are dealing with two orders of minds. "For my thoughts are not your thoughts, neither are your ways my ways, saith the Lord. For as the heavens are higher than the earth, so are . . . my thoughts than your thoughts." (Isaiah 55:8-9.)

But why this crippling limitation on our thoughts if we are God's children? It is precisely this limitation which is the essence of our mortal existence. If every choice I make expresses a preference; if the world I build up is the world I really love and want, then with every choice I am judging myself, proclaiming all the day long to God, angels and my fellowmen where my real values lie, where my treasure is, the things to which I give supreme importance. Hence, in this life every moment provides a perfect and foolproof test of your real character, making this life a time of testing and probation. And hence the agonizing cry of the prophet Mormon speaking to our generation. ("I speak unto you as if ye were present, and yet ye are not. But behold, Jesus Christ hath shown you unto me, and I know your doing" [Mormon 8:35].) He calls upon us, "Be wise in the days of your probation . . . ask not, that ye may consume it on your lusts" (Mormon 9:28); i.e., that you may use up or consume your probation time just having a good time or doing what you feel like doing — nothing could be more terrible than that: "But *woe* unto him . . . that *wasteth* the days of his probation, for *awful* is his state!" (2 Nephi 9:27. Italics added.) It is throwing our life away, to think of the wrong things, as we are told in the next verse that "the cunning plan of the evil one" is to get us to do just that; trying, in Brigham Young's phrase, to "decoy our thoughts," to get our minds on trivial thoughts, on the things of this world against which we have so often been warned.

Sin is waste. It is doing one thing when you should be doing other and better things for which you have the capacity. Hence, there are no innocent idle thoughts. That is why even the righteous must repent, constantly and progressively, since all fall short of their capacity and calling. "Probably 99 percent of human ability has been wholly wasted," writes Arthur Clarke, "even today we operate . . . most of our time as automatic machines, and glimpse the profounder resources of our minds only once or twice in a lifetime."[6] "No nation can afford to divert its most able men into such essentially noncreative and occasionally parasitic occupations as law, advertising, and banking."[7] Those officials whom Moroni chides because they "sit upon [their] thrones in a state of thought-less stupor" (Alma 60:7) were not deliberately or maliciously harming anyone — but they were committing grave sin. Why do people feel guilty about TV? What is wrong with it? Just this — that it shuts out all the wonderful things of which the mind is capable, leaving it drugged in a state of thoughtless stupor. For the same reason a mediocre school or teacher is a *bad* school or teacher. Last week it was announced in the papers that a large convention concerned with violence and disorder in our schools came to the unanimous conclusion — students and teachers alike — that the main cause of the mischief was *boredom*. Underperformance, the job that does not challenge you, can make you sick: work which puts repetition and routine in the place of real work begets a sense of guilt; merely doodling and noodling in committees can give you ulcers, skin rashes, and heart trouble. God is not pleased with us for merely sitting in meetings: "How vain and trifling have been our spirits, our conferences, our councils, our meetings, our private as well as public conversations," wrote the Prophet Joseph from Liberty Jail, "— too low, too mean, too vulgar, too condescending for the dignified characters called and chosen of God."[8]

This puts a serious face on things. If we try to evade the responsibility of directing our minds to the highest possible object, if we try to settle for a milder program at lower stakes and safer risks, we are immediately slapped and buffeted by a power that will not let us rest. Being here, we must play the probation game, and we pay an awful forfeit for every effort to evade it. We must think — but what about? The substance of thought is knowledge. "The human brain depends for its normal alertness, reliability and efficiency on a continuous flow of information about the world . . . the brain craves for information as the body craves for food."[9] "Both individuals and societies can become insane without sufficient stimulus."[10] If the mind is denied functioning to capacity, it will take terrible revenge. The penalty we pay for starving our minds is a phenomenon that is only too conspicuous at the BYU: Aristotle pointed out long ago that a shortage of knowledge is an intolerable state and so the mind will do anything to escape it; in particular, it will invent knowledge if it has to. Experimenters have found that "lack of information quickly breeds insecurity in a situation where any information is regarded as better than none."[11] In that atmosphere, false information flourishes and subjects in tests are "eager to listen to and believe any sort of preposterous nonsense."[12] Why so? We repeat, because the very nature of man requires him to use his mind to capacity. "The mind or intelligence which man possesses," says Joseph Smith, "is co-equal with God himself." What greater crime than the minimizing of such capacity? The Prophet continues: "All the minds and spirits

265

that God ever sent into the world are susceptible of enlargement. God himself, finding he was in the midst of the spirits and glory, because he was more intelligent, saw proper to institute laws whereby the rest could have a privilege to advance like himself. The relationship we have with God places us in a situation to *advance* in *knowledge*."[13] *Expansion* is the theme, and we cannot expand the boundaries unless we first reach those boundaries, which means exerting ourselves to the absolute limit.

Now we come to a subject with which the Prophet Joseph was greatly concerned. To keep the Saints always reaching for the highest and best, the utmost of their capacity, requires enormous motivation — and the gospel supplies it. Nothing can excite men to action like the contemplation of the eternities. The quality in which the Saints have always excelled is zeal. Zeal is the engine that drives the whole vehicle, without it we would get nowhere. But without clutch, throttle, brakes, and steering wheel, our mighty engine becomes an instrument of destruction, and the more powerful the motor, the more disastrous the inevitable crack-up if the proper knowledge is lacking. There is a natural tendency to let the mighty motor carry us along, to give it its head, open up and see what it can do. We see this in our society today. Scientists tell us that the advancement of a civilization depends on two things: a) the amount of energy at its disposal, and b) the amount of information at its disposal.[14] Today we have unlimited energy — nuclear power, but we still lack the necessary information to control and utilize it. We have the zeal but not the knowledge, so to speak. And this the Prophet Joseph considered a very dangerous situation in the Church. Speaking to the new Relief Society, he "commended them for their *zeal*, but said that sometimes their zeal was not according to *knowledge*."[15] He advised restraint in an effort to keep things under control. The Society, he observed, "was growing too fast. It should grow up by degrees," he said, and "... thus have a select society of the virtuous, and those who would walk circumspectly."[16] What good is the power, he asks, without real intelligence and solid knowledge? He gives the example of those Saints who were carried away at the thought and prospect of "a glorious manifestation from God." And bids them ask, "a manifestation of what? Is there any intelligence communicated? ... All the intelligence that can be obtained from them when they arise, is a shout of 'glory,' or 'hallelujah,' or some incoherent expression; but they have had the 'power.' "[17] Another time he warned the sisters against being "subject to overmuch zeal, which must ever prove *dangerous*, and cause them to be rigid in a religious capacity."[18] Zeal makes us loyal and unflinching, but God wants more than that. In the same breath, the Prophet said that the people "were depending on the Prophet, hence were darkened in their minds, in consequence of neglecting the duties devolving upon *themselves*."[19] They must do their own thinking and discipline their minds. If not, that will happen again which happened in Kirtland: "Many, having a zeal not according to knowledge," said the Prophet, " . . .have, no doubt, in the heat of enthusiasm, taught and said many things which are derogatory to the genuine character and principles of the Church."[20] Specifically, "soon after the Gospel was established in Kirtland . . . many false spirits were introduced, many strange visions were seen, and wild, enthusiastic notions were entertained . . . many ridiculous things were entered into, calculated to bring disgrace upon the Church of God."[21] This was the time when some of the brethren in Kirtland were out to prove that they were smarter than the Prophet and produced the so-called "Egyptian Alphabet and Grammar," to match *his* production of the Book of Abraham.

This illustrates another point — that knowledge can be heady stuff. It easily leads to an excess of zeal — to illusions of grandeur and a desire to impress others and achieve eminence. The university is nothing more nor less than a place to show off: if it ceased to be that, it would cease to exist. Again, the Prophet Joseph is right on target when he tells us that true knowledge can never serve that end. Knowledge is individual, he observes, and if a person has it, "who would know it? . . . The greatest, the best, and the most useful gifts would be known nothing about by an observer. . . . There are only two gifts that could be made visible — the gift of tongues and the gift of prophecy."[22]

Our search for knowledge should be ceaseless, which means that it is open-ended, never resting on laurels, degrees, or past achievements. "If we get puffed up by thinking that we have much knowledge, we are apt to get a contentious spirit," and what is the cure? "Correct knowledge is necessary to cast out that spirit."[23] The cure for inadequate knowledge is "ever more light and knowledge." But who is going to listen patiently to correct knowledge if he thinks he has the answers already? "There are a great many wise men and women too in our midst who are too wise to be taught; therefore they must die in their ignorance."[24] "I have tried for a number of years to get the minds of the Saints prepared to receive the things of God; but we frequently see some of them . . . [that] will fly to pieces like glass as soon as anything comes that is contrary to their traditions: they cannot stand the fire at all. . . .[25] [If I] go into an investigation into anything, that is not contained in the Bible . . . I think there are so many over-wise men here, that they would cry 'treason' and put me to death."[26] But, he asks, "why be so certain that you comprehend the things of God, when all things with you are so uncertain?"[27] True knowledge never shuts the door on more knowledge, but zeal often does. One thinks of the dictum: "We are not seeking for truth at the BYU; we have the truth!" So did Adam and Abraham have the truth, far greater and more truth than what we have, and yet the particular genius of each was that he was constantly "seeking for *greater* light and knowledge."

The young, with their limited knowledge are particularly susceptible to excessive zeal. Why do it the hard way, they ask at the BYU, when God has given us the answer book? The answer to that is, because if you use the answer book for your Latin or your math, or anything else, you will always have a false sense of power and never learn the real thing. "The people expect to see some wonderful manifestation, some great display of power," says Joseph Smith, "or some extraordinary miracle performed; and it is often the case that *young* members of this Church, for want of better information, carry along with them their old notions of things, and sometimes fall into egregious errors."[28] "Be careful about sending boys to preach the Gospel to the world," said Joseph Smith. Why? Certainly not because they lacked zeal, that's the one thing they had. The Prophet explains: "Lest they become puffed up, and fall under condemnation . . . beware of pride . . . apply yourselves diligently to *study*, that your *minds* may be stored with all necessary *information*."[29] That is doing it the hard way. Can't the Spirit hurry things up? No — there is no place for the cram course or quickie, or above all the superficial survey course or quick trips to the Holy Land, where the gospel is concerned. "We consider that God has created man with a mind capable of instruction, and a faculty which may be enlarged in proportion to the heed and diligence given to the light communicated from heaven to the *intellect* . . . but . . . no man ever arrived in a moment: he must have been instructed . . . by *proper degrees*."[30] "The things of God are of deep import; and time, and experience, and careful and ponderous and solemn thoughts . . . stretch as high as the utmost heavens."[31] No short-cuts or easy lessons here! Note well that the Prophet makes no distinction between things of the spirit and things of the intellect. Some years ago, when it was pointed out that BYU graduates were the lowest in the nation in all categories of the graduate record examination, the institution characteristically met the challenge by abolishing the examination. It was done on the grounds that the test did not sufficiently measure our unique "spirituality." We talked extensively about "the education of the whole man," and deplored that educational imbalance that comes when students' heads are merely stuffed with facts — as if there was any danger of that here! But actually, serious imbalance is impossible if one plays the game honestly: true zeal feeds on knowledge, true knowledge cannot exist without zeal. Both are "spiritual" qualities. All knowledge is the gospel, but there must be a priority, "proper degrees," as he says, in the timing and emphasis of our learning, lest like the doctors of the Jews, we "strain at a gnat and swallow a camel." Furthermore, since one person does not receive revelation for another, if we would exchange or convey knowledge, we must be willing to have our knowledge *tested*. The gifted and zealous Mr. Olney was "disfellowshipped, because he would not have his writings *tested* by the word of God," according to Joseph Smith.[32] Not infrequently, Latter-day Saints tell me that they have translated a text or interpreted an artifact, or been led to an archaeological discovery as a direct answer to prayer, and that for me to question or test the results is to question the reality of revelation; and often I am asked to approve a theory or "discovery" which I find unconvincing, because it has been the means of bringing people to the Church. Such practitioners are asking me to take their zeal as an adequate substitute for knowledge, but like Brother Olney, they refuse to have their knowledge tested. True, "it needs revelation to assist us, and give us knowledge of the things of God,"[33] but only the hard worker can expect such assistance: "It is not wisdom that we should have all knowledge at once presented before us; but that we should have little at a time; then we can comprehend it."[34] We must know what we are doing, understand the problem, live with it, lay a proper foundation — how many a Latter-day Saint has told me that he can understand the scriptures by pure revelation and does not need to toil at Greek or Hebrew as the Prophet and the Brethren did in the School of the Prophets at Kirtland and Nauvoo? Even Oliver Cowdery fell into that trap and was rebuked for it. (D&C 9.) "The principle of knowledge is the principle of salvation. This principle can be comprehended by the faithful and diligent," says the Prophet Joseph.[35] New converts often get the idea that, having accepted the gospel, they have arrived at adequate knowledge. Others say that to have a testimony is to have everything — they have sought and found the kingdom of heaven; but their minds go right on working just the same, and if they don't keep on getting new and testable knowledge, they will assuredly embrace those "wild, enthusiastic notions" of the new converts in Kirtland. Note what a different procedure Joseph Smith prescribes: "[The] first Comforter or Holy Ghost has no other effect than pure intelligence [it is not a hot, emotional surge]. It is more powerful in expanding the mind, enlightening the understanding, and storing the intellect with present knowledge, of a man who is of the literal seed of Abraham, than one who is a Gentile."³⁶ "For as the Holy Ghost falls upon one of the literal seed of Abraham, it is calm and serene; and his whole soul and body are only exercised by the pure spirit of intelligence."³⁷ "The Spirit of Revelation is in connection with these blessings. A person may profit by noticing the first intimation of the spirit of revelation; for instance, when you feel pure intelligence flowing into you, it may give you sudden strokes of ideas . . . thus, by learning the Spirit of God and understanding it, you may grow into the principle of revelation."³⁸ This is remarkably like the new therapeutic discipline called "biofeedback."

The emphasis is all on the continuous, conscientious, honest acquisition of knowledge. This admonition to sobriety and diligence goes along with the Prophet's outspoken recommendation of the Jews and their peculiar esteem and diligence for things of the mind. "If there is anything calculated to interest the mind of the Saints, to awaken in them the finest sensibilities, and arouse them to enterprise and exertion, surely it is the great and precious promises to . . . Abraham and . . . Judah. . . . and inasmuch as you feel interested for the covenant people of the Lord, the God of their fathers shall bless you. . . . He will endow you with power, wisdom, might and intelligence, and every qualification necessary: while your minds will expand wider and wider, until you can . . . contemplate the mighty acts of Jehovah in all their variety and glory."³⁹ In Israel today, they have great contests in which young people and old from all parts of the world display their knowledge of scripture and skill at music, science, or mathematics, etc., in gruelling competitions. This sort of thing tends to breed a race of insufferably arrogant, conceited little show-offs — *and* magnificent performers. They tend to be like the Jews of old, who "sought for things that they could not understand," ever "looking beyond the mark," and hence falling on their faces: "they needs must fall." (Jacob 4:14.) Yet Joseph Smith commends their intellectual efforts as a corrective to the Latter-day Saints, who lean too far in the other direction, giving their young people and old awards for zeal alone, zeal without knowledge — for sitting in

270

endless meetings, for dedicated conformity, and unlimited capacity for suffering boredom. We think it more commendable to get up at 5:00 A.M. to write a bad book than to get up at nine o'clock to write a good one — that is pure zeal that tends to breed a race of insufferable, self-righteous prigs and barren minds. One has only to consider the present outpouring of "inspirational" books in the Church which bring little new in the way of knowledge: truisms, and platitudes, kitsch, and clichés have become our everyday diet. The Prophet would never settle for that. "I advise you to go on to perfection and search deeper and deeper into the mysteries of Godliness. . . . It has always been my province to dig up hidden mysteries, *new things,* for my hearers."[40] It actually happens at the BYU, and that not rarely, that students come to a teacher, usually at the beginning of a term, with the sincere request that he refrain from teaching them anything new. They have no desire, they explain, to hear what they do not know already! I cannot imagine that happening at any other school, but maybe it does. Unless we go on to other new things, we are stifling our powers.

In our limited time here, what are we going to think about? That is the all-important question. We've been assured that it is not too early to start thinking about things of the eternities. In fact, Latter-day Saints should be taking rapid strides toward setting up that eternal celestial order which the Church must embody to be acceptable to God. Also, we are repeatedly instructed regarding things we should *not* think about. I would pass this negative thing by lightly, but the scriptures are explicit, outspoken, and emphatic in this matter; and whenever anyone begins to talk about serious matters at the BYU, inevitably someone says, "I would like to spend my time thinking about such things and studying them, but I cannot afford the luxury. I have to think about the really important business of life, which is making a living." This is the withering effect of the intimidating challenge thrown out to all of us from childhood: "Do you have any money?" With its absolute declaration of policy and principle: "You can have anything in this world for money!" and its paralyzing corollary: "Without it, you can have *nothing!*" I do not have to tell you where that philosophy came from. Somebody is out to "decoy our minds," to use Brigham Young's expression, from the things we should be thinking about to those which we should not care about at all. The most oft-repeated command in the scriptures, repeated verbatim in the Synoptic Gospels, the Book of Mormon, and in the Doctrine and Covenants[41] is "Take ye no thought for the morrow, for what ye shall eat, or what ye shall drink, or wherewithal ye shall be clothed. For consider the lilies of the field. . . ." We cannot go here into the long catalog of scripture of commandments telling us to seek for knowledge in one direction but not in another. "Seek *not* for riches, but for wisdom"; "lay *not* up treasures on earth," but in heaven, for where your treasure is, there will your heart be also. You *cannot* serve two masters, you must choose one and follow him alone: "Whatsoever is in the world *is not* of the Father but is of the world," etc. We take comfort in certain parables; for example, "Which of you, intending to build a tower, sitteth not down first, and counteth the cost. . . ." (Luke 14:28ff. Italics added), as if they justified our present course. But the Lord is not instructing people to take economic foresight in such matters — they already do that: "Which of you does *not?*" says the Lord. He points out that people are only too alert and provident where the things of *this* world are concerned and says, to their shame: "If you're so zealous in such matters, why can't you take your eternal future seriously?" And so he ends the parable with this admonition: "Whosoever he be of you that forsaketh not all that he hath, he cannot be my disciple." That is the *same* advice, you will observe, that he gave to the rich young man. The Lord really means what he says when he commands us *not* to think about these things; and because we have chosen to find this advice hopelessly impractical "for our times" (note that the rich young man found it just as impractical for *his* times!), the treasures of knowledge have been withheld from us. "God [has] often sealed up the heavens," said Joseph Smith, "because of covetousness in the *Church.*"[42] You must choose between one route or the other. If we go on "lusting after the grovelling things of this life," says Brigham Young, we remain "fixed with a very limited amount of knowledge, like a door upon its hinges, moving to and fro from year to year without any visible advancement or improvement. . . . Man is made in the image of God, but what do we know of Him or of ourselves when we suffer ourselves to love and worship the God of this world — riches?" "I desire to see everybody on the track of improvement . . . but when you so love your property as though all your affections were placed on the changing, fading things of earth, it is impossible to increase in knowledge of the truth."[43]

What things should we think about then, and how? Here the Prophet is very helpful. In the first place, that question itself is what we should think about. We won't get very far on our way until we have faced up to it. But as soon as we start seriously thinking about that, we find ourselves covered with confusion, overwhelmed by our feelings of guilt and inadequacy — in other words, repenting for our past delinquency. In this condition, we call upon the Lord for aid and he hears us. We begin to know what the Prophet Joseph meant about the constant searching, steadily storing our minds with knowledge and information — the more we get of it, the better we are able to judge the proper priorities as we feel our way forward, as we become increasingly alert to the promptings of the Spirit which become ever more clear and more frequent, following the guidance of the Holy Ghost: and as we go forward, we learn to cope with the hostile world with which our way is sure to bring us into collision in time. That calls for sacrifice, but what of that? Eternal life is not cheaply bought.

This may sound very impractical to some, but how often do we have to be reminded of the illusory and immoral nature of the treasures we are seeking on earth? Even without the vast powers of destruction that are hanging over our heads at this moment, even in the most peaceful and secure of worlds, we would see them vanishing before our eyes. Such phenomena as ephemeralization and replication, once dreams of the science-fiction writers, are rapidly becoming realities. Speaking of the ephemeralization, of technological obsolescence, A. R. Clark writes, "Within the foreseeable future all the most powerful and lucrative callings in our world will exist no more. Because of new processes of synthesizing, organizing, programming basic materials of unlimited supply into the necessities of life, we shall soon see the end of all factories and perhaps of all transportation of raw materials and all farming. The entire structure of industry and commerce ... would cease to exist ... all material possessions would be literally as cheap as dirt. ... Then when material objects are intrinsically worthless, perhaps only then will a real sense of values arise."[44]

Yes, you say, but meantime "we must live in the world of the present." Must we? Most people in the past have got along without the institutions which we think, for the moment, indispensable. And we are expressly commanded to get out of that business. "No one supposes for one moment," says Brigham Young, "that in heaven the angels are speculating, that they are building railroads and factories, taking advantage of one another, gathering up the substance in heaven to aggrandize themselves, and that they live on the same principle that we are in the habit of doing. ... No sectarian Christian in the world believes this; they believe that the inhabitants of heaven live as a family, that their faith, interests, and pursuits have one end in view — the glory of God and their own salvation, that they may receive more and more. ... We all believe this, and suppose we go to work and imitate them as far as we can."[45] It is not too soon to begin right now. What are the things of the eternities that we should consider even now? They are the things that no one ever tires of doing, things in themselves lovely and desirable. Surprisingly, the things of the eternities are the very things to which the university is supposed to be dedicated. In the Zion of God, in the celestial and eternal order, where there is no death there will be no morticians, where there is no sickness there will be no more doctors, where there is no decay there will be no dentists, where there is no litigation there will be no lawyers, where there is no buying and selling there will be no merchants, where there is no insecurity, there will be no insurance, where there is no money there will be no banks, where there is no crime there will be no jails, no police, where there are no excess goods there will be no advertising, no wars, no armies, and so on and so on.

But this happy condition is not limited to celestial realms of the future; it actually has been achieved by mortal men on this earth a number of times, and represents the only state of society of which God approves. All the things that are passing away today are the very essence of "the economy," but they will be missing in Zion. They are already obsolescent, every one of them is made work of a temporary and artificial nature for which an artificial demand must be created. Moreover, few people are really dedicated to them, for as soon as a man has acquired a super-quota of power and gain, he cuts out and leaves the scene of his triumphs, getting as far away as he can from the ugly world he has helped create — preferably to Tahiti. The race has shown us often its capacity to do without these things we now find indispensable. "The Devil has the mastery of the earth: he has corrupted it, and has corrupted the children of men. He has led them in evil until they are almost entirely ruined, and are so far from God that they neither know Him nor his influence, and have almost lost sight of everything that pertains to eternity. This darkness is more prevalent, more dense, among the people of Christendom than it is among the heathen. They have lost sight of all that is great and glorious — of all principles that pertain to life eternal."[46] "Suppose that our Father in heaven, our elder brother, the risen Redeemer, the Savior of the world, or any of the Gods of eternity should act upon this principle, to love truth, knowledge, and wisdom, because they are all-powerful," says Brigham Young, "they would cease to be Gods; ... the extension of their kingdom would cease, and their God-head come to an end."[47] Are we here to seek knowledge or to seek the credits that will get us ahead in the world? One of the glorious benefits and promises of the gospel given the Saints in these latter days that "inasmuch as they *sought* wisdom they might be instructed; And inasmuch as they were humble they might be made strong, and blessed from on high, and receive *knowledge* from time to time."(D&C 1:26, 28. Italics added.) But they had to want it and seek for it. What is that state of things? The late President Joseph Fielding Smith wrote: "We are informed that many important things are withheld from us because of the hardness of our hearts and the unwillingness as members of the Church to abide in the covenants and seek divine knowledge."[48] "Our faculties are enlarged," said Joseph Smith, "in proportion to the heed and diligence given to the light communicated from heaven to the intellect." "If [a man] does not get knowledge, he will be brought into captivity by some evil power in the other world, as evil spirits will have more knowledge, and consequently more power than many men who are on the earth. [We need] revelation to assist us, and give us knowledge of the things of God."[49] There is indeed an order of priority. The things of God come first, and the seeker ever tries to become aware of that priority. "All science," says Karl Popper, "is eschatology," concerned fundamentally with the questions of religion. The most important question of all is that of our eternal salvation.

I once acted as counselor to students in the College of Commerce for a couple of years. Most of these students were unhappy about going into business and admitted that Satan rules this earth and rules it badly, with blood and horror, but they pointed out the intimidating circumstance that you cannot have money without playing his game because he owns the treasures of the earth. They could see he owns them as loot, and by virtue of a legal fiction with which he has, in Joseph Smith's terms, "riveted the creeds of the fathers," but still the students would ask me in despair, "If we leave his employ, what will become of us?" The answer is simple. Don't you trust the Lord? If you do, he will give you the guidance of the Holy Spirit and you will not end up doing the things that he has expressly commanded us not to do.

May God help us all in the days of our probation to seek the knowledge *he* wants us to seek.

NOTES

1. Nigel Calder, *The Mind of Man* (London: BBC, 1970), p. 25.

2. *Ibid.*, p. 169.

3. *Loc. cit.*

4. *Ibid.*, p. 29.

5. *Ibid.*, pp. 29, 184.

6. Arthur Clarke, *Profiles of the Future* (N.Y.: Harper and Row, 1962), p. 197.

7. *Ibid.*, p. 96.

8. *DHC*, 3:295f.

9. Calder, p. 33.

10. Clarke, p. 83.

11. Lyall Watson, *Supernature* (N.Y.: Anchor Press, 1973), p. 239.

12. Calder, p. 77.

13. Joseph Fielding Smith, comp., *Teachings of the Prophet Joseph Smith*, (Salt Lake City: Deseret Book Co., 1967), p. 354. Italics added. Hereafter cited as *TPJS*.

14. Carl Sagan, *The Cosmic Connection* (N.Y.: Dell, 1973), Ch. 34.

15. *TPJS*, p. 201. Italics added.

16. *Ibid.*

17. *TPJS*, p. 204.

18. *TPJS*, p. 238. Italics added.

19. *Ibid.* Italics added.

20. *TPJS*, p. 80.

21. *TPJS*, pp. 213, 214.

22. *TPJS*, p. 246.

23. *TPJS*, p. 287.

24. *TPJS*, p. 309.

25. *TPJS*, p. 331.

26. *TPJS*, p. 348.

27. *TPJS*, p. 320.

28. *TPJS*, p. 242. Italics added.

29. *TPJS*, p. 43. Italics added.

30. *TPJS*, p. 51. Italics added.

31. *TPJS*, p. 137.

32. *TPJS*, p. 215. Italics added.

33. *TPJS*, p. 217.

34. *TPJS*, p. 297.

35. *Ibid.*

36. *TPJS*, p. 149.

37. *TPJS*, pp. 149, 150.

38. *TPJS*, p. 151.

39. *TPJS*, p. 163.

40. *TPJS*, p. 364. Italics added.

41. Matthew 6:25ff, Mark 13:11ff, Luke 12:11ff, 3 Nephi 13:25ff, D&C 84:81ff.

42. *TPJS*, p. 9. Italics added.

43. Brigham Young in *Journal of Discourses*, 26 vols. (London: Latter-day Saints' Book Depot, 1855-86), 7:337: hereafter cited as *JD*.

44. Clarke, p. 16.

45. *JD* 17:117f.

46. *JD* 8:209.

47. *JD* 1:117.

48. Joseph Fielding Smith, *Answers to Gospel Questions*, Melchizedek Priesthood Manual, 1972-1973, p. 229.

49. *TPJS*, p. 217.

Beyond Politics

13

In most languages the Church is designated as that of the Last Days, and so this speech, which is only a pastiche of quotations from its founders, is unblushingly apocalyptic. Did our grandparents over-react to signs of the times? For many years a stock cartoon in sophisticated magazines has poked fun at the barefoot bearded character in the long nightshirt carrying a placard calling all to "Repent, for the End is at Hand". But where is the joke? Ask the smart people who thought up the funny pictures and captions: Where are they now?

For all of us as individuals the fashion of this world passeth away; but the Big Bang is something else. How near is that? Should we be concerned at all? The problem may be stated in the form of a little dialogue:

We: Dear Father, whenever the end is scheduled to be, can't you give us an extension of time?

He: Willingly. But tell me first, what will you do with it?

We: Well . . . ah . . . we will go on doing pretty much what we have been doing; after all, isn't that why we are asking for an extension?

He: And isn't that exactly why I want to end it soon — because you show no inclination to change? Why should I reverse the order of nature so that you can go on doing the very things I want to put an end to?

We: *But is what we are doing so terribly wrong? The economy seems sound enough. Why shouldn't we go on doing the things which have made this country great?*

He: *Haven't I made it clear enough to you what kind of greatness I expect of my offspring? Forget the statistics; you are capable of better things – your stirring commercials don't impress me in the least.*

We: *But why should we repent when all we are doing is what each considers to be for the best good of himself and the nation?*

He: *Because it is not you but I who decide what that shall be, and I have told you a hundred times what is best for you individually and collectively – and that is repentance, no matter who you are.*

We: *We find your inference objectionable, Sir – quite unacceptable.*

He: *I know.*

My story goes back to the beginning, and to some very basic propositions. This world was organized in the light of infinite knowledge and experience and after due thought and discussion, to offer multiple facilities to an endless variety of creatures and especially to be the home and dominion of a godlike race who would take good care of it and have joy therein. Being a highly favored breed, much was expected of them, and their qualifications for advancement were to be put to the test by allowing an adversary, a common enemy to God and man, to tempt them and try them. It was decided before even the world was that, if man should yield to this temptation and thus lower his defenses and make himself vulnerable to repeated attacks of the adversary, steps would immediately be taken to put into operation a prearranged plan to restore him to his former status.[1]

What God tells us in effect is, "Now that you have fallen and forfeited your paradise by deliberately, knowingly disobeying me, I will give you another chance, a chance to get back to that paradise by deliberately and knowingly obeying me. To get back where you were and beyond, you must repent — forever give up doing it your way, and decide to live by the law of God, or by the law of obedience, which means, doing it my way." Adam agreed to do it God's way, though Satan lost no time in trying to sell him on another plan.

Adam's own children and their posterity, however, chose to achieve salvation *their* way, not God's way, and ever since then there has been trouble. The Lord Jesus Christ told the young Joseph Smith in the First Vision that men were no longer doing things his way, that as a result that way was no longer upon the earth, but it was about to be brought again: "I was answered that I must join *none* of them, for they were all wrong . . . that *all* their creeds were an abomination in his sight; that those professors were *all* corrupt." (Joseph Smith 2:19. Italics added.) The Lord's actual words were (according to the 1832 version in the handwriting of Frederick G. Williams): "Behold the world at this time lieth in sin, and there is *none* that doeth good, *no not one.* . . . And mine anger is kindling against the inhabitants of the earth to visit them according to this ungodliness."[2] The message of the restored gospel is that one phase of the earth's existence is coming to a close, and another phase, a phase in which God's will will be done on earth as it is in heaven, is about to become the order of life on earth.

Politics, as practiced on earth, belongs to the ways of men; it is the essential activity of the city — the city of man, not the city of God. As used by the Greek writers, the *polis* is "the community or body of citizens," that is, a body of citizens not taking orders from anyone else. *Politeia* is "a well-ordered government, a common-wealth." Politics, *ta politika*, is concern for the social order, things done civilly or courteously, "the weal of the state." In practice the emphasis has been on civility. Thus, in modern Greek, civilization is *politismos*, a civilized person is *politismenos*, etc. Even at a superficial view, if it is not God's way, it is still not all bad, and we can understand why God approves of men engaging in politics, and even encourages the Saints, at times, to participate.

The problem of conflicting obligations to the city of man and the city of God is basic to every dispensation of the gospel. We have Abraham in Egypt, Joseph in Egypt, Moses in Egypt, not as enslaved subjects but as top government officials, high in the favor of Pharaoh, serving him faithfully for years until the inevitable showdown. The classic treatment of the theme is found in the book of Daniel. Daniel's three friends were not only in high favor with the king — he made them his special advisers, his right-hand men (Daniel 1:19-20) — for years they served him devotedly and they owed all they had to him. Daniel was made, next to the king himself, the highest official in the state, and he showed all respect and reverence to Darius. But then in each case came the showdown: jealous and ambitious men contrived special laws forcing the king's hand and forcing the king's favorites to take a public stand between serving God and serving the king. In each case it was nothing more than a public gesture of loyalty, which anyone might make without hypocrisy. The three young men who bowed to the king each day were asked to bow to his image when the band played in the Plain of Dura at a great public testimonial of loyalty. Why not? Didn't they owe all to the king? It was only a symbol! Yet here they drew the line — they would be thrown into a fiery furnace rather than make this one simple concession. Daniel insisted on continuing with his private prayers after a bit of trick legislation, a mere technicality, had made them illegal for one month. The king pleaded with him but to no avail — he chose the lions' den. In all this there is not a trace of jaunty defiance or moral superiority on either side: the king is worried sick — he refuses to eat or listen to music, he can't sleep, and before daybreak there he is outside the lion's den, biting his nails and asking Daniel if he is all right, and Daniel respectfully wishes him good morning — "O King, live forever!" Nebuchadnezzar personally appeals to the three young men to change their minds — but they cannot change their position, and he cannot change his. The moral is clear: the children of God can work well with the men of the world, and bestow great blessings by their services — but there comes a time when one must draw the line and make a choice between the two governments. Such a choice was forced on the Mormons very early, and a very hard choice it was, but they did not flinch before it. "We will go along with you as far as we can; but where we can't we won't," and no hard feelings.

The question arises, If we decide to do things God's way will not all discussion cease? How could there be a discussion with God? Who would disagree with him? If we go back to our basic creation story we are neither surprised nor shocked to hear that there was free discussion in heaven in the presence of God at the time of the Creation, when some suggested one plan and some another. "In the beginning was the *Logos* [counsel, discussion], and the *Logos* was in the presence of God, and all things were done according to it. . . ." (John 1:1, translated by the author). Satan was not cast out for disagreeing, but for attempting to resort to violence when he found himself outvoted. If we cannot clearly conceive of the type of discussion that goes on in the courts on high, we have some instructive instances of God's condescending to discuss things with men here on earth. "Come, let us reason together," he invites the children of Israel. Accordingly Abraham and Ezra both dared, humbly and apologetically, but still stubbornly, to protest what they considered, in the light of their limited understanding, unkind treatment of some of God's children. They just could not see why the Lord did or allowed certain things. So he patiently explained the situation to them, and then they understood. Enoch just couldn't see the justification for the mass destruction of his fellows by the coming flood; he too was stubborn about it: "And as Enoch saw this, he had bitterness of soul, and wept over his brethren, and said unto the heavens: *I will refuse to be comforted;* but the Lord said unto Enoch: Lift up your heart, and be glad; and look." (Moses 7:44. Italics added.)

God did not hold it against these men that they questioned him, but loved them for it: it was because they were the friends of men, even at what they thought was the terrible risk of offending him, that they became friends of God. The Lord was not above discussing matters with the brother of Jared, who protested that there was a serious defect in the vessels constructed according to the prescribed design: "Behold there is no light in them. . . . wilt thou suffer that we shall cross this great water in darkness?" (Ether 2:22.) Instead of blasting the man on the spot for his impudence, the Lord very reasonably asked the brother of Jared: "What will you that I should do that ye may have light in your vessels?" (Ether 2:23.) So they talked it over and, as a result, the brother of Jared prepared some beautiful fused quartz, that was as clear as glass but could not shine by itself. Again he went to the Lord, almost obliterated with humility, but still reminding the Lord that he was only following orders: "We know that thou art holy and dwellest in the heavens, and that we are unworthy before thee; because of the fall our natures have become evil continually [a vivid reminder of the gulf between the two ways — that our ways are not God's ways]; nevertheless, O Lord, thou hast given us a commandment that we must call upon thee, that from thee we may receive according to our desires." (Ether 3:2.) So he screws up his courage and asks the Lord to do him a favor: "Touch these stones, O Lord, with thy finger . . . that they may shine forth in darkness. . . ." (Ether 3:4.) The sight of God's finger quite overpowered the brother of Jared, knocked him flat, and that led to another discussion in which the Lord explained certain things to him at length. Moroni, recording these things, also recalls, "I have seen Jesus, and . . . he hath talked with me face to face, and . . . he told me in plain humility, even as a man telleth another in mine own language, concerning these things." (Ether 12:39.) Note the significant concept of humility set forth here — humility is not a feeling of awe and reverence and personal unworthiness in the presence of overpowering majesty — anyone, even the bloody Khan of the Steppes, confesses to being humble in the presence of God. Plain humility is reverence and respect in the presence of the lowest, not the highest, of God's creatures. Brigham Young said he often felt overawed in the presence of little children or any of his fellowmen — for in them he saw the image of his Maker. Even so, God is willing to discuss things with men as an equal: "In their weakness, after the manner of their language, that they might come to understanding." (D&C 1:24.) Note that God, far from demanding blind obedience, wants us to *understand* his commandments.

A discussion with God is not a case of agreeing or disagreeing with him — who is in a position to do that? — but of understanding him. What Abraham and Ezra and Enoch asked was, "Why?" Socrates showed that teaching is a dialogue — a discussion. As long as the learner is in the dark he *should* protest and argue and question, for that is the best way to bring problems into focus, while the teacher patiently and cheerfully explains, delighted that his pupil has enough interest and understanding to raise questions — the more passionate the more promising. There is a place for discussion and participation in the government of the kingdom; it is *men* who love absolute monarchies, it was the Israelites, the Jaredites, the Nephites, who asked God to give them a king, overriding the objections of his prophets who warned them against the step.

Leaders of the Church have repeatedly taught that earthly rulers exercise their authority illegitimately; that the only legitimate authority upon the earth is that which is founded and recognized by God, whose *right* it is to rule.[3]

As John Taylor points out, it is the priesthood that should rule: "Some people ask, 'What is Priesthood?' I answer, 'It is the legitimate rule of God, whether in the heavens or on the earth'; and it is the only legitimate power that has a right to rule upon the earth; and when the will of God is done on earth as it is in the heavens, no other power will bear rule."[4]

Politics, at best, is the free discussion of people running their own common affairs. Until men are willing to accept God's way, he is willing that they should do their best on that lower level, and even encourages them in such activity. "All regularly organized and well established governments," said Joseph Smith, "have certain laws . . . [that] are good, equitable and just, [and] ought to be binding upon the individual who admits this."[5] At the same time, "It is not our intention . . . to place the law of man on a parallel with the law of *heaven*; because we do *not* consider that it is formed in the same wisdom and propriety ... [it is not] sufficient in itself to bestow anything on man in *comparison* with the law of heaven, even should it promise it."[6] In an important statement in 1903, the First Presidency of the Church said that the Church

> does not attempt to exercise the powers of a secular government, but its influence and effects are to strengthen and promote fidelity to the law and loyalty to the nation where its followers reside.... It is solely an ecclesiastical organization. It is separate and distinct from the state. It does not interfere with any earthly government.... The Church, therefore, instructs in things temporal as well as things spiritual.... But it does not infringe upon the liberty of the individual or encroach upon the domain of the state.... The Church does not dictate a member's business, his politics, or his personal affairs. It never tells a citizen what occupation he shall follow, whom he shall vote for or with which party he shall affiliate.
> Sermons, dissertations and arguments by preachers and writers in the Church concerning the Kingdom of God that *is to be* are *not* to be understood as relating to the *present*. If they ... convey the idea that the dominion *to come* is to be exercised *now*, the claim is incorrect....

Meantime:

> Every member of the organization in every place is absolutely free as a citizen.... In proclaiming "the kingdom of heaven's at hand," we have the most intense and fervent convictions of our mission and calling.... But we do not and will not attempt to force them upon others, or to control or dominate any of their affairs, individual or national.[7]

It is precisely because we never for a moment think of the two systems as competing with each other that we can make the most of the one until the other is established. They are in the same game, they are in the same arena, though both have rules and both require qualities of character in their players.

The governments of men and their laws are completely *different* from those of God. "We do not attempt to place the law of man on a parallel with the law of heaven; but ... the laws of man are binding upon man."[8]

When God establishes his way among men it is by special

divine messengers who come to men well prepared, "of strong faith and a firm mind in every form of godliness." (Moroni 7:30.) Every restoration of the gospel has been accomplished through a series of heavenly visitations and glorious manifestations, with the divine plan fully and explicitly set forth for that dispensation, with all the divine authority and revealed knowledge necessary to establish the kingdom at that time. But since Satan is given explicit permission to tempt men and to try them, it is not long before a familiar trend begins to appear, a weakening of the structure as discussion deteriorates into power politics and political skulduggery:

> Christ... proposed to make a covenant with them [the Jews] but they rejected Him and His proposals.... The Gentiles received the covenant... but the Gentiles have not continued... but have departed from the faith... and have become high-minded, and have not feared; therefore, but few of them will be gathered.[9]
> Man departed from the first teachings, or instructions which he received from heaven in the first age, and refused by his disobedience to be governed by them. Consequently, he formed such laws as best suited his own mind, or as he supposed, were best adapted to his situation. But that God has influenced man more or less... in the formation of law... we have no hesitancy in believing.... And though man in his own supposed wisdom would not admit the influence of a power superior to his own, yet... God has instructed man to form wise and wholesome laws, since he had departed from Him and refused to be governed by those laws which God had given by His own voice from on high in the beginning.[10]

Here we learn that over against the perfect way of life which God proposes for us and entirely removed from that way are all the other ways that men have proposed for themselves. These last are not equally good or bad, but some are much better than others, and God encourages and even assists men in adopting the best ones.

There is, then, virtue in politics even at the human level. The energy, the dedication, courage, loyalty, selflessness, zeal and industry, the intelligence that have gone into the political actions of men are immense, and the excitement, color, dash and humor bring out some of the best in human nature. But, as we have just noted, there are various levels at which the political dialogue takes place —

all the way from the *Federalist Papers* to the local crackpot's letters to the editor; and many arenas and different forms of the game, differing as widely as a chess match from a slugging contest. Let us by all means retain the drive and dedication of politics, but do we still need the placards and the bands, the serpentine parades, funny hats, confetti, squabbling committees, canned speeches, shopworn clichés, patriotic exhibitionism, Madison Avenue slogans, to say nothing of the bitter invective, the poisonous rhetoric, the dirty tricks and shady deals, payoffs, betrayals, the blighted loyalties, the scheming young men on the make, the Gadianton loyalty, the manipulated ovations and contrived confusion of the last hurrah? The furiously mounting infusion of green stuff into the political carnival in our day is enough to show that the spontaneity is not there, and even if some of it may remain, those running the show know very well from tried and tested statistics that all that sort of thing is to be got with money — lots and lots of money — and with nothing else.

An important part of the message of the restored gospel is that God's way has now been restored to the earth and is available to men; and that there is no excuse for their not embracing it inasmuch as it is entirely within their capacity to receive it and live by it, beginning, of course, with a complete turning away from their own ways:

> I think that it is high time for a Christian world to awake out of sleep, and cry mightily to that God, day and night, whose anger we have justly incurred. . . . I step forth into the field [said the Prophet] to tell you what the *Lord* is doing, and *what you must do* . . . in these last days. . . . I will proceed to tell you what the *Lord* requires of all people, high and low . . . in order that they may . . . escape the judgments of God, which are almost ready to burst upon the nations of the earth. Repent of all your sins.[11]

Even at its best man's way is not God's way: "Some may pretend to say that the world in this age is fast increasing in righteousness; that the dark ages of superstition and blindness have passed . . . the gloomy cloud is burst, and the Gospel is shining . . . carried to divers nations of the earth [etc., etc.]. . . . But a moment's candid reflection . . . is sufficient for every candid man to draw a conclusion *in his own mind whether this is the order of heaven or not.*"[12] The best of human laws leaves every man free to engage in his own pursuit of happiness,[13] without presuming for a moment to tell him where that happiness lies; that is the very thing the laws of God can guarantee. At *best*, the political prize is negative.

Important in the record of the dispensations is that when men depart from God's way and substitute their own ways in its place they usually do not admit that that is what they are doing; often they do not deliberately or even consciously substitute their ways for God's ways; on the contrary, they easily and largely convince themselves that *their way is God's way.* "The apostasy described in the New Testament is not a *desertion* of the cause, but a *perversion* of it, a process by which 'the righteous are removed and none perceives it.' "[14] The wedding of the Christian Church and the Roman state was a venture in political dialectics, a restatement of the age-old political exercise of demonstrating that our way is God's way. "There's such divinity doth hedge a king" — *vox populi, vox Dei,* etc. The Lord told the apostles that in time "whosoever killeth you will think that he doeth God service." (John 16:2.) The horrible fiasco of the Crusades went forward under the mandate of the *Deus Vult* — God wills it: it is his idea; the Inquisition was carried out by selfless men "for the greater glory of God."[15] In every age we find the worldy powers hypnotized by the image of the world as a *maidan,* a great battleground, on which the forces of good and evil are locked in mortal combat.[16] True, there is a contest, but it is within the individual, not between ignorant armies — that solution is all too easy. Recall the statement of Joseph Smith that "every candid man" must "draw the conclusion in his own mind whether this [any political system] is the order of heaven or not."[17] Banners, trumpets, and dungeons were early devised to help men make up their minds. But God does not fight Satan: a word from him and Satan is silenced and banished. There is no contest there; in fact we are expressly told that all the power which Satan enjoys here on earth is granted him by God. "We will allow Satan, our common enemy, to try Man and to tempt him." It is man's strength that is being tested — not God's. Nay, even in putting us to the test, "the devil," to quote Joseph Smith, "has no power over us only as *we* permit him."[18] Since, then, "God *would* not exert any compulsory means, and the devil *could* not . . . ,"[19] it is up to us to decide how much power Satan shall have on this earth, but only in respect to ourselves; the fight is all *within us.* That is the whole battle. But how much easier to shift the battle to another arena, and externalize the cause of all our misfortune.

It is easy enough to see how a world willingly beguiled by the devil's dialectic is bound to reject God's way and continue with its own. Even the Saints are guilty: "Repent, repent, is the voice of God to Zion; and strange as it may appear, yet it is true, mankind will persist in *self-justification* until all their iniquity is exposed, and their character past being redeemed.[20] As in every other dispensation, the world will continue to go its way, which is one of *progressive deterioration:*

> The great and wise of ancient days have failed in all their attempts to promote eternal power, peace, and happiness.... They proclaim as with a voice of thunder... that man's strength is weakness, his wisdom is folly, his glory is his shame.... Nation has succeeded nation.... History records their puerile plans, their short-lived glory, their feeble intellect and their ignoble deeds. Have we increased in knowledge or intelligence?... Our nation, which possesses greater resources than any other, is rent, from center to circumference, with party strife, political intrigues, and sectional interest... our tradesmen are disheartened, our mechanics out of employ, our farmers distressed, and our poor crying for bread, our banks are broken, our credit ruined.... What is the matter? Are we alone in this thing? Verily no. With all our evils we are better situated than any other nation.... England... has her hands reeking with the blood of the innocent abroad.... The world itself presents one great theater of misery, woe, and 'distress of nations with perplexity.' *All, all, speak with a voice of thunder, that man is not able to govern himself, to legislate for himself, to protect himself, to promote his own good, nor the good of the world.* [After all is said, there is nothing for it but to accept God's way — nothing else will work.] *It has been the design of Jehovah, from the commencement of the world, and is His purpose now, to regulate the affairs of the world in His own time, to stand as a head of the universe, and take the reins of government in His own hand.* When that is done... 'nations will learn war no more.'[21]

Here the Prophet lays it on the line:

> The world has had a fair trial for six thousand years; the Lord will try the seventh thousand Himself.... To bring about this state of things, there must of necessity be great confusion among the nations of the earth. God is coming

289

out of His hiding place... to vex the nations of the
earth. . . . It is for us to be righteous, that we may be wise
and understand; for none of the wicked shall understand. . . . As a Church and a people it behooves us to be
wise, and to seek to know the will of God, and then be
willing to do it. . . . *Our only confidence can be in God. . . .*
We have treated lightly His commands, and departed
from His ordinances, and the Lord has chastened us
sore. . . . In regard to the building up of Zion, it *has to be
done by the counsel of Jehovah, by the revelations of Heaven.*[22]

From these sayings of the Prophet one would hardly expect the
world to have improved since his day, and the words of Brigham
Young are eloquent in describing the steady deterioration that has
continued unabated up to the present moment. No wonder "thinking men, inquiring minds, ask whether it is really necessary for the
Government of God to be on the earth at the present day; I answer,
most assuredly; there never was a time when it was more needed
than it is now. Why? Because *men do not know how to govern themselves
without it.*"[23] "I acknowledged to him [Col. Thomas Kane] that we
have the best system of government in existence, but queried if the
people of this nation were righteous enough to *sustain its institutions.*
I say they are not, but will trample them under their feet."[24]

But is not Satan a politician with his love of confusion and
controversy? Isn't the adversary an arch-politician? "There shall be
no disputations among you. . . ." said the Lord to the Nephites,
"for . . . he that hath the spirit of contention is not of me, but is of the
devil, who is the father of contention, and he stirreth up the hearts
of men to contend with anger, one with another." (3 Nephi 11:28-
29.) Let us make one thing clear: contention is not discussion, but
the opposite; contention puts an end to all discussion, as does war.
Cedant leges inter arma, said the Romans — when war takes over
politics are in abeyance. The most famous dictum of Clausewitz is
that war is simply a continuation of the political dialogue in another
arena, but — as he points out at great length and with great clarity —
it is an arena in which the appeal is all to brute force and in which
any talk of laws or rules or principles cannot be anything but a
strategic ruse. In reality a declaration of war is an announcement
that the discussion is over. War is beyond politics, and God has said:
"[I] will that all men shall know that the day speedily cometh; the
hour is not yet, but is nigh at hand, when peace shall be taken from
the earth, and the devil shall have power over his own dominion."
(D&C 1:35.) That is the end of politics for now.

God discusses things with men "in all humility" for the sake of our enlightenment. Satan too loves to "discuss," but what a different type of discussion! He is not teaching but laying traps; his whole line is a sales pitch with his own advantage as the end. He is not enlightening but manipulating. He does not reason, but bargains: his proposition as put before Adam, Cain, Abraham, Moses, Enoch, and the Lord himself is the same one he puts to Faust and Jabez Stone: "If you will worship me I will give you unlimited power and wealth — everything this world has to offer — all you have to do is sign away your rather dubious expectations for the other world." If his proposition is refused outright, he has no other resort but to have a tantrum, falling down, rending upon the earth, screaming madly, "I am the Son of God! Worship me!" for his sole objective from the beginning has been to be number one.

> There are men who . . . wish to destroy every power in Heaven and on earth that they do not hold themselves. *This* is the spirit of Satan that was made so visibly manifest in Heaven and which proved his overthrow, and he *now* afflicts *this people* with it; *he* wants to dictate and rule every principle and power that leads to exaltation and eternal life.[25]

To be number one is to be beyond politics. It is his command of the ultimate weapon that places Satan — like God — beyond politics.

Recently a piece appeared in the press noting that businessmen are insisting with increasing zeal on searching the minds and the hearts of their employees by means of polygraph tests. If any arm of government[26] were to go so far they would be met by horrified protests at this vicious attack on individual freedom, and rightly so. What is it that gives ordinary businessmen a power greater than that of the government? It is the capacity for giving or withholding money — nothing else in the world. This is the weapon that Satan chose from the beginning to place him and his plans beyond politics, and it has worked with deadly effect. There is only one thing in man's world that can offer any check on the unlimited power of money — and that is government. That is why money always accuses government of trying to destroy free agency, when the great enslaver has always been money itself.

We do not have time here to review Satan's brilliant career in business and law: how he taught Cain the "great secret" of how to "murder and get gain" while claiming the noblest notions, "saying: I am free" (Moses 5:31, 33); how he inspired the Jaredites and then the Nephites "to seek for power, and authority, and riches" (3 Nephi 6:15); how he tried to buy off Abraham (in the *Apocalypse of Abraham*), and Moses and Jesus by promising them anything in the world if they would only worship him; how he coached Judas in the art of handling money; how he corrupts the Saints by covetousness and the things of the world; how his disciple, Simon Magus, offered Peter cash on the line for the priesthood. To be beyond politics does not place one, in President John Taylor's words, "above the rule of Mammon." Only a celestial order can do that.

Largely because of this dominion, the human dialogue has a tendency, as many ancient writers observed, to deteriorate unless there is divine intervention;[27] and since men normally insist on rejecting such intervention the end result is periodic catastrophe. This is the standard message found in the apocalyptic literature. "Every system of civil polity invented by men, like their religious creeds, has been *proved by experiment wholly inadequate to check the downward tendency* of the human race."[28]

When this downward tendency passes the *point of no return*, the process accelerates beyond control, ending in general catastrophe to be followed by God's intervention and a new dispensation. "Wherefore, I the Lord, *knowing the calamity* which should come upon the inhabitants of the earth, called upon my servant Joseph Smith, Jun., and spake unto him from heaven, and gave him commandments. (D&C 1:17.) Joseph Smith intended to follow those commandments: "The object with me is to obey and teach others to obey God in *just what He* tells us to do."[29] "One truth revealed from heaven is worth all the sectarian notions in existence."[30] "A man is his own tormentor and his own condemner. . . . All will suffer until they obey Christ himself."[31] "The sinner will slay the sinner, the wicked will fall upon the wicked, until there is an utter overthrow and consumption upon the face of the whole earth, until God reigns whose right it is."[32]

The Church has been put to great trouble and expense through the years by its insistence on sticking to its long and awkward title: plainly the second part of the name is very important — the Church of the *latter days*. These are the *last days* — the last days of what? Neither we nor the outside world have ever bothered to explore or argue definitions about that — because the answer is obvious: it is the perennial message of the apocalyptic teaching which is now recognized as the very foundation of the Old and the New Testaments. The last days are the last days of everything as we know it. "The Lord declared to His servants, some eighteen months since

[1833], that He was then withdrawing His Spirit from the earth . . . the governments of the earth are thrown into confusion and division; and *Destruction*, to the eye of the spiritual beholder, seems to be written by the finger of an invisible hand, in large capitals, upon almost every thing we behold."[33] "God hath set His hand and seal to change the times and seasons, and to blind their minds, that they may not understand His marvelous workings. . . ."[34] "While upon one hand I behold *the manifest withdrawal of God's Holy Spirit*, and the *veil of stupidity* which seems to be drawn over the hearts of the people; upon the other hand, I behold the judgments of God . . . sweeping hundreds and thousands of our race, and I fear unprepared, down to the shades of death."[35]

At the present time the political dialogue throughout the world has deteriorated catastrophically. In most countries it has degenerated into such mechanical and stereotyped forms that it is no longer profitable or meaningful — it is no longer a dialogue at all. If you are a private citizen you just do not "discuss" things with colonels, commissars, or corporations — you do what they tell you to do or at best manipulate you into doing. Has it ever been different? Not much, but on October 17, 1973, the junta in Chile officially put an end to *all* political activity of any kind or by any party. This is something unique, a final step by rulers who do not even make a *pretense* of consulting the ruled. Where do we go from here? We are beyond politics indeed. Another and even more fateful development has recently come to the fore in our midst, indicating beyond question that we have at last reached that point of no return[36] which heralds the last of the last days.

God has never given us a time schedule for the developments of the last days. There are a number of reasons for this; for example, if we knew the time and the hour, we would gauge our behavior accordingly and conveniently postpone repentance — whereas God wants us to live *as if* we were expecting his coming at any moment. He comes as a thief in the night, "Watch, therefore, for ye know not the time. . . ." But though he does not give us dates and figures, he does give us unmistakable signs of the times, and urges us to pay the closest possible attention to them. Simply by looking at a fig tree, for example, one can estimate quite closely about how far away the harvest is. The word *historia* was borrowed by Hecateus from the medical profession, the *historia* being progressive symptoms of a disease or illness; just as there are signs by which the doctor can tell how far along the patient is and how long he has to go, so there are such signs in the body politic of any society.

Specifically, if we want to know the sure sign of the end, we are instructed to look for *ripeness* or *fullness*. The end comes when, and *only* when, "the time is *ripe*," when "the harvest is ripe"; when the people are "ripe in iniquity." Or, to use the other figure, when "the cup of His wrath is *full*," which will be when "the cup of *their* iniquity is *full*." Or, to combine both terms, when the world is *fully ripe* in iniquity. Fruit is fully ripe at that moment when further ripening would not mean improvement but only deterioration. ("And so from day to day we ripe and ripe, and then from day to day we rot and rot.") And a vessel is *full* when nothing more can be added to it; when its contents can no longer be improved or damaged by adding any more ingredients. When the fruit is ripe there is no point in letting it remain longer on the tree. And when the cup is full nothing further remains to be done about its contents. Ripeness and fullness are that state of things, in short, when nothing further remains to be done in the direction of filling or ripening, and the process has reached the end. A society has reached such a point when it can no longer go in the direction it has been taking, when the only hope of motion lies in a change or a direct reversal of direction, and repentance is that change of direction. It is when men reach the point of refusing to *repent* that they have reached the point of fullness: "And it shall come to pass, because of the wickedness of the world, that I will take vengeance upon the wicked, for they will not repent; for the cup of mine indignation is full." (D&C 29:17.) The moment Adam found himself going in the wrong direction because of the Fall, he was to repent and call upon God forevermore — that is, to reverse his course, and ever since then "the days of the children of men were prolonged, according to the will of God, that they might repent while in the flesh; wherefore, their state became a state of probation, and their time was lengthened. . . . For he gave commandment that all men must repent." (2 Nephi 2:21.) The reason that our lives are extended as they are beyond the age of reproduction is to allow us the fullest possible opportunity to repent. Therefore, when men have lost the capacity to repent they forfeit any right to sojourn further upon the earth; the very purpose of this extended span of life being to practice repentance, when men announce that they have no intention of repenting there is no reason why God should let them stay around any longer to corrupt the rising generation. "And now cometh the day of their calamity . . . and their sorrow shall be great unless they speedily repent, yea, very speedily." (D&C 136:35.)

There is a time limit, then, and I believe that the time limit has now been reached — the cup is full. For we have in our time the terrifying phenomenon of men who refuse to repent. Why should they repent? Because God commands it. "Behold, I command all men everywhere to repent." (D&C 18:9.) "And surely every man must repent or suffer, for I, God, am endless." (D&C 19:4.) "Therefore, I command you to repent — repent, lest I smite you by the rod of my mouth. . . . For behold, I, God, have suffered these things for all, that they might not suffer if they would repent." (D&C 19:15-16.) "Wherefore, I command you again to repent, lest I humble you with my almighty power." (D&C 19:20.) "And I command you that you preach naught but repentance" (D&C 19:21); "Wherefore, I will that all men shall repent, for all are under sin, except those which I have reserved unto myself, holy men that ye know not of." (D&C 49:8.) "Hearken and hear, O ye inhabitants of the earth. Listen, ye elders of my church together, and hear the voice of the Lord; for he calleth upon all men, and he commandeth all men everywhere to repent." (D&C 133:16.)

Yet throughout the world today, few, it would seem, have any intention anymore of repenting. That is the ominous note! Mormon describes this condition as marking the last stand of the Nephites:

> And now behold, my son, I fear lest the Lamanites shall destroy this people; for they do not repent. . . . When I speak the word of God with sharpness they tremble and anger against *me;* and when I use no sharpness they harden their hearts against it; wherefore, I fear lest the Spirit of the Lord hath ceased striving with them. . . . I cannot any longer enforce my commands. And they have become strong in their perversion. . . . without principle, and past feeling. . . . and I pray unto God . . . to witness the return [repentance] of his people unto him, or their utter destruction. (Moroni 9:3-4, 18-22. Italics added.)

They sorrowed at the loss of their wealth, "but, behold this . . . was vain," Mormon continues, "for their sorrowing was not unto repentance . . . but . . . because the Lord would not always suffer them to take happiness in sin." (Mormon 2:13.) "And . . . I saw that the day of grace was passed with them, both temporally and spiritually." (Mormon 2:15.) When the day of repentance is past, so is the day of grace. They had reached the *point of no return.* This is what the Greeks called *ate,* and is the telling moment of tragedy. Take that greatest of tragedies, *Oedipus Rex.* Oedipus had in his youth committed a terrible compound crime: but he had done it unknowingly and was therefore given every opportunity, not only to repent and be forgiven, but also to achieve higher glory than ever. The question was not whether or not he was guilty, but, whether or not, being guilty, he would repent. At the beginning of the play he drops hints that betray a subconscious awareness of his guilt; he, as the king, insists on a thorough investigation. Then, as more and more evidence accumulates against him, he insists even more loudly that he has done no wrong; he looks for one party and then another to fix the blame on, but each time it becomes clear that it could not have been that person. In the end even his wife cannot deny his guilt any longer and pleads with him to drop the case; his reply is to blame her for everything in a fantastically forced and vicious argument. When finally he is forced to recognize that he and he alone is the enemy he seeks, the results are terrible. His whole trouble is that he will not repent: after his meteoric career, his matchless fame, his unfailing cleverness and strong character had held the reins of power for twenty years, he was in no mood to repent of everything. The last words spoken to him in the play are significant when his brother Creon says to him: "Don't think you can be *number one* all the time." This is also the tragedy of Lear, that most tragic of tragedies, of Richard II, and of King Laertes in *The Winter's Tale:* each king, because he *is* the king, cannot tolerate the idea of repenting — that would be a fatal confession of weakness — and so each one digs himself deeper and deeper into a devastating situation from which he cannot escape: because the only escape hatch is repentance. In each case the trouble is the insistence on being number one — and this takes us back to the primal tragedy, and the character of Lucifer, whose example all our tragic figures are following. "Now, in this world," said Joseph Smith, "mankind are naturally selfish, ambitious and striving to excel. . . . Some seek to excel. And this was the case with Lucifer when he fell"[37] — he had to be number one. Since all have sinned, there is no question of whether one has done wrong or not, but only of whether one will repent. But what is now the approved school solution? Since all have sinned, why should anybody be the goat? Why should anybody repent?

When President Harold B. Lee said that the Saints are above politics, he was referring to the brand of politics that prevails in the world today. "The government of heaven, if wickedly administered, would become one of the worst governments upon the face of the earth. No matter how good a government is, unless it is administered by righteous men, an evil government will be made of it."[38] Men caught red-handed, charged, tried, confessed, and convicted, now come forth to plead innocent: they were merely carrying out orders, they were doing what everyone does, they have done no wrong. The winningest of slogans when the national conscience became burdened with the guilt of relentless shedding of innocent blood day after day, month after month, and year after year, could only be the slogan: *we have done no wrong!* Any politician foolish enough to so much as hint at a need for repentance certainly was asking for the drubbing he would get. King Claudius and Macbeth were bloody villains, and they knew it, and even in their darkest hours speculated with a wild surmise on the possibility, however remote, of repentance and forgiveness. The fatal symptom of our day is not that men do wrong — they always have — and commit crimes, and even recognize their wrongdoing as foolish and unfortunate, but that they have *no intention of repenting,* while God has told us that the first rule that he has given the human race is that all men everywhere must repent.

Joseph Smith tells us that there are crimes and sins which are wrong no matter who does them or under what condition: they are wrong in and of themselves, at all times and at all places. You cannot deceive one party to be loyal to another. "Any man who will betray the Catholics will betray you; and if he will betray me, he will betray you."[39] Compare this with Mr. Stone's recent declaration that he found nothing shocking in public officials' lying under oath, since they were trained to do that very thing. "All [men] are subjected to vanity," according to Joseph Smith, "while they travel through the crooked paths and difficulties which surround them. Where is the man that is free from vanity?"[40] Granted that, it is still true that "all men have power to resist the devil,"[41] which leaves them without excuse.

The dialogue between men has always been remarkably superficial, devoid of any substance and depth, since men must always be on the go and only make brief contact like jet planes passing in the night as each goes about his business, looking out first of all for his own interests with little time left over for the common interest. Busy modern men and women feel they are too busy for the rigors of serious discussion necessary for genuine politics. Senator Proxmire recently deplored the fact, as all public-spirited people always have, that very very few people take a real and active part in the political process. How could it be otherwise? Politics by its very nature is superficial: the practitioner can never go into depth because too many things have to be considered. If in physics the problem of three bodies has been solved only by approximation, how can we expect to cope wisely and fully with the infinite complexity of human affairs? Politics, in the proper Greek sense, was a full-time job for the citizen who spent his day in the Agora and his nights in long discussions and debates, while servants and slaves took care of petty and menial matters.[42] Even that, however, was an ideal which neither the Greeks nor anyone else could live up to. After all, the first interest of every citizen is to make money: *"O cives, cives, quaerenda pecunia primum est; virtus post nummos!"*[43] And so politics degenerated quickly into subservience to private interests — it yields subservience to wealth. If Greece produced the most enlightened politicians, it also, as Thucydides informs us, produced the most sordid. Politics is often a forlorn and hopeless affair, because it is not really a dialogue unless it is strictly honest, and the ulterior motives of power and gain always vitiate it in the end. It is then the tricky lawyer who takes over. Eventually someone seeks a stronger tool than mere talk — we start talking and end up condemning and smiting. "Man shall not smite, neither shall he judge" (Mormon 8:20), is the final wisdom of the Book of Mormon. "Man should not counsel his fellow man, neither put trust in the arm of flesh" (D&C 1:19-20) is the initial wisdom of the Doctrine and Covenants. What was to be a meeting of the minds often degenerates into a trial of arms. Politics gravitate in the direction of an ever stronger clout, inevitably leading to the trial of arms. Someone seeks a stronger tool than mere talk. Consider again Clausewitz's famous dictum that war is the natural end of politics — also that war lies beyond politics. It is the arena that smells of death — and we are trapped in the arena.

The wide difference, amounting to complete antithesis, between men's ways and God's ways should always be kept in mind. If we would remember that fact, it would save us from a pitfall that constantly lies before us — especially here at Brigham Young University. Nothing is easier than to identify one's own favorite political, economic, historical, and moral convictions with the gospel. That gives one a neat, convenient, but altogether too easy advantage over one's fellows. If my ideas are the true ones — and I certainly will not entertain them if I suspect for a moment that they are false! — then, all truth being one, they are also the gospel, and to oppose them is to play the role of Satan. This is simply insisting that our way is God's way and therefore, the only way. It is the height of impertinence. "There have been frauds and secret abominations and evil works of darkness going on [in the Church] ... all the time palming it off upon the Presidency ... practicing in the Church in their name."[44] Do you think these people were not sincere? Yes, to the point of fanaticism — they wholly identified their crackpot schemes with the Church and with the gospel. Some of the most learned theologians, such as Bossuet, have shown from every page of the scripture that God is an absolute monarchist, while others, equally learned and dedicated, have formed religious communities dedicated to the equally obvious scriptural proposition that the Saints are Communists. You can search through the scriptures and find support for any theory you want, and it is your privilege to attempt to convince yourself of any position you choose to take — but not to impose that opinion on others as the gospel. God certainly does not subscribe to our political creeds. The first issue of the *Times and Seasons* contained a lead editorial to the elders: "Be careful that you teach not for the word of God, the commandments of men, nor the doctrines of men, nor the ordinances of men . . . study the word of God and preach it and *not your own opinions,* for no man's opinion is worth a straw."[45]

We may seem to be speaking out of order because we insist on bringing into the discussion of political science certain theological propositions which are simply not acceptable to those outside of our Church. But I am speaking for myself. There is the basic proposition: "The Spirit of God will . . . dwell with His people, and be withdrawn from the rest of the nations." Accordingly, among the Saints, "party feelings, separate interests, exclusive designs should be lost sight of in the one common cause, in the interest of the whole."[46] If the world cannot accept such a proposition, we are still committed to it — wholly and irrevocably — whether we like it or not. "The government of the Almighty has always been very dissimilar to the governments of men. . . . [It] has always tended to promote peace, unity, harmony, strength, and happiness," while on the other hand, "the greatest acts of the mighty men have been to depopulate nations and to overthrow kingdoms. . . . Before them the earth was a paradise, and behind them a desolate wilderness. . . . The designs of God, on the other hand, [are that] . . . 'the earth shall yield its increase, resume its paradisean glory, and become as the garden of the Lord.' "[47]

How you play the game of politics is important, but the game you are playing is also important. It is important to work, but what you work for is all-important. The Nephites, "by their industry," obtained riches — which then destroyed them ; "[for] the laborer in Zion shall labor for Zion; for if they labor for *money* they shall perish" (2 Nephi 26:31, italics added) — work does not sanctify wealth, as we try to make ourselves believe. The zeal and intelligence that our political commitments demand — to what should they be directed? At present we have a positive obsession with the *economy* — the economy is all. But the Lord told Samuel the Lamanite that when a people " . . . have set their heart upon riches . . . cursed be they and also their treasures." (Helaman 13:20.)

While listening to Senator Proxmire's address recently, I was impressed by the clear-headed intelligence and zeal he brought to his task: it made one almost think that the show was going on — that there still is a genuine politics after all. What then of the prophecies? Both in manner and appearance the senator recalled to my mind certain dashing, wonderful men who, during World War II, used to brief the various units of the 101st Airborne Division which they were leading into battle. (The classic Leader's Oration Before the Battle enjoyed a revival in airborne operations where the army, a short hour before the battle, could sit quietly on the grass one hundred miles from the enemy and listen to speeches.) It was the high point of their careers, the thing they had been working and hoping and looking forward to all their lives — to lead a crack regiment or division into battle, and they made the most of it. The feeling of euphoria was almost overpowering — they were smart, sharp, vigorous, compelling, eager, tense, exuding optimism and even humor, but above all excitement. Invariably General Maxwell Taylor would end his oration with: "Good hunting!" It was wonderful, thrilling; you were ready to follow that man anywhere. *But* before the operation was a day old every man in the division was heartily wishing that he was anywhere else, doing anything else but that; everyone knew in his mind and heart that he was not sent to earth to engage in this nasty and immoral business. The heroism and sacrifice were real — the situation was utterly satanic and shameful; the POWs we rounded up to interrogate were men just as good as we were, the victims of a terrible circumstance that the devil's game of power and gain had woven around them.

So I like Senator Proxmire — like General Taylor, a splendid man — I admire his style and approve his zeal, but wisdom greater than man tells me that we are not playing the right game: "Behold, the world at this time lieth in sin, and there is *none* that doeth good — no, not one!" The game is not going to last much longer. "They seek not the Lord to establish his righteousness, but every man walketh in his own way, and after the image of his own God, whose image is in the likeness of the world, and whose substance is that of an idol, *which waxeth old* and shall perish in Babylon, even Babylon the great, *which shall fall.*" (D&C 1:16. Italics added. See also 2 Nephi 9:30.) According to Joseph Smith, "The most damning hand of murder, tyranny and oppression . . . that spirit which has so strongly riveted the creeds of the fathers, who have inherited lies, upon the hearts of the children, and filled the world with confusion, has been growing stronger and stronger, and is now the very mainspring of all corruption, and the whole earth groans under the weight of its iniquity."[48] This is our heritage.

The news of the world today reminds me of nothing so much as those bulletins which a short while ago were being issued by the doctors attending the late King Gustave of Sweden and by those treating Pablo Casals. The king was in his nineties, Casals, ninety-six; and both were very ill — what really good news could come out of the sickroom? That the patient had rested well? That he had had some lucid moments? That he had taken nourishment? Could any of that be called good news, hopeful news — in view of the inevitable news the world was waiting for? What is your own idea of an encouraging and cheering item in the news today? That the next Middle Eastern war has been postponed? That a new oil field has been discovered? "This physic but prolongs thy sickly days!"[49] We shall achieve lasting peace when we achieve eternal life. Politics has the same goal as the gospel: complete happiness. But to achieve that requires eternal life. The most painful thing in the world, says Joseph Smith, is the thought of annihilation;[50] until that gnawing pain is relieved all the rest is a forlorn and wistful game of make-believe. The solution of all our problems is the resurrection: only God knows the solution. Why not follow his advice? And only the gospel can remove that pain. The final relief of all our woes lies beyond all worldly politics. So when Joseph Smith says, "My feelings revolt at the idea of having anything to do with politics," he is not being high and mighty but putting his priorities in order. "I wish to be let alone," he says, "that I may attend strictly to the spiritual welfare of the Church."[51] Specifically, "the object with me is to obey and to teach others to obey God in just what He tells us to do."[52] For "one truth revealed from heaven is worth all the sectarian notions in existence."[53] And so he pursues his way: "It matters not to me if all hell boils over; I regard it only as I would the crackling of thorns under a pot. . . . I intend to lay a foundation that will revolutionize the whole world. . . . It will not be by sword or gun that this kingdom will roll on."[54]

How should the Saints behave? Brigham Young believed that "the elders cannot be too particular to enjoin on all the Saints to yield obedience to the laws, and respect every man in his office, letting politics wholly, entirely, and absolutely alone, and preaching the principles of the Gospel of salvation; for to this end were they ordained and set forth. We are for peace, we want no contention with any person or government."[55] "Amid all the revolutions that are taking place among the nations, the elders will ever pursue an undeviating course in being subject to the government wherever they may be, and sustain the same by all their precepts to the Saints, having *nothing to do with political questions* which engender strife, remembering that the weapons of their warfare are not carnal but spiritual, and that the Gospel which they preach is not of man but from heaven."[56] "As for politics we care nothing about them one way or the other, although we are a political people. . . . It is the Kingdom of God or nothing with us."[57] The kingdom is beyond politics — one way or the other, i.e., it is beyond partisan party politics.

On the last night of a play the whole cast and stage crew stay in the theater until the small or not-so-small hours of the morning striking the old set. If there is to be a new opening soon, as the economy of the theater requires, it is important that the new set should be in place and ready for the opening night; all the while the old set was finishing its usefulness and then being taken down, the new set was rising in splendor to be ready for the drama that would immediately follow. So it is with this world. It is not our business to tear down the old set — the agencies that do that are already hard at work and very efficient — the set is coming down all around us with spectacular effect. Our business is to see to it that the new set is well on the way for what is to come — and that means a different kind of politics, beyond the scope of the tragedy that is now playing its closing night. We are preparing for the establishment of Zion.

NOTES

1. When man yielded to the temptations of the adversary, certain drastic corrections had to be made; the original plan and design for the use of the earth would not be scrapped at any rate, since it is not only the best but the only plan that will work here. No, the original plan was to be preserved as a beacon, and the minute fallen man realized his fallen state every inducement would be given him to turn his back on that condition and make his way back to the presence of God and to the only kind of life that is endurable throughout eternity.

2. Dean C. Jessee, "The Early Accounts of Joseph Smith's First Vision," *BYU Studies 9* (Spring 1969): 280.

3. See John Taylor and Orson Pratt in *Journal of Discourses* (Liverpool: F. D. Richards, 1855), 1:221-233 and 8:101-106, respectively. Hereafter cited as *JD*.

4. *JD* 5:187.

5. Joseph Fielding Smith, comp., *Teachings of the Prophet Joseph Smith* (Salt Lake City: Deseret Book, 1938), p. 49; hereafter cited as *TPJS*.

6. *TPJS*, p. 30. Italics added.

7. James R. Clark, ed., *Messages of the First Presidency* (Salt Lake City: Bookcraft, 1970), 4:78, 82. Italics added.

8. *TPJS*, pp. 51-52, cf. also p. 50.

9. *TPJS*, pp. 14-15.

10. *TPJS*, p. 57.

11. *TPJS*, pp. 14, 16. Italics added.

12. *TPJS*, pp. 48-49. Italics added.

13. At best man's laws are negative — "Congress shall make no law...." "The laws of men," says Joseph Smith, "may guarantee to a people protection in the honorable pursuits of this life ... and when this is said, all is said.... The law of heaven is presented to man, and as such guarantees to all who obey it a reward far beyond any earthly consideration.... The law of heaven ... transcends the law of man, as far as eternal life the temporal." (*TPJS*, p. 50.)

14. See Hugh Nibley, "The Passing of the Church: Forty Variations on an Unpopular Theme," *Church History* 30 (June 1961):134; reprinted in Nibley, *When the Lights Went Out: Three Studies in the Ancient Apostasy* (Salt Lake City: Deseret Book, 1970), p. 4, quoting Justin, *Dialogue*, 110, Hilary, *Contra Constant, Imp.*, 4, in Migne, ed., *Patralogia Latina*, 10.581B. "The Christian masses do not realize what is happening to them: they are 'bewitched' by a thing that comes as softly and insidiously as a slinging noose." Nibley, *When the Lights*, p. 6.

15. See Hugh Nibley, "The Ancient Law of Liberty," in *The World and the Prophets* (Salt Lake City: Deseret Book, 1954), pp. 166-173, for a more detailed treatment of this theme.

16. See Hugh Nibley, "The Hierocentric State," *Western Political Quarterly*, 3(1951):226-253.

17. *TPJS*, p. 49.

18. *TPJS*, p. 181. Italics added.

19. *TPJS*, p. 187. Italics added.

20. *TPJS*, pp. 18-19. Italics added.

21. *TPJS*, pp. 249-251. Italics added.

22. *TPJS*, pp. 252-254. Italics added.

23. *JD* 10:320. Italics added.

24. *JD* 12:119. Italics added.

25. *JD* 10:97. Italics added.

26. Except, say, the CIA or FBI.

27. Cf. for example, Hesiod's law of decay. This is, incidentally, the basic principle of apocalyptic literature.

28. *Millennial Star*, 17(1855):675. Italics added.

29. *TPJS*, p. 332. Italics added.

30. *TPJS*, p. 338.

31. *TPJS*, p. 357.

32. *JD* 2:190.

33. *TPJS*, p. 16.

34. *TPJS*, p. 135.

35. *TPJS*, pp. 13-14. Italics added.

36. The point of no return marks the stroke of doom in classical tragedy.

37. *TPJS*, p. 297.

38. *JD* 10:177.

39. *TPJS*, p. 375.

40. *TPJS*, p. 187.

41. *TPJS*, p. 189.

42. This was their genius and the secret of their success. Whether the Greek pursued philosophy, art, religion, pleasure, science, or money, he was willing to give the search everything he had — sacrificing every convenience and amenity: the ideal of the Greeks was the *Sophos* — completely selfless, oblivious to his own comfort, health, appearance, and appetites as his mind came to grips with the problem of achieving one particular objective. That is why the Greeks were anciently way out in front of others in almost every field of human endeavor — and still remain unsurpassed and

even unequalled in many of them. The Greek citizen not only spent the day in the Agora, but in the evenings at home he carried on the dialogue in discussion and study groups, for the Greek citizen knew that the only work worthy of the name, a work a hundred times harder than the repetitious routines and seemingly virtuous bootlicking that we call work, was the terribly demanding and exhausting task of cutting new grooves and channels with the sharp edge of the mind. He felt that if politics was all that important, it was worth our best hours.

43. Horace, *Epistles*, 1. 1. 53-54.

44. *TPJS*, pp. 127-128.

45. *Times and Seasons* 1(1839):13.

46. *TPJS*, p. 231.

47. *TPJS*, pp. 248-249.

48. *TPJS*, p. 145.

49. *Hamlet*, 3.iii.96.

50. *TPJS*, p. 296.

51. *TPJS*, p. 275.

52. *TPJS*, p. 332.

53. *TPJS*, p. 338.

54. *TPJS*, pp. 339, 366.

55. Brigham Young History, manuscript in the Office of the Church Historian, The Church of Jesus Christ of Latter-day Saints, Salt Lake City, May 7, 1845.

56. General Epistle, *Millennial Star*, 13 (1851): 21.

57. *Millennial Star*, 31 (1869):573.

BIBLIOGRAPHY

Compiled by

Louis C. Midgley

1926

1. "Of Birthdays," *Improvement Era,* 29 (June 1926), 743. [Poem written for his grandmother.]

1939

2. The Roman Games as a Survival of an Archaic Year-cult (Berkeley: University of California Ph.D. thesis, 1939). 235 pp.

1942

3. "New Light on Scaliger," *Classical Journal,* XXXVII (1942), 291-295.

1945

4. "Sparsiones," *Classical Journal,* XL (1945), 515-543.

1946

5. *No, Ma'am, That's Not History: A Brief Review of Mrs. Brodie's Reluctant Vindication of the Prophet She Seeks to Expose* (Salt Lake City: Bookcraft, 1946). 62 pp. This is a short, witty reply to Fawn Brodie's *No Man Knows My History* 1st ed. (New York: Knopf, 1945; 2nd ed., 1971).

1948

6. Review of S. B. Sperry's *Our Book of Mormon,* in *Improvement Era,* 51 (Jan. 1948), 42.

7. "The Book of Mormon as a Mirror of the East," *Improvement Era,* 51 (April 1948), 202-204, 249-251. [Reprinted in the *Improvement Era,* 73 (Nov. 1970), 115-120, 122-125.]

8. "Baptism for the Dead in Ancient Times," a series of articles in the *Improvement Era.*
8-1. "Part I," 51 (Dec. 1948), 786-788, 836-838.

1949

8. "Baptism for the Dead in Ancient Times," — continued:
8-2. "Part II," 52 (Jan. 1949), 24-26, 60.

8-3. "Part III," 52 (Feb. 1949), 90-91, 109-110, 112.
8-4. "Part IV," 52 (March 1949), 146-148, 180-183.
8-5. "The Dilemma: Part V — Conclusion," 52 (April 1949), 212-214.

[Reviewed and discussed by Bernard M. Foschini, " 'Those Who are Baptized for the Dead,' I Cor. 15:29," *Catholic Biblical Quarterly*, 13 (1951), 51-53, 70-73.]

9. "The Arrow, the Hunter, and the State," *Western Political Quarterly*, II (1949), 328-344. [A study of the role of the marked arrow in ancient statecraft.]

1950

10. "Lehi in the Desert," a series of articles in the *Improvement Era*.
10-1. "Part I," 53 (Jan. 1950), 14-16, 66-72.
10-2. "Part II," 53 (Feb. 1950), 102-104, 155-159.
10-3. "Part III," 53 (March 1950), 200-202, 222, 225-226, 229-230.
10-4. "Part IV," 53 (April 1950), 276-277, 320-326.
10-5. "Part V," 53 (May 1950), 382-384, 448-449.
10-6. "Part VI," 53 (June 1950), 486-487, 516-519.
10-7. "Part VII," 53 (July 1950), 566-567, 587-588.
10-8. "Part VIII," 53 (Aug. 1950), 640-642, 670.
10-9. "Part IX," 53 (Sept. 1950), 706-708, 744.
10-10. "Part X," 53 (Oct. 1950), 804-806, 824, 826, 828, 830.

[Reprinted without illustrations as the first half of *Lehi in the Desert . . .* (1952).]

11. Review of J. W. Swain's *The Ancient World*, in *The Historian*, XIII (Autumn 1950), 79-81.

12. "The Christmas Quest," *Millennial Star*, 112 (Jan. 1950), 4-5.

1951

13. "The Hierocentric State," *Western Political Quarterly*, IV (1951), 226-253. [A study of the role of ritual centers and kingship in ancient statecraft.]

14. "The World of the Jaredites," a series of articles in the *Improvement Era*. [These articles were written in the form of expository letters to Professor F.]
14-1. "Part I," 54 (Sept. 1951), 628-630, 673-675.
14-2. "Part II," 54 (Oct. 1951), 704-706, 752-755.
14-3. "Part III," 54 (Nov. 1951), 786-787, 833-835.
14-4. "Part IV," 54 (Dec. 1951), 862-863, 946-947.

1952

14. "The World of the Jaredites" — continued:
14-5. "Part V," 55 (Jan. 1952), 22-24.
14-6. "Part VI," 55 (Feb. 1952), 92-94, 98, 100, 102, 104-105.
14-7. "Part VII," 55 (March 1952), 162-165, 167-168.
14-8. "Part VIII," 55 (April 1952), 236-238, 258, 260-265.
14-9. "Part IX," 55 (May 1952), 316-318, 340, 342, 344, 346.

14-10. "Part X," 55 (June 1952), 398-399, 462-464.

14-11. "Conclusion," 55 (July 1952), 510, 550.

15. Review of Ph. Hitti's *History of Syria, Including Lebanon and Palestine,* in *Western Political Quarterly,* V (June 1952), 312-313.

16. Review of T. Cuyler Young (ed.), *Near Eastern Culture and Society: A Symposium on the Meeting of East and West,* in *Western Political Quarterly,* V (June 1952), 315-316.

17. *Lehi in the Desert and the World of the Jaredites* (Salt Lake City: Bookcraft, 1952). VIII, 272 pp. [The bulk of these materials appeared in the *Improvement Era* between 1950 and 1952. The original illustrations and some other materials were not included in the book.]
Contents:
Foreword (by John A. Widtsoe)
Lehi in the Desert
  I. The Troubled Orient
  II. Men of the East
  III. Into the Desert
  IV. Desert Ways and places
  V. The City and the Sand
  VI. Lehi the Winner
The World of the Jaredites
  I. A Twilight World
  II. Departure
  III. Jared on the Steppes
  IV. Jaredite Culture: Splendor and Shame
  V. They Take up the Sword
  VI. A Permanent Heritage
Appendix
  I. East Coast or West Coast?
  II. How Far to Cumorah?

1953

18. "The Unsolved Loyalty Problem: Our Western Heritage," *Western Political Quarterly,* VI (1953), 631-657. [An examination of the problem of loyalty in the 4th century, with obvious significance for our own time.]

19. "Columbus and Revelation," *The Instructor,* 88 (Oct. 1953), 319-320.

20. "The Stick of Judah and the Stick of Joseph," a series of articles in the *Improvement Era:*
20-1. "I: The Doctors Disagree," 56 (Jan. 1953), 16-17, 38-41.
20-2. "II: What Were the Sticks?" 56 (Feb. 1953), 90-91, 123-127.
20-3. "Part III," 56 (March 1953), 150-152, 191-195.
20-4. "Part IV," 56 (April 1953), 250-267.
20-5. "Conclusion," 56 (May 1953), 331-333, 334, 336, 338, 341, 343, 345.

[Cf. Lesson (or chapter) XXIV in *An Approach to the Book of Mormon* (1957/1964).]

21. "New Approaches to Book of Mormon Study," a series of articles in the *Improvement Era*.
    21-1. "Part I: Some Standard Tests," 56 (Nov. 1953), 830-831, 859-862.
    21-2. "Part II: Some Standard Tests," 56 (Dec. 1953), 919, 1003.

1954

21. "New Approaches to Book of Mormon Study" — continued:
    21-3. "Part 3," 57 (Jan. 1954), 30-32, 41.
    21-4. "Part 4," 57 (Feb. 1954), 88-89, 125-126.
    21-5. "Part 5," 57 (March 1954), 148-150, 170.
    21-6. "Part 6," 57 (April 1954), 232-233, 246, 248-250.
    21-7. "Part 7," 57 (May 1954), 308-309, 326, 330.
    21-8. "Part 8," 57 (June 1954), 389, 447-448, 450-451.
    21-9. "Conclusion," 57 (July 1954), 506-507, 521.

22. *Time Vindicates the Prophets* (Salt Lake City: The Church of Jesus Christ of Latter-day Saints, 1954). [Published as 31 separate pamphlets (part 20 was never published). These were addresses given over radio station KSL at 9:00 p.m. on the regular Sunday Evening Program.]
    22-1 "How Will It Be When None More Saith 'I Saw'?" (3pp.) March 7.
    22-2. "A Prophet's Reward." (4pp.) March 14.
    22-3. "Prophets and Scholars." (3pp.) March 21.
    22-4. "The Prophets and the Scriptures." (3pp.) March 28.
    22-5. "Prophecy and Tradition." (3pp.) April 11.
    22-6. "Easter and the Prophets." (4pp.) April 18.
    22-7. "Prophecy and Office." (4pp.) April 25.
    22-8. "Prophets and Crisis." (4pp.) May 2.
    22-9. "Prophets and Preachers." (4pp.) May 9.
    22-10. "Prophets and Philosophers." (4pp.) May 16.
    22-11. "Prophets and Creeds." (4pp.) May 23.
    22-12. "Two Ways to Remember the Dead." (4pp.) May 30.
    22-13. "The Prophets and the Plan of Life." (4pp.) June 6.
    22-14. "The Prophets and the Search for God." (4pp.) June 20.
    22-15. "Prophets and Martyrs." (4pp.) June 27.
    22-16. "The Ancient Law of Liberty." (4pp.) July 4.
    22-17. "Prophets and Gnostics." (4pp.) July 11.
    22-18. "The Schools and the Prophets." (4pp.) July 18.
    22-19. "A Prophetic Event." (4pp.) July 25.
    22-20. never published
    22-21. "St. Augustine and the Great Transition." (4pp.) Aug. 1.
    22-22. "A Substitute for Revelation." (4pp.) Aug. 8.
    22-23. "Prophets and Mystics." (4pp.) Aug. 15.
    22-24. "Rhetoric and Revelation." (4pp.) Aug. 22.
    22-25. "Prophets and Miracles." (4pp.) Aug. 29.
    22-26. "The Book of Mormon as a Witness." (4pp.) Sept. 5.
    22-27. "Prophets and Reformers." (4pp.) Sept. 12.
    22-28. "The Prophets and the Open Mind." (4pp.) Sept. 19.
    22-29. "Prophets and Ritual." (3pp.) Sept. 26.
    22-30. "The Church of the Prophets." (4pp.) Oct. 10.
    22-31. "Prophets and Glad Tidings." (4pp.) Oct. 17.

23. *The World and the Prophets* (Salt Lake City: Deseret Book, 1954). 250 pp. [This is a collection of addresses originally given over station KSL on the Sunday Evening Program at 9:00 p.m. from March to October 1954.]
Contents: (Number of the radio address is in parentheses.)
   1. "How Will It Be When None More Saith 'I Saw'?" (1)
   2. "A Prophet's Reward" (2)
   3. "Prophets and Preachers" (9)
   4. "Prophets and Scholars" (3)
   5. "Prophets and Philosophers" (10)
   6. "Prophets and Creeds" (11)
   7. "Prophets and the Search for God" (14)
   8. "Prophets and Gnostics" (17)
   9. "The Schools and the Prophets" (18)
   10. "St. Augustine and the Great Transition" (21)
   11. "A Substitute for Revelation" (22)
   12. "Prophets and Mystics" (23)
   13. "Rhetoric and Revelation" (24)
   14. "Prophets and Reformers" (27)
   15. "The Prophets and the Open Mind" (28)
   16. "Prophets and Miracles" (25)
   17. "Prophets and Ritual" (29)
   18. "Easter and the Prophets" (6)
   19. "Two Ways to Remember the Dead (12)
   20. "Prophets and Martyrs" (15)
   21. "The Ancient Law of Liberty" (16)
   22. "Prophets and Crisis" (8)
   23. "The Prophets and the Scriptures" (4)
   24. "The Book of Mormon as a Witness" (26)
   25. "Prophecy and Tradition" (5)
   26. "The Prophets and the Plan of Life" (13)
   27. "A Prophetic Event" (19)
   28. "Prophecy and Office" (7)
   29. "What Makes a True Church" (30)
   30. "Prophets and Glad Tidings" (31)
   Index

1955

24. "Do Religion and History Conflict?" in *Great Issues Forum*, Series 2 (Religion), No. 5 (Salt Lake City: University of Utah, Extension Division, 1955), 22-39. [The published version of the first of several famous "debates" with Sterling M. McMurrin held on March 23, 1955, under the sponsorship of the Department of Philosophy at the University of Utah. McMurrin's address, "Religion and the Denial of History," is published on pp. 5-21 and therefore precedes Nibley's, although Nibley spoke first.]

25. "The Way of the Church," a series of articles in three parts in the *Improvement Era*. [This series was to have been continued, but was actually abandoned. The materials were eventually used in "The Pas-

sing of the Church," *Church History*, XXX (June 1961), 131-154 and reprinted in *When the Lights Went Out* (1970), 1-32; and in *BYU Studies*, 16 (Autumn 1975), 135-164.]

"The Way of the Church," I:

25-1.   "Controlling the Past (A Consideration of Methods)," 58 (Jan. 1955), 20-22, 44-45.

25-2.   "Controlling the Past," 58 (Feb. 1955), 86-87, 104, 106-107.

25-3.   "Controlling the Past: Part III," 58 (March 1955), 152-154, 166, 168.

25-4.   "Controlling the Past: Part IV," 58 (April 1955), 230-232, 258, 260-261.

25-5.   "Controlling the Past: Part V," 58 (May 1955), 306-308, 364-366.

25-6.   "Controlling the Past: Part VI," 58 (June 1955), 384-386, 455-456.

"The Way of the Church," II:

25-7.   "Two Views of Church History," 58 (July 1955), 502-504, 538.

25-8.   "Two Views of Church History: Part II," 58 (Aug. 1955), 570-571, 599-600, 602-606.

25-9.   "Two Views of Church History: Part III," 58 (Sept. 1955), 650-653.

25-10. "Two Views of Church History: Part IV," 58 (Oct. 1955), 708-710.

25-11. "The Apocalyptic Background, I: The Eschatological Dilemma," 58 (Nov. 1955), 817, 835-838, 840-841.

25-12. "The Apocalyptic Background, II: The Eschatological Dilemma" 58 (Dec. 1955), 902-903, 968.

1956

26.   "Victoriosa Loquacitas: The Rise of Rhetoric and the Decline of Everything Else," *Western Speech*, XX (1956), 57-82. [A study of the rhetoric of the second Sophistic movement and its influence on politics and culture generally, with obvious significance for our own time because of remarkable parallel developments in the current world of business, politics and education.]

27.   Review of E. A. Shils' *The Torment of Secrecy*, in *American Political Science Review*, L (Sept. 1956), 887-888.

28.   "More Voices from the Dust," *The Instructor*, 91 (March 1956), 71-72, 74.

29.   "There Were Jaredites," a series of articles in the *Improvement Era*.

29-1.   "There Were Jaredites," 59 (Jan. 1956), 30-32, 58-61.

29-2.   "I: Egypt Revisited," 59 (Feb. 1956), 88-89, 106, 108.

29-3.   "II: Egypt Revisited," 59 (March 1956), 150-152, 185-187.

29-4.   "III: Egypt Revisited," 59 (April 1956), 244-245, 252-254, 258.

29-5.   "IV: Egypt Revisited," 59 (May 1956), 308-310, 334, 336, 338-340.

29-6.   "V: Egypt Revisited," 59 (June 1956), 390-391, 460-461.

29-7. "The Babylonian Background, I," 59 (July 1956), 509-511, 514, 516.

29-8. "The Babylonian Background, II," 59 (Aug. 1956), 566-567, 602.

29-9. "The Shining Stones — Continued," 29 (Sept. 1956), 630-632, 672-675.

29-10. "Epic Milieu in the Old Testament," 29 (Oct. 1956), 710-712, 745-751.

29-11. " 'Our Own People'," 59 (Nov. 1956), 818-819, 857-858.

29-12. "Our Own People — Continued," 59 (Dec. 1956), 906-907.

1957

29. "There Were Jaredites" — continued:

29-13. "Our Own People — Continued," 60 (Jan. 1957), 26-7, 41.

29-14. "Our Own People — Concluded," 60 (Feb. 1957), 94-95, 122-124.

30. *An Approach to the Book of Mormon* (Salt Lake City: Council of the Twelve Apostles, The Church of Jesus Christ of Latter-day Saints, 1957; Salt Lake City: Deseret Book, 1964). XVI, 416 pp. (XXII, 416 pp.) [This book was originally published as the lesson manual for the Melchizedek Priesthood quorums of The Church of Jesus Christ of Latter-day Saints. The 2nd ed. contains a new preface, one new chapter and deletes the questions which were originally appended to each chapter. The pagination differs in the two editions.]

Contents:
Preface (by Joseph Fielding Smith)
Foreword
I. The Changing Scene
   1. Introduction
   2. A Time for Re-examination
II. Lehi's World
   3. An Auspicious Beginning
   4. Lehi as a Representative Man
III. Lehi's Affairs
   5. The Jews and the Caravan Trade
   6. Lehi and the Arabs
   7. Dealings with Egypt
IV. The Doomed City
   8. Politics in Jerusalem
   9. Escapade in Jerusalem
   10. Portrait of Laban
V. The Meaning of the Wilderness
   11. Flight into the Wilderness
   12. The Pioneer Tradition and the True Church
   13. The Church in the Wilderness
VI. The Dead Sea Scrolls and the Book of Mormon
   14. Unwelcome Voices from the Dust
   15. Qumran and the Waters of Mormon

1958

31. "The Idea of the Temple in History," *Millennial Star*, 120 (Aug. 1958), 228-237, 247-249. [Reprinted as *What Is a Temple? The Idea of the Temple in History* (1963 and 1968).]

32. "Mixed Voices," A series of articles (on so-called Book of Mormon "criticism"), in the *Improvement Era*.
    32-1. "Kangaroo Court: A Study in Book of Mormon Criticism," 62 (March 1959), 145-148, 184-187.
    32-2. "Kangaroo Court: Part Two," 62 (April 1959), 224-226, 300-301.
    32-3. "Just Another Book? Part One," 62 (May 1959), 345-347, 388-391.
    32-4. "Just Another Book? Part Two," 62 (June 1959), 412-413, 501-503.
    32-5. "Just Another Book? Part Two, conclusion," 62 (July 1959), 530-531, 565.
    32-6. "The Grab Bag," 62 (July 1959), 530-533, 546-548.
    32-7. "What Frontier, What Camp Meeting?" 62 (Aug. 1959), 590-592, 610, 612, 614-615.
    32-8. "The Comparative Method," 62 (Oct. 1959), 744-747, 759.
    32-9. "The Comparative Method," 62 (Nov. 1959), 848, 854, 856.

33. "Strange Ships and Shining Stones," in *A Book of Mormon Treasury: Selections from the Papers of the Improvement Era* (Salt Lake City: Bookcraft, 1959), pp. 133-151. [See also the *Improvement Era*, 59 (Sept. 1959), 630-632, 672-675, and cf. *An Approach to the Book of Mormon*, Lesson XXV.]

34. "Christian Envy of the Temple," a two-part essay in the *Jewish Quarterly Review*. [A study of the reaction of early Christian writers to the destruction and disappearance of the temple. Reprinted with the same title in *When the Lights Went Out* (1970), 55-58.]

34-1. "Christian Envy of the Temple," *Jewish Quarterly Review*, L (1959), 97-123.

1960

34. "Christian Envy of the Temple" — continued:
34-2. "Christian Envy of the Temple," *Jewish Quarterly Review*, L (1960), 229-240.

1961

35. "The Liahona's Cousins," *Improvement Era*, 64 (Feb. 1961), 87-89, 104, 106, 108-111.

36. "The Boy, Nephi, in Jerusalem," *The Instructor*, 96 (March 1961), 84-85.

37. "The Passing of the Church: Forty Variations on an Unpopular Theme," *Church History*, XXX (June 1961), 131-154. [An examination of the expectation of early Christian writers of the passing of the Church. Nibley presents forty different arguments for the apostasy in the lead article of the journal of the American Association of Church Historians. Hans J. Hillerbrand wrote a passionate letter protesting the publication of Nibley's article because, among other reasons, of the possibility that, if widely accepted, Nibley's thesis would preclude his teaching "Church history." See Hillerbrand, "The Passing of the Church: Two Comments on a Strange Theme," *Church History*, XXX (Dec. 1961), 481-482; and a defense of Nibley by R. M. Grant, "The Passing of the Church: Comments on Two Comments on a Strange Theme," *Church History*, XXX (Dec. 1961), 482-483. Nibley's article has been reprinted under the title "The Passing of the Primitive Church" in *When the Lights Went Out* (1970), 1-32.]

38. "Literary Style Used in Book of Mormon Insured Accurate Translation," in *Deseret News*, "Church News," July 29, 1961, 10, 15.

39. "Censoring the Joseph Smith Story," a series of articles in the *Improvement Era*.
39-1. "Part I: The Problem," 64 (July 1961), 490-492, 522, 524, 526, 528.
39-2. "Part II: Suppressing the First Vision Story after 1842," 64 (Aug. 1961), 577-579, 605-609.
39-3. "Part III," 64 (Oct. 1961), 724-725, 736, 738, 740.
39-4. "Conclusion," 64 (Nov. 1961), 812-813, 865-869.

40. *The Myth Makers* (Salt Lake City: Bookcraft, 1961). 293 pp. [This is an examination of the early criticisms of Joseph Smith.]
Contents:
Foreword
Part I. The Crime of Being a Prophet
Part II. Digging in the Dark
Part III. The Greek Psalter Mystery Bibliography

1962

41. "The Book of Mormon: True or False?" *Millennial Star*, 124 (Nov. 1962), 274-277.

42. "How to Write an Anti-Mormon Book," Lecture II, Feb. 17, 1962 in *Seminar on the Prophet Joseph Smith* (BYU Extension Publications, 1962), pp. 30-41. [Reprinted (1964), pp. 31-42; essentially a preview of *Sounding Brass* (1963).]

43. *The World and the Prophets*, 2nd "enlarged ed." (Salt Lake City: Deseret Book, 1962). 281 pp.

1963

44. *Sounding Brass* (Salt Lake City: Bookcraft, 1963). 294 pp. [This book carries the subtitle "Informal Studies in the Lucrative Art of Telling Stories About Brigham Young and the Mormons" and is a response to Irving Wallace's *The Twenty-seventh Wife* (New York: Simon & Schuster, 1961).]
Contents
Introduction
Part I.   "In My Mind's Eye Horatio..."
Part II. The Two-faced Monster
Part III. How to Write an Anti-Mormon Book (A Handbook for Beginners)
Part IV. It Fairly Sears the Screen — A Romance You Will Never Forget!
Part V.   Is There a Danite in the House? You Never Know
Bibliography

45. " 'Howlers' in the Book of Mormon," *Millennial Star*, 125 (Feb. 1963), 28-34.

46. *What Is a Temple? The Idea of the Temple in History* (Provo: BYU Press, 1st ed., 1963; 2nd ed., 1968). II, 18 pp. (16 pp.). [Reprinted from the *Millennial Star*, and as "Die Templesidae in der Geschichte," *Der Stern*, 85 Jahrgang, no. 2 (Feb. 1959), 43-60.]

47. *New Discoveries Concerning the Bible and Church History* (Provo: BYU Extension Publications, 1963). 12pp. [A series of quotations by various writers on six general topics.]

48. "The Dead Sea Scrolls: Some Questions and Answers," *The Instructor*, 98 (July 1963), 233-235. [Originally given as an address on July 5, 1962, to the Seminary and Institute Faculty at Brigham Young University.]

1964

49. *The Early Christian Church in Light of Some Newly Discovered Papyri from Egypt* (Provo: BYU Extension Publications, 1964). 20 pp. [A talk delivered to the BYU Tri-Stake Fireside, March 3, 1964.]

50. *An Approach to the Book of Mormon*, 2nd ed., (Salt Lake City: Deseret Book, 1964). XXII, 416 pp. [Originally published in 1957, this edition contains a new "Preface to Second Edition" by HN, one new chapter (#25) entitled "Strange Ships and Shining Stones," which is reproduced here from a 1959 publication. The questions originally appended to each chapter in the 1957 edition have been deleted and the pagination of the two editions is different.]

Bibliography

51. "Since Cumorah: New Voices from the Dust," series of articles on the Book of Mormon in the *Improvement Era*.
    51-1. [Part I], 67 (Oct. 1964), 816-821, 844-847.
    51-2. "Part I. (Continued)," 67 (Nov. 1964), 924-928, 974-975, 977-978, 980-983.
    51-3. "Part I. (Continued)," 67 (Nov. 1964), 1032-1035, 1126-1128.

1965

51. "Since Cumorah" — continued:
    51-4. "Part I. (Continued)," 68 (Jan. 1965), 34-37, 60-64.
    51-5. "Part II. Hidden Treasures: The Search for the Original Scriptures," 68 (Feb. 1965), 100-103, 146-147.
    51-6. "Part II. Hidden Treasures: The Search for the Original Scriptures (continued)," 68 (March 1965), 210-213, 226, 228, 230, 232, 234.
    51-6. "Part III: Secrecy in the Primitive Church," 68 (April 1965), 308-311, 326, 330-332.
    51.7. "Part III: Secrecy in the Primitive Church (continued), 68 (May 1965), 406-407, 444.
    51-8. "Part III: Secrecy in the Primitive Church (concluded)," 68 (June), 482-483, 574-575.
    51-9. "The Testament of Lehi/Part I," 68 (July), 616-617, 645-648.
    51-10. "The Testament of Lehi/Part I, continued," 68 (Aug. 1965), 696-699, 702, 704.
    51-11. "The Story of Zenos," 68 (September, 1965), 782-783, 792.
    51-12. "The Olive Tree," 68 (Oct. 1965), 876-877, 916-917.
    51-13. "The Bible, the Scrolls, and the Book of Mormon — A Problem of Three Bibles," 68 (Nov. 1965), 974-977, 1013, 1040.
    51-14. "The Bible, the Scrolls, and the Book of Mormon — the Problem of Three Bibles — continued," 68 (Dec. 1965), 1090-1091, 1165-1168.

1966

51. "Since Cumorah" — continued:
    51-15. "The Bible, the Scrolls, and the Book of Mormon: A Problem of Three Bibles," 69 (Jan. 1966), 32-34, 44-46.
    51-16. "The Bible, the Scrolls, and the Book of Mormon: A Problem of Three Bibles (continued)," 69 (Feb. 1966), 118-122.
    51-17. "The Bible, the Scrolls, and the Book of Mormon: A Problem of Three Bibles (continued)," 69 (March 1966), 196-197, 232-234.
    51-18. "The Mysteries of Zenos and Joseph," 69 (April 1966), 296-297, 334-336.
    51-19. "Problems, Not Solutions," 69 (May 1966), 419-420, 422, 424.
    51-20. [Continuation of "Problems, Not Solutions"], 69 (June 1966), 582-583.
    51-21. "Epilogue: Since Qumran," 69 (July 1966), 636-638.
    51-22. [Continuation of "Since Qumran"], 69 (Aug, 1966), 710-712.
    51-23. "(Since Qumran)," 69 (Sept. 1966), 794-795, 799-800, 802, 804-805.
    51-24. "(Since Qumran)," 69 (Oct. 1966), 884-885.

51-25. "(Since Qumran)," 69 (Nov. 1966), 974-975, 1028-1031.

51-26. "(Since Qumran)," 69 (Dec. 1966), 1084-1085, 1162-1165.

[These materials were reprinted in *Since Cumorah* (1967/1970) with two large and important additions.]

52. "Qumran and the Companions of the Cave," *Revue de Qumran*, V (1965), 177-198. [This is a remarkable and complex study of stories that turn up in both Muslim sources and in the Dead Sea Scrolls; these stories and their strange appearances have more significance than appears on the surface.]

53. "Early Accounts of Jesus' Childhood," *The Instructor*, 100 (Jan. 1965), 35-7.

54. "The Expanding Gospel," *BYU Studies*, VII (Autumn 1965), 3-27. [2nd annual BYU Faculty lecture.]

1966

55. "Evangelium Quadraginta Dierum," *Vigiliae Christianae*, XX (1966), 1-24. [An essay on the teachings of the resurrected Jesus to his disciples. Reprinted under the title "The Forty-day Mission of Christ — The Forgotten Heritage," in *When the Lights Went Out* (1970), 33-54.]

56. "Tenting, Toll, and Taxing," *Western Political Quarterly*, XXIX (December 1966), 599-630. [A third important study of ancient statecraft.]

57. *Writing and Publication in Graduate School* (Provo: Mimeographed by the BYU Graduate School, 1966). 11 pp. [This is a reproduction of an address given on May 12, 1965 to the BYU History Department Honors Banquet.]

58. *Since Cumorah: The Book of Mormon in the Modern World* (Salt Lake City: Deseret Book, 1967) XIII, 451 pp.
Contents:
Preface: H.N.
Foreword: Richard Lloyd Anderson
Part 1. The Book of Mormon as Scripture
    Chapter 1. "...There Can Be No More Bible."
    Chapter 2. A New Age of Discovery
    Chapter 3. The Illusive Primitive Church
    Chapter 4. "...But Unto Them It Is Not Given" (Lk. 8:10)
    Chapter 5. The Bible in the Book of Mormon
Part II. Philosophical Notes
    Chapter 6. Strange Things Strangely Told
    Chapter 7. Checking on Long-forgotten Lore
Part III. Some Scientific Questions
    Chapter 8. "Forever Tentative..."
Part IV. The Real Background of the Book of Mormon
    Chapter 9. Some Fairly Foolproof Texts
    Chapter 10. Prophets in the Wilderness
    Chapter 11. A Rigorous Test: Military History
Part V. The Prophetic Book of Mormon

Chapter 12. Good People and Bad People
Chapter 13. Prophecy in the Book of Mormon: The Three
Periods.
Conclusion
Index

[This book reprints materials from the *Improvement Era* in 1964-66, but with some additional materials, specifically on "Military History" (pp. 328-370) and "The Prophetic Book of Mormon: (pp. 373-444). See L. Midgley, "The Secular Relevance of the Gospel," *Dialogue*, IV (Winter, 1969), 76-85, for a commentary on the last seventy pages of *Since Cumorah*. The book is also reviewed by Robert Mesle, *Courage*, 2 (Sept. 1971), 331-332.]

1967

59. "The Mormon View of the Book of Mormon," *Concilium: Theology in the Age of Reviewal*, XXX (New York: Panlist Press, 1968), 170-173; also printed in England under the same title in *Concilium: An International Review of Theology*, X (Dec. 1967), 82-83, and in other foreign-language editions of this Catholic journal in French, pp. 151-153; Portuguese, pp. 144-147; German, pp. 855-856. [An interesting summary statement of the content and purpose of the Book of Mormon prepared for a volume of *Concilium* concerned with scripture.]

1968

60. "Phase One," *Dialogue: A Journal of Mormon Thought*, III (Summer 1968), 99-105. [This essay concerns the debate over the Joseph Smith Papyri and the bulk of the number contains materials on this issue.]

61. "Prolegomena to Any Study of the Book of Abraham," *BYU Studies*, VIII (Winter 1968), 171-178.

62. "Fragment Found in Salt Lake City," *BYU Studies*, VIII (Winter 1968), 191-194. [The discovery of the Joseph Smith Papyri.]

63. "Getting Ready to Begin: An Editorial," *BYU Studies*, IX (Autumn 1968), 69-102. [The debate over the Joseph Smith Papyri.]

64. "As Things Stand at the Moment," *BYU Studies*, IX (Autumn 1968), 69-102. [The debate over the Joseph Smith Papyri.]

65. "A New Look at the Pearl of Great Price," a series of articles in the *Improvement Era*.
65-1. "Part 1, Challenge and Response," 71 (Jan. 1968), 18-24.
65-2. "Part 1 (Continued), Challenge and Response," 71 (Feb. 1968), 14-18, 20-21.
65-3. "Part 1 (Continued), Challenge and Response," 71 (March 1968), 16-18, 20-22.
65-4. "Part 1 (Continued), Challenge and Response," 71 (April 1968), 64-69 (including a long note entitled "We Should Explain," 65-66).
65-5. "Part 2, May We See Your Credentials?" 71 (May 1968), 54-57.

65-6. "Part 2 (Continued), May We See Your Credentials?" 71 (June 1968), 18-22.
65-7. "Part 3, Empaneling the Panel," 71 (July 1968), 48-55.
65-8. "Part 4, Second String," 71 (Aug. 1968), 53-64.
65-9. "Part 5, Facsimile No. 1: A Unique Document," 71 (Sept. 1968), 66-80.
65-10. "Part 5, Facsimile No 1: A Unique Document," 71 (Oct. 1968), 73-81.
65-11. "Part 6, Facsimile No. 1: A Unique Document (Continued)," 71 (Nov. 1968), 36-38, 40, 42, 44.
65-12. "Part 6, Facsimile No. 1: A Unique Document (Continued)," 71 (Dec. 1968), 28-33.

1969

65. "A New Look at the Pearl of Great Price" — Continued:
65-13. "Part 7: The Unknown Abraham," 72 (Jan. 1969), 26-33.
65-14. "Part 7 (Continued): The Unknown Abraham," 72 (Feb. 1969), 64-67.
65-15. "Part 7 (Continued): The Unknown Abraham," 72 (March 1969), 76, 79-80, 82, 84.
65-16. "Part 7 (Continued): The Unknown Abraham," 72 (April 1969), 66-72.
65-17. "Part 7 (Continued): The Unknown Abraham," 72 (May 1969), 87-91.
65-18. "Part 7 (Continued): The Unknown Abraham," 72 (June 1969), 126-128, 130-132.
65-19. "Part 7 (Continued): The Unknown Abraham," 72 (July 1969), 97-101.
65-20. "Part 8: Facsimile No. 1, By the Figures," 72 (July 1969), 101-111.
65-21. "Part 8: Facsimile No. 1, By the Figures," 72 (Aug. 1969), 75-87.
65-22. "Part 8 (Continued): Facsimile No. 1, By the Figures," 72 (Sept. 1969), 85-95.
65-23. "Part 8 (Continued): Facsimile No. 1, By the Numbers," 72 (Oct. 1969), 85-88.
65-24. "Part 9, Setting the Stage — The World of Abraham," 72 (Oct. 1969), 89-95.
65-25. "Part 9 (Continued), Setting the Stage — The World of Abraham," 72 (Nov. 1969), 116-126.

66. "How to Have a Quiet Campus Antique Style," *BYU Studies*, IX (Summer 1969), 440-452.

1970

65. "A New Look at the Pearl of Great Price" — Continued:
65-26. "Part 9 (Continued), Setting the Stage — The World of Abraham," 73 (Jan. 1970), 56-65.
65-27. "Part 10, The Sacrifice of Isaac," 73 (March 1970), 84-94.
65-28. "Part 11, The Sacrifice of Sarah," 73 (April 1970), 79-95.
65-29. "Conclusion: Taking Stock," 73 (May 1970), 82-89, 91-94.

67. "Educating the Saints — A Brigham Young Mosaic," *BYU Studies*, XI (Autumn 1970), 61-87.

68. *Since Cumorah* (Salt Lake City: Deseret Book, 1970). [A reprint of 1967 edition.]

69. *When the Lights Went Out: Three Studies on the Ancient Apostasy.* (Salt Lake City: Deseret Book, 1970). 94 pp. [Three of Nibley's important essays in academic journals in 1959-60, 1961 and 1966 are reprinted and indexed for the Mormon audience.]
    Contents;
    1. The Passing of the Primitive Church (Forty Variations on an Unpopular Theme)
    2. The Forty-day Mission of Christ — The Forgotten Heritage
    3. Christian Envy of the Temple

70. "The Book of Mormon as a Mirror of the East," *Improvement Era*, 73 (Nov. 1970), 115-120, 122-125. [Reprinted from *Improvement Era*, 51 (April 1948), 202-204, 249-251.]

71. "Brigham Young and the Enemy," in *The Young Democrat*, privately printed leaflets, ed. by Omar Kadar and published in two separate parts in 1970. 4 pp. and 11 pp.

1971

72. "The Day of the Amateur," *New Era*, I (Jan. 1971), 42-44.

73. "Myths and the Scriptures," *New Era*, I (Oct. 1971), 34-38.

74. "What is 'The Book of Breathings'?" *BYU Studies*, XI (Winter 1971), 153-187. [An early version of one part of *The Message of Joseph Smith Papyri* (1975).]

75. "The Meaning of the Kirtland Egyptian Papers," *BYU Studies*, XI (Summer 1971), 350-399.

76. "If There Must Needs Be Offense," *The Ensign*, I (July 1971), 53-55. [See also Nibley's anti-war letter of March 29, 1971 in *BYU Daily Universe*.]

1972

77. "Brigham Young on the Environment," in T. G. Madsen and C. D. Tate, eds., *To the Glory of God*, the B. West Belnap Memorial Volume (Salt Lake City: Deseret Book, 1972), pp. 5-29. [See the 6-page mimeo. of quotes from Brigham Young used by Nibley for his Earth Week Lecture, April 21, 1971, on file in the Harold B. Lee Library at BYU.]

78. "Jerusalem: In Christianity," *Encyclopedia Judaica*, IX (Macmillan, N.Y./Encyclopedia Judaica Publishing, Jerusalem, 1972), columns 1568-75.

79. "Islam and Mormonism — A Comparison," *The Ensign*, II (March 1972), 55-64. [Footnotes with evidence and explanation were not published with this essay.]

80. "Ancient Temples: What Do They Signify?" *The Ensign;* II (Sept. 1972), 46-49.

81. "Man's Dominion," *New Era,* II (Oct. 1972), 24-31.

1973

82. "The Genesis of the Written Word," *New Era,* III (Sept. 1973), 38-50. [Reprinted from the Commissioner's Lecture Series, 1972.]

83. "Our Glory or Our Condemnation," in *Last Lecture Series, 1971-72* (Provo: BYU Press, 1973), pp. 1-14.

84. "What Is Zion? A Distant View," in *What Is Zion? Joseph Smith Lecture Series, 1972-73* (Provo: BYU Press, 1973), pp. 1-21. [This was circulated earlier as "Waiting for Zion" (1973), 34 pp.]

85. "Common Carrier: Author Defends Image of Joseph Smith As Prophet," *The Salt Lake Tribune,* Sunday, Nov. 25, 1973, p. 2 G. [Reply to "Common Carrier" article by Jerald and Sandra Tanner, Nov. 11, 1973, p. 6 B; Nibley focuses on debate over the *Book of Abraham.*]

86. "The Best Possible Test," *Dialogue* VIII (Spring 1973), 73-77. [Nibley's views on revelation, the negro and the priesthood. See the reply of M. R. Gardner in *Dialogue,* VIII (Summer 1973), 102-106.]

87. Review essay on Yigael Yadin's *Bar-Kokhba: The Rediscovery of the Legendary Hero of the Second Jewish Revolt Against Rome,* in *BYU Studies,* XIV (Autumn 1973), 115-126.

88. *Genesis of the Written Word* (Provo: BYU Press, 1973). [Commissioner's lecture delivered in 1972 and reprinted (without the complete footnotes) in *New Era.*]

1974

89. "Treasures in the Heavens: Some Early Christian Insights into the Organizing of Worlds," *Dialogue,* VIII (Autumn/Winter 1974), 76-98.

90. "Beyond Politics," *BYU Studies,* XIV (Autumn 1974), 3-28.

1975

91. "The Passing of the Church," *BYU Studies,* XVI (Autumn 1975), 139-164.

92. "Zeal Without Knowledge," academic awareness lecture, 26 June 1975. Available in mimeographed form, 17 pp.

93. *The Message of the Joseph Smith Papyri: An Egyptian Endowment* (Salt Lake City: Deseret Book, 1975). XIII, 305 pp.
    Contents:
    Explanation
    Chapter I: What Manner of Document?
    Chapter II: Reproduction and Translation of Papyri X and XI
    Chapter III: Translated Correctly?
    Chapter IV: A More Complete Text of the Book of Breathings
    Commentary

Part I: Nature and Purpose of the Book of Breathing(s)
Part IIa: Purification Rites
Part IIb: Entering the Temple
Part III: The Creation of Man
Part IV: The Garden Story
Part V: The Long Road Back
Part VI: The Fearful Passage
Part VII: Culmination and Conclusion
Apendixes
   I.   From the Dead Sea Scrolls (IQS)
   II.   From the Odes of Solomon
   III.   The Pearl
   IV.   From the Pistis Sophia
   V.   Cyril of Jerusalem's Lectures on the Ordinances
   VI.   From the Gospel of Philip
Bibliography
Index

[For a review of this book, see C. Wilford Griggs, "A Great Fuss About a Scrap of Papyrus," *The Ensign,* 5 (Oct. 1975), 84.]

94.   " 'A Strange Thing in the Land': The Return of the Book of Enoch," a series of articles in *The Ensign:*
94-1.   "Part 1," 5 (Oct. 1975), 78-84.
94-2.   "Part 2," 5 (Dec. 1975), 72-76.

1976

94.   " 'A Strange Thing in the Land': The Return of the Book of Enoch" — continued:
94-3.   "Part 3," 6 (Feb. 1976), 64-68.
94-4.   "Part 4," 6 (March 1976), 62-66.
94-5.   "Part 5," 6 (April 1976), 60-64.
94-6.   "Part 6," 6 (July 1976), 64-48.
94-7.   "Part 7," 6 (Oct. 1976), 76-81.
94-8.   "Part 8," 6 (Dec. 1976), 73-78.

1977

94.   " 'A Strange Thing in the Land': The Return of the Book of Enoch" — continued:
94-9.   "Part 9," 7 (Feb. 1977), 66-75.
94-10. "Part 10," 7 (March 1977), 86-90.
94-11. "Part 11," 7 (April 1977), 78-89.
94-12. "Part 12," 7 (June 1977), 78-90.
94-13. "Part 13," 7 (Aug. 1977), 66-65.

95.   "The Uses and Abuses of Patriotism," in *American Heritage: A Syllabus for Social Science 100* (Provo: Brigham Young University Press, 1977), 188-197.

Book designed by Bailey-Montague and Associates
Composed by Column Type
in Palatino Medium with display lines in Palatino Italic
Printed by Publishers Press
on Bookcraft Natural Vellum
Bound by Mountain States Bindery
in Devon "19990" Black Vellum